UNDER THE INFLUENCE

THE
DESTRUCTIVE
EFFECTS
OF GROUP
DYNAMICS

UNDER THE INFLUENCE

JOHN D. GOLDHAMMER

 Prometheus Books

59 John Glenn Drive
Amherst, New York 14228-2197

Published 1996 by Prometheus Books

00 99 98 97 96   5 4 3 2 1

Library of Congress Cataloging-in-Publication Data

Goldhammer, John D.
    Under the influence : the destructive effects of group dynamics / John D. Goldhammer.
       p.   cm.
    Includes bibliographical references and index.
    ISBN 1–57392–006–1 (alk. paper)
    1. Social groups. 2. Group identity. 3. Conformity. 4. Individuality. I. Title.
HM131.G564   1996
302.3—dc20
[B]   95–43779
                                          CIP

Printed in the United States of America on acid-free paper

To my sons
Mark and David
and for all who have the integrity to be themselves
and the courage to travel their own unique path

Contents

Acknowledgments   13

Prologue   15

I: The Nature of the Beast

1. Collective Enchantment   23
Death by Group   24
   Cultural Conditioning   26
   The Heart of the Dilemma   28
   Chaos and Assimilation   30
Implications for People and the Planet   31
   Our Common Humanity   34
Individuation: Differentiating from the Herd   36
   The Differentiated Psyche   38
Barbarians in the City   39
   The Problem of Opposites   41
   Psychological Opportunity Cost   41
The Collective God Hole: The Quest for Meaning   42

2. Trapped in Paradise   49
My Experience in a Religious Group   49

Filling the God Hole   50
Meeting My Spiritual Teacher . . . Oops!   51
The Kingdom Collapses   56
The Exodus   58
The Collective Holocaust   60

3. Fatal Persuasion   63

Soul Psychology   63
The Meaning in Words   65
Group Speak: The Language of the Group Mind   66
Cultural Editing and Censorship   69
A Vocabulary of Prejudice   72
Propaganda   75
The Statistical Wasteland in Groups   77
Statistical Murder   80
Collective Narcissism   81
The Totalistic Nature of the Collective   82
The Collective Need for Power   83

4. The Dark Side of Groups   85

The Trap of One-Sidedness   86
Eros and the Will to Power   91
The Flat Earth One-Sided Personality   92
Loss of Soul in Groups   95
The Disease of Exclusiveness   99
An Arrogant Cosmology   100
Existential Sacrifice   101
Deadly Superiority: Group Egocentricity   102
Exporting Our Moral Ideas   106
Peer Pressure   108
Under the Influence: Hypnotic Effects of Groups   109
The Social Trance   110
Collective Complexes   111
Destruction of the Individual   113
Collective Panic   114
Gangs: Street Cults   116
Patriarchal Rules   117
Suicide and the Collective   117
Repressed Collective Tension   118
Collective Tension Producers   119

5. Systems: Mega Groups   **121**

The Serpent in Our Free Market Paradise   122

Slavery American Style   125

Turning the Heart Into Stone   127

In the Shadows: Black Markets   128

    The Religion of Organized Gambling   130

Capitalist Heaven and Hell   131

Putting a Conscience in the Machine   133

    Corporate Murder   134

    Monotheistic Capitalism   136

Educational Systems   137

    The New Inquisition and the Religious Right   138

The Industrialized Psyche   139

    Characteristics of Business Totalism   141

Cultism in Politics   142

    The Religion of Politics   146

    The Welfare System   148

    The FDA: A Political Cult   152

    The Environmental Protection Agency   155

    The Department of Energy   156

    Unions: Legalized Extortion   157

The Medical Establishment   159

Drugs: Putting the Soul to Sleep   162

Reclaiming Our Economic Integrity   163

6. The Collective Machine   **165**

Robotization of the Human Psyche   165

    Extroverts, Introverts, and Groups   171

Mind Control and Thought Reform in Groups   174

How Groups Control Inner and Outer Communication   177

Mystical Control: Calculated Spontaneity   179

Rationalizing Evil   180

Fanatical Separation of Pure and Impure   181

Control Through Confession   185

The Quicksand of Knowing   186

7. Going Backward: Developmental Regression in Groups   **189**

Survival Mode   189

Trapping the Inner Child   193

    Developmental Stages   194

8. Creating Gods   **197**

Escaping Life Through Religion   197
Bewitchment: Projection and Groups   199
Identification: Unconscious Conformity   203
    Cultural Cloaking   206
What Is This Thing Called "Self"?   206
    The Empty Self   208
Archetypal Paralysis   212

9. The Neurotic Side of Religion   **215**
The Shadow of Christianity   216
    Collective Compulsions   219
    Salem Revisited: Mass Paranoia   222
    Stigmata: Our Collective Hysteria   224
The Savior Business   224
    The Born Again Phenomenon   225
    Electronic Hypnosis: The Cult of Evangelism in America   226
Dogma-Free Meditation   227
Integrity and Evil   230
    When Obedience Is Evil   231
    Fundamentalism: A Social Plague   232
Finding Values Outside the Religious Community   234
    The Dark Side of Illumination   234
Dualism in Religion   235

10. The Color of the Dream   **237**
The American Dream   237
Pre-Packaged Dreams   239
Dream Eaters   242
Group-Induced Racism   244
The Cult of Color in America   246
Our Collective Costumes   249

II: Breaking Free

11. Slaying the Collective Dragon   **253**
Collective Deprogramming   254
    The Hero's Adventure   254
    Active Imagination: Animating Our Symbolic World   255
    Thirteen Steps for Recovery from the Group Mind   260
Becoming Your Own Soul Therapist   262
    Creating Your Personal Totem   262

Polytheism: Connecting with Our Inner Community   263
The Inner Shaman   266
Dreams and Groups   267
Psychotherapy: Mind Control or Soul Work?   271
Characteristics of Destructive Psychotherapy   273
Characteristics of Constructive Psychotherapy   275

12. Putting Soul into Relationships   **277**
Holding Tension Between the Individual and the Collective   277
Life's Oppositeness   278
Relationship: Finding the Space of the In-Between   281
Where Inner and Outer Worlds Meet   286
Tension and Integrity   287
Creating Healthy Tension: Soul Work   290
Acknowledgment   290
Process Over Results   293
Creating Insight Gaps   295
Seeing Through Feelings   296
Words that Express Feelings   297
Repression: Nurturing a "Poison Tree"   301
Exploring Our Blind Side: Shadow Work   302
Criteria for a Healthy Group   303

13. Life After Group   **305**
An Archetypal Perspective   306
Building a Healthy Community   307
Our Need for Community   308
Endings and Beginnings   310

Appendix: Marks of a Destructive Group   313

Notes   315

Bibliography   337

Index   345

Acknowledgments

I owe a great debt to these individuals who helped provide the philosophical and psychological background for *Under the Influence*: Carl Gustav Jung, the extraordinary Swiss psychologist, thinker, and writer who broke with his mentor Sigmund Freud and proceeded to develop his own theories of the personal and collective unconscious, of archetypes, techniques of dream analysis, and of the individual's role in a collective world; Marie-Louise Von Franz, who worked with Carl Jung for twenty-seven years and founded the C. G. Jung Institute in Zurich; Joseph Campbell, perhaps the most influential mythologist of this century; writer and lecturer Sam Keen, a close colleague of Joseph Campbell; James Hillman, a prolific, provocative thinker and founder of "archetypal psychology"; Robert J. Lifton, the distinguished psychologist, editor, and writer who developed the "psychology of totalism"; R. Buckminster Fuller, scientist, philosopher, and inventor of the geodesic dome; Eric Hoffer, one of our great contemporary philosophers; psychiatrist W. R. Bion, who developed important concepts about group psychology; Erik Erikson, a Pulitzer Prize winner, and leading figure in the study of human development; Steven Hassan, a psychotherapist and well-known expert on cult mind-control techniques; Daryl Sharp, a prominent Jungian editor and publisher; Jungian analyst and author Robert Johnson; poet Robert Bly, for his excellent translations of Rainer Maria Rilke's poetry; Connie Zweig and Jeremiah Abrams for their remarkable collection of essays on the human shadow; psychologist Robert Godwin for his paper on "The Function of Enemies"; author, theologian, and lecturer John Bradshaw for his work on "cultic fam-

13

ilies"; Peter McWilliams, a best-selling author and former cult member for his research and work on destructive groups and consensual crime. Also, I would like to thank the Cult Awareness Network for their excellent research and information about destructive cults.

I especially want to thank W. Shep Brown for his continuing friendship and most valuable help and support over the years. Many friends and colleagues gave excellent advice, encouragement, and in many cases contributed portions of their experiences to this book, among them: Joseph Bottone, Monica Davis, Richard Davis, Chyrelle Martin, Rick Martin, Becky Taylor, Laurie Casnel, Virgil Smith, Loren Schmidt, Jaitay-Linda Good, and Khalisa Lord. Additionally, I am grateful for Andrew Schmookler's advice and feedback, and Clement M. Brown, Jr.'s encouragement. And what would the life of this writer be without my wonderful wife, Terri, who also happens to be an excellent literary critic.

Finally, the thoughtful insights, observations, and reactions of my courageous editors at Prometheus Books, Steven L. Mitchell and Mary A. Read, proved to be invaluable.

Prologue

There is an accumulative cruelty in a number of men, though none in particular are ill-natured.

Marquess of Halifax[1]

Significant events and experiences shape our lives and in many ways create our future. My life was forever altered by my experience in a religious cult. Not only did I abandon my passions in life, I spent fifteen years following someone else's path. When I finally awakened from my enchantment, I found myself with near-zero self-esteem, a lot of regret for many wasted years, and plenty of anger at my own naivete, as well as being furious with my former group. I felt that a gigantic chunk of my real identity had been stolen from me without my conscious consent. At the same time, I felt a euphoric sense of freedom and complete delight that I now had my life back in my own hands.

Renowned mythologist Joseph Campbell (1904–1988) explained how, in trying to find our passion or "bliss," we recapitulate to what he refers to as the "hero's journey." He wrote: "The mythological hero, setting forth from his commonday hut or castle, is lured, carried away, or else voluntarily proceeds, to the threshold of adventure. There he encounters a shadow presence that guards the passage. The hero may defeat or conciliate this power and go alive into the kingdom of the dark (brother-battle, dragon-battle; offering, charm), or be slain by the opponent and descend in death (dismemberment, crucifixion)."[2] The dragon I met was the *group mind.* You could say that my group experience was my *involuntary* "hero's journey," my unwilling trial by fire. I had no understanding of the power-

15

ful psychological group dynamics that made the group an almost irresistible force—a force that effectively crushed my hopes and dreams—easily entrapping me in a collective mission.

How did this seemingly idealistic, loving community so completely annihilate my identity? Ironically, people everywhere are searching for meaning and purpose, trying to find their passion. Yet they are losing themselves in one group after another. I had to find out how this collective beast operated. Much to my astonishment, I began to realize that my experience was not at all unusual, but quite common. In fact, while researching group psychology, I discovered that many different types of groups and organizations shared a deadly but common theme: a typical set of destructive dynamics that has lethal implications for individuals, for our future, and for our environment. Hence this book.

Groups have a dark side that destroys individual freedom and autonomy, aborting the individual's quest for meaning, integration, and fulfillment. Even the slightest contact can expose one to these destructive dynamics. Gradually we start classifying people: there are those *in* our group, those *outside* our group, and those who *could be* in our group. And there are always those inner-core people who cluster around the leader. They become our role models as we slip down the icy slope of self-deception, ego-inflation and collective adaptation. Before you know it, we're feeling superior and exclusive—better than the unenlightened masses. If only everyone knew what *we* knew.

Although not all persons are directly affiliated with a particular group, everyone is deeply affected by destructive collective influences and abuse whether religious, political, social, or economic. Such influences often take the form of covert psychological manipulation that loads one's psyche with alien, self-destructive ideologies.

In authoritarian collective hands, "surrender," "idealism," "loyalty," and many other perceived virtues become psychological, soul-numbing traps. Holding the tension between powerful collective impulses and one's integrity and authentic sense of self becomes one of life's greatest challenges. In *Under the Influence* I explore the self-destructive aspects of the relationship between the individual and this collective dark side, examining destructive group characteristics such as mind control, propaganda, developmental regression, the "social trance," loss of soul, projection and identification, existential sacrifice, dualism, loaded language, and "ideological totalism." Through a group-perpetuated one-sidedness, people lose their *sense of relationship,* and consequently are unable to relate to others, to their environment, or to themselves.

More than ever, destructive group dynamics pose one of the gravest threats to individual human potential and liberty. Knowing how to recognize and deal with this collective dark side has never had such urgency as the often deadly effects of the group-mind bombard our innate humanity and common sensibilities.

This is a good place to explain some terminology. While I use the words "group" and "collective" in this book to address their destructive influences on the individual, all groups gravitate toward a totalistic organization—their ever-present dark side. I use "group" in a specific sense, and "collective" to refer to groups in general. When using the words "cult" or "cultlike," I refer to a cluster of common destructive group dynamics that include what the dictionary refers to as "obsessive devotion or veneration for a person, principle, or ideal," as well as empowering "an exclusive group of persons sharing an esoteric interest."[3] (In the Appendix, I've listed the most common characteristics of destructive groups.) However, it's important to keep in mind that our popular usage of the term "cult" tends to narrow the concept of abuse to small religious sects, which is far from accurate. Many larger religious organizations have ideologically trapped billions of people in authoritarian, patriarchal belief systems. Now we see people following a spiritual guru, a charismatic CEO, a fanatical movement, a mesmerizing evangelist.

I use the word "soul" in a Neoplatonic sense that views the soul as residing in an *in-between place*—a mysterious, personal, experiential realm filled with imagination and fantasy, encompassing *both* good and evil, joy and sorrow. This experiential soul is the thrashing ground of realness in the individual—one's authenticity, honesty, eccentricities, and moods—a place of interconnectedness linking one to the soul in all things, animate and inanimate. From this perspective, having "soul" means being a *distinct, unique individual,* and it means having an empathy that knows no boundaries. "Psyche," although similar in meaning to the soul, I use as a descriptive, all-inclusive term indicating a totality of all psychological processes in the individual, both conscious and unconscious.

In referring to groups, I include all types: families, political parties, unions, religions, corporations, institutions, countries, communities (racial, ethnic, and social), churches, spiritual groups, self-improvement groups, recovery and support groups, street gangs, hate groups, one's peer group, the in-group, one's age group, and even psychological schools of thought. The point is that no group is immune from slipping into destructive patterns. Additionally, "systems," such as the "free-market," political, and educational systems, are extremely powerful *mega-groups* that, in turn, spawn innumerable subgroups, which, like parasites, feed off the larger "systems." This holds particular relevance for our political and economic systems.

Moreover, destructive groups come in all shapes and sizes, ranging from small, but nonetheless deadly, religious cults to massive global organizations. In general, groups have three basic modalities: economic (money-based), political (power-based), and religious/philosophical (belief-based). Society is structured in a hierarchy of groups ranging from nation-states, cities, and communities on down to the family unit. Whether a missionary religious group, a political party, a cosmetic company, or a local union, the intent and methods used by each group to recruit and indoctrinate new members are stunning in their similarity. In fact, the number of persons caught by destructive collective influences is incalculable, extending far beyond religious organizations and significantly affecting all of us whether we belong to a particular group or not.

According to the Cult Awareness Network, there are over three thousand documented, seriously destructive religious groups in the United States, with about three million members.[4] Each of these groups has a "mission": agendas that range from locally spreading their particular belief system to converting the entire world to their ideology. These religious cults are but a microcosmic snapshot of a much larger problem. The religious right, backed by over one hundred thousand churches with a membership in the tens of millions, continues to gain political power across the United States, and at this writing has formidable and ominous influence in the Republican party.

Certainly many groups are helpful and constructive forces in society. Support groups, various recovery groups, common-interest groups, and community groups *can* be invaluable and often are forums for important new ideas and information sharing, *provided they maintain a balance of power between individual autonomy and the group.* Some groups are in fact breaking down cultural barriers. Examples abound in the high-tech world of computers and telecommunications where a growing global interconnectedness points to the potential for a major shift in intercollective relationships, from an ideologically isolated, unconnected, many-group, fragmented social order, to one global community with *healthy tension* between a growing diversity of participants.

In *Under the Influence* we examine the implications of the rush to join groups—this *cultural clotting* process. Our mobile, hi-tech age has wreaked havoc with our sense of community and with our traditional relationships. Often alone, feeling rootless and disconnected, we long for meaningful connections with others, feelings of belonging and acceptance.

We will look at new approaches to help those caught in abusive, repressive, and addictive situations in groups: practical techniques we can use to extricate ourselves from the clutches of the collective mind-set. And, drawing on the rich heritage of Jungian depth psychology, we will explore the dynamic of *identification* with a group and its impact on what Carl Jung called "individuation," a critical developmental process of integration and differentiation—the psychological equivalent of self-realization. Carl Jung explained, "It [individuation] is the development of the psychological individual as a being distinct from the general, collective psychology."[5] We will see how the phenomenon of projection works to entrap people: how we lose our souls by projecting inner parts of the self—our inner gods and goddesses—onto organizations and group leaders. We will look at collective deprogramming techniques, returning the human soul to our relationships with each other, recovering the self from collective hands, and life after *group*.

This collision of the individual with the collective poses a formidable predicament: how can one be a contributing member of a group or community and yet retain one's soul, one's passion, and one's original identity? How do we walk in the great stream of humanity and not drown in it? What specific traps do groups fall into that are so devastating to individuals? How do groups slip into patterns of abuse that cause them to become dysfunctional, deteriorating, closed systems in society? Equally important, what is it in human nature that makes us so vulnerable to group influences? What archetypes, mythologies, and longings do groups awaken in the human psyche? What is the metaphor of the current headlong rush to join, like sheep jumping off a cliff, to become an "ism," to belong to "something bigger"? What exactly do groups offer that is so addictive and so compelling? What is in back of our collective "urge to merge"? Moreover, how does one *hold the tension between the collective and the individual* in a manner that adds richness, vitality, and meaning to both?

The following chapters probe the collective beast and attempt to clarify why we so willingly volunteer to be victims of groups, and why we are often so afraid to step outside of our group even when we know something is wrong and it has become destructive. Joseph Campbell saw groups as divisive, self-destructive entities in society and wrote:

> Every single one of the old horizon-bound mythologies reserved love for the in-group, and aggression and denigration for the out-group. But I see people pulling back into in-group associations. Just look all around you. This group, that group, the other: "we're it." And the challenge of the day of opening out to humanity is being ducked because it means giving up what we have and are sure of. We are afraid to un-shell.[6]

We cannot altogether escape collective influences, but we can become more aware of how this Shakespearean "beast with many heads" functions, and what we can do to protect ourselves from being manipulated and consumed by its dark side.

I

The Nature of the Beast

┌──┐
│ 回回回 │
└──┘

The tyrant grinds down his slaves and they don't turn against him; they crush those beneath them.

> Heathcliff in Emily Bronte, *Wuthering Heights* (1847)

When people are said to be in good company, often the reason is simply that they have the more civilized kinds of vices; perhaps it is the same as with poisons, the subtlest of which are also the most dangerous.

> Montesquieu, *Persian Letters* (1721)

The community today is the planet, not the bounded nation; hence the patterns of projected aggression which formerly served to co-ordinate the in-group now can only break it into factions.

> Joseph Campbell, *The Hero with a Thousand Faces* (1949)

And what rough beast, its hour come round at last, Slouches towards Bethlehem to be born?

> William Butler Yeats, "The Second Coming" (1919)

1

Collective Enchantment

Every society is compelled, for its very survival, to structure itself for power. These societies, in turn, compel their members to adapt to social demands that are in many ways antagonistic to their inborn natures.

Andrew Bard Schmookler[1]

Nothing novel, kind, or hopeful can be created in the future unless we kill this God, the idol of the tribe, unless we cease offering our blood to Moloch.

Sam Keen[2]

No perverseness equals that which is supported by system, no errors are so difficult to root out as those which the understanding has pledged its credit to uphold.

William Wordsworth[3]

The stacking together of the paintings of the great masters in museums is a catastrophe, and a collection of a hundred good intellects produces collectively one idiot.

Carl Jung[4]

Death by Group

What the crowd requires is mediocrity of the highest order.

Auguste Préault[5]

As this century draws to a close, we find ourselves immersed in a culture that is heavily influenced and, to a large extent, controlled by group ideologies—a collective enchantment. We seem under a spell, a social trance, convinced that collective organizations, whether political, religious, or economic, somehow have the solutions and answers we need to cope with life's challenges. Like Odysseus's crew in the *Odyssey,* the seductive collective voice lures us into the castle where we are fed a mysterious potion and turned into pigs.[6] In drinking the group elixir, we lose our humanity, our essential, inherent character and distinctiveness.

Groups have trapped millions of individuals, destroying individual freedom of expression, enforcing collective rules and norms, indoctrinating people into their belief systems, and ostracizing those who do not conform to group values. Groups, like individuals, have both light and dark sides and therefore have the innate destructive potential to compromise individual integrity. Collective integrity in a society comes from embracing *individual* diversity, not culturing *sameness.*

Destructive groups cross the line that separates a relatively benign organization from one that is immediately dangerous: *The group becomes more important than the individual.* Consequently, members lose their freedom and autonomy, becoming *things* instead of human beings. The renowned mythologist Joseph Campbell (1904–1988) observed, "The ego that sees a 'thou' is not the same ego that sees an 'it.' "[7] "Thou" acknowledges another human being, while "it" dehumanizes the other. It is easier to demean or kill an "it" than a "thou." Destructive groups turn human beings into objects or things. Collectivized egos view life through the "crowd soul," a sharklike feeding machine.

Hitler, Stalin, Mao, Gandhi, Jesus, Buddha, Luther—what do all these individuals have in common? They were leaders or founders of mass movements and all led and controlled groups, in some cases benefiting humankind, but in many instances propagating unimaginable evil and terror.

What do Rwanda, Bosnia, Russia, China, the United States, Iraq, Iran, and Israel all have in common? They are all nation-states, some freer than others, some violent and dictatorial—and they are all *organized groups.* Public education, the FDA, unions, business enterprise, religions—all are groups that appear to embody many noble and idealistic goals, yet their dark sides, placing the group's agenda ahead of the individual, far too often predominate.

A fairy tale by Richard Roberts titled *The Mask that Wore the Man* illustrates the essential dilemma between the collective and the individual. In his story, a child is born without a face. Looked upon as a fool by the local villagers, he is constantly teased and humiliated. One day, while wandering in the forest, the child happens upon a clearing where a theatrical play is underway. He watches for hours, fascinated by the elaborate costumes and masks. After the play is over and everyone has gone, he determines to make for himself a magician's mask, reflecting the "face of every man," so that he, too, can be applauded and admired. Wearing his new mask, the child returns to the village. Much to his surprise, he discovers that each person he meets sees in him exactly what they wanted to see. As a result, he quickly becomes very popular and very busy. To the sick, he is a wise healer; to the religious, his is the word of God; to the common folk, he is a magnificent wise stranger who seems to know their innermost desires.

For many days the child continues in his new role, putting his mask on each morning and carefully removing it each evening. One evening, after an especially long and tiring day, he falls into a deep sleep, forgetting to take off the mask. Not realizing that he no longer removed the mask, many weeks pass. The child is elected to high political office, and wined and dined as the town's number-one celebrity. Eventually he decides that he needs a vacation, thinking that he would take some time off, return to the forest, and contemplate his situation and all that had happened. Looking in a mirror, the child begins to remove the mask, but it will not budge. Horrified, he tears at the edges, but to no avail. The mask will not come off. In fact, his skin now seems to have grown into the mask. Terror-stricken, he realizes that for the rest of his life, the mask is now wearing him![8]

Groups do not have a personal conscience. What they do have is a collective center of gravity where some ideal or higher purpose becomes the driving force for a collective mission. But the dark side of common idealism always builds around sex, money, and power over others, with individual human beings becoming the fuel to drive the mass mind. Collective agencies have a built-in propensity toward accumulating more centralized power. And when centralized authority and power increase in a group, individual responsibility and autonomy decrease.

Our group-oriented society shapes us in a collective image. Collective influences in our culture work to keep everyone within a *normal* range of culturally specific and socially demanded behavior, a collective imperative to *fit in* or be cast out. Groups impose their reality upon individuals, and individuals base their self-image on a collective or group ideal. This group-derived identity points to the insidious tendency of groups to assume responsibility over the individual's process of differentiation: the necessary separation from the mass that marks a mature adult, able to stand on his own feet. Only the individual can complete this task. Differentiation does not mean that we leave our community or social group. Rather it implies a growing up combined with a detached involvement where groups no longer shape our reality and manipulate our consciousness. A group will continually frustrate this essential developmental process. Carl Jung, in his autobiography *Memories, Dreams, Reflections,* observed: "All collective identities, such as memberships in organizations, support of 'isms,' and so on, interfere with the fulfillment of this task [differentiation]. Such collective identities are crutches for the lame, shields for the timid, beds for the lazy, nurseries for the irresponsible."[9]

The individual's *right of choice* to believe anything, regardless of how unorthodox, is not the issue. Rather the problem is with groups that utilize potent psychological techniques such as propaganda, thought reform, and mind control to eliminate individual freedom of choice, alter personality and behavior, and cause people to believe something *without their informed consent.* Merging with the collective seriously erodes the freedom to choose one's own way in life and the ultimate inner freedom to *choose one's attitude* toward life. Subtle but powerful and organized collective influences now threaten the last bastion of human freedom, one's private inner stream of consciousness.

Containment in a group means we filter our view of the world through the group or collective system to which we belong. But a *relationship to a group* is utterly different from being *contained in it.* From containment *inside* a group, we become culturally and socially shut off from other views, psychologically and spiritually crippled. To remain free of collective influences, one needs the perspective of individual autonomy or self-determination, which is the first thing one loses in most groups.

CULTURAL CONDITIONING

> The danger of the past was that men became slaves. The danger of the future is that men may become robots. True enough, robots do not rebel. But given man's nature, robots cannot live and remain sane, they become "Golems," they will destroy their world and themselves because they cannot stand any longer the boredom of a meaningless life.
>
> Erich Fromm[10]

The totality of literature, art, religion, mythology and the entire range of human endeavor combine in a process of cultural conditioning—a collective shaping of individuals within a cultural milieu. Whenever a particular ideology such as Christianity or a particular system like the market system become dominant influences, individuals suffer as powerful collective forces gradually exclude and destroy all that is alien to their view.

Logic suggests that the human soul is a nonexclusive creature—that confining the psyche to one particular system or theology is therefore unnatural. Life on earth presents us with an endless panorama of diversity. Indeed, even our dreams reveal an inner multiplicity of figures, a plural psyche, a self with many faces. The soul's natural state would appear to require a milieu of rich diversity in contrast to a milieu of implanted cultural and religious dogma that pressures individuals into adaptive, absolutist, exclusive positions. The human psyche is inherently multifaceted and "polytheistic,"[11] not monotheistic or totalitarian. Our prevalent monotheism can be thought of as more a cultural implant of the times than a natural state of affairs. Depth psychology has shown that the psyche is comprised of many parts, inner child, shadow, hero, witch, wise old woman/man, and so on. James Hillman, the eminent Jungian analyst, prolific writer, and founder of archetypal psychology, maintains that the psyche is "not only multiple, it is a communion of many persons, each with specific needs, fears, longings, styles, and language." Calling this multiplicity "psychological polytheism," Hillman adds, "It implies a life that can embrace conflicting directions, one that doesn't resort to hierarchies and overarching principles to impose order."[12]

We must ask, what does it mean to be human in an age of machines—an age of intellectual supremacy? In America, we fought for freedom from the tyranny of European totalitarian religious/political systems. Ironically we now live under the influence of totalitarian collective systems that provide the illusion of freedom. There are no U.S. dictators in our semidemocracy. In his landmark study of Chinese Communist thought reform practices, "Thought Reform and the Psychology of Totalism," Robert Lifton, a distinguished professor of psychiatry at New York's John Jay College, synthesized the underlying psychological dynamics found in destructive groups and religious cults. Lifton refers to these recurring dynamics as "psychological" and "ideological totalism." Robert Lifton's "ideological totalism"[13] is alive and well in our collective culture as multitudes of groups compete for *shares of mind.* This subtle, often unseen tyranny—our invisible dictatorship—insidiously erodes human will and freedom, threatening the future of all life on our planet.

The former Communist Soviet mind-set will not end so easily because its ideology is embedded in the collective psyche of Russia. We cannot be sure where this totalistic bent will take the new Russia. We can be sure that it will be a significant influence on the political scene regardless of that nation's political alignment. We can also count on the Russian people to "expect" their new government to solve all their problems. Having been under the authoritarian fist of communism for so long, they will unconsciously project a parental image onto any new system.

THE HEART OF THE DILEMMA

> Ultimately everything depends on the quality of the individual, but our fatally short-sighted age thinks only in terms of large numbers and mass organizations, though one would think that the world had seen more than enough of what a well-disciplined mob can do in the hands of a single madman.
>
> Carl Jung[14]

Can we benefit from and value the best in our collective culture without being possessed by it? How does one differentiate the human psyche philosophically, emotionally, and spiritually not only from one's family, but from larger collective influences in the world? Innovative ways to harness the creative potential within groups without sacrificing individual autonomy and freedom need to be found if the world is to survive the present chaos and violence.

Much of our society is locked into a *conforming-to-group* structure, which demands that the individual take sides. One is deemed a "good Christian" based on regular church attendance and the following of a particular ideology. The intellectual establishment accepts members into its ranks provided they have proper academic credentials as proof of having jumped through the system's hoops; the rewards are money, social status, and privilege. In this manner the institutionalized system rewards those who play the game, those whom the system trains to maintain and perpetuate the system. Thus group dynamics manipulate and control our lives far more than we care to admit.

Any such system of societal reward and punishment is inherently totalistic in nature. A soul-based depth psychology encompassing both the individual and the collective has the potential to break this pattern of maintaining the collective status quo and preserving systems at the expense of human beings. Any psychology that endeavors to break our collective chains must keep itself free of the "fix it and make it feel better" mode of psychotherapy, the therapeutic dogma that encourages individuals to *reconform* to their social group. Psychology, to be effective once more, must be taken out of the patriarchal role of reinforcing an ideological one-sidedness of the psyche—the role of being a pawn for a greater collective agency (for example the mental health system)—which defines neuroses within the context of conforming or not conforming to a collective agenda. I can't be depressed because in our society, feeling bad is unacceptable.

Depth psychology honors the depths, the soul. As such, depth psychology is a psychology of soul-making. Modern psychotherapy has in most cases become an acculturating and socializing tool of the state, shaping individuals into *acceptable* collective roles.

Around 1433 C.E., the *Corpus Hermeticum,* an alchemical underground bible of sorts, was considered a heretical writing because it held the belief that individuals had a dual nature, mortal and immortal, and that the world was *incomplete,* requiring the individual soul to undertake the task of creation itself. This unfinished soul-work became each person's work as a co-creator with God. The alchemists worked with the imagination, believing that one must let an image work upon the soul—that the painting is not complete until it is seen by the viewer.

Perhaps our real modern heroes are those individuals who manage to slay (differentiate themselves from) the collective dragon. In a collective sense, the seducer of souls (true evil) is anything or anyone that lures us from being who we are, taking us from our own unique path, remaking the individual in a group image and crushing the unique insight of the individual soul. Jung, in *The Undiscovered Self,* elaborated on the dangers inherent in mass movements. He wrote:

> As experience unfortunately shows, the inner man remains unchanged however much community he has. His environment cannot give him as a gift something which he can win for himself only with effort and suffering. On the contrary, a favorable environment merely strengthens the dangerous tendency to expect everything from outside—even that metamorphosis which external reality cannot provide.[15]

Living an authentic life means seeing things as they really are, from the inside out, not from a collective outside in. Our collectively suppressed and long ignored, unintegrated shadow side more and more possesses people. Driven underground, these dark energies, which are in all of us, become our personal as well as our collective demons, eventually erupting from the unconscious into consciousness. Like puppets on a string, we encounter unknown forces controlling and propelling us; our cultural complexes (our collective dark side) has us by the scruff of our collective necks. Experts at playing our roles, the freedom we naively believe we enjoy is actually a formidable psychological prison of our own creation.

From the dawn of time we've lived in groups, classes, tribes. The inclination and apparent deeply seated need to be with others of our kind, to belong to a community, creates a primary existential conflict—a collision of opposites. On the one hand, it is a part of human nature to differentiate from the collective organism; on the other hand, no one wants to feel isolated or outcast. The balance of power between these two polarities usually favors the group. According to Mother Teresa of Calcutta, God "called" her to her vocation. By following her "calling," her passion, she has attracted a large following of those who want to be like her. Individuals who live their passion impart a mystique and intensity to whatever they love. This makes their work extraordinarily attractive and intriguing. Mother Teresa may be able to live authentically as the spiritual leader of a large subgroup, which has its own strict militaristic-style hierarchy embedded within the larger Catholic church. But, are her followers living their own authentic lives or are they living a mirror of Mother Teresa's passion?

CHAOS AND ASSIMILATION

> Nearly all the international debt accumulated by African states, and nearly half of all other Third World debt, comes from the purchase of weapons by states to fight their own citizens. Most of the world's twelve million refugees are the offspring of such conflicts, as are most of the 100 million *internally* displaced people who have been uprooted from their homelands. Most of the world's famine victims are nation peoples who are being starved by states that attempt to *assimilate* them while appropriating their food supplies. (Emphasis added)
>
> Jason W. Clay[16]

During chaotic social transitional periods, there is an increase in the tendency for people to join groups in order to achieve a sense of stability and security amid chaos. In the midst of chaotic world change, a group often appears to be a safe refuge. However, a "safety in numbers" approach to life is dangerously flawed; if all the numbers are zeros, people find themselves in a communal morass—a collective existential vacuum—that is not only unsafe, but marks the end to one's individuality, freedom, and autonomy.

Cultural *spaces-in-between* are dangerous periods for any nation-state, for in such gaps there is a powerful movement toward polarization, a moving toward *one* viewpoint that supposedly will save the day and heal the social ills of the times. But *only the individual* can save and revitalize the community.

The totalitarian mind is a group-oriented *assimilating mind* that cannot tolerate difference. A modern nation-state *ethnically cleanses* itself through *assimilation,* a consuming, transforming collective process in which the predominate culture cannibalizes other cultures, often resulting in their disappearance. In the process, persons lose their individual uniqueness and their cultural integrity. Such absorption in the hands of a nation-state is the political equivalent to a "One God" monarchic theology that seeks to make everything "one" and the same.

In the documentary "The War Against the Indians," the Discovery Channel reported that when Columbus "discovered" the Americas, he wrote back to Spain that the American Indians "had no religion and would make good slaves."[17] He really meant that the Indians did not have Christianity yet! Thus for most cultures, assimilation means extermination.

People everywhere are in the midst of intense psychological warfare with the mass mind—a battle that threatens complete assimilation into the collective mind-set where we will no longer *exist* as individuals, but only as dehumanized working parts of the collective machinery. The human psyche is our new frontier; the battle for control of individual mental and psychological processes defines our struggle to attain a greater dimension of freedom and integrity in the midst of widespread devastating group dynamics.

Implications for People and the Planet

The world has become a stage for the collective shadow.

Connie Zweig[18]

The mass of men must satisfy the needs of the social organism in which they live far more than the social organism must satisfy them.

Norman Mailer[19]

The implications for our society and our culture derive from the consequences of a collective ideology characterized by a *we/they* split. A tribal propensity to split everything into warring factions is wreaking havoc throughout the world. Our global breakdown in human relationships suggests an overwhelming urgency to free individuals from this trap of identification with one side of a pair of *group-defined* opposites. A soul-honoring depth psychology has within its approach to life an important key to resolving these opposites: not to escape from them, but to *hold* them in our consciousness, and in so doing shift the human spirit from a rigid patriarchal dualism into a *three-dimensional* soul-centered perspective.

Such cultural dualism produces a partitioned society with a proliferation of opposing groups, from street gangs to nations, each reacting against a perceived enemy or threat to its position, its turf. Collective splitting finds expression in *acting out* far too often through war, violence, and terror. We can only wonder how much child abuse and spouse abuse is the result of such polarization.

By joining forces with either camp, we lose our freedom and step out of the most creative and exquisite *space of the in-between,* the androgynous point, home of the Self, the changing changelessness, the coming together of masculine and feminine, wholeness, integration, integrity, the razor's edge.

Rampant throughout the world, collective symptoms and complexes increasingly perplex sociologists, national leaders, and politicians: gangs, violence, war, pollution, starvation, genocide, mass immigrations and displacements, political and social upheavals—the not-always-silent screams erupting from the collective fabric of the late twentieth century. During 1993, we had ethnic violence in forty-eight countries around the globe.[20]

What exactly is the message in suffering, both psychological and physical, both personal and collective? Perhaps the "collective unconscious," through which we are all interconnected, is trying to get our attention. It would seem that the very body of humanity desperately needs therapeutic intervention. What then can be ill if not the groups, systems, and institutions that formulate, shape, and regulate our lives? The cause of our widespread social disorders certainly rests more in dominant collective dynamics than in the personal. Our increasing masses of "have nots," the twentieth century's dispossessed citizens, are rapidly becoming the fuel of discontent and frustration that threaten revolution and upheaval.

Ultimate responsibility, however, belongs to you and me, for we have empowered "others" to take care of all our problems. A growing list of "rights" increasingly excuses government confiscation and redistribution of wealth and property with the resultant decrease in personal freedom and self-responsibility. More reliance on groups means less self-reliance, less self-respect, and more *disrespect*. A collective dogma of "let some group or public agency take care of it" numbs our human sensibilities and natural empathy, destroying our self-esteem along with our integrity and sense of purpose. Of what use are families when the government does everything for us? Increasingly mechanized by collective rules and regulations, we become little more than robots attached to the mass culture, programmed to be "normal" and ostracized if we're not.

Our growing indifference and intolerance to each other mirrors our collective hardening—the authoritarian dark side that so pervades most groups. We don't know our neighbors anymore and quite often we don't care to. Writing about our collective numbing, Joe Klein, senior editor and columnist for *Newsweek,* wondered: "Is it possible that the 1990s are the 1930s on Prozac?"[21] Our gods, heroes, and neighbors now live in the TV set and in the stereo system. We have an electronic media family that we can turn on or off. Our *relationships* with others have become projective illusions. We are more comfortable with Phil Donahue or Jay Leno than the person next door. Our neighbors have become faceless, nameless persons caught in collective obscurity. If our neighbor has a problem, we wonder why some state agency hasn't taken care of it; it's not *our* problem. It's some *group's* problem.

Hence our relationships continue to disintegrate—as does our individual distinctiveness—under the collective bewitchment that has *trained us* to expect a mysterious collective "they" to solve all our problems. "They" are now in charge of you and me, and we expect "them" to turn off our depressions and moods, and turn on our happiness and joy. When we want to be happy, we spend $200 at a "theme park" instead of using our time creatively, living our own lives. Or we medicate ourselves with system-approved drugs so that we don't *feel* anything uncomfortable. The collective has trained us to be "on or off" binary machines with no relationship to the many parts of ourselves and no relationship to others. Machinelike, if we experience a little discomfort, we "fix it," losing the opportunity to expand our self-awareness and soulfulness by *going into* what ails us. Instead, we rewire the brain's circuitry because our behavior doesn't "fit" the popular mold, and rewiring the brain's circuitry is *exactly* what groups and drugs do to individuals.

The phenomenon of "death and disinterest" has become the subject of talk shows.[22] Intense interest in the caning of an American teenager in Singapore and the nearly zero media interest in the slaughter of hundreds of thousands of Rwandan citizens indicate how numbed our human sensibilities have become. We simply cannot relate to death and destruction that is *unconnected* to our group, in this case the United States. Completely identified with the Western culture, most Americans are disconnected from any sense of relationship to human beings outside their group.

This insensibility insidiously erodes "human heartedness," restricting our natural empathy to members of our social and cultural group. Having first lost the connection to our own authenticity and integrity, we find it an easy task to similarly turn our backs on suffering masses in a distant land. You may say, "We have sent aid to help them." Once more, we rely on "someone else," that collective anonymous "they" to do something, anything, so that we can continue to live a drugged, guilt-free, heart-deadening, conscience-killing, collectively approved life.

The Berlin Wall acted as a barrier that enabled East and West Berlin (two opposing group ideologies) to remain relatively unconscious of each other. Now that the wall is down, an inevitable struggle is taking place between two opposite societies, with individuals caught in the middle. The integration of these two collective entities will be difficult but it holds the potential of synergetically producing something unique and new for the world. Most assuredly, neither East or West Berlin will ever be the same, and the struggle for individuals will be to retain their freedom and autonomy in the midst of the conflict.

We live in a world bumping up against collective walls that have separated nations and individuals for eons. R. Buckminster Fuller, the world-

acclaimed thinker, scientist, inventor, and mathematician, referred to nation-states as "150 blood clots."[23] In this process there is bound to be
struggle, especially for those who refuse to acknowledge and work with
opposite points of view. Thus, for a time, bigotry and racism will increase
as people are directly confronted with opposites and with difference.

A cold war is a state of accumulating tension, while a hot war is a stage
of releasing and acting out repressed collective tension. In a sense, we are
in the midst of a psychological/spiritual war where the battlefield is within
the human spirit, and the individual soul is up for grabs to the most powerful collective agency. The more we give in to collective domination, the
more excessive *tension* accumulates between who we really are as individuals and our collective roles.

R. D. Laing, the noted psychiatrist and author of *The Divided Self,*
maintained that a psychosis results from a breakdown of society's mask—
a tension between one's real self and the collective persona that becomes
intolerable. Thus when the distance between who we really are and the collective role we play becomes too great, the psyche breaks down.

Depression and melancholy, which are epidemic in our society, may be
not so much from what we have done as from what we have not done. The
"existential crisis," the psychological cancer of our age, may be the result
of living illusory collective lives, lives covered over with the iron masks
of totalistic one-sidedness. Split off from our own dark gods, we consequently miss the hidden gold to be found in the shadow.

More than ever the world needs unique, *individual* creativity to solve the
critical problems now facing humankind. Individuals remove themselves
from humanity the moment they believe their particular organization or tradition is special, with some unique purpose or wisdom. This *dark dynamic*
in groups needs to be confronted, for we are in an age of rapidly increasing
conflict between group ideologies: racial, political, religious, and economic.

Human consciousness is so interconnected with the earth that our environment tends to become like us. As our consciousness widens, becoming more soul-full, the earth will be healed. Our planet is rapidly losing its
ability to heal itself and its capability to be *self-governing.* The earth, like
you and me, is losing its autonomy as a result of the patriarchal predomi-
nance of a *conscienceless* group mind-set. Our world needs not "rugged individualism" so much as what the Tao philosophy calls "Jen," a soulful
"human heartedness."

OUR COMMON HUMANITY

A single song is being inflected through all the colorations of the human
choir. General propaganda for one or another of the local solutions, there-

fore, is superfluous—or much rather, a menace. The way to become human is to learn to recognize the lineaments of God in all of the wonderful modulations of the face of man.

Joseph Campbell[24]

Both collective and individual impulses war with one another within the individual psyche. We need a certain degree of compromise with the collective for survival. However, when collective thinking and feeling predominate, we become alienated from the real self. Thus whenever a group ideology becomes the mainstay of the personality and consciousness, one sacrifices living his own unique life.

A healthy relationship with the collective demands a balance, *a state of tension* between general expectations and the creative expression of one human soul. While some degree of compromise with the collective is necessary in order to function in society, too much is deadly for individuals and for the collective as well.

What Jung called the "collective unconscious" comprises a common link between all life: an underlying interconnectivity containing "the whole spiritual heritage of mankind's evolution, born anew in the brain structure of every individual."[25] It is important to differentiate between the collective unconscious and general influences from cultural and societal agencies. Jung explained:

> The collective unconscious—so far as we can say anything about it at all— appears to consist of mythological motifs or primordial images [archetypes], for which reason the myths of all nations are its real exponents. In fact, the whole of mythology could be taken as a sort of projection of the collective unconscious. . . . We can therefore study the collective unconscious in two ways, either in mythology or in the analysis of the individual.[26]

The importance of teaching mythology to our children becomes apparent. Through our stories and myths we develop an understanding, empathy, and tolerance for those who are different. What a tragic loss that often we are exposed to only one religious or philosophical view. In this group-facilitated (our educational system) narrow-mindedness we find the roots of prejudice, bigotry, and hatred.

Mythology, relegated to unscientific foolishness in modern times, has the potential to transform relationships between citizens of all nations. Paradoxically, the collective unconscious, as a bearer of our common archetypal roots, strikes a death blow to divisiveness and separateness perpetuated by so many groups. The effects of an increased understanding of the collective unconscious are profound, not only enlarging one's consciousness, but freeing one from the ego-prison of fixed ideas and judgments. As Jung said, "it [consciousness] is a function of relationship to the world of objects, bringing the individual into absolute, binding, and indissoluble communion with the world at large."[27] Here we find the basis for real community—not so much similar beliefs, but instead a *similar humanity.* It is precisely our lack of a "relationship" to the world of objects and the world of other peoples that wreaks havoc environmentally and socially.

The word "evolution" comes from the Latin *evolutio,* meaning "an opening, an unrolling." Therefore to "evolve" implies *movement*—movement in consciousness, not in the sense of up or down, but in a sense of greater inner-outerness, an awareness and insight about who we are and the psychological mechanics of how we relate to others.

Human nature resists change (movement) unless it comes without effort or expense, i.e., *some*thing for *no*thing. To evolve, to move, creates tension. We all have an innate inertia, a gravity of thinking and feeling that easily succumbs to collective "shoulds." Holding evolutionary tension means we have to let go, "unroll," move, and *allow* ourselves to take risks, be frightened, be uncomfortable. In other words, evolution depends on the principle of *tension.*

Thus the evolution of consciousness becomes the real work of each individual, not in the sense of group-defined material or technological progress, but in the sense of deepening insight into our individual unique potential and our common humanity as passengers on this tiny planet hurtling through space in the outer reaches of our galaxy.

Individuation: Differentiating from the Herd

> If you bring forth what is within you, what you bring forth will save you.
> If you do not bring forth what is within you, what you do not bring forth
> will destroy you.
>
> Jesus, The Gospel According to Thomas[28]

Jung wrote, "the aim of individuation is nothing less than to divest the self of the false wrappings of the persona on the one hand, and of the suggestive power of primordial images on the other."[29] Jung's reference to "primordial images" indicates the danger inherent in collective images such as religious figures, sports heroes, political leaders, celebrities, and other popular figureheads. These collective images, when cloaked in an archetypal mystique, become all-powerful collective gods in the human psyche, thwarting the individuation process where each person must "slay their Buddhas" whenever met on one's journey.

Often misunderstood as some variation of "individualism," the individuation process "is a process of differentiation, having for its goal the development of the individual personality. As the individual is not just a single, separate being, but by his very existence presupposes a collective relationship, it follows that the process of individuation must lead to more intense and broader collective relationships and not to isolation."[30]

When we internalize and identify with popular icons, they become the dragons we must slay in order to become whole human beings. This does not in any way mean that we cannot draw inspiration and glean much wisdom from the example of others, but eventually we must come to the realization that each of us is totally unique. To realize our own potential, we must take back our projections by psychologically slaying our outer heroes to become our own hero whose task is to bring a whole individual to consciousness. This cannot be done as long as we idolize others, whether gods, devils, or humans. The process of individuation implies far more than simply attaining greater consciousness. It means an eventual "synthesis of the Self," a state of wholeness where we gather together our many fragmented, projected parts, where our inner reality and authenticity form the ground of the conscious ego.

The process of individuation means a vital and ever-changing, passionate exchange and involvement between the personal and collective. In this late twentieth century, we are on anything but an equal footing with the collective. Jung maintained, "Individuation does not shut one out from the world, but gathers the world to itself."[31] Daryl Sharp, a Jungian analyst and author of *Personality Types: Jung's Model of Typology,* points out that:

> Individuation and a life lived by collective values are nevertheless two divergent destinies. In Jung's view they are related to one another by guilt. Whoever embarks on the personal path becomes to some extent estranged from collective values, but does not thereby lose those aspects of the psyche which are inherently collective. To atone for this "desertion," the individual is obliged to create something of worth for the benefit of society.[32]

It is precisely the "creation of something of worth" that *enmeshment* in groups prevents, while differentiation from the collective enables one to make a worthwhile contribution. *Only the individual* can initiate this "hero's journey." In fact, Jung maintained that, "Without this production of values, . . . individuation is immoral and—more than that—suicidal."[33]

Organized religions, or organized "anything" means someone else (some group) is organizing our life. And a collectively organized life is a compromised life to the extent that it prevents one from expressing one's true nature. Granted, living requires a certain degree of compromise with the collective, but there is a vast difference between a degree of compromise and complete surrender to a group ideology. The former may be a social necessity, while the latter annihilates our individual reality and integrity.

The process of individuation depends upon maintaining the tension between the conscious ego and the unconscious. For only by consciously tolerating a state of tension can we give birth to the authentic Self, our true individuality, our unique personality. Similarly, we must hold the tension between collective and individual autonomy and freedom.

In this process, perfection is not a goal; instead, one strives to become more conscious—a never-ending process throughout life. The process of becoming more conscious, of becoming a responsible individual complete with good and bad qualities, limitations, and strengths, makes us more *human,* able to empathize with others.

Only by respecting and guarding our own integrity and uniqueness do we come to respect others, and in the process differentiate ourselves from the collective—no longer children but adults, expressing who we really are, which is the greatest contribution one can ever make. Only by living our own lives, by being true to ourselves, do we, in the words of poet William Wordsworth, "trail clouds of glory."

THE DIFFERENTIATED PSYCHE

> If each thing follows its own *li* [principles] it will harmonize with all other things following theirs, not by reason of rule imposed from above but by their mutual resonance and interdependence.
>
> Alan Watts[34]

Greater consciousness demands separation of parts from a whole; it demands both "resonance" and interconnectedness, which precludes one-sided alignment with a particular viewpoint—even one's own point of view. As long as people identify completely with a collective ideal or system, they are unable to access the consciousness-producing tension between individual parts of the psyche. Instead, conflicting parts are repressed, submerged into the unconscious where they are left to ferment, causing all sorts of psychological and physical mischief. Unfortunately, all movement toward increased insight and greater awareness grinds to a halt. For example, I agree with some Republican ideas and strongly disagree with others. Some Democratic principles appeal to me, yet I vigorously disagree with others. If I became totally enmeshed in *either* political party's beliefs, I would have to push part of my conscience and integrity underground, denying an authentic part of myself and compromising who I really am. Of course, it automatically follows that my identification with any political party forces me to make other political groups my adversaries. By total identification with a group, I become a "label" that dehumanizes me; I become an appendage of a collective organism, and in order to maintain my group's position, I must disown all other conflicting parts of my psyche. In this sort of collective compromise, everybody loses: the individual and the group. The undifferentiated mind is a lost, trapped mind incapable of independent thinking, for all thought processes are *conditional*: they must confirm and help perpetuate the *group*.

Ironically, every adamant position we take helps to form its opposite, which, in the situation of group-enmeshed individuals, means they collectively create their own enemies. These psychologically engineered enemies then become the carriers of all the collective disowned energies. Thus our group dislikes another group that appears to represent the opposition to our group's views. We then spend our lives hating parts of ourselves we refuse to acknowledge; then, projected onto others, our own darkness enables our group to be pure, free of error, and superior. Ultimately, we cannot direct our own lives unless we function within a differentiated psyche, a psyche free of enmeshment with any group or collectivity.

Barbarians in the City

> The man of today, who resembles more or less the collective ideal, has made his heart into a den of murderers, as can easily be proved by the analysis of his unconscious, even though he himself is not in the least disturbed by it. And in so far as he is normally "adapted" to his environment, it is true that the greatest infamy on the part of his group will not disturb him, so long as the majority of his fellows steadfastly believe in the exalted morality of their social organization.
>
> Carl Jung[35]

Destructive groups have exited their Trojan horses. What first appeared as beneficial to society has become a malignant cancer eating out the heart and soul of the human spirit. Organized religions that market toxic spirituality, political special interest groups, industry groups and lobbyists that make a shambles of representative democracy, and commercial enterprises that sell deadly products are all barbaric in the sense that, as groups, they impose their agendas/products/ideas on individuals. Using the dark side of technology, destructive groups market their wares on a global scale. What is the difference if depression, smog, polluted food, cigarettes, or bullets kill us? The end result, death, is the same.

ABC News reported in 1993 that cigarettes kill 434,000 people each year in the United States alone.[36] R. J. Reynolds, in *one* North Carolina plant, makes 300 million cigarettes per day. The tobacco industry is one of many examples of destructive business groups. They design their advertising to persuade or brainwash individuals into believing that smoking is acceptable. Destructive commercial groups place profits above human life—this is economic barbarism and *uncivilized* behavior. It is an example of how a business acts out a collective complex: money is all-powerful, a green-backed god. Such groups work to "protect" their special interests at the expense of human beings. They have no soul, no empathy, and no mercy. They are the great white sharks in our collective sea.

Unfortunately, many employees of such enterprises are victims of what becomes an endless round of compromise between one's innate sense of right and wrong, the need to survive and to support their families, and their company's policies. Is any job worth sacrificing even a small portion of one's integrity? Not an easy question. Certainly part of the solution rests upon the shoulders of those individuals who choose to stop supporting corrupt organizations, either leaving or working from within to expose and change destructive practices. Individuals caught up in groups of one sort or another are responsible for the vast majority of violence around the world. Whether Los Angeles street gangs or the Irish Republican Army, groups, convinced of the singular righteousness of their cause, instill a brute mob mentality, empower a "crowd soul," numbing individual sensibilities and obliterating self-responsibility. Does this mean we should dismantle such groups? No, just *disempower them by making the individual more important than any group.* The formation of violence-prone groups provides valuable insight about what ails society. Indeed, when channeled into nonviolent pursuits and creative expression, rage can transform our communities and the world. Constructive change usually requires intense emotion. But, even more ominous than organized physical violence, group-based emotional and psychological abuse silently, and often unseen, eats away at our humanity.

It doesn't take a lot of intellectual prowess to know what is controlling whom. In Washington, D.C., lobbying is the fourth largest industry with revenues in excess of $60 million each year, employing over 20,400 people.[37] The American Petroleum Institute has a staff of 350 people and an annual budget of $50 million. Political Action Committees (PACs) number over 2,000 groups spending $370 million each year. [38] So much for democracy! While many lobbyists do provide important information and help counteract unreasonable and unjust legislation, many go far beyond that role, influencing public officials to enact laws that insure immense profit and exclusive advantages to special interest groups. For example, the Senate, under pressure from timber lobbyists, recently (October 1995) passed a bill allowing loggers to clear-cut sections of Alaska's Arctic National Wildlife Refuge, the nation's last rainforest and home to many endangered species, including grizzlies and bald eagles.[39]

THE PROBLEM OF OPPOSITES

> There is no freedom at either end; only in the middle position, between
> . . . opposites, does a certain amount of consciousness and with it of individual freedom seem to be possible.
>
> Marie-Louise Von Franz[40]

The notion of opposites and our reflexive mechanical fixation on concretizing pairs of opposites must be transcended *not* by leaving the oppositeness, but by entering into the *space between them* and maintaining the relationship (tension) between the two.

The inexorable tendency of groups and systems toward polar opposites constitutes a formidable obstacle to continued development of the human spirit. What's more, the splitting (patriarchal) nature of groups has so decimated our environment that it will take a concerted global effort to even begin to repair the damage, let alone reverse the deadly progress of what has now become a collective disease: groups and systems that tyrannize the individual, both psychologically and physically. You and I would not even consider, as individuals, dumping poisonous waste in the ocean, but groups and systems we voluntarily support and empower do just that, everyday! We have given up our integrity and our power on a vast scale.

PSYCHOLOGICAL OPPORTUNITY COST

> We often experience more regret over the part we have left, than pleasure over the part we have preferred.
>
> Joseph Roux[41]

In economics, "opportunity cost" refers to the situation where in order to pursue a particular goal, something else must be given up. In other words there is no "free lunch." If I spend ten dollars on lunch, I must give up spending that ten dollars on anything else. In a group context, when we "spend" our resources, physical and psychological, on the group's agenda, we incur hidden costs: we lose what we *could have done* with our time and energy. In the process of living we must *select*—we must make choices. The choices we make demand the exclusion of those things that are irrelevant to the direction we have chosen. This fact of life means there is an automatic propensity to take sides, to get caught in one particular viewpoint. Psychologically, what happens to the excluded, lost possibilities and energies of consciousness? Depth psychology has shown that these excluded and repressed contents move into our unconscious, stirring up all sorts of images, fantasies, dreams, and in cases of extreme one-sidedness, appearing as autonomous complexes and disease.

In this manner we create entropic chaos within our personal unconscious, and we certainly construct more of our own demons than we care to admit.

Jungian psychology postulates that, "Depression should therefore be regarded as an unconscious compensation whose content must be made conscious if it is to be fully effective. This can only be done by consciously regressing along with the depressive tendency and integrating the memories so activated into the conscious mind—which was what the depression was aiming at all along."[42] This predicament is compounded when our depression is causally related to repressed material in order to "support" a group ideology. To work on our own depression automatically means being at odds with our group. To speak *one's own mind* invites the wrath of the collective mind, which prefers to keep its own shadow hidden and buried. This is one of the reasons so many religious cults and even many twelve-step groups oppose psychotherapy. They don't want you and me to think for ourselves in spite of what they publicly proclaim. They want members to follow *their* program or system. Thus we have the spectacle of former addicts now newly addicted to a self-help or support group.

The Collective God Hole: The Quest for Meaning

> With the selection for the ways of power beyond the ability of humankind to stop, people became the servants rather than the masters of their systems. Under the reign of power, human creativity did not so much drive the engine of social evolution as become grist for its mill.
>
> Andrew Bard Schmookler[43]

Groups encourage what I call "creativity in a box," which means we can be creative as long as it furthers the group's agenda and purpose. This conditional creativity leads to existential creative frustration and the uneasy gut feeling that *something* is wrong with us—there's something missing, a void. According to the *New York Times,* Americans spent $8.1 billion in 1992 on over 100 million therapy sessions attempting to figure out what was wrong with them.[44]

As a nation, we seem to be in the midst of a desperate search for meaning: a way to make sense out of the senseless violence, chaos, and de-

struction that permeates twentieth-century civilization. The majority of
our therapy is state-licensed, directed to returning individuals to socially
acceptable group-defined behavior. We medicate our emptiness, loboto-
mize our souls, with all manner of drugs, legal and illegal, so that we may
become "normal," docile, good citizens. Our social group dictates our
therapy and we are psychologically "fixed" so that we can once more play
our "well-adjusted" role within our particular set of groups we belong to.
As Schmookler points out, this is not freedom but enslavement to an outside system. Little wonder that we find ourselves in the midst of a search
for meaning. In fact, as long as we look to outside organizations to provide
meaning, our search will be futile. Indeed, Eric Hoffer maintained that,
"Faith in a holy cause is to a considerable extent a substitute for the lost
faith in ourselves. . . . Hence the embracing of a substitute will necessarily be passionate and extreme."[45] Additionally, our culture conditions us to
be collectively parented by institutions, groups, and systems, so we expect
others—that mysterious, all-powerful "they"—to solve our problems.

Many mental health professionals are finding that political, social,
and economic *systems* are directly responsible for a lot of mental illness
formerly thought to have originated in the individual. In a *Los Angeles
Times* article, "Psyched Out," Mary Blakeley writes that many therapists
now "recognize political systems that force individuals into conformist
roles and dehumanizing lifestyles are a huge part of their client's suffering."[46]

Desperately medicating our existential boredom with all manner of
foods and drugs, we try to cure what has become a massive identity crisis.
Following collective patterns and ideals, we lose the vital connections
with our own uniqueness, with other human beings, and with our environment. Thus we create a spiritual heart disease, for without a deep sense
of interconnectedness and participation as *distinct* individuals, we blend
with the common herd. The "crowd soul" assumes possession of our lives
and we disappear, committing spiritual and psychological suicide.

We have allowed state, commercial, and political systems to define
health and happiness for us: if I drive that car, live in this house, wear these
clothes, stay as thin as a model, I will be happy. Like sheep led to the
slaughter, we follow the collective rules. In the collective, innumerable
groups, which we have empowered through our obedience to authority figures, rob us of our existence—the right to live our own lives.

Each generation of parents teaches their children to follow a patriarchal social system, to be *good* little girls and boys, and to adapt and to fit
in to the larger social systems. The noted psychologist James Hillman believes that much of our depression has its source in social issues. In other
words, it is in the nature of our *relationship to society*—in our collective

and cultural entanglements—that we find many dangerous pathologies responsible for our individual existential crises.

Viktor Frankl, the Austrian psychiatrist who survived imprisonment at Auschwitz, concluded that individual happiness is dependent on finding meaning in life. Frankl has spent his life trying to understand how otherwise rational human beings can allow themselves to become mere puppets within an authoritarian and destructive social system. He believes *tension* to be a critical ingredient in the search for meaning:

> Mental health is based upon a certain degree of tension, the tension between what one has already achieved and what one still ought to accomplish, or the gap between what one is and what one should become. . . . What man actually needs is not a tensionless state but rather the striving and struggling for a worthwhile goal, a freely chosen task.[47]

What Frankl describes as a "freely chosen task" strikes at the heart of the imperative to "fit in to your social group."

This conforming-to-group pathology prevents individuals from acting in a state of true freedom. Consistently making life choices *that must first be acceptable* to some outside group or system means that we are following someone else's task and digging our own grave in the process, drowning our souls in the masses.

Life has more to do with the *experience* of being alive than simply "meaning." The experience of being who we really are imparts meaning. It takes both experience and meaning to round out a life and make it whole. In our desperate longing to "experience" life we flock to movies filled with on-the-edge excitement, death, and destruction. We skydive, bungee jump, race cars, and attend wild men or women weekends in search of the feeling of being alive, with some measure of *tension,* whether emotional, psychological, or physical. We look for ways to create extraordinary quantities of tension. We approach the possibility of death in order to feel more alive, animating the greatest existential tension—that between life and death.

Jung believed experience to be foremost and is credited with saying, "Religion is a defense against religious experience." Organized religion comes between the individual and self-realization. When we place our spiritual development into collective hands, we abort our own process of self-understanding and self-awareness. The real threat to our existence, as Joseph Campbell asserts, is "living life in relation to a system instead of to our humanity."[48]

The individual's existential vacuum may well be a microcosmic representation of a massive collective existential "God Hole," as indicated by a questioning of who we in the West are as a people and what is our purpose in the world. In the United States, it would appear that without a major enemy, a nuclear threat, or some far-off evil dictator, our totalistic plutocracy loses its sense of purpose. As a nation-state, we have nowhere to place our national shadow. Hence we desperately search for the enemy in inner cities, in satanists, in abortion clinics, in another race, in the legal system, in big business, in abused childhoods.

Can any group or association derive meaning and purpose in and of itself? The answer is no, for all such alliances are but reflective abstractions, mathematical averages of individuals. The group does not exist without its members. Only individuals can give meaning to their lives, and in so doing, imbue a group with the *appearance* of meaning and purpose. Thus, when the search for our missing piece (something to fill the God Hole) is directed to outside groups instead of within, we become *outside-polarized* and empty *inside,* and the God Hole, paradoxically, becomes ever deeper and blacker, which then mirrors itself in a collective emptiness and lack of meaning.

The rush to collective value systems that are *dominant and superior* to individual human values indicates the extent to which humanity has lost soul, our relationship and interconnectedness to life. *Things* that carry projected group images and ideals become more important than people, and in order to get *things,* people are expendable.

The British politician Disraeli once said, "The sense of existence is the greatest happiness."[49] A "sense of existence" then is of paramount importance in our quest for meaning. A group can temporarily provide a sense of purpose. Our existence often gains a feeling of importance and significance (inflation) in a group. But this group-provided feeling of existence is not real, but rather a *conditional existence.* Only as long as we follow the group's agenda are we allowed to feel good about ourselves. This unreal, conditional existence eventually collapses, leaving the individual with a massive identity crisis—a dark void without apparent meaning.

The human need to derive value and meaning for life is contained within the innate desire to belong to something that gives us an acceptable, collective identity. Belonging implies that one is *needed.* In a group, our self-worth and self-esteem are based in large part upon the fact of belonging to it.

Existentialists argue that we need some anxiety, and that "normal anxiety" can be used creatively. Without anxiety ours is a lifeless, drugged state of consciousness. Existentialism further places *freedom* in a position of paramount importance; freedom means we have and can make independent choices in our lives. Making independent choices requires self-responsibility. In fact, meaning in life is not possible without a sense of self-responsibility.

Existentialists describe two major *distractions* from normal anxiety: fantasies of being *special* and the fantasy that one will be *rescued.* Existentialists maintain that the purpose of life is doing something meaningful in the world, and we have to find it. A sense of purpose in life is far more important than attaining a particular goal. We have to find the *gradient* for our life, the space to channel our singular potential.

The struggle to find the meaning-fullness of one's life necessarily requires tension. Tension and anxiety become our energy source for the journey, an inward journey to find the "treasure hard to attain"—the authentic expression of one's Self.

Thus life takes on meaning when we finally *experience it within the context* of our own uniqueness and individuality. Searching for meaning from someone or something outside of ourselves is a psychological trap. Each person's real quest begins, paradoxically, only when one lets go of the ego's collectively driven viselike grip on popular images and ideals. This means differentiating from one's social group, leaving the palace (and all its comforts), journeying into the desert, the "wasteland," there to find our own path—the justification for our existence. Of course this journeying forth is a metaphor for an inner adventure; in practical terms, it means growing up. In *The Hero with a Thousand Faces,* Joseph Campbell explains this necessary *rite of passage*—the search for the real Self: "A hero ventures forth from the world of common day into a region of supernatural wonder: fabulous forces are there encountered and a decisive victory is won: the hero comes back from this mysterious adventure with the power to bestow boons on his fellow man."[50]

When we allow ourselves the freedom to express and work with our real passion in life, a unique value is added to society, and we find simply accepting the struggle launches us on our "hero's journey." Thus the collective is enriched through those individuals who, with tremendous courage and effort, differentiate themselves from it.

The universe does not respond to our demands for meaning and explanations. It is you and I who give meaning to life by doing something with our lives *outside the range of any destructive group influences.* Whatever does not belong to us from the masses must pass through us, not move or change us; this is "walking in the stream but not getting wet." The task then is to find one's life in the midst of powerful societal currents that would sweep one up in an endless pursuit of group-idealized treasure that on close examination turns out to be fool's gold. Our relationships with each other and with groups are in desperate need of transformation. Even in the animal world, according to zoologist Adolph Portmann, *creative changes of behavioral patterns can only be initiated by individuals.*[41]

Unfortunately, the world abounds with groups that prey upon our search for meaning and purpose. When the seductive collective hooks of belonging, purpose, love, a sacred mission, a holy war, wealth, and power are dangled in front of the human psyche, many fish are caught in the collective nets. To search for justification for our existence in the masses is an exercise in futility. Only in accessing our deepest inner resources, our singular soul making, do we find our treasure, that transcendent mysterious elixir capable of breaking our collective chains.

By creating meaning in our lives, we add meaning and integrity to the universe. Life becomes a process to be lived, not a problem to be solved. And *individual integrity* becomes a soul relationship with the rest of humanity.

2

Trapped in Paradise

‖░‖▓▓▓▓▓▓▓▓▓▓▓▓▓▓▓▓▓▓▓▓▓▓▓▓▓▓▓▓▓▓░‖

> No easy thing to bear,
> the weight of sweetness.
>
> Li-Young Lee[1]

I now perceive one immense omission in my *Psychology*—the deepest principle of Human Nature is the *craving to be appreciated.*

William James[2]

Part of the blame lies with the student, because too much obedience, devotion and blind acceptance spoils a teacher. Part also lies with the spiritual master because he lacks the integrity to be immune to that kind of vulnerability.

Dalai Lama[3]

If you have been put in your place long enough, you begin to act like the place.

Randall Jarrell[4]

My Experience in a Religious Group

For one's own part, one is a mere disciple, but nonetheless a joint guardian of the great treasure which the Master has found. One feels the full dignity and burden of such a position, deeming it a solemn duty and a moral necessity to revile others not of a like mind, to enroll proselytes

49

and to hold up a light to the Gentiles, exactly as though one were the prophet oneself. And these people who creep about behind an apparently modest persona, are the very ones who, when inflated by identification with the collective psyche, suddenly burst upon the world scene. For, just as the prophet is a primordial image from the collective psyche, so also is the disciple of the prophet.

Carl Jung[5]

The individual's instinctual drive to merge with something godlike, to belong, to be loved and accepted—far too often drives persons into groups that seem to fill these basic human needs.

My interest in destructive group dynamics resulted from my association from 1976 to 1990 with a New Age spiritual group, the Ann Ree Colton Foundation of Niscience (which I will refer to as "Niscience"), an authoritarian and manipulative religious group having a membership of about four hundred. The word "Niscience" ("omniscience" without the "om"), was supposedly received directly from God by our illumined guru and minister, Ann Ree Colton, and comes from the Latin *sciens*, "to know." Oddly, *Ni*, in both Sanskrit and Germanic, means "down" or "lower." Hence the literal interpretation of the word "Niscience" means "lower knowing," a fit and true name for any ideological dogma.

The criteria that determine whether or not a group is destructive are covered at length in the following chapters. Additionally, the appendix provides information about common characteristics of destructive groups.

FILLING THE GOD HOLE

Jeanne Mills, a former member of the People's Temple and subsequent victim of assassination a year following the November 18, 1978, Jonestown suicides and murders of 911 church members, wrote these words:

When you meet the friendliest people you have ever known, who introduce you to the most loving group of people you've ever encountered, and you find the leader to be the most inspired, caring, compassionate and understanding person you've ever met, and then you learn that the cause of the group is something you never dared hope could be accomplished, and all of this sounds too good to be true, it probably is too good to be true! Don't give up your education, your hopes and ambitions, to follow a rainbow.[6]

With a very successful business, a wife and two small children, a Mercedes in the garage, a big home in the suburbs, I thought, "There must be more to life." I had suddenly become aware of what some call the "God

Hole," an unfulfilled, empty feeling that psychologists often describe as an "existential vacuum." So, my search for the meaning of life began. I redirected all the energy and ambition that had gone toward building a large business into my search for God. I was as determined to become enlightened as I had been determined to succeed in business. I devoured hundreds of books, reading everything I could find about the inner life: meditation, psychology, the writings of mystics, gurus, poets, and philosophers of many different religions. These early efforts were exceedingly egocentric. My search focused on attaining an "enlightened" state of consciousness. I had no interest at all in the dark side of my nature, but wanted to experience "Illumination," which I equated to union with God, whatever that meant.

Not realizing what remarkable consequences this seemingly innocent searching and curiosity would have, I jumped, practically overnight, off the edge of a familiar world into a collective pit. My spiritual adventure became a soul-churning trial by fire; it also proved to be a priceless study in human nature, particularly how and why groups become dysfunctional. Yet my group experience also had its ecstatic, deeply moving, and profound moments. Niscience appeared to have all the answers in addition to providing a social and family structure. Combine these factors with an extremely charismatic leader, Ann Ree Colton (1898–1985), and you have one very dedicated new member!

Paradoxically, when we begin to find our true selves, to differentiate from the collective, we are also most likely to rejoin some group. Precisely at the moment we attempt to set foot on our own path in life, the "threshold guardian," what I call the "collective dragon," challenges us. And this dragon represents a collective voice that tells us we can't be ourselves. The "call to adventure" means undertaking the journey to find ourselves, to be who we really are as unique individuals, as Joseph Campbell eloquently explains:

> Whether small or great, and no matter what the stage or grade of life, the Call rings up the curtain, always, on a mystery of transfiguration—a rite, or movement, of spiritual passage, which, when complete, amounts to a dying and a birth. The familiar life horizon has been outgrown; the old concepts, ideals, and emotional patterns no longer fit; the time for the passing of a *threshold* is at hand.[7] (Emphasis added)

MEETING MY SPIRITUAL TEACHER . . . OOPS!

> The eagle never lost so much time as when he submitted to learn of the crow.
>
> William Blake[8]

Ann Ree Colton, a silver-haired elderly woman in her late seventies, was supposedly an "illumined" spiritual teacher. Ann Ree was born in Atlanta, Georgia, in 1898 and had a Methodist upbringing. She had written several books, one of which on dreams particularly interested me. I sent away for monthly lessons called the "White Paper," which contained detailed rituals and practices for each day. The White Paper lessons were for members only, and we were not to show them to outsiders because "less spiritually evolved souls would not be able to understand them." A short time later I began attending regular meetings with other Niscience members, including frequent travel to group conclaves and seminars in Washington, D.C., Pennsylvania, California, and New Mexico.

The Niscience system combined bits and pieces of New Age metaphysics, fundamentalist Christianity, Theosophy, Buddhism, and Hinduism. Niscience, according to Ann Ree, was "the most advanced spiritual teaching in the world." The Niscience system had been "received telepathically" by Ann Ree from the "ascended Masters," purportedly to save the world in the scientific age. Niscience spiritual exercises included meditation, prayer, repeating certain mantras and mantrams, regular fasting, and taking the Sacrament. We observed, often with elaborate rituals, most Christian and many Eastern holy days. Our "spiritual practices" were time consuming and complicated, leaving little time or energy for any socializing outside the group.

The Niscience ideology became so deeply implanted in my psyche that after leaving the group, it took me several years to get some of the Niscience mantras, vocabulary, and ideas out of my mind. To this day I still struggle with group attitudes and with the lingering effects of mind control, to determine what belongs to me and what was implanted by the group.

Of course it followed that persons who were "guided" to Ann Ree's group were "chosen"—select souls who Ann Ree called "the Golden Horde." Golden Horde persons were more spiritually evolved than ordinary people. I was told that members of Ann Ree's group had been very prominent figures in their past lives. Naturally I felt extremely special and superior. My ego underwent an immediate and enormous inflation! I *accepted without question* everything Ann Ree said, because to question Ann Ree now would threaten my own hard-won spiritual stature. I could not attack the system without destroying myself. My identity had become completely dependent upon the group. Ironically, I believed I was in a unique and special spiritual place, but in actuality I had stepped into a deep pit of collective quicksand.

As my personal spiritual guide and guru, Ann Ree became God incarnate. I was absolutely captivated by this lady who seemed to have an answer for everything. In one dream, shortly after meeting Ann Ree, she and

I merged into one being. In fact, I became "possessed" by the ideology that Ann Ree represented. This dream, which I thought was a miraculous "confirming," was really warning me that I was becoming possessed. For me, Ann Ree became a living saint, a kind, loving, wisdom-filled, prophetic, enlightened being; in my eyes she was beyond perfect—she could do no wrong. I hung on every word she said, and I always carried a notebook with me so that I could write down everything. All the other members conscientiously took notes whenever Ann Ree spoke, meaning that recording the Teacher's wisdom was the mark of a dedicated and sincere student; of course, I followed this example of my peers. I felt Ann Ree knew me as no other person in the world could know me—even more than I knew myself.

Looking back on this experience, I believe that I went through what Christians would call a "born again" experience, which for me was the psychological process of allowing a particular image of God (Ann Ree) to take control of my consciousness. Initially, this process had beneficial effects. My meditations deepened; yoga exercises relaxed and energized me; I felt better physically; my blood pressure which was moderately high soon dropped back to normal; and I was in a nearly constant state of spiritual euphoria. But I was naively unaware of the dangerous implications of following *another person's path* and looking to this person for all the answers.

This turning of my journey into a group-directed, guru-guided experience was the beginning of a psychological and spiritual disaster. Meeting Ann Ree Colton was like meeting my own self (God) in another person. I was totally entranced, enchanted, under a spell. This enchantment produced a tremendous spiritual high, but I was spiritually drugged and addicted to a group illusion. I remember making tremendous efforts to be in Ann Ree's presence. Just sitting in the same room with her became a spiritual experience for me. However, when I gave up my will to another person, I stepped into a collective trap that took a major chunk of my life and proved to be extraordinarily difficult to get out of.

In the first few months after joining, I was showered with attention from the other members. Special loving attention given to new members is a common technique used by many groups and appeals to a person's innate longing to be accepted and loved. All this attention is an immediate, intoxicating, and potent hook, not only making it difficult for a new member to leave, but reinforcing the addictive need to keep returning to the group. It is a powerful reinforcement of the joining process in many different types of groups: I call this the *warm fuzzies trap*.

Because of my zeal and "dedication" to Niscience and to Ann Ree, she soon placed me in charge of the Colorado Niscience members. I became a "Unit Moderator," which meant I was a group leader for all Colorado meetings and services. We met in my home three times each week and later in a leased building. I became an accomplished recruiter of many new members for Niscience. In my new position, I was a zealous and exceedingly sincere advocate for the Niscience system. I spent the next thirteen years in a flurry of endless activity, planning meetings and conclaves, preparing and giving hundreds of lectures, enrolling new members, studying White Paper lessons, and traveling extensively all over the United States.

Abusive groups use rituals to bind members to their system or ideology. They accomplish this by making even trivial acts into rituals. For example, in Niscience, we folded and blessed our money in a specific way before spending it, to cleanse it and pass along blessings to others. We even had a prayer to speak before entering our cars. After leaving the group, I recall being shocked at the difficulty of stopping myself from automatically repeating these prayers and mantras in my head whenever I held a dollar bill or went to my car. This is MIND CONTROL, not religion or spirituality!

When asked about mind control, a Methodist minister explained:

> What is mind control? Very simply, it is causing people to think a certain way. Every minister practices mind control every time he preaches, teaches or writes. Is it not the goal of ministers to get their flock to think and act like Jesus?[9]

Destructive groups tend to keep their members endlessly busy. This former member of a destructive religious group describes what it was like during a typical week:

> It was Tuesday night. I was exhausted from juggling a full-time job with the endless activities at church. After working as a nurse all day, I stood for hours at choir rehearsal.
>
> After work on Wednesday evening, I am in the sewing room at church frantically sewing costumes for an upcoming dance production. The light is inadequate and I am tired.
>
> Thursday night and I attend the required Bible Study group meeting which lets out at 11:30 p.m. And I go home to prepare my uniforms for the next day's work, eat my dinner (or not), and prepare food for the next day's church luncheon.
>
> Friday, lunch time, I rush to church from work for group prayers.
>
> Friday evening, fifteen minutes before the Children's party, I am still wrapping their gifts. I haven't had dinner and I am still in my work clothes. I haven't seen my husband since 6 A.M. yesterday.
>
> Saturday morning at 9 A.M. I sit in the Chapel waiting for the weekly fast ritual. Following this, I will take my turn at baby-sitting and then do my volunteer gardening. At 11 A.M. there are group prayers and at 1 P.M. group meditation. At 1:30 we will leave for a rigorous three-hour re-

hearsal of the dance production. From not eating all day, I am exhausted. I miss my husband. I have a headache. I am cold in the unheated auditorium. We have one hour for dinner to break the fast and to get dressed for the evening ritual performance. At 11 P.M., after the performance, we attend the cast party until 1 A.M.

Sunday morning choir rehearsal commences at 10 A.M. I mouth the words to the new songs while my mind is searching through the day trying to find time to finish normal household chores.[10]

Ann Ree became the glasses through which I looked at God, and I was becoming more and more like Ann Ree. She once told me, "John, you have become the White Paper." She was right. I had completely absorbed the Niscience version of truth along with its unique vocabulary. My thinking and reasoning processes were entirely within the Niscience belief system, and I interpreted and rationalized all life's circumstances through the group mind-set. I had become a perfect disciple.

We were told that any criticism or doubts about Ann Ree were inspired by "ancestral negativities" or satanic forces. Conflicting ideas or philosophies from other religions or groups were the result of what Ann Ree called that particular group's "dweller action." We had to watch out for the "Hebrew dweller," the "psychological dweller," the "Catholic dweller," the "Hindu dweller," the "family dweller," "astral gurus," and on and on. Any ideology that conflicted with Ann Ree's system either had a dweller or the people were less spiritually evolved. What's more, these dweller forces could cause accidents, mishaps, and even death. In this manner all sorts of mishaps were simply explained away; if a member had an auto accident, he or she was just being attacked by dark forces. According to Ann Ree, "there were no accidents."

This explanation-for-everything approach prevented members from critically thinking about the dark side of life. It prevented any in-depth thinking at all. This logic of nonthought is similar to many traditional religious groups who explain away any event as simply "God's will." I remember one of our ministers telling a member whose fifteen-year-old son died of bone cancer that *she* had caused her son's death because she did not teach him the Ten Commandments.

Ann Ree put her spin on many words. She used the word "karma" essentially in a negative context: by karma, Ann Ree referred to one's bad deeds in this life or in a past incarnation as the cause of present problems. "Karma," simply stated, means "act, deed or work," and can be good or bad.

Persons who were "sifted out" of the group had karmically fallen back into "family genesis," which was considered an inferior state of evolvement. After all, didn't Jesus say, "He that loveth father or mother more than me is not worthy of me" (Matthew 10:37)? We were told that individuals who left the group did not have the "atom (spiritual atoms) evolvement" or "grace" to remain in the "group body." We had to be on constant guard for initiatory trials that could "knock us off the Path." Of course, the only God-approved "Path" turned out to be the group's doctrine; anything else was a fall from the Grace of God, which had guided us to our teacher, Ann Ree Colton.

THE KINGDOM COLLAPSES

> There is nothing but water in the holy pools.
> I know, I have been swimming in them.
> All the gods sculpted of wood or ivory can't say a word.
> I know, I have been crying out to them.
> The sacred books of the East are nothing but words.
> I looked through their covers one day sideways.
>
> Kabir[11]

My own disillusionment began when Ann Ree chastised me for following her advice in a Colorado recruitment project that attracted many new members. Ann Ree accused me of trying to "take the Teacher's mantle." I was naively and obediently doing everything Ann Ree suggested, and her accusation shocked me. For the first time, I began to realize that my spiritual teacher was immensely interested in maintaining her own authority and position. I could not reconcile Ann Ree's behavior, and the resulting conflict eventually grew to such agonizing proportions that I was compelled to leave the group.

During my last two years as a member of Niscience, I began to experience repeated dreams of Ann Ree having difficulty breathing, almost dying, or too weak to walk—the *belief system* was dying in my psyche. I was no longer breathing life into it. My spiritual teacher's outward behavior was less and less compatible with my image of a saint. Ann Ree's actions, as well as those of other Niscience group leaders and "elders," became more and more concentrated around gaining power and influence instead of spiritual wisdom. Along with the dreams about Ann Ree I began to have repeating dreams of trying to escape from Russia. And shortly before leaving, I had this dream: Members of Niscience were working in an ancient Egyptian stone quarry, chiseling the outline of an immense block of stone which was to be cut from the wall. There was a heavy air of oppression, death, and servitude, and I knew we were building a tomb, a monument for some dead person—most likely me!

Often, during meetings, members would be asked (without any prior notice) to pledge their loyalty and dedication to Niscience by standing and repeating group vows that any normal person would want time to consider and reflect on. The peer pressure in these group declarations was overwhelming! It was virtually impossible for me and others not to go along with the group. To go against the "Teacher's guidance" would mean being ostracized and, in essence, cast off the spiritual path—a karmic fate worse than death. In these situations, I felt utterly compromised and more and more devoid of any shred of integrity or self-esteem. Whatever was left of my identity as a person was slowly being crushed out of existence.

Phobias—fears about what will happen if a person leaves the group—are a common occurrence in destructive groups. That I stayed so long after knowing something was seriously wrong is incredible to me now, but leaving so many apparent friends was scary. We had all been brainwashed to believe that if we left, lightning would strike us. Steven Hassan, himself a former cult member, explains in *Combatting Cult Mind Control:*

> Today's cults know how to effectively implant vivid negative images deep within members' unconscious minds, making it impossible for the member to even conceive of ever being happy and successful outside of the group. When the unconscious is programmed to accept the negative images, it behaves as though they were true. The unconscious mind is made to contain a substantial image-bank of all the bad things that will occur if anyone should ever betray the group.[12]

Groups accomplish this programming by repeating—over and over and over—what happens to those who leave, who betray the collective *mission,* or who desert the *spiritual path,* which is really no path at all but the total destruction of the individual's path, which is replaced by a collective agenda. I found out in later research that these group-implanted images and fears are characteristic of many different types of groups. Members who left believed all their negative karma would implode in on them, causing all manner of problems: sickness, accidents, or even death. In Niscience, like many other destructive groups, we were programmed to expect that bad things would happen.

During my last few months in the Niscience group, a sense of dread haunted me, as though I were going to die. I was overwhelmed, suffocated by the horror of what I had allowed to happen, and by what had happened to a beautiful group of people under mind control and propaganda hiding behind the mask of spirituality. I knew that to remain in Niscience any longer would obliterate any scraps of integrity left in me. I felt suicidal and I had a deep fear that I would die with a little plaque around my neck that read "Perfect Attendance." To miss any meeting, or to be absent when the Teacher was speaking, was considered a great sin of "ingratitude for enlightened instruction."

The Exodus

> Agony and ecstasy—
> authenticity ground down
> into a collective morass.
> Leaving life-drained smiles
> standing on nails—
> hollowed-out shell friends—
> my flat cardboard family.
>
> John D. Goldhammer

> I was angry, then the freedom was exhilarating!
> Former member's comment after leaving a destructive group[13]

In spite of what had become a crushing agony of being in the group, it was excruciatingly painful and frightening to finally walk off the Niscience grounds, knowing that I could never return. For the last two years, I had rationalized staying for the "Work," for Ann Ree's sake, to serve God. And I could not imagine leaving friends I had known for fifteen years, who had become like family. I continually thought that things would somehow be better, that God would save the situation at the eleventh hour, a state of mind some psychologists call "delusion of reprieve," which often occurs when individuals who have been condemned to death become convinced that they will be saved at the last minute. Leaving the group was like ending my life as I knew it—like the prospect of dying. I could not imagine my life without the spiritually "chosen" inflated self-image that was maintained by belonging to the group. I can now appreciate why so many people stay in dysfunctional groups for years even after realizing something is terribly wrong. When the tension between what the group was turning me into and my own reality finally became unbearable, I walked out.

What is it like to leave the group? Life is new and wonderful! It is *living* life with a deep and profound gratitude for being alive. It is being *free to choose* from the depths of my own reality. My increasing moodiness and depression have all but disappeared. My wife tells me that I am humming, smiling, and whistling so often she is amazed at the change. A deep and rollicking sense of humor has returned. But also I am angry at having been so misled and deceived—angry at Ann Ree and myself. I feel frustrated and helpless knowing former friends are trapped in such an oppressive environment. There is something about the "group mind" that is barbaric and frightening to me—like a lynch mob.

Joseph Bottone, shortly after leaving Niscience, wrote this poetic letter to the minister who supposedly received Ann Ree's "spiritual mantle" after she died in 1985:

You are not an anointed teacher,
>nor of Cosmos Consciousness,
>but a man clinging to power who has lost his purse.
You never gave me the time of day,
>never displayed that sweet calm of profound wellspring, love.
The Philokalia said it better years ago:
>"There is no water in your words."
I set you loose for that place all must go that are prideful,
>full of lies and deception,
>who steal from the blind,
>who claim and keep down
>those not strong enough to know the certainty of God within.
But I say, persist in your teaching separation and retaliation,
>neglect devotion and you will surely fall
>with the rubble and debris upon your head of all that you have created.
>Hypocrite!
Should you see me on the road or the busy street,
>put down your eyes and look away
>until pride is transformed into humility
>and fear is fled from the hearts of those who look to you.
I shake the rattle and dust falls away from my feet.
I shake the rattle and dust falls away from my eyes and the ten directions.
You as a teacher of Truth are Anti-Christ and this dust fills your mouth.
Feel free to read my letter on the Altar for that is where Truth belongs
>as money-changers belong in banks.[14]

The modern hero's journey can be likened to the individual shedding the group's collective influences that have gradually gained control of one's life. Campbell observed three basic stages in the hero's journey: "separation—initiation—return."[15] Following our theme of collective entrapment, the hero ventures forth into the world, encountering "threshold guardians." The threshold guardians are the institutions, the degrees, behavior, and demeanor "acceptable" to our collective culture. We must pass through, becoming institutionalized products molded, trained, and shaped in a collective image. Thus we assume our place in the popular order; we perform our "duties." Initially, this conformity often produces feelings of accomplishment, a feeling that we've "made it."

But after years spent playing our assumed roles, our collective persona—the mask we wear—becomes more and more disturbing; we begin to feel uneasy, disillusioned, restless, empty. A deep, unnameable frustration nibbles away at the soul. We attempt to explain the feelings away by saying it's just a mid-life crisis. But in fact we're having an "existential crisis," a deep gnawing dread that somehow *we've missed living our own life,* missed doing some unknown something, which, if not discovered and undertaken soon, will vanish forever and life will become a living death. Thoughts of suicide (because we've been killing our own uniqueness) and feelings of "being lost" arrive like an invading army storming the walls of our consciousness. Now we're in the hero's initiation. Collective dragons and monsters surface, beating us down into a morass of collective "shoulds," a deadening and mind-numbing drumbeat of how we "should" live our lives.

What's happening? The authentic individuality is struggling to be born out of collective dominance. The battle has begun and the stakes are enormous. One's very soul is at stake—one's existential fundamental prerogative to live life as a singular, unique expression. That is our obligation, to live our own life, a life that if unlived, becomes dead and stagnant, a pollutant in the cosmos, a place without meaning and reason to exist.

The hero, beaten down by the collective, wearing the leaden armor of institutionalized systems, now must step off the treadmill, and resurrect (rescue) the Self. Of course, the collective responds to such "selfishness" with vicious attacks. Mustering all their forces, groups bombard the hero with fear, doubt, and especially guilt—guilt that supposedly stems from "doing one's own thing." In fact, only when we do "our own thing" do we live a life that has meaning and value for the whole. We add meaningful value to any group *only through our distinctiveness, not our sameness.*

Having survived the collective armies, our hero returns from slaying the collective dragon, empowered with new-found strength and courage. We now have access to our real treasure, and that hard-won treasure is our unique gift that has survived the "valley of the shadow of death."

After twenty-two years, Caryn Aman takes early retirement from the phone company so that she can start her own creative therapy practice, her real passion, her treasure. But first she has to leave the apparent security of working for a large organization, "stripped like Inanna of all my 'me' of the organization [her collective identity]—I. D. pass, building pass, keys, company credit card, company calling card, electronic mail access."[15] Now, in work she loves, by being herself, Caryn can spend her treasure.

THE COLLECTIVE HOLOCAUST

> So, let us be alert—alert in a twofold sense: Since Auschwitz we know
> what man is capable of. And since Hiroshima we know what is at stake.
>   Viktor E. Frankl[17]

The Nazi Holocaust was a "slaughter of innocents." Similarly, destructive groups prey upon and then annihilate *innocence.* In fact, dreams of Hitler's Germany or other military organizations often portray the dark side of the collective and its lethal effect on individuals. While in my group, I had this dream: I found myself inside a German concentration camp, in a prisoners' barracks. Even though abandoned long ago, I saw and felt the atrocities committed there from looking at bloodstained patterns on the concrete floor. Then looking out a window I saw a German firing squad executing seals, who were helplessly trying to get out of a large open grave. Horrified by what I had seen, I left. Walking down a long hallway, I encountered a very angry seal who proceeded to bite me on my left hand.

The seals were certainly out of their element—water—disconnected from the ocean so necessary for their life. In the earthen pit, they were truly helpless and were being executed. On collective authoritarian ground, we are cut off from the unconscious, the source of our individuality, our spiritual essence, our connection to water which sustains life. Like the seals, we find ourselves helpless and powerless under the collective onslaught, which mechanically executes our individuality, our distinctiveness, and our creative potential. Like the angry seal, we have tremendous rage at ourselves because of our willing "sacrifice" to collective tyranny.

Terri, a gifted artist and former member of a destructive group, had this dream shortly after joining the group: "I was painting a picture on the beach at Pompei. Suddenly I realized an immense tidal wave was coming and that I would be killed. Next I remember being under water and drowning."[18] Terri's dream clearly illustrates how a group ideology, the tidal wave, destroyed her creativity—her reality and identity as an artist.

Self-hatred further reinforces ideas of "original sin" and other twisted religious viewpoints that glorify self-immolation. Hence the collective grip of patriarchal tyranny tightens as we slip deeper into the group dynamic where we bury our souls. The fact that I willingly did this to myself is a source of both immense anger at such systems and also rage at my own naive, voluntary self-destruction. No drug or addiction could have effected a greater demise of who I am and who I had hoped to become. I had been thoroughly conned, but could not face the enormity of my naivete. I had been "captured by my bamboozle" as Carl Sagan put so well:

> One of the saddest lessons of history is this: If we've been bamboozled long enough, we tend to reject any evidence of the bamboozle. We're no longer interested in finding out the truth. The bamboozle has captured us. It is simply too painful to acknowledge—even to ourselves—that we've been so credulous. So the old bamboozles persist as the new bamboozles arise.[19]

In the group, I experienced a regression to childlike attitudes and dependencies. Looking back on my experience, I am amazed that my own thinking processes could be so completely altered without my realizing what was happening. No wonder I now feel grown up at last! I had lost the ability to think for myself, to make my own choices. I gave up my autonomy and my own existential legitimacy to a group. Understandably, I value freedom and individual autonomy as life's most priceless gifts.

After the extremely traumatic experience of leaving the group I became intrigued by the psychological reasons why persons give up their volition, will, autonomy, and identity for the sake of some collective ideal. Although my experience had a religious orientation, the underlying dynamics proved to be relevant for many other types of groups. Manipulation and mind-control techniques are startling in their similarity over a broad spectrum of groups in our collective culture—a tyranny of groups with many different faces.

Not long after leaving the group, I had this dream: I was standing with a woman on an enormous high bridge overlooking a vast river of water so wide that it was not possible to see the other side. I was told in the dream, "We have worked long and hard to get you out of the pit." In this dream, I felt the most *exquisite sense of freedom* imaginable!

> Leaving everything— exquisite freedom
>   washes over my heart.
> Life opens to awesome immensity—grandeur.
> The Great Spirit awakens from submersion in the herd,
>   and the Gods once more become nameless—
>   mysterious.
> On the great bridge
>   far vistas unfold over shining waters,
>   and a dream tells me:
> "We have worked a long time to get you out of the pit."

3

Fatal Persuasion

There are three forces, the only three forces capable of conquering and enslaving forever the conscience of these weak rebels in the interests of their own happiness. They are: the miracle, the mystery, and authority.

Fyodor Dostoevsky[1]

The successful persuasion tactic is one that directs and channels thoughts so that the target thinks in a manner agreeable to the communicator's point-of-view; the successful tactic disrupts any negative thoughts and promotes positive thoughts about the proposed course of action.

Anthony Pratkanis and Elliot Aronson[2]

The effect of power and publicity on all men is the aggravation of self, a sort of tumor that ends by killing the victim's sympathies.

Henry Adams[3]

Whatever deceives seems to produce a magical enchantment.

Plato[4]

Soul Psychology

You could not discover the limits of the soul, even if you traveled every road to do so; such is the depth of its meaning.

Heraclitus[5]

In this study I draw on the tradition of depth psychology, perhaps better called soul-psychology, that began with the Greek philosopher Heraclitus (c. 540–c. 480) and moved through the centuries to the present time with Freud and Jung being its most prominent luminaries. In his book *The Undiscovered Self* (1958), Jung points out the central conflict between the individual and the collective:

> Let it [society] band together into groups and organizations as much as it likes—it is just this banding together and the resultant extinction of the individual personality that makes it succumb so readily to a dictator. A million zeros joined together do not, unfortunately, add up to one. Ultimately everything depends on the quality of the individual, but our fatally short-sighted age thinks only in terms of large numbers and mass organizations.[6]

Immersion in a group establishes a collectively dictated mind-set *within the individual.* When a group ideology reigns supreme over the individual, a patriarchal totalism becomes embedded in one's thought processes, and the individual becomes a programmed clone for some group "ism."

The nature of the individual's relationship to the collective is the issue. Separation from the collective then becomes a matter of relationship, with the emphasis being on *relatedness* as opposed to one's *containment* within the collective. The former enables the individual to make a unique contribution to the collective, while the latter makes the individual obsolete. Containment in a group means that the group defines the individual, while relatedness implies an equal footing, *a tensional connection* between the group and the individual, where individuals maintain their autonomy free of collective definitions and ideological constraints. Jung maintained, "But the individual is precisely that which can never be merged with the collective and is never identical with it. That is why identification with the collective and voluntary segregation from it are alike synonymous with disease."[7]

When we are contained within collective impulses, carried along in the currents of "public opinion," we are under the spell of *mass suggestion*— in a "social trance." One unknowingly becomes a numbered mechanical part of a group—a corporate, state, or religious body—which in reality is simply a group-embodied abstract idea that individuals have empowered. Myriad special interest subgroups seeking power, influence, and control further corrupt the larger collective entity, which always has something for sale or exchange to the highest bidder or to the most dedicated supporters.

The psychology formulated by Jung was a major watershed event in our understanding of consciousness, especially in the manner in which it returns the experiential nature of myth and deity to the individual psyche, thereby moving psychology out from under the imagination-deadening, soul-killing collective influence of religious and political institutions. In fact, Jung insisted that *only individual experience* counted in religious matters. The significance of the individual's unique experience and the relationship of this experience to the collective is the point of tension that this book addresses.

Involvement in a group promotes an inner imbalance between masculine and feminine polarities. The "anima," a man's inner feminine counterpart, and the "animus," a woman's inner masculine polarity, can cause one's psyche to slip into a state of "possession." What Jung called "animus possession" produces a totalitarian attitude in women: fixed concepts, group ideology, and opinions along with one-sided positions based upon *absolute* truth. Animus possession means the masculine side of a woman becomes an active functioning complex, although one is unconscious of the spell one is under. Jung maintained that such women are "always in danger of losing [their] femininity."[8] In this manner, patriarchy rules within a woman's psyche. Destructive groups reinforce this *inner patriarchal possession* in both men and women.

In a healthy psyche, the animus becomes a mediator (a tension holder) between the conscious and the unconscious, a helpful spirit, nourishing one's philosophical and spiritual ideas. The animus, as mediator, is like Hermes, a messenger of the gods and a spiritual guide.

Animus attitudes invariably reflect *collective* impulses and ideas. Thus a woman must constantly question from where her ideas come. She must differentiate between collective voices and her own authentic voice. To accomplish this, she must become her own critic, searching out the origins of her ideas and concepts. In contrast, a man gets in touch with his feminine side (anima) by connecting with his feelings and imaginative faculties.

The Meaning in Words

Language is by its very nature a communal thing; that is, it expresses never the exact thing but a compromise—that which is common to you, me, and everybody.

T. E. Hulme[9]

I am deep in the old book—
caught in the mystery.
And the words have taken over;
they are living—
throbbing with purpose,
with momentum—

dancing on my desk.
They refuse to follow my plans,
my deadlines.
They are warriors on a sacred quest,
and I am in the middle of the battle.
                                        John D. Goldhammer

This monograph exists only by virtue of its relationship to you, the reader, a relationship *between* my words and your understanding of them. As such your reading of these words is a unique experience that cannot be duplicated; it is a one-to-one relationship. In this respect, my writing is part of *me* that is dependent on you, the reader. Your reading completes this book, the point being that consciousness and cognition require a relationship. Similarly, the dynamic in the relationship between the individual and a *collective other* comprises the psychological landscape we will explore.

My ideas necessarily build upon my own unique experience with uncountable others whom I have met, many through my own reading, souls trapped in time between the covers of some book. So for me a bibliography would be more aptly called "an honoring of souls," a meeting of friends, a collaboration of thoughts, a collision of concepts—out of which this work was born. It is a *re-searching* aided by countless others, to whom I am most grateful.

We also need to clarify the concept of evolution. Holding evolutionary tension means letting go, "unrolling," moving, and allowing ourselves to be uncomfortable, frightened, and at times chaotic. The idea of a linear evolution does not fit our soul-centered psychological approach, but belongs to a monolithic, anthropomorphized god who is *up there* on top of everything: a linear hierarchy. According to T. S. Eliot (1888–1965), the concept of a linear evolution tends to be a "means of disowning the past."[10] A dualistic, one-sided collective wants to split off the past, discard, and get rid of painful experiences. Linear evolution implies an up-sided, one-directional escapism: a "fix it and forget it" mentality that is a supporting ideology for collective modern life caught in the inexorable grip of collectively defined progress.

Group Speak: The Language of the Group Mind

Syllables govern the world.

                                        John Seldon[11]

> A striking expression, with the aid of a small amount of truth, can surprise
> us into accepting a falsehood.
>
> Vauvenargues[12]

There is no such thing as the "greater good"; it is a total illusion, a collective phantom! But there *is* an interconnectivity with all life based upon the individual's linkage—both physically and psychologically—with the universe. A "greater good" cannot exist because it refers to a generalization, not individual human consciousness.

The "thought-terminating cliché" exemplifies what Robert Lifton refers to as "loading the language":

> The most far-reaching and complex of human problems are compressed
> into brief, highly reductive, definitive-sounding phrases, easily memo-
> rized and easily expressed. These become the start and finish of any ide-
> ological analysis. . . . [T]hese clichés become . . . "ultimate terms": either
> "god terms," representative of ultimate good; or "devil terms," repre-
> sentative of ultimate evil. Totalist language, then, is repetitiously centered
> on all-encompassing jargon, prematurely abstract, highly categorical, re-
> lentlessly judging, and to anyone but its most devoted advocates, deadly
> dull: in Lionel Trilling's phrase, "the language of nonthought."[13]

Examples of linguistic, mind-stopping solutions and clichés abound in our collective culture. From the religious view, people suffer because they're unsaved, not following the commandments, not doing their spiritual practices, not thinking positively, not meditating, not praying, not repeating their mantras, not accepting Jesus in their lives, not confessing their sins, or they are unrepentant. And, "it's just your karma," "it's an initiation," "it's your past-life karma," "it's dweller action," "you're being contested," "they (persons outside the group) are contesting your spiritual life," "lesser evolved persons can't understand our system," "it's an etheric clot," or "you've just got a jammed chakra.*" If you're not making it in a twelve-step program, it's because "you're not working the steps." Psychotherapy has its therapy-stopping solutions as well. When therapy isn't working, the patient is "resistant," "in denial," or "not getting their feelings out." Jungians have problems because they have not worked through all their complexes and are still unindividuated. Like Orwell's "Newspeak," collective agencies use language that reveals their totalitarian shadow.

> The purpose of Newspeak was not only to provide a medium of expres-
> sion for the world-view and mental habits proper to the devotees of Ing-

---

*Chakra: one of seven centers of spiritual energy within the body accessed by yoga practices.

soc, but to make all other modes of thought impossible. It was intended
that when Newspeak had been adopted once and for all and Oldspeak forgotten, a heretical thought—that is, a thought diverging from the principles of Ingsoc—should be literally unthinkable, at least so far as thought
is dependent on words.[14]

On the August 29, 1993, broadcast of the CBS television program "Sunday Morning," Governor Roy Romer of Colorado said, "If *we* [referring to
the state government] give *them* [parents] the *right* . . ." Although Romer
speaks for an elected governmental group empowered by citizens to enact
laws, it is his choice of words—his "we versus them" language—that illustrates how potent group-think is, how effortlessly one's point of view
shifts from citizen to elitist, forgetting that a democracy means government
by the people, that elected officials must represent and protect the rights of
citizens. Suddenly he is no longer a citizen. Instead he identifies with an
elite "we" separated from the people. Romer's totalistic language exemplifies the basic linguistic ideology of a supreme, superior group controlling assumed-to-be-less-intelligent individuals. Such binary language always operates out of a patriarchal "we and they" split. Political tyranny and
abuse of power comes as no surprise to a long-disillusioned and fed up
electorate. Romer's remark concerned a debate over the issue of school
voucher systems that would give parents a *choice.* Freedom of choice is a
prerequisite to economic, social, and political freedom. Without the ability to make *informed choices,* we are totalistically unfree and our choices
are determined by others, usually a group.

   Totalistic ideology, wearing the mask of altruism, purports to protect
us from evil by taking away or diminishing the choices we make. To accomplish this, political groups make choices for us through the legal system, enacting laws that penalize nonconformist, noncriminal behavior instead of *enabling* greater freedom of choice. No choice equals no freedom!
The vast proliferation of entrenched federal and state agencies, government
bureaucracies, and lobbyists have created an overwhelming maze of powerful, usually unstoppable groups, each with their own mission and virtually beyond the control of our elected officials, not to mention individual
voters. The incredible waste and corruption within the multitude of such in-
tergovernmental groups stagger the imagination. We will explore more
about the destructive effects of political groups in chapter 5.

   In the West we have been lulled into a comfortable captivity, with our
high-tech adult toys, big homes, and luxurious life styles. But when it
comes to choosing where or what type of school for our children, we run
into an institutional collective wall that has its own agenda: preserving the
status quo. This is not unlike a religious group's "preservation of the

dharma" or "truth" or "God's word." The reality of such group self-preservation always means less individual freedom and a sickening slide into a collective quagmire of waste, inefficiency, and corruption.

The "group voice" says:

- Absolutely
- Either, or
- God willing
- If only they would . . .
- I'm *entitled* to . . .
- It's God's will
- Keep the big picture in mind
- My God is the only God
- My system is the best system
- My way is the only way
- Them
- They
- They're not as enlightened, not as highly evolved
- Thou shalt not . . .
- Us
- We
- We (I) should . . . You should . . .
- We must . . .
- We're special

George Orwell's classic novel *1984* pointed out the awesome power of language to control people. Orwell demonstrated how a totalitarian state used what he termed "Newspeak," the official world language, to censor all "politically incorrect" thoughts. Although science fiction, *1984* has proven to contain more fact than fiction. In his essay "Politics and the English Language," Orwell wrote:

> The great enemy of clear language is insincerity. . . . In our time, political speech and writing are largely defenses of the indefensible. . . . Political language has to consist largely of euphemism, question-begging and sheer cloudy vagueness. . . . Political language . . . is designed to make lies sound truthful and murder respectable, and to give an appearance of solidity to pure wind.[15]

CULTURAL EDITING AND CENSORSHIP

> The fact is that censorship always defeats its own purpose, for it creates, in the end, the kind of society that is incapable of exercising real discre-

tion. . . . In the long run it will create a generation incapable of appreciating the difference between independence of thought and subservience.

Henry Steele Commager[16]

Wheresoever manners and fashions are corrupted, language is. It imitates the public riot.

Ben Johnson[17]

According to Jung, modern translations of the Bible reflect the projected-out parts of the individual psyche, which further influence the collective orientation:

> Recently, "within you" (*intra vos*) has been translated as "among you," therefore, . . . in the visible and bodily gathering together of men. This shows the modern tendency to replace man's inner cohesion by outward community, as though anyone who had no communion with himself would be capable of any fellowship at all! It is this deplorable tendency that paves the way for mass-mindedness.[18]

Such modifications of the original meaning of scriptural language exemplify how a totalistic ideology gradually pollutes and embeds itself not only in our religious and mythological traditions, but more ominously within the human mind, which then becomes an instrument for the furtherance of collective tyranny.

What is popularly called "politically correct" language represents a powerful way groups pervert and cover up reality. To be "politically correct," we use words that water down authenticity and in so doing we repress legitimate feelings and experiences. Such manipulated and guarded language is a potent form of group-inspired self-censorship, an example of mass denial.

The "politically correct" crowd, referred to as "thought police" by their critics, represents a subtle but nonetheless deadly form of increasing collective manipulation and control over our use of language. Once more, in order to supposedly "protect" minority "groups," we must censor our speech. This is patently against the constitutional right to free speech. Syndicated columnist Robert Novak points out that political correctness "destroys meaning. It also demeans the ethnic groups it supposedly protects. Do we really think that these groups are so unintelligent as to be unable to distinguish between conventional idioms and genuine prejudice? Is their identity so fragile that it must depend on censorship?"[19] Novak's insightful comments take on new significance when we consider that an individual who identifies with a group will be all the more affected by language. Those who lack a strong sense of self will no doubt experience a collective feeling of offense from direct and open language. On the other hand, groups do have a stake in destroying the meaning in words. They do not want their real character openly displayed. Instead, they want to use language to their own ends, to obfuscate the individual's reality.

Collective logic that limits individual freedom is a serious form of tyranny and an imposed morality by those whose inquisitional fanaticism undermines the heart and essence of a free society, which depends on each individual's freedom to say or write anything no matter how controversial. The politically correct crowd does not like any language, including humor, that portrays others in a bad light or makes fun of a stereotype. Hence, political correctness reinforces a person's group identity and encourages people to think through a collective mind-set.

One of the hallmarks of destructive nation-states and religious groups throughout history is the attempt to control freedom of expression in order to obliterate opposing views. In a democracy, attempts to control often uncomfortable viewpoints and ideas that oppose the status quo are disguised as altruism. We are told that we should not use these words because it is disrespectful of a certain perceived minority group; it is *almost always* a particular group.

Only by labeling and thus grouping individuals through some common racial, gender, ethnic, or other group characteristic can we become offended by what someone says about *our* group. By submissively accepting a collective label, we turn ourselves into stereotypical clones, little more than puppets whose strings are controlled by the prevailing popular ideology.

Group Speak then is numbing language, most commonly used when those in power do not want the public to realize the full impact of politically damaging events. Of course all groups have their unique words and phrases, their group jargon, which helps people communicate in specialized fields. However, a lot of group jargon actually stops critical reasoning and free inquiry, suppresses honest feelings, and keeps individuals contained within the group belief system. I am indebted to William Lutz, whose excellent book *Doublespeak* illuminates the remarkable extent of deception that has crept into our collective vocabulary. Lutz explains that, "Jargon as doublespeak often makes the simple appear complex."[20] Here are some common examples:

Group Speak	Actual Meaning
Duty	Follow the group's dogma
Self-sacrifice	Put the group first, not yourself
Most admired persons	Media-installed implants (images), collective projections

Group Speak	Actual Meaning
Therapeutic misadventure	A fatal dose of anesthesia
Collateral damage	Civilians killed in a war
Mechanical deficiencies	Rear axles can fall off
Failed to proceed	The car broke down
Revenue enhancement	A tax increase
Unauthorized withdrawal	Armed robbery at an ATM machine
Diagnostic misadventure	Patient died
Radiation enhancement device	A neutron bomb
A discontinuity	A crack in a support beam
Surgical strike	Kill only those targeted

As our language proliferates with words that avoid reality and direct meaning, we increasingly obscure our own authenticity and reinforce our collective masks. In the Vietnam War, napalming villages became "resource control problems," while capturing enemy villages was termed "pacification." We have "collateral damage" instead of killing innocent civilians accidentally. "Surgical strikes" imply something cancerous being removed, implying the enemy is like a cancer. Allowing obscuring language to come between us and reality is a dangerous practice, eroding our ability to empathize with others and enabling us to sanction and commit atrocities without really thinking about or seeing them. Words evoke images, and words that evade reality create a false world. In this manner the collective distorts language in order to lull the masses into a communal, hypnotic stupor of unknowing. When we build false self-identities, our environment reflects our illusions; we become dangerous to ourselves and to others.

In a group context, "duty" becomes a trap empowering the group and enslaving individuals. When we don't "do our duty" or "do what's *right,*" we place ourselves outside the group laws and rules, both written and unwritten; we become criminals subject to some sort of punishment. Duty also precludes any critical examination of group rules and laws. It was Voltaire who said, "Where it is a duty to worship the sun it is pretty sure to be a crime to examine the laws of heat."[21]

A VOCABULARY OF PREJUDICE

Prejudice: An adverse judgment or opinion formed beforehand or without knowledge or examination of the facts. The act or state of holding unreasonable preconceived judgments or convictions. Irrational suspicion or hatred of a particular group.

American Heritage Dictionary[22]

Collective labels such as the words "black" and "white" evoke collective images that superficially define individuals based on affiliation with an ethnic group. Such collective classifying words are demeaning and demoting, making one a faceless part of a group without one's consent. The mass projection of hatred onto another race is, paradoxically, just what many blacks do to the white race and what whites do to blacks. Black power (militant) groups have made *color* (whiteness) the enemy. Through a militant blaming stance, blacks, as well as whites, become what they each hate most. Tragedy results when any group sinks into a one-sided extreme viewpoint, which necessarily requires an enemy who occupies an adversarial position; if we are not responsible for our problems, someone else must be the cause. One sees a collective mask and not the individual. Accordingly we prejudge others based on a group identity: color, belief, race, culture, or other collective affiliation. Hence the life and dignity of the individual soul is not honored or recognized.

Both blacks and whites, through their militant anticolor viewpoints, have fallen into the mass-mind trap, losing the *only* characteristic that can make a difference in any society: the uniqueness and creativity of the individual. Instead of a relationship between individual human beings, we have only a mob-to-mob confrontation of opposites.

Such totalistic approaches to complex life situations block individuals from any in-depth self-analysis and reflection. Furthermore, polarized groups commonly use descriptive words that are sweeping generalizations of some other social or cultural group. Such generalizations do not define the individual human being, but instead refer to a fictitious collective persona, with dehumanizing effects on anyone who is so mass-categorized.

Better to know the person instead of a *group-defined* individual. The fact that so-and-so is a Democrat or Republican speaks to a particular group's ideology, but does not tell me much about another human being. In politics, when a highly individual personality runs for office, voters tend to cross party lines.

Moreover, destructive organizations, in developing their own unique vocabulary, often add their own meaning to existing words. A collective thought-stopping vocabulary means that group-implanted definitions and mechanistic word phrases that tend to prevent any further questioning and analysis automatically censor (often unconsciously) outside information. We filter or reinterpret any information that conflicts with the group doctrine; we only allow *acceptable* information in, information that always confirms and reinforces the group ideology.

Further restricting the individual, loading the language adds to one's isolation and separateness from those on the outside who have difficulty understanding the group jargon. A group lingo also has the effect of making members feel special and superior, but at the same time it is a horrific compromise of one's soul-autonomy, seriously limiting one's ability to communicate with the outside world. Using the group's vocabulary insures increased control by the group. By using a unique vocabulary, the group mind reaches its tentacles deep inside the individual's psyche, limiting one's ability to express any feelings, ideas, and emotions except in ways that substantiate the group's viewpoint. This mental reprogramming also has the effect of making previously acquired knowledge useless unless it happens to fit within group parameters and definitions.

The individual who succumbs to these language implants must become fanatical and quite adept in reducing all life experiences into the context of this exclusive vocabulary in order to survive in the group. We lose the original soul-genealogy, the rich heritage of authentic meaning in words. Lifton writes, "This loading may provide an initial sense of insight and security, eventually followed by uneasiness. . . . [H]is imagination becomes increasingly dissociated from his actual life experiences and may even tend to atrophy from disuse."[23]

Groups also tend to use *polarizing jargon,* words and phrases that reinforce and sustain a one-sided position: the "higher life," the "Great Satan," "Devil worshippers," a "higher purpose," "perfection," "sin," "good," "evil," "blacks," "whites," "Jews," a "positive experience" (which requires a negative experience), and "God is good" (which requires evil), as well as the common "we/they," "us/them" separating phrases that reduce other individual human beings to an amorphous mass. Who are the "they" that apparently are responsible for doing all the wrong things to "us"?

And who are "we"? In a psychological sense, "we" could refer to my inner community: psychic parts of myself that are aspects of my "I." We have the editorial "we," the writer and the reader. Am "I" ever a "we"? In the context of one's outside relationships to others, I am always "I," an individual; the instant I become a "we" by entanglement in a group, "I" have been diminished or destroyed. "We" refers to a group, and where has my "I" gone? My "I" has been compromised with some degree of enmeshment with the collective, which may be a spouse, a political party, or a religion. In my inner collectively inspired patriarchal nature, "I" would like to think I'm in control of "we," my inner psychic community. But just as we seek our own autonomy from the group influences in the world, it follows that we must grant an inner autonomy of sorts to the many diverse parts of the self.

A dangerous word, "we," as collective *groupese,* should not be used without being sure that one is authorized to speak for the "other" part of the "we." When "we" or "they" speak, the collective mind speaks, and we (the editorial you and I) need to be clear about it. A "we" person often is not speaking as an individual, but as a spokesperson for a group. The *ego/I* that so many religions, businesses, and institutions try to suppress illustrates a mind-control technique intent upon extinguishing the individual in favor of a body politic, a collective doctrine. Persons under the influence of totalistic collective thinking—a group mind-set, commonly use "we" far more than "I" to express themselves. There is a saying that, "Crafty men deal in generalizations" (anonymous).

"We" and "they," in the collective sense, become verbal escapes from self-responsibility. Language then becomes a denial/avoidance mechanism: "It's a trade-off," "In a larger sense," "Society says . . . ," "THEY. . . ." If we can assign blame to a "they," we are off the hook so to speak. When "we" explain *our* beliefs, I hide in the collective, and am less visible—and less vulnerable—as a human being. This type of collective vocabulary promotes *binary thinking*: everything is either yes or no, on or off, wiring in a monocratic dualism through one's vocabulary. Such language-bound groups, whether religious, economic, or political, are full of *rules,* doctrine, and dogma, saturated with "shoulds" and "should nots."

Propaganda

> The chief use to which we put our love of the truth is in persuading ourselves that what we love is true.
>
> Pierre Nicole[24]

Authoritarian agencies use propaganda, a powerful form of milieu control that reinforces a group's belief system. To blindly accept group propaganda as the truth makes one subservient to a monolithic collective structure whose basic motive is to perpetuate itself and increase its power and control over masses of individuals. Propaganda makes an idea or viewpoint into a mass movement, and a collective idea, once totally accepted by the individual, reduces one to nothing more than a programmed robot. Through propaganda, people are *persuaded to persuade themselves.* Psychoanalytic principles, according to Anthony Pratkanis and Elliot Aronson, prominent social psychologists at the University of California, Santa Cruz, are used by many successful advertising agencies:

> To produce such ads, marketers were busily engaged in finding the hidden meaning of things. One handbook on the subject actually listed common objects and what they mean, in theory, to the unconscious—for example, rice means fertility, removing one's gloves is erotic and intimate, soup is the magic elixir of life, and eggs mean growth and fertility. Once the unconscious meaning of a thing is uncovered, an advertiser can de-

sign a campaign that appeals to our deepest motivations and thus can be quite powerful.[25]

For example, by packaging products like panty hose in egg-shaped containers, marketers associate their products with numinous* archetypal motifs.[26] Purchasing panty hose suddenly carries an aura of growth, fertility, and rebirth.

A dualistic, dictatorial business enterprise will promote "the big picture" to its employees, and the "big picture" or "company policy" is always more important than the individual. If the individual has an idea that does not fit into company policy, he or she does "not see the big picture." Teamwork, in such an environment, becomes analogous to slaves pulling stones to the pyramid, tied together by a common purpose, a company mission.

Destructive business enterprises employ workers in the same sense that a totalitarian state does—to their collective ends, and not in any manner that empowers individuals. Workers, who are expendable "things," part of the machinery, become caught in a completely one-sided preservation of a business group at the expense of individual autonomy. Sadly, this business autocracy stifles badly needed innovation and creativity that would insure a commercial enterprise's survival. The company mission takes on a spiritual quality, and promoting the company's "mission" becomes a form of economic evangelism, a "just cause." The "God Hole" is filled with the group's purpose; meaning is temporarily provided to the individual through the company ideal. We become workaholics. Winning (recruiting) new customers or clients becomes equivalent to "winning souls for Jesus." Persons who do not use *the company product* are considered ignorant and unenlightened.

Sam Keen, a colleague of Joseph Campbell and contributing editor for *Psychology Today,* writes, "You are what you want."[27] In many ways we in the West are both victims and beneficiaries of the media. By the time the average American reaches age sixty, he/she will see 350,000 TV commercials. A potent form of mass suggestion, this media saturation does provide useful information. But when the media become the primary way through which we absorb our collective culture, we are going to be inevitably brainwashed into a fantasized image of how life *should* be lived. When we confront situations in real life that do not meet our expectations, we become angry, frustrated, and often rage-filled, sometimes propelled by our frustration to the point of killing and violence in a desperate attempt to at-

---

*Numinous, from the Latin *numinosum,* refers to a dynamic agency or effect independent of the conscious will, a quality belonging to a visible object or the influence of an invisible presence that causes a peculiar alteration of consciousness. See Carl G. Jung, "Psychology and Religion," in *The Collected Works,* vol. 11 (Princeton, N.J.: Princeton University Press, 1954), par. 6.

tain the things that are somehow absent from our media-implanted expectations.

Hence, the necessity of a broad and diverse exposure to the world we live in—an *unbiased* exposure through different media including books, history, mythology, art, education—representing the innate *difference* and diversity of human experience and belief systems. In this sense, a good liberal arts education would build a foundation for a global individual—an individual not bound by a single viewpoint or cultural system. Of course, an essential openness to *all* views—religious, economic, and political—would counterbalance the tendency toward manipulation by *one worldview.* Fostering a broad diversity of viewpoints with opposition and conflict is essential for a healthy and vital media. The recent increase of interest in talk shows indicates the pent-up need for individuals to express their views.

In the West, we have succumbed to the notion of *exclusivity,* believing that our way of life and our beliefs are *superior* to other cultures. Such "we're better" collective thinking turns patriotism into tyranny. When we are one-sided, we claim the *cosmic center* as our exclusive possession, our property, when it is in reality, as Nietzsche said, "everywhere."

Sam Keen concluded, "The purpose of propaganda is to paralyze thought, to prevent discrimination, and to condition individuals to act as a mass."[28] By "discrimination" Keen refers to our ability to differentiate the better from the worse, to make fine qualitative judgments based on one's unique perception. Political, religious, and economic groups are saturated with conformity-producing slogans and sayings designed to change individual behavior and block out contradictory messages.

The Statistical Wasteland in Groups

> Life taken in general can be no sacred thing. It has enslaved and brutalized the globe.
>
> Sir Charles Sherrington[29]

Power in a group increases as individual members are disempowered. Not knowing the extent of our servitude and manipulation, we continue to play our assigned parts. Jung alluded to this mostly unconscious support of our oppressors:

> Although we human beings have our own personal life, we are yet in large measure the representatives, the victims and promoters of a collective spirit whose years are counted in centuries. We can well think all our lives long that we are following our own noses, and may never dis-

cover that we are, for the most part, supernumeraries on the stage of the world theater.[30]

One can be "normal" only in the context of being a member of a group. Persons are grouped by collective entities even without actual membership in them. We are counted, classified, and averaged into the masses. We find ourselves in that no-man's (and no-woman's) land called "normal." A normal family consists of a married couple with 1.2 children, 2 cars, 2.6 TV sets. Statistical profiles of groups like "baby boomers" are distributed to the mass media who busy themselves making us aware of "wants" that we never realized we wanted.

In mathematics, the "law of large numbers" argues "that in any very large ensemble of probabilistic events, things will always average out to the point where *individual deviations and happenings can be ignored*" (emphasis added).[31] Hence mathematics confirms the disappearance of individuality in any large group.

What if the mass media inform us that some other group threatens our social group? Accordingly, we project our unconscious rage at having given up our freedom and our passion in order to *fit into* (be accepted by) the collective onto our newly discovered enemy who has been the cause of our problems all along. So we are against those people or that country or this religion.

The primary difficulty with trying to make ourselves into a statistical person is the task's inherent unreality and impossibility, for there are always exceptions, differences, and irregularities that make up one's true identity. You and I cannot be classified because we are unique, exceptions to the rule. To identify with a collective statistic, to believe I am something that I am not, is to lose my identity through immersion in a group.

These collective classifying, averaging, and normalizing characteristics of groups are, by their rational scientific nature, prejudicial and inherently biased against the individual. If you or I deviate too far from our group norm, we are in trouble and will be *labeled* as social misfits: eccentric, mentally ill, or antisocial. Hence, the group has its statistical hooks in us and it is no simple task to remove them. At the same time, this tension between the *unreal normal* person and the real individual provides a necessary self-referencing point for the process of differentiation from a group.

However, it is important to keep in mind the manipulative psychological effects of a collective *statistical person* on the individual; statistical stereotypes keep us immersed in a group ideology as a frame of reference for our self-image and self-esteem. In other words, the danger lies in deriving our sense of self-worth based upon how closely we can approximate the accepted statistical average. For example, our collective culture creates poverty by defining its statistical limits (income levels) and characteristics. These collective definitions close the door on alternatives and maintain the status quo, in this case the statistical "normal person." Through this striving for the ideal of normalcy, people are controlled—the central dynamic in all totalistic groups—to maintain collective authority over the individual.

We have to decide to be "ordinary." Being ordinary means succumbing to an "ordered" life, a life whose limits are defined by the masses. Being ordinary also means we have inadvertently succumbed to an affliction called "normalizing judgment (the 'gaze'),"[32] a *totalistic* social behavior modification process where our peers force our conformity to group standards, often by little more than facial expressions and body language. The raised eyebrows, a certain expression, are all that we need to immediately know we have deviated from the collective norm or from collective authority. Once we give in to such collective leveling, we lose our ability to think independently and make free choices, for the mass mind has implanted a censoring mechanism inside our heads; any feelings or thoughts that are not in alignment with our social group are censored and repressed. Like a child who becomes acutely aware of a parent's disapproving glance, we are taught to repress unacceptable behavior, ideas, and language.

Granted, life requires some degree of compromise, since we are by and large "social animals," and if we don't relish complete isolation from others, peer group feedback provides guidelines about what may or may not be acceptable. However, collective feedback usually does not let up until we have made ourselves into a false self, wearing the iron mask of sameness.

Our collective culture has already decided who we "should" be. All we can do is "measure up" to the collective standard. If we don't meet the acceptable standards, we feel somehow inferior, less intelligent, and defective; something must be wrong with us. Our self-esteem, when measured against the popular culture, can only exist within a context of being like popular images, which requires not being ourselves. Similarly, John Bradshaw, counselor, theologian, writer, and host of the PBS series "Bradshaw on: The Family," describes the process of "mystification" as society's way of saying "the way you are is not OK."[33] This antiself collective message determines our fate when we allow the mass culture to dominate our lives. We also enter a mystified illusory state when we make gods of parents, sports figures, political leaders, priests, gurus, ideas, beliefs, and money. A somewhat mystical state may be beneficial to children, but to adults, mystification means living a false life, following someone else's god. In a mystified state we lose touch with our authenticity and with who we really are.

Our society has constructed an unending series of collective media images of heroes: *perfect* virile men who never lose their hair and *perfect* eternally youthful women who likewise do not really exist—a state of perfection that is unattainable, but nevertheless keeps the real self submerged while individuals exhaust themselves on an endless treadmill pursuing impossible collective ideals. In this fruitless attempt to be like some group ideal, people compromise both their dignity and integrity in addition to losing their individuality. A *normal* person has no soul, no distinctiveness.

We need information, data, and statistics to give us a sense of where we are in general, but generalized information can never define one authentic individual. The most perceptive autobiography can only peek into the self, the great estate, glimpse an occasional room, wonder at the distant tower that reaches into the heavens.

STATISTICAL MURDER

> Direction is essential for the continuing existence of the crowd. Its constant fear of disintegration means that it will accept *any* goal. A crowd exists so long as it has an unattained goal.
>
> Elias Canetti[34]

Groups commonly use statistics to justify their continued existence. In group hands, statistics often become weapons to control people. For example, a recent ABC News program, "Are We Scaring Ourselves to Death?" (April 21, 1994), explored how certain government groups commit "statistical murder." Given as an example, the Environmental Protection Agency's Super Fund is spending billions to clean up pollution that certainly causes sickness and death. But the EPA spends only a miniscule amount of money to fund research that would help to prevent auto deaths that kill and injure thousands daily. Hence, "statistical murder" because of a group, in our example the EPA, responding to a politically hot issue that gets lots of media attention, the media being another broad, loosely linked group that often develops its own collective hysteria when following certain news stories. Groups in the public sector, like the EPA, are especially vulnerable to what appears to be "public opinion," but is often little more than small yet highly vocal special interest groups.

This type of political persuasion between groups poses disastrous consequences for individuals. Thousands of auto deaths might have been prevented had taxpayer money been spent in areas where there is the greatest human suffering. Statistical murder provides an excellent example of how groups themselves are manipulated by other groups into making faulty and sometimes deadly decisions.

Less and less individual freedom inevitably results from increasing government regulation. In the EPA's case, their purpose may be honorable, but the way they go about enforcing their approach to regulation translates into a gradual socialization of private property. Again, when a government agency says it is protecting you and me, we are sure to lose some degree of individual freedom. The only valid exceptions to this axiom arc the court system, the police, and the military, whose legitimate function is to protect individual lives and property.

Government regulators, also infected with "original sin" theology, assume human nature to be essentially evil, and that without strict control and ever-increasing laws people will run amuck. This "original sin" theology motivates and permeates our political institutions.

No amount of money will reduce the risk in life to zero. Life will remain a hazardous state. However, we *significantly increase* the statistical odds that we will meet with some tragedy when we entrust multiple billions of our dollars to groups who are so easily swayed, not by legitimate concerns of individuals, but by currently "popular" trends or political issues.

Collective Narcissism

> Behind manifest grandiosity, there constantly lurks depression, and behind a depressive mood there often hide unconscious (or conscious but split off) fantasies of grandiosity. In fact, grandiosity is the defense against depression, and depression is the defense against the deep pain over the loss of the self.
>
> Alice Miller[35]

I would be remiss if I did not include the narcissistic characteristic of collective agencies. Alexander Lowen, prominent psychoanalyst and author, wrote:

> On the cultural level, narcissism can be seen in a loss of human values—in a lack of concern for the environment, for the quality of life, for one's fellow human being. A society that sacrifices the natural environment for profit and power betrays its insensitivity to human needs. The proliferation of material things becomes the measure of progress in living, and man is pitted against woman, worker against employer, individual against community. When wealth occupies a higher position than wisdom, when notoriety is admired more than dignity, when success is more important than self-respect, the culture itself overvalues "image" and must be regarded as narcissistic.[36]

Lowen's "loss of human values," in a collective milieu, results from dehumanizing collective influences that obliterate individual autonomy. When people give up their own humanity in favor of some group ideal, they cannot value or empathize with others as individuals. Maintaining the group's power structure and images becomes a matter of life and death for people, who depend upon the group for their identity and purpose in life. Furthermore, Lowen points out that individuals are caught in collective influences without actually subscribing to a particular group's ideology. Such subtle collective influences point out the need for people to become more aware of the ramifications and effects of unconscious manipulation by group images and ideals.

Extreme narcissism commonly masquerades in the guise of spiritual leadership. The idea of being "chosen" or being "anointed" feeds a grandiose ego-inflation. Collective positions of power and control over others lead to the false assumption of power—power that is in reality stolen projectively from idealizing and deluded followers who themselves are caught in extremes of narcissism.

Characteristics of narcissism include fantasies of power, a lack of empathy for others, attitudes of entitlement, and emotions that range between extremes of cool indifference and explosive rage—all excused automatically and never subject to question because one has been selected by God, or by the shareholders, or by the voters.

In a group context, narcissism refers to individuals who believe they are supporting a unique idealistic cause, but are actually furthering a loss of soul and the resultant lack of feeling for other human beings and for the earth. The group ideal image becomes more important than the individual. Whether a CEO, guru, priest, president, or self-appointed dictator, the group dynamic of elevating the leader to superhuman heights remains one of the greatest challenges to ethical leadership in any context. The adoration, admiration, and expectations of expertise by followers makes for a seductive, ego-inflating elixir that few individuals have the integrity to resist. Recent history is jam-packed with corrupt leaders in every walk of life, leaders and celebrities who believe the projections of infallibility from the mystified group mind.

The Totalistic Nature of the Collective

> Human beings become the means, as the systems of power pursue their own purposes. So long as power flows from the outside in, human life is turned inside out. The systems surrounding us encage the nature within us.
> Andrew Bard Schmookler[37]

Society is stuck in a collective, either/or totalism that is polarizing and alienating people instead of bringing people together. A fragmented society, divided into hostile factions, does not honor the individual diversity and difference that help make a community vital and whole. When everything is "sacrificed for the greater good," you're in a destructive group.

We in the West look at the inevitable chaos stemming from the disintegration of totalitarian regimes and believe things are different here. But our "free world" is deeply affected by similar influences, often subtle, but none the less deadly. In our free world, most groups do not openly advocate abuse, suicide, and murder, but their *ideological totalism* (authoritative centralized control) directly undermines individual autonomy and self-responsibility. In a totalistically organized group, and in a totalistically influenced culture, we cannot be authentic.

Robert Lifton's landmark work, *Thought Reform and the Psychology of Totalism,* is a major contemporary study of the ways totalistically structured groups influence human behavior. Lifton explained eight criteria for defining mind control: milieu control, mystical manipulation, the demand for purity, the cult or confession, sacred science, loading the language, doctrine over person, and the dispensing of existence. He called the underlying motif for these criteria "ideological totalism," explaining, "Each [criterion] has a totalistic quality; each depends upon an absolute philosophical assumption; and each mobilizes certain individual emotional tendencies, mostly of a polarizing nature. . . . In combination they create an atmosphere which may temporarily energize or exhilarate, but which at the same time poses the gravest of human threats."[38] As we continue to explore destructive group dynamics, we will look at how Lifton's important research applies to many different types of contemporary organizations. His research began with studying how the Chinese practiced thought reform during and after the Korean War.

THE COLLECTIVE NEED FOR POWER

Psychologist David McClelland, in his life-long study of the relationship between motivation and achievement, found that the desire for power was a fundamental motivational factor.[39] Because we have given up our power to systems and groups, we have made "power"—the chief characteristic of totalism—a social goal. This need for individual power provides one explanation for our fascination with the *tools and symbols* of power, i.e., money, status, titles, credentials, powerful positions, guns, and so on.

A power-based totalitarian group mind-set organizes the titanic, abnormal drive for power in individuals. Unfortunately, this drive for power takes place within the context of the prevailing collective systems like the market system, political systems, or religious systems.

In the following chapters, we will examine the potential applications of past and present research into group dynamics, attempting to connect depth psychology concepts to practical interventions enabling the individual to develop a healthy coexistence with groups, while reclaiming one's soul-integrity and personal destiny. How do we cope with a totalistic collective dynamic stuck in the push-pull of opposites?

4

The Dark Side of Groups

```
回卪卪卪卪卪卪卪卪卪卪卪卪卪卪卪卪卪卪卪卪卪卪卪回
```

Any large company composed of wholly admirable persons has the morality and intelligence of an unwieldy, stupid, and violent animal. The bigger the organization, the more unavoidable is its immorality and blind stupidity.

Carl Jung[1]

I guess I have been to over a hundred of these wonderful evenings. Beautiful people. Soft. Gentle. Spiritual. Visionary. Fascinating. But underlying all of this beauty lurks a darkness, only thinly veiled by beatific platitudes of sweetness. I call this beast New Age Fundamentalism, a belief that I am right and everyone else is wrong, stupid or evil; a belief that I represent the forces of light and goodness, while everyone else is duped by the forces of evil.

John Babbs[2]

There is no pleasure comparable to the not being captivated by any external thing whatever.

Thomas Wilson[3]

To ripen a person for self-sacrifice, he must be stripped of his individual identity and distinctness. . . . The most drastic way to achieve this end is by the complete assimilation of the individual into a collective body. The fully assimilated individual does not see himself and others as human beings.

Eric Hoffer[4]

85

The Trap of One-Sidedness

> We show greatness not by being at one extreme, but by touching both at
> once and occupying all the space in between.
>
> Blaise Pascal[5]

English author Rudyard Kipling is credited with saying, "Everyone is
more or less mad on one point." Such "madness on one point" is the result of being trapped by one side of a pair of opposites: on the one hand remaining unconscious of the opposite viewpoint, or on the other hand, making
the opposite into the enemy, the devil. "Madness on one point" exemplifies a
hallmark of toxic groups and toxic individuals. Systems locate and define happiness within their system, which restricts one to activity that fits the system;
personal fulfillment results from following group-dictated roles.

In the Tao philosophy, the ability to see both sides of a conflict, understanding that each viewpoint contains *both* right and wrong, is called the
"Pivot" of Tao. This means moving to the center, into the space between
opposites; this is soul work, the "still point" of Zen Buddhism. One stands
in the center "while 'Yes' and 'No' pursue each other around the circum-
ference. . . . Abandoning all thought of imposing a limit or taking sides, he
rests in direct intuition."[6]

Identification with one side and opposition to the other is part of human
nature. It is a primitive instinctual defense mechanism, but nevertheless a totalistic patriarchal response. Our spiritual and physical survival depends
upon our acknowledgment of and working *through* opposites, instead of the
instinctual knee-jerk dynamic of one-sidedness. In the early years of this century, the renowned Indian poet and writer Rabindranath Tagore realized the
overwhelming patriarchal one-sidedness of civilization. He wrote:

> Civilization is almost exclusively masculine, a civilization of power in
> which woman has been thrust aside in the shade. Therefore it has lost its
> balance and is moving by hopping from war to war. Its motive forces are
> the forces of destruction and its ceremonials are carried through by an ap-
> palling number of human sacrifices. This one-sided civilization is crash-
> ing along a series of catastrophes at a tremendous speed because of its
> one-sidedness. And at last the time has arrived when woman must step
> in and impart her life rhythm to the reckless movement of power.[7]

Marion Woodman, a well-known Toronto Jungian analyst and author
of *Addiction to Perfection*, describes the shadow-making consequences of
this one-sided identification dynamic:

Rather one recognizes that these poles are the domain of the gods, the extremes of black and white. To identify with one or the other can only lead to plunging into its opposite. The ratio is cruelly exact. The further I move into the white radiance on one side, the blacker the energy that is unconsciously constellated behind my back: the more I force myself to perfect my ideal image of myself, the more overflowing toilet bowls I'm going to have in my dreams.[8]

Sadly, most ideal images people would like to emulate are not their own but are collective (cultural) implants. Such idealism further alienates individuals from themselves (Jung's "disunion"). This disunion from the self results in greater ignorance of who we really are as individual souls, and it further splits and fragments the human psyche. The more we try to make ourselves into some outside, idealized image, the more irrational and abusive will be our reactions to others and to our environment. We have only to go into any sizable inner city to see the overflowing collective toilet bowl. The ominous shadow of all that we suppress and ignore in ourselves and as a society inevitably expresses itself in our society and environment.

Unreflective identification with one side is a consequence of a psyche split into a totalistic *we/they* viewpoint, producing an ever-increasing fragmentation of our world into warring factions—economic, religious, political, ecological, and cultural—outer conflicts that mirror our own inner split. We project our own shadow onto others instead of working out the conflict within—a psychological and spiritual irresponsibility with tragic results for all life. This has immediate consequences for the individual: all growth stops and one regresses to more primitive levels of unconsciousness. The psyche becomes frozen, caught in an absolute, either/or, black-and-white toxic thinking; we become fixed, brittle, immovable, and threatened by any group or person who disagrees with us. All the while, an inexorable psychological equation is operating unseen: the consequence of ignoring one side of a pair of opposites creates a gradual accumulation of tension until it's no longer tolerable, often resulting in violent acting out. People lose control, something snaps, monstrous shadow material erupts out of the psyche, individually and collectively. The collective keeps people in an "either/or" mind game. Moving out of enmeshment in collective agencies means transitioning from either/or, black-and-white thinking to a "both/and" process.

In this fashion we create our most fearsome demons from our inability to simply be true to ourselves, which means having the courage to follow one's own heart, conscience, and sense of self—it means being self-responsible as well as self-honest. Above all, it means not compromising our innate integrity, character, and distinctiveness by allowing any group or outside influence to assume ideological or psychological control over our lives and our identity. According to Jung, as a result of *one-sidedness* "the psyche disintegrates and loses its capacity for cognition. It becomes an unreflective succession of psychic states, each of which fancies itself its own justification because it does not, or does not yet, see any other state."[9] The inability to *reflect* on issues out of one's own depth and honest feelings creates psychological blindness. Self-reflection cultivates understanding and human heartedness, and nurtures the soul-making process. Self-reflection locates us within a relationship, first within our own psyche and then in our relationship to others. Reflection is the antithesis to *reaction*, a hallmark of the one-sided personality.

In the reaction mode, we react without thinking—shoot first and ask questions later. In groups we bypass reflection when we mechanically turn to the group's belief system for answers instead of working through an issue out of our own insight and unique experience. Enmeshed in the group mind-set, we become victims of psychological bypass surgery on our souls.

One-sidedness is an experience in robotics while reflection places one in a third aspect of consciousness, utilizing the tension created the moment we stop and *reflect* instead of mechanically reacting. Belonging to a particular group exerts a nearly irresistible pull on one to conform to the group viewpoint. In such a milieu of group pressure, individual reflection often produces feelings of guilt and betrayal of the group cause. Destructive groups often see self-reflection as expressing doubt and questioning the leader's good intentions.

But what about physical threats? If someone is about to kill us, it's kill or be killed with no time to reflect. Are there situations when life demands instant reactions—animal instinct—one-sided self-preservation? Of course this depends on individual judgment of the value of human life and the consequences of self-sacrifice or killing another human being, a dilemma that has no simple answer.

One-sidedness produces a certain sort of blindness, an inability to "see" the whole picture. The personality becomes one-sided, two-dimensional, flat, and trapped in a perpetual defensive reactive mode. Communication and getting along with such a person becomes an exercise in futility unless you completely give in and support their point of view.

One unavoidable result of one-sidedness is that we become stuck in a particular viewpoint. In this sense, we are all extremists, caught in our particular cultural viewing point. A one-sided viewpoint always creates conflict. By identifying with one position, we automatically make an enemy out of any opposing position. We wage "holy war" with those who do not follow our version of God. We see other nations as backward, uncivilized, or barbaric because their culture is alien to *our viewing point*. Being caught in one viewpoint breeds war and violence on every level. Nation-states build Berlin Walls between peoples. We subdivide ourselves and the world into ideological fragments. One-sidedness demands struggle against some perceived enemy, who must be defended against or be destroyed.

Extricating oneself from a particular viewpoint can be next to impossible. A life-long implantation of collective and cultural bias robotizes the psyche, ominously concretizing a false self, without which we feel isolated and lost. Only when we can *hold the tension between two viewpoints* are we free to think and reason as autonomous individuals. As long as we are blinded by one-sidedness, prejudice, racism, bigotry, or some "ism" will contaminate everything we do; we become *isimites,* no longer individuals, but appendages of the crowd mind. Successful diplomats see *both sides* and arrive at solutions, a *mixture* that resolves (dissolves) the conflict. Describing the consequences of repressing one side of a pair of opposites, Jung wrote, "The tension leads to conflict, the conflict leads to attempts at mutual repression, and if one of the opposing forces is successfully repressed a dissociation ensues, a splitting of the personality, a disunion with oneself."[10]

Well aware of the danger of a one-sided attitude of mind, one of my psychology professors once remarked, "Someone [who] tells you to 'think positively' yokes you to a system of tyranny."[11] Freudian psychology has important relevance for group dynamics, especially regarding what Freud called "denial." Freud concluded that the unconscious exists because he observed people defending against *something.* And this "something" he called the "unconscious." Freud's proof of the existence of the unconscious was our "resistance" to it. Dreams, humor, slips of the tongue are all cracks in the floor opening one to the unconscious. The fact that we defend ourselves so fervently against the unconscious became the essence of Freud's psychoanalysis. Freud also believed that the unconscious was the headquarters for desires and hungers, and that we resist and suppress our desires, resulting in an unconscious acting out of repressed material—a state of being mechanized (because of our unawareness) by unconscious forces.

Groups especially enhance unconsciousness with the resultant increase in blind acting out. The greater our involvement in the collective, the less conscious we become and the more we become victims, not only of our own shadows, but of massive quantities of collectively repressed energy from assuming a group's necessarily one-sided viewpoint.

Denial means we are saying, "It doesn't exist." In order to maintain a collective position, our true individuality falls into this nonexistent (shadow) underground, which must be increasingly suppressed in order to play our collective role. There are basic ways we maintain a state of denial through what Freud called "defense mechanisms." While important concepts for individuals, Freud's defense mechanisms become awesome forces when wielded in a collective context:

Projection: In the dynamic of projection we find the primary root of collective evil. One's own unacknowledged (unconscious) and unwanted attributes are projected onto others. Projection, an essential and permanent ingredient in all destructive groups, enables members to create outside enemies of the group's cause. Within a group, projection also empowers leaders with ego-inflating adoration of *followers* who project their inner gods and spiritual self-hood onto outer personalities. In this process we sadly defend against understanding ourselves, who we really are, and how we can uniquely contribute as individuals.

Rationalization: Another prevalent defense mechanism in groups, rationalization excuses behavior that ordinarily would be considered unacceptable to the individual. From the Inquisition to Hitler's "racial purification," to killing abortion doctors, to genocide in Rwanda, history reverberates with an unending stream of *groups* rationalizing torture, destruction, and death in order to accomplish their "mission."

Spiritual and psychological suicide for the individual, "self-sacrifice" becomes a lethal rationalization in any group. Self-sacrifice for a collective ideal means death for the individual and perpetuation of the group. We are made to feel selfish and guilt-ridden if we resist living a group-defined life. Thus, the height of collective virtue turns individuals into mechanized and dehumanized slaves.

Reaction Formation: Closely related to rationalization, reaction formation occurs when we *neutralize* an event by turning it into its opposite. For example, we thank a speaker for a lecture we either did not like or did not agree with. Peer pressure in groups easily pushes us into this dynamic. We are afraid to be honest and instead repress our feelings. On a collective level, this sort of reaction-formation repression takes on gargantuan proportions, feeding on itself as individuals become little more than mindless appendages of the crowd. And leaders become more and more unassailable, out of reach of constructive criticism, more and more believing in their own infallibility. Members grow increasingly unreal and the group takes on airs of one-sided fanaticism; their agenda becomes *absolutely necessary* for survival.

Regression: An extremely common characteristic of dysfunctional groups from families to nation-states, regression means becoming childlike as a defense. All authoritarian groups push psychological and spiritual development backward. Parental authority, whether in a family, a religion, or in the state, keeps one in an infantile state. Childlike behavior may be natural for children, but in an adult, it becomes the greatest hindrance imaginable. In my own experience in a religious group, I felt increasingly as though I were being treated like a child, and indeed I was. My growing discomfort with this particular dynamic was a significant part of my waking up from my group hypnosis. Groups capitalize on naive, uncomplaining, obedient hopefulness characterizing childhood qualities, using these traits to totally control and manipulate their constituents. Thus we have the spectacle of otherwise intelligent people swallowing utterly ridiculous, unfounded information like so much pablum and dedicating their lives and resources to a collective illusion.

EROS AND THE WILL TO POWER

> A mouth that prays, a hand that kills.
>
> Arabian proverb

Depth psychology has shown that a one-sided conscious attitude creates an opposite, unconscious shadow. In a group context, one-sided viewpoints generate collective opposites—a group *shadow* that exerts subtle yet potent influences on individual members. Hence, the church group expressing a sickening sweet love justifies all sorts of abuse in the guise of love for its members' own good: we abuse you because we love you and care for you. Thus an Eros-centered group uses "love" to control members. In religious groups, excessive displays of love are known psychologically as "love bombing." Love bombing in a group makes people feel loved, needed, and appreciated. In return, the group expects undying loyalty and dedication. Beware of any group that expresses *profuse* loving attitudes toward its members. Rest assured that such loving groups are intent, often unconsciously, on controlling you.

The will to power, a patriarchal attribute found in both men and women, makes individuals, relationships, and groups destructive. Power, in a group, means that controlling others becomes the dominant factor in relationships between people. The "will to power" may be either conscious or unconscious. According to Jung, an "unconscious Eros" [12] always expresses its conscious opposite as a "will to power." Attempting to keep us somewhat balanced (a state of normal tension), the compensatory nature of the psyche guarantees that a one-sided viewpoint will come under attack by its unconscious opposite. In Jung's example of power and Eros, a conscious attitude of extreme Eros constellates an equally extreme unconscious lust for power. For example, where the attitude of "love" overly dominates a group, the collective group unconscious will build a powerful lust after power. This unconscious lust for power in spiritual organizations commonly manifests itself as a strong desire to master and control one's life. In metaphysical New Age groups, members repeat "affirmations" and prayers designed to attain self-mastery—absolute power over all aspects of life. The greater the obsession with a shadowless loving attitude, the more ominous and threatening becomes the unconscious collective power shadow.

Individuals caught up into this power-eros dynamic often find themselves driven to control not only their own lives, but others as well. In business groups, the will to power expresses itself through absolute control of employees and the relentless increase in control of economic resources; one is never satisfied.

The Flat Earth One-Sided Personality

> Norms without pathologizing in their images perform a normalizing upon our psychological vision, acting as repressive idealizations which make us lose touch with our individual abnormalities.
>
> James Hillman[13]

The increasing use of psychotropic drugs illustrates a striving for perfection in the form of an even, *flat personality* with no highs and no lows, no oppositeness, and consequently no tension. Through such *social chemistry* we make ourselves *socially acceptable*—"normal" at the expense of being nonhuman. We have been culturally and socially conditioned to expect unreal and nonhuman behavior with little or no feeling. Being a human being encompasses ups and downs, opposites that are a normal part of life. Without struggle and tension there can be no soul work, no empathy, no humaneness, and no further development of consciousness. We have to ask ourselves, whose ideal are we attempting to conform to? Who are we trying to be like, other than ourselves?

Interestingly, cocaine and heroine use has exploded around the globe, and, according to an April 4, 1994, NBC Evening News report by Tom Brokaw, Nigeria and Russia now account for 35 to 40 percent of the world supply.[14] The increasing use of these drugs indicates a massive collective neurosis. What are so many people trying to medicate? Has the impossibility of living up to collective images and standards reached a global crisis? It is quite possible that we have become supersaturated with impossible group expectations and images, combined with a deep and massive sense of loss from allowing groups to define our lives.

These are common characteristics of individuals caught in a group dynamic of one-sidedness. Such people often:

Show abusive behavior	Are arrogant
Have authoritarian attitudes	Blame others

Carelessly disregard others	Classify and label others, use name calling
Have a closed-minded stance	Are overly competitive
Show dogmatic inclinations	Have ego-inflation
Believe people are either with them or against them	Exhibit hatred, rage, temper tantrums
Seem exclusive and elitist	Act retributive
Are fanatical	Fear difference
Act overly good or sweet	Believe they are right, everyone else is wrong
Are excessively idealistic	Are self-righteous
Behave judgmentally	Demonstrate missionary zeal
Moralize	Have narcissistic traits
Display obsessive behavior	Are perfectionists
Are prejudicial	Have racist, intolerant views
Retaliate	Scapegoat
Are stubborn, obstinate	Try to make others be like them
See winning as all-important	Act superior and condescending

There is always an "opposite" lurking nearby. In our naiveté we are like Little Red Riding Hood. When we ignore and repress the unpleasant side of life, we create the wolf stalking us; it may be fear, depression, poverty, sickness, famine, or war. All our repressed energies become the "wolf pack at our door" intent on devouring us. Our spiritual, mental, and physical health depend upon defining, dialoging with, and observing the "wolf" within. Seeing the wolf—our shadow—requires holding opposites. It means becoming consciously aware of both sides of a problem at the same time—holding two contrasting views by giving equal weight or consideration to both, without being caught by one side. The psychological tension produced by the collision of such oppositeness brings about a solution that transcends both extremes yet also incorporates something of each. "The wolf also shall dwell with the lamb, and the leopard shall lie down with the kid."

An ever-present, dangerous group-reinforced dynamic always exists that we will *unconsciously* fall into one extreme or the other; become a victim of the dark or the light; or develop a fanatical obsession with an idea, a person, a guru, a religion, a political party, some movement, or a way of life.

Depression, especially the bipolar variety with its extreme mood swings, so common in contemporary society, suggests the extent to which we have become one-sided: caught in a dualistic world of opposites; neglecting, ignoring, and repressing our authenticity, and our true feelings: and avoiding working through (holding) the tension between opposites. Cut off from our individual and collective shadows, we turn our rage inward on ourselves or project it outward onto others, creating scapegoats for what we will not face in ourselves.

Individuals identified with group ideologies such as Christianity find themselves confined within doctrinal constraints. The religious idea of "original sin" implies that we must escape our depressions and our dark moods; thus, theology demonizes the tension-producing elements in life that make one a whole person. One of the world's most eminent Jungian psychologists, a prolific writer, and founder of archetypal psychology, James Hillman maintains that "to be conscious" necessitates the full range of feelings: "Drawn to extremes, consciousness and depression have come to exclude each other, and psychological depression has replaced theological hell. . . . As long as our actions in regard to depression are resurrective, implying that being down and staying down is sin, we remain Christian in theology."[15]

A stupa in Kathmandu, Nepal, reveals the eyes of Buddha looking out from a *place in between* the earth dome and the heavens above. In Sanskrit, *Buddha* means "awakened." And in the Christian Bible we find a *both and* divinity described:

> I am the Lord and there is none else.
> I form the light
> and create the darkness;
> I make peace and create evil.
> I, the Lord,
> do all these things.
>
> (Isaiah 45:6–7)

Perhaps Jesus warned against becoming one-sided in this apocryphal saying:

> . . . the two shall be one,
> and the outside as the inside,
> and the male with the female neither male nor female.
> Clement of Rome, Second Epistle to the Corinthians 12[16]

Loss of Soul in Groups

> There may be intelligence or sparks of the divinity in millions—but they
> are not Souls till they acquire identities, till each one is personally itself.
>
> John Keats[17]

When we eventually step off the collective treadmill, the effects of loss of
soul and the resultant loss of meaning in life confront us. We find ourselves
in an identity crisis, seriously wounded by our attempt to be something else
instead of being ourselves. Loss of soul, a paramount characteristic of individuals caught in a group ideology, lays the groundwork for a whole society devoid of meaning and purpose.

Thomas Moore, a leading lecturer and writer in the area of archetypal
psychology, maintains that persons who lose touch with the soul "fall into
extremes of literalism and destructive fanaticism."[18] "Destructive fanaticism" increasingly occurs in many groups that rationalize destructive behavior, violence, and even murder as justifiable methods in order to force
their presumed superior morality systems on others. This propensity for loss
of soul in groups results from an inherent group dynamic toward extreme
one-sided positions, which accompany fanatical behavior to support a particular position. To survive, groups have to adhere to their viewpoint.

Our largely *unconscious* support of collective ideologies has dangerous ramifications. Carl Jung wrote, "The mass crushes out the insight and
reflection that are still possible with the individual, and this necessarily
leads to doctrinaire and authoritarian tyranny."[19] Jung's "crushed-out insight" is analogous to our loss of soul.

Mass movements appropriate the deep-seated human need to surrender to something greater than the ego, what we might call the *conversion
factor.* Instead of surrendering to our inner potential, we objectify this archetypal longing and sell our souls to the crowd, extinguishing the inner
flame and spirit. In fact, groups must disparage Individual autonomy, making it a sin. Thus we shut off our only source of help—the Self. Indeed, sacrificing for the good of a group perfects an estrangement from the Self and
results in the building of a false Self.

Groups provide an escape from self-responsibility, which brings a
temporary sense of great relief, as Von Franz illustrates: "In the group,
therefore, the sense of security increases *and the feeling of responsibility
decreases* [emphasis added]. Suggestibility also increases enormously, a
fact which includes, however, a loss of freedom, because one falls into the
hands of good or evil environmental influences."[20]

Cartesian influence saturates the topology of the group landscape. The
Cartesian way of thinking splits the universe in two, on one side living per-

sons and on the other side dead matter. This dualistic mentality typifies totalistically structured groups. Scriptures become literalized, reduced to historical facts; mankind down here, God up there, producing a flat-earth isolationist theology. Destructive groups express a "either you are with us or you are against us" enemy-creating dogma with no *middle ground,* no soul. Metaphor, myth, dream, and imagination die in this milieu of concretistic dualism.

Loss of soul in the collective means an accompanying loss of *empathy,* a dehumanizing of the individual, a loss of the feminine ability to *feel.* Such desouled group-identified persons develop a mob mentality, able to kill without feeling or conscience. They function exclusively to perpetuate their respective groups, and they eliminate anyone who impinges on their ideological or physical territory. The effects of the dehumanized dark side of groups are all around us. We see and read about them daily in the media.

James Hillman maintains that the "gods are in social disease just as they are in the problems of the individuals."[21] One wonders, what gods are loose in our inner-city gangs, in racial hate groups, and in fanatical religious groups? Identification of these gods provides a way to see through the chaos and perhaps begin to understand the horrible ramifications of giving up our souls in exchange for the infantile illusion of some collective security, power, and false sense of grandiosity. Furthermore, what becomes of the tremendous repressed rage at a dehumanizing collective that has stolen one's soul?

Where does the soul go when we lose it? I don't think it goes anywhere. I think it gets irritated as hell from being ignored, and starts causing all sorts of psychological and physical suffering to get our attention. It begins a process of poking us in all the wrong places. The understanding we lack—the very thing we need is in the poking—the pathology. For instance, one's spouse keeps remarking that one does not listen or pay attention. Or, one enters a deep unexplainable depression, which is the soul's way of drawing us down. Trying to medicate ourselves out of our melancholy desensitizes and aborts the inner transformation of consciousness, anesthetizing the human spirit.

According to Jungian thought, loss of soul equates to a lessening or lowering of consciousness, what we commonly refer to as depression. In particular, Jung observed that a "loss of soul" entailed a "slackening of the tensity of consciousness."[22] The soul needs and comes alive through tension—not destructive tension, but rather creative dynamic tension—the kind of tension that keeps one awake, aware and *conscious,* and creative. For example, in my psychotherapy practice, I often ask a client to construct a collage of pictures or art work that illustrates two conflicting, opposite aspects of their nature, placing them next to each other on what I call a *ten-*

sion board. One might portray a wild, impulsive side next to a controlled, subdued side. The tension created by this visual collision of opposites helps individuals to creatively integrate different parts of the psyche, to imagine creative ways, in our example, to utilize needed attributes of both sides, without letting either one dominate the personality.

Another example of creative tension involves learning to tolerate what can be thought of as *healthy tension.* One of my clients, a thirty-five-year-old man, wanted to improve his communication skills with his wife. After finding out the key words he used to avoid arguments, I asked him to "hold the tension" in their conversations by first eliminating the tension-reducing word "but" when he replied to his wife's comments, which he used to defend and defuse difficult issues. Eliminating "but" had the effect of leaving the tension out in the open—something that had to be dealt with. He was then to stay with the issue, talking it through completely irregardless of his resistance to it or how uncomfortable it might feel. My client did this, explaining that he had to really struggle with himself (holding the tension) to keep from defending, defusing, and thus ending the conversation. However, he was able to work through the issue with his wife, and as they were talking, he explained to me that he clearly felt the presence of an inner little boy who was terrified of an extremely hypercritical, controlling mother. And to his astonishment, his wife remarked afterward that for a moment she had seen a "frightened little boy" in his eyes as they were talking! This was a profound experience for my client and for me as well. And both he and his wife opened a new level of empathy and understanding in their relationship. Here was an example of Jung's "transcendent function," the frightened little boy, which appeared out of the tension between opposites—a synergetic event. My client was learning to tolerate some uncertainty and the resulting tension.

This dynamic easily extends itself into a group setting where individuals with opposing views can get together and agree to respectfully disagree; to listen to each other; to tolerate ambiguity, uncertainty, and conflict; and to work through issues on both sides until some resolution arrives. This requires allowing a *process to unfold* as opposed to expecting certain results.

Creative tension can also be used to create new ideas, products, processes, designs, and concepts. For instance, a company can create a brainstorming session that includes bringing together bizarre and disconnected ideas, humor, or playfulness that is totally out of context (opposite) from normal company decorum. In this tension-producing collision of preposterous elements, creative ideas are born.

In a group setting, a lack of tension has a deadening effect. We can attribute loss of soul in destructive groups to a lessening of tension between members since all are of a "like mind." Such like-minded groups usually maintain a minimal degree of tension by creating scapegoats, enemies outside the group who replace and receive the members' own repressed shadow material. By keeping the tension outside the individual, the group prevents and even regresses individual understanding while keeping up the illusion of something vital going on.

One could argue that many of the most beautiful and creative masterpieces of art have been done when the power of a group (i.e., the Roman Empire, the Greek city-states, or the Catholic church) was at its peak. But this logic attributes *individual* creativity to a group, when in fact, such genius more likely occurs in spite of a group. On the other hand, even destructive groups can be catalysts for individual creativity. For example, a major factor in any successful religious group's attractive power has to do with a core ideology based upon a mythological motif. Archetypal stories of virgin births (of which there are seventy that predate Christianity), saviors, avatars, enlightenment, great floods, paradise lost, conquering heroes, resurrection, good against evil, saints, and mystics resonate with deep-seated "mytho-genetic" patterns inherent in all individuals, engraved upon what Carl Jung called our "collective unconscious." This inner resonance no doubt accounts for a large portion of our fascination with groups that build their doctrine and rituals around these timeless stories about the human experience.

In contrast to group-oriented creativity, we have the Renaissance, where creative effort often involved rebelling against church and state. Science, art, literature, and individual reason that deviated from official dogma made one a heretic. In fact, during the Renaissance, some city-states, like Florence, supported the arts in ways far beyond our present culture. Indeed, even healthy groups channel creativity in directions that are *only favorable and confirming for the group*. Hence we have art and architecture that glorifies a particular ideology or political system. In this sense, we can only wonder what we have lost to ages of immense group-directed creative effort in every field of human endeavor—our collective brain drain. In the end, the singular individual—not a group—creates a Mona Lisa, designs an inspiring building, sculpts a Pietà. Each inspiring and exquisite masterpiece reaffirms the unique ability of creative individuals to ennoble and lift the masses, to rise above the common herd.

While groups do not possess souls, they often do *possess* the souls of their members. This collective grasp on the individual has been referred to by some writers as a "crowd soul." For a brief period of time, joining a group provides a high degree of tension because persons are struggling to suppress their individuality in favor of a collective position; this marks the "conversion" period common to many groups when one "surrenders" to a greater cause. This surrender may be to a religious idea or to a business mission of generating greater profits; we create our gods in the form of our obsessions and projections. It takes contrast, struggle, difference, diversity, conflict, and emotion to maintain tension, which maintains consciousness, which *is* soul at work.

The Disease of Exclusiveness

We must reassert that no Christian is ever called upon to give unquestioning obedience to anyone. We ultimately must accept only the lordship of Christ.

Ronald M. Enroth[23]

Ronald Enroth, supposedly rescuing persons from religious cults, makes abundantly clear Christianity's cult of exclusiveness and its demand that adherents worship "only the lordship of Christ." This sad paradox of one cult member trying to recruit other cult members is far too common in our society. While Enroth correctly identifies many characteristics of destructive cults in his book, *The Lure of the Cults,* his own entrapment in a particular religious ideology seriously undermines his work. Hopping from cult to cult is not a solution to the collective madness that grips modern civilization.

Exclusiveness in any group alludes to a claim that the group has some unique purpose or knowledge and therefore membership in the group implies that the members are likewise special in some manner. Of course, along with this exclusiveness, outsiders must be classified as ignorant and inferior. Campbell insists, "The whole idea of a chosen people, for example, is pathology."[24] If the group has the answers to existence, then it follows that those outside the group do not have the answers.

What Lifton refers to as "the dispensing of existence,"[25] makes human beings chattel—property of the group—and ownership includes mind, body, and soul, a modern-day version of feudalism. Existential legitimacy is restricted to those within the group. Those outside the group do not have this collectively dispensed existential right, and are automatically subject to psychological elimination. Elimination does not mean physical death, but even more ominously, the death of opposing ideas, conflicting images, unfamiliar life styles—anything or anyone who is different.

A collective "dispensing of existence" has a profound dehumanizing effect on anyone outside the group. Outsiders are not seen as individuals, but as *things,* expendable enemies of the state, e.g., immigrants stealing jobs from American citizens, or unsaved primitives worshipping unfamiliar gods who must be convinced to worship *our group's version of God.* Persons are caught in mass polarizations—ideological camps constantly at war with some other group that is responsible for all their problems. Lifton compared the collective presumption of existential property rights to, "what the Greeks called *hubris*, of arrogant man making himself God,"[26] adding:

> Yet one underlying assumption makes this arrogance mandatory: the conviction that there is just one path to true existence, just one valid mode of being, and that all others are perforce invalid and false. Totalists thus feel themselves compelled to destroy all possibilities of false existence as a means of furthering the great plan of true existence to which they are committed. Existence comes to depend upon creed (I believe, therefore I am), upon submission (I obey, therefore I am) and beyond these a sense of total merger with the ideological movement.[27]

The Mormon church controls access to temple space, even excluding many of their own members from certain rituals reserved for those in positions of authority and privilege. All totalistically organized groups, whether religious, business, or political, have restricted places reserved for those with special status.

AN ARROGANT COSMOLOGY

> The Bible is the inerrant word of the living God. It is absolutely infallible, without error in all matters pertaining to faith and practice, as well as in areas such as geography, science, history, etc.
>
> Jerry Falwell[28]

> In all the broad universe, there is no other hope for man than ourselves. This is a tremendous responsibility. I have borne it too long alone. You share it with me now.
>
> L. Ron Hubbard[29]

Only a "flat-earth" arrogance would demand, without knowing, that we are the exclusive inhabitants of the universe, the only intelligent life. Primarily characteristic of organized religions, such elitist theology results from a fundamentalist stance that literalizes mythology, desperately trying to turn legend into historical fact, coupled with a deep fear and denial of the possibility and ramifications of other worlds and other gods.

Similarly, Sam Keen explains, "Claims that we alone are protecting the flame, incarnating the purpose of history, must be seen as propaganda masquerading as theology, as atheism covering itself in false piety."[30] Assuming the group has the "only truth" or way automatically implies that all others are somehow inferior, in a less evolved state, and that they are economically, morally, and spiritually less advanced. Those in the group experience a great satisfaction and smugness in being part of such a select, superior, "good," elite community. As William James wrote, ". . . goodness casts the last stone."[31]

Psychologist and former cult member Steven Hassan explains the ramifications of exclusiveness: "This feeling of elitism and destiny, however, carries a heavy burden of responsibility. Members are told that if they do not fully perform their duties, they are failing all of mankind."[32] Hence, the other side of this *savior consciousness* embodies the assured disillusionment that occurs when the group fails to "save" humanity from what the group perceives as undesirable. The opposite experiences of *savior* and *failure* are inseparable and guaranteed for individuals caught in such systems.

Groups claiming the right to existence create a serious inner conflict for individuals that can be characterized as the classic existential "being versus nothingness." Only by conforming to and identification with the group's dogma does one maintain a valid claim to one's right to exist. As a result, leaving the group immediately has the effect of compounding an *existential crisis* as one is faced with the immense effort of finding one's *pregroup reality and original identity*—the self that has been repressed for so long. Even the expectation of leaving often creates gnawing fear of divine retribution, internal collapse, and ego-extinction. How can one leave such a unique and special place without somehow incurring the wrath of the gods? What colossal ingratitude! How selfish and self-centered.

EXISTENTIAL SACRIFICE

> To be able to live among men and women we must allow everyone to exist with his given individuality. If we condemn another man absolutely, there is nothing for him but to treat us as a mortal enemy; for we are willing to grant him *the right to exist* only on condition that he becomes different from what he invariably is. (Emphasis added)
>
> Arthur Schopenhauer[33]

> Because your mind troubles you, give it to me. It won't trouble me.
>
> Guru Maharaj Ji, Divine Light Mission[34]

Robert Lifton calls the collective belief that reality belongs to a certain group, their *exclusive* possession, the "assumption of omniscience."[35] The fundamental human right to one's own existence (reality) is taken from the individual and placed into collective hands. The group possesses reality, hence *those not in the group* are in a state of unreality and nonexistence.

Once individuals abdicate their own existence to a collective ideal, they become a sort of psychological capital—fuel for a machinelike conscienceless mass. Such existential sacrifice destroys the only source of creativity and innovation that in fact has the potential to change groups in a constructive manner that is soul-empowering and supportive of individual integrity and initiative. Unfortunately, conforming to the collective mindset is often more comfortable than standing on one's own feet. Resisting collective indoctrination processes requires tremendous integrity and a strong sense of self apart from any group.

Belief systems—organized "isms"—are usually closed systems, with mental barbed wire and collective electric fences that keep out alien ideas and critical thinking. In reality, a healthy individual's beliefs are always in a state of transition, changing, moving, choosing this, reclaiming that, discarding one thing while adding something else. Once we make life into a fixed system, organizing our beliefs into neat explanatory boxes, we kill human imagination, ingenuity, and creativity—the spirit and essence of consciousness and of the soul itself.

Dysfunctional groups have a bent toward an increasing narrowness of view. As a result, members have fewer and fewer options. Mentally filtering outside information through the group's belief system, people find themselves trapped in a narrow worldview that admits zero contradiction. Unbending and inflexible, fanaticism grows with its accompanying ironclad adherence to the "letter" of dogma. There is no space for conflict other than collective enmity directed at all who oppose the group's views.

Stepping out of a totalistic ideology has the effect of leaving one with a sense of homelessness, of having stepped off the edge of a familiar world. One suddenly feels quite alone. Without a belief system to fill the God Hole, one is left with a void—what feels like an enormously empty and meaningless life. But the real problem becomes one of rediscovering one's own center, one's soul, and one's unique human potential. Eventually we discover that *being* has a great deal to do with *being one's self,* standing on our own two feet, as opposed to standing in collective shoes walking someone else's path.

DEADLY SUPERIORITY: GROUP EGOCENTRICITY

> The building up of prestige is always a product of collective compromise: not only must there be one who wants prestige, there must also be a public seeking someone on whom to confer prestige.
>
> Carl Jung[36]

One-sidedness maintains and perpetuates inequality and prejudice. If we believe we are *superior,* we have to appoint a person, religion, group, or race to be *inferior.* Superiority only exists in contrast to inferiority. The entire notion of superiority perpetuates a see-saw world: if I am better, you have to be worse so that I can stay on top. I am up only if you are down. When there is a clear outside enemy, our group is elevated and superior. In fact, we need to find inferior people so that we can stay superior. Conversely, when we perceive others as superior and more successful, we feel *put down,* depressed.

Group and cultural elitism is one consequence of being caught in extremes: blacks against whites, whites against blacks, Protestants against Catholics, Catholics against Protestants, Arabs against Jews, Jews against Arabs, and on and on. If we have been particularly persecuted as a group, revenge can easily trap us in another extreme. A basic characteristic of all totalistic organizations is the fact that the system, the doctrine, the program, the mission, and the beliefs are *superior to the individual and always come first.* This is precisely the reverse of a healthy group where the individual comes first and the group fulfills a supportive role. A slave-master relationship with a group automatically results from this doctrinally superior stance. Of course, a slave-master relationship requires an attitude of *surrender and obedience* on the part of the slave. Surrender then becomes a major prerequisite to mind control. And in a collective context, surrender often triggers the acting out of one's retrospective longing to return to an effortless, blisslike childhood where someone else takes care of us.

Being overly impressed with oneself is the hallmark of those who are possessed by a collective ideology. In fact, nowhere does ego-inflation find so willing a resting place as in the hearts and minds of religious and political fanatics. Such zealots, having identified with a mass ideal, fancy themselves "chosen" people, selected by God or destiny to lead and inspire the masses. Many CEOs also fall into this trap, believing that their material success equates to economic divinity. Some of the most arrogant and dehumanized individuals alive are heads of giant business enterprises that operate in a totalitarian milieu.

Inflated egos develop from collective influences in two ways. First, leaders or celebrities begin to *believe* the mass projections they receive from dutiful followers, employees, and admirers as to their abilities, talents, and wisdom. Second, the individual members of a group so completely identify with a collective mission that they, too, experience tremendous ego-inflation, viewing themselves, through their association with their group, as anointed persons, uniquely gifted and appointed as emissaries of a world-saving cause which, of course, all others must be converted to. Monica, a former member of a religious cult, remarked, "The greatest disservice my former spiritual home has done is to label, categorize, and judge people— putting them in a false light and keeping them locked into either a negative image (false), or a glorified saintly superhuman image (also false) totally absent from what is real or true, lacking clear-sightedness."[37]

Ironically, outwardly displayed attitudes of self-sacrifice, humility, and dedication in such group-identified individuals reveal they are caught in the most arrogant and narcissistic of roles in addition to being alienated from the self, totally cut off from a sense of their own distinctiveness and humanity. These individuals willingly dedicate their lives to a corporate mission and die for a cause—for a holy war. Bereft of their own real value as individual human beings, they willingly torture and kill others whom they perceive as enemies to their mission. Curiously, traits that we consider virtues, like selflessness and humility, become sources of tremendous ego-inflation. Eric Hoffer maintained, "The burning conviction that we have a holy duty toward others is often a way of attaching ourselves to a passing raft."[38] His "passing raft" is often some group. Hoffer contends that self-lessness produces its opposite of grandiosity: "There is no doubt that in ex-changing a self-centered for a selfless life we gain enormously in self-es-teem. The vanity of the selfless, even those who practice utmost humility, is boundless."[39] How easy it is to see the smugness and superiority of those who claim to be on a "God-sent" mission. Of course, you and I are automatically inferior, part of the "unsaved" masses.

In additional, inflated personalities require the unconscious opposites of deflation and inferiority. Both are extremes and indicate a state of pos-session when either manages to gain control of the psyche. Psychologically both states have value. When we are feeling a little too big for our britches, we need a dose of humility; and when we are too much putting ourselves down, we need to draw on some badly needed ego-inflation. But when ego-inflation is collectively inspired, we are in danger of becoming dispos-sessed of our individuality in favor of a group view. Jung maintained that along with inflation, one loses the faculty of discrimination.

> It [an inflated consciousness] is hypnotized by itself and therefore can-not be argued with. It inevitably dooms itself to calamities that must strike it dead. Paradoxically enough, inflation is a regression of con-sciousness into unconsciousness. . . . [Inflation] should not be interpreted as . . . conscious self-aggrandizement. Such is far from being the rule. In general we are not directly conscious of this condition at all, but can at best infer its existence indirectly from the symptoms. These include the reactions of our immediate environment. Inflation magnifies the blind spot in the eye.[40]

Those who so identify with a collective position—whether a religious, political, or economic viewpoint—that they cannot see the other side of an issue, live in a state of true possession. We encounter such possessed in-dividuals daily in the media and in our everyday lives: "religious" persons who are intent upon converting others to their beliefs and who dedicate their lives to imposing their morality on the rest of the world; members of political groups who are determined to force their system on everyone; members of business enterprises who, with profit-blinded hearts, mechanically enable the machinery of the market place to crush the life out of our planet; celebrities who, reeling under the intoxication of mass worship, become sudden experts imbued with profound wisdom on any subject.

Moreover, whatever people surrender to becomes their god—whether it be a political party, a stone, an idea, or a guru. Regardless, the outcome is the same: the other side of surrender is *empowerment,* and one can be sure that whatever or whomever we empower will be antiself and antisoul. Lifton described the consequences of this slave-master relationship as a struggle with integrity:

> The individual person who finds himself under such doctrine-dominated pressure to change is thrust into an intense struggle with his own sense of integrity, a struggle which takes place in relation to polarized feelings of sincerity and insincerity. In a totalist environment, absolute "sincerity" is demanded; and the major criterion for sincerity is likely to be one's degree of doctrinal compliance—both in regard to belief and to direction of personal change.[41]

The demand for "absolute sincerity" requires total dedication to a group's cause, which means not letting any outside interest interfere with one's dedication. In religions, this dedication often takes the form of giving one's life to a particular deity (to a doctrinally defined god or goddess), or in the business world, making a company the most important activity in one's life. Subordination of the individual to the group is a deadly blow to the individuation process. Consequently, individual development not only halts but regresses into more and more infantile attitudes of complete trust in the group's mission or trust in the will of God, which, not surprisingly, always turns out to be identical with the group's agenda and doctrine.

In the case of religious leaders, *God's will is always whatever the leader wants or decides*—and no one dares to question the leader's "divine guidance," or for that matter, their own doubts. Under such psychological tyranny, even one's own thoughts become suspect as potential enemies of the system.

Absolute sincerity within a group effects an alienation from the self and from one's own will, volition, and critical thinking. Our natural feelings and real self then become inner adversarial parts of our psyche; we find ourselves in a constant inner power struggle, which exhausts and depletes our energy. Collective sincerity requires unflinching support of the group agenda, while individual responsibility and autonomy require questioning and examining the behavior and ideas of others. Hoffer submits that "the chief preoccupation of an active mass movement is to instill in its followers a facility for united action and self-sacrifice, and . . . it achieves this facility by stripping each human entity of its distinctiveness and autonomy and turning it into an anonymous particle with no will and no judgment of its own."[42] Of course, groups of all sizes and types use the human propensity for "self-sacrifice" to enslave and at the same time inflate their members' egos.

In a process of endless compromise, individuals lose their integrity. And without integrity, one loses the ability to *hold together* the human psyche; our original identity *disintegrates* as we assume a new collective identity, creating a false self—a placating, fit-into-the-collective persona—while the real person is locked up in some dark dungeon of repression and death.

EXPORTING OUR MORAL IDEAS

> I am the way, the truth, and the life.
>
> Jesus (John 14:6)

When the United States, or any nation-state, tries to impose its moral and ethical systems on other nations, we become a proselytizing invading army, crusaders for a collectively sanctioned self-righteousness disguised as concern for "human rights." I am not implying that there are not atrocities committed every day, but when we identify with any group, in this case our Western political culture, we tend to feel superior to other cultures based on our group's views.

The entire notion that "we" can "save" them from their "third world," "underdeveloped" cultural status is but another indication of a group's fateful inclination to establish hierarchies with, of course, *our* group occupying the supreme position of cultural and political correctness. Incredibly, we in the United States still seem to be stuck in a "convert the natives to our obviously best way of life or get rid of them" attitude. The "human rights" movement, under its do-gooder cloak, reveals the same callous disregard for other cultures as did the Indian Wars earlier in our history. Human rights really means imposing our morality on other nation-states—an example of *group-think*, a "we/they" view of the world instead of a "both/and" view. It is the time-worn patriarchal splitting of everything and everyone without any middle ground of *relationship* and interconnectedness; it evokes a politics of separateness and exclusion that destroys diversity and encourages deadening sameness—the kind of Orwellian equality that stamps out human ingenuity, creativity, and distinctiveness.

From a collective viewpoint, we in the West judge other cultures based on our own *culturally specific values.* We are horrified to hear about child abuse, yet paradoxically we purchase items every day that are produced by, what from our view is, child slave labor. That "Made in India," 100 percent wool carpet that I got for such a low price—who made it? Should I care who made it?

In a typical fourteen-hour day, an estimated twenty thousand child slaves in India's carpet industry are making all manner of rugs and carpets. The carpet industry in India is reportedly controlled by the Indian Mafia. According to the U.S. Department of Labor, two hundred million children around the world are *forced* to work.[43]

In Egypt, where one child in ten works, some children work all night picking jasmine flowers for the world's perfume markets. After their all-night shift is over, they are admonished, "Weigh in and get out of here or you'll get the stick!"[44] In Colombia, over three thousand children work in coal mines. This sounds terrible. We should "save the children." But, for example, consider the reality of life in India. The Indian children who work fourteen-hour days making carpets for global markets have some interesting choices. Primarily children of impoverished families, their labor often means the difference between existence or starvation for their families. In other cases, Indian children are intentionally crippled or maimed, a hand or arm cut off so they can beg on the streets.

The current "popular" surge of interest in human rights has good intentions in back of it, but if we as a nation-state were to carry out the implications of such a policy, we would have to refrain from purchasing any product produced by child labor, or prisoners, and so on. The real-world consequences of trying to force our collective values on other nation-states would, in our Indian example, perhaps force families into even more desperate measures with much more horrible abuse of children. Rather than helping such children or their families, such arrogant intrusion by a self-righteous superior group actually impedes and interferes with "human rights" in other lands.

Only a global *free* exchange of *individual* ideas and information from a standpoint of mutual respect for individual choices will advance the human spirit in ways *unforeseen and unanticipated* by any bureaucratic or other collective organization. In this manner, the vital cultural diversity of planet earth will be preserved, immeasurably adding to the richness of all life.

What's more, such morally superior collective views are hypocritical in the extreme. How many children work on farms in this country, and for that matter, how many millions are and have worked in the most horrible polluted factory conditions in supposedly civilized countries? Is it not equally abhorrent for U. S. business firms to knowingly poison workers and pollute our environment or for the military to secretly test the effects of radiation on soldiers and civilian populations? Who are the real slaves: American workers who spend their lives working for a company and are suddenly dumped like unwanted trash on the street, or the frail children picking night-blooming jasmine petals so that their families will have food to eat?

Peer Pressure

> Naturally the disciples always stick together, not out of love, but for the very understandable purpose of effortlessly confirming their own convictions by engendering an air of collective agreement.
>
> Carl Jung[45]

Voluntarily giving up one's identity sooner or later produces a deep resentment and inner anguish—a feeling of impending death and frequent suicidal thoughts—for one inevitably feels the immensity of voluntary self-destruction. According to Steven Hassan, a disruption and replacement of the individual's identity, in large part due to peer pressure, is "a social process, often involving large groups of people who reinforce it. . . . [A] person's original identity becomes replaced with another identity, often one that he would not have chosen for himself without tremendous social pressure."[46]

Many groups, both commercial and religious, have frequent "sharing" or "testimony" sessions, similar to confessions, which reinforce behavior that conforms to the group doctrine—a potent form of group peer pressure. The sales associate describes how he or she sold record numbers of the company product, implying that similar behavior by other members will achieve the same results, the real purpose being to perpetuate the group. Flattery and praise are given to members whose testimony supports the group mission, while the rare antidoctrinal sharings are met with icy silence and ostracism. A mass of people who all think alike exerts an awesome influence on the individual. Viktor Frankl describes one of his experiences with peer pressure as a prisoner in a Nazi death camp: "Each time Hitler gave a public speech, the inmates were lined up and had to stand at attention while the speech was broadcast over the camp's loudspeakers." He said the urge to raise his arm in the German salute was overpowering at these times, and that it took all his will power to keep his arm in place.[47]

Group peer pressure is a formidable behavior modifier and identity shaper. Peer pressure from even a small group results in individuals acting in ways they would never even consider on their own. A potential "lynch mob," brute-mind mentality forms a part of all totalistic groups to some degree. Pressure to conform promotes the constructing of a false self-image, which further alienates one from family, friends, and outsiders. A new group identity strikes at the basic structure of the human psyche, robbing one's life of meaning outside of the group, and collapsing one's integrity. The instant we consider *compromising* our feelings and beliefs we are in a self-destruct mode, losing our integrity, crushing out our unique insight. And once the group self firmly implants itself, leaving the group means self-abandonment.

Under the Influence: Hypnotic Effects of Groups

> Becoming accustomed to certain sounds has a profound effect on character; soon one acquires the words and phrases and eventually also the ideas that go with these sounds.
>
> Friedrich Nietzsche[48]

Steven Hassan, in his comprehensive study of destructive groups, found that seemingly harmless activities often become a form of mass hypnosis:

> Mind control involves little or no overt physical abuse. Instead, *hypnotic processes* are combined with *group dynamics* to create a potent indoctrination effect. The individual is deceived and manipulated—not directly threatened—into making the prescribed choices. . . . In many cults which claim to be religious, what is often called "meditation" is no more than a process by which the cult members enter a trance, during which time they may receive suggestions which make them more receptive to following the cult's doctrine. Non-religious cults use other forms of group or individual induction. . . . Repetition and forced attention are very conducive to the induction of a trance.[49]

Hypnosis (mass hypnosis and self-hypnosis) is a major factor in the indoctrination process, especially for religious groups where members repeat mantras, prayers, affirmations, chants, songs, and practice lengthy meditations. In addition, many groups commonly have lengthy meetings, weekend conclaves, and seminars, which last for many hours without a break where people sit passively listening to highly repetitious material. Since group dynamics encourage one-sidedness and repression, unconsciousness increases, and as Jung observed, "The greatest danger about unconsciousness is proneness to suggestion. Hence the ever-widening split between conscious and unconscious increases the danger of psychic infection and mass psychosis."[50]

Moreover, destructive groups fill members' infrequent spare time with an endless series of projects: writing papers, preparing lectures, research, endless volunteer work, and frequent travel. People can literally exhaust themselves both mentally and physically with these endeavors. When we are exhausted and worn out we are far more vulnerable to hypnotic influences. In religious groups this *intentional suffering* plays right into religious self-torture and martyrdom ideas that glamorize abuse and self-denial as behavior making one more "spiritual," when in fact such group-induced suffering simply lends legitimacy to inhuman acts of cruelty and sadism.

When individuals are taught to mentally repress ideas that conflict with a group's viewpoint, and collective ideas are constantly reinforced through mind-control techniques disguised as spiritual practices or rituals, one becomes highly suggestible—a blank slate for someone else's mission. Imprisoned in a suggestible childlike role, one easily accepts without question vast amounts of complex new material, concepts, definitions, and values. Such techniques gradually force individual critical thinking out of one's thought processes. Group values gradually replace our former ethical and moral values.

THE SOCIAL TRANCE

> What anthropologists know as "participation mystique," or "a mysterious communal mind," sounds lovely, but it can mean that tribal members all know exactly the same thing and no one knows anything else.
>
> Marie-Louise Von Franz[51]

Joe Berghold's recent (1991) research has confirmed the existence of a "social trance . . . a general social reality of hypnotic trance as unconscious submission to authoritarian rules and figures."[52] Individuals subjecting themselves to supposed spiritual disciplines, if not using some prayer or mantra as self-hypnosis, are often putting themselves in light trance states through hours of passive listening. Instead of attaining a "higher consciousness," they are simply practicing self-hypnosis.

Many of these trance-inducing practices are highly addictive, producing drugged-like states and the *illusion* of a spiritual high. In fact, Hassan found that in some groups members become addicted to the mind-control techniques, turning members into addicts with a "variety of deleterious side effects, including severe headaches, involuntary muscle spasms, and a diminution of cognitive faculties like memory, concentration, and decision making."[53] Relating brain chemistry to spiritual highs, Hassan explains: "Such mind-stilling generates strong releases of brain chemicals which cause not only a dissociated mental state but also a 'high' similar to that created by illegal drugs."[54]

Immersion in and total identification with a group ideology paradoxically can be a "peak experience." People feel they have found the perfect solution to life's problems and have entered a transcendent environment of absolute truth and enlightenment—a loving, accepting, nurturing community of kindred, likeminded persons. In fact this addictive group "high" is actually part of the process of becoming embedded in collective concrete. We find ourselves trapped, immovable, and with our real identity pushed into the shadows!

COLLECTIVE COMPLEXES

According to Jung, complexes are autonomous "splinter psyches" that "interfere with the intentions of the will and disturb the conscious performance; they appear and disappear according to their own laws; they can temporarily obsess consciousness, or influence speech and action in an unconscious way. In a word, complexes behave like independent beings."[55] We are all too familiar with some complex taking over and compelling us to do something against our better judgment or moral values. In fact, it is precisely powerfully organized complexes—"splinter psyches"—that fuel the engines of evil, the ego mania of dictators, and economic, religious, and political fanatics. However, complexes are not necessarily negative. They are essential functioning components of a consciousness that maintains a healthy tension. Only when this tension between complexes slips into a one-sided outlook do complexes become dangerous to our mental and physical health.

Extreme one-sidedness splits the psyche, giving birth to powerful and often dangerous complexes that assume total control of individuals as well as groups. A religious group, caught into a single point of view or belief system, generates an awesome, monsterlike collective complex that takes over the minds and souls of its members. Religious cults are an extreme example of how a group complex can utterly destroy the independent thinking of masses of people, turning otherwise intelligent persons into prejudiced and bigoted shadows of the crowd.

Movement in life requires that we make choices and let go of other alternatives. However, when a one-sided view assumes command of the psyche, we are in deep trouble. We unwittingly join forces with the fanatics and zealots of the world; we align ourselves with evil, lose our freedom, and become destructive, dysfunctional influences in our own lives and in society.

The tremendous social and group pressure to live inauthentic lives, to assume other moral ideas, and to follow popular belief systems all combine to exert nearly irresistible pressure on onc to take sides and to push underground one's true Self and original authenticity.

For most of us, complexes operate without our conscious awareness. The entire thrust of Jungian psychology is directed at making unconscious contents of the psyche conscious, making one consciously aware of formerly unconscious psychic operations. As long as we remain unaware of our complexes, they easily manipulate and control our life. Thus it follows that the more inner work we do and the more time we take for reflection and for individual self-therapy, the more we will understand ourselves, and the freer we will become from complexes, both personal and collective, that seek to live our life. This means confronting our complexes head-on and facing those parts of ourselves that are often utterly foul and bitter.

Jung pointed out that complexes are necessary parts of the psyche, that "The possession of complexes does not in itself signify neurosis . . . and the fact that they are painful is no proof of pathological disturbance. Suffering is not an illness; it is the normal counterpole to happiness. A complex becomes pathological only when we think we have not got it."[56] Indeed, we find ourselves in dangerous waters when an unconscious complex begins to control our life. Even worse, group complexes exert horrific influence over the masses.

Jung described complexes as "feeling toned ideas that center around certain archetypes."[57] For example, one believes that he or she is a savior when, in actuality, a complex centered around a savior archetype has taken over. In such a case, one *identifies* with the complex; one becomes and lives through an archetypal "splinter psyche." A similar situation often occurs involving other archetypal figures like the shadow, anima, animus, hero warrior, wise old man, the mother, and the child. In fact, a complex in control of an individual is a form of possession and obsession; one becomes possessed by an idea or an image. Racism, war, abuse, hate groups, prejudice, elitism, and enemy-making are all examples of *collective complexes* responsible for unfathomable inhumanity and destruction.

What Christians call being "under the anointing" or "speaking in tongues" may be simply allowing a complex, a repressed daimon, to take over and assume control—a group-induced outburst of shadow material. Interestingly, the one who is "under the anointing" often knows who is sick just as so-called demons also seem to know unusual information.

The whale sees two opposite views through eyes on the side of its head. Like whales who must surface to breathe, when a complex surfaces and enters our awareness, it becomes useful as a potential transformative energy.

Destruction of the Individual

For the development of personality, then, strict differentiation from the collective is absolutely necessary, since partial or blurred differentiation leads to an immediate melting away of the individual in the collective. . . . [F]or identity with the collective psyche always brings with it a feeling of universal validity—"godlikeness"—which completely ignores all differences in the personal psyche of his fellows. . . . [T]hat means a ruthless disregard not only of individual differences but also of differences of a more general kind within the collective psyche itself, as for example differences of race.

Carl Jung[58]

I can think of no state so insupportable and dreadful, as to have the soul vivid and afflicted, without means to declare itself.

Montaigne[59]

To begin with, personality is necessarily a compromise between the individual and the collective—a survival mechanism common to all. The extent of this compromise then creates a critical conflict. Recent research indicates that one's psychological profile actually changes under group influence. In 1982, Dr. Flavil Yeakley, a psychologist from Abilene Christian University, tested the psychological profiles of hundreds of cult members using the Meyers-Briggs Type Indicator (MBTI).* He found that, "People in certain cults appeared to be all moving toward having the same kinds of personalities, regardless of the original personalities they brought with them into the group."[60] This "cloning," as Yeakley calls it, further indicates how effectively groups alter peoples' behavior and personalities, creating a new *group persona* replacing a person's pregroup personality.

By individual, I refer to one's innate uniqueness, that which distinguishes one from the crowd. Individuals cannot be classified, labeled, normalized; these are dehumanizing collective mechanisms reducing people to *things*. As Jung articulated, "The individual is precisely that which can never be merged with the collective and is never identical with it,"[61] and, "The larger a community is, and the more the sum total of collective factors peculiar to every large community rests on conservative prejudices detrimental to individuality, the more will the individual be morally and

---

*The Meyers-Briggs Type Indicator, a modern personality type model of typology. It consists of eight typological groups: two personality attitudes—introversion and extroversion—and four functions—thinking, sensation, intuition, and feeling. Each function may operate in an introverted or extroverted way. Daryl Sharp, *C. G. Jung Lexicon: A Primer of Terms and Concepts* (Toronto: Inner City Books, 1991), p. 141.

spiritually crushed, and, as a result, the one source of moral and spiritual progress for society is choked up."[62] Here Jung points to the paradox of the community's utter dependence upon the integrity of the individual: that human and social progress hinge upon the ability of individuals to function in a state of freedom, autonomy, and independence. A community, nation-state, or group that impinges upon these necessary individual freedoms condemns itself to stagnation and dissolution. In this sense, the individual perspective supports and enhances the community only so long as individuals remain completely free to express their unique points of views. As such, the individual is not anticommunity, but rather provides *the* vital ingredient in an effective, healthy community.

Communities and other collective organizations remain dynamic and supportive elements in society only as long as *they do not dominate individuals.* Survival of the individual within a group depends upon being, in Jung's words, "as well organized in his individuality as the mass itself,"[63] hence the importance of a strong sense of self, a healthy self-respect, and self-esteem. Being well organized requires that we become more aware of the unconscious and how the multifaceted aspects of the psyche, including the full range of internal opposites, work together and complement each other. We know that deindividualization and dehumanization partly result from attitudes of selfless dedication in a group context. Arthur Koestler in *The Ghost in the Machine* describes his own experience in a political cult: "I now lived in a mental world which was a 'closed system,' comparable to the self-contained universe of the Middle Ages. All my feelings, my attitudes to art, literature and human relations, became reconditioned and moulded to the pattern."[64]

COLLECTIVE PANIC

> A mob in action displays an extreme form of group mentality. But to be affected by it, a person need not be physically present in a crowd; mental identification with a group, nation, church or party is quite often sufficient.
>
> Arthur Koestler[65]

Collective panic affects us all. The recent Iraq war provides a good example of how most Americans, including this writer, found themselves caught up in a national panic; we had to act immediately, rescue the underdog, and save the day. Perhaps as a nation we had no other choice. Perhaps we cannot escape war as a final event because of the complex web of circumstances created over time by political and economic systems, which, through their totalitarian stance, set into motion lethal accumulations of good and evil polarized collective forces that must ultimately release their pent-up energy in physical destruction. Failing to see our own national shadow of selling arms and promoting dictatorships as long as they were friendly to U. S. interests, we became victims of our own dark side.

Panic disorders derive their name from the Greek god Pan, who was half human and half goat. Pan delighted in scaring shepherds. The "hour of Pan" was high noon—a time when we cast no *shadow*. We can theorize that a good candidate for a "panic attack" is someone who cannot see their own shadow. Adherence to any one group ideology requires that we deny some portion of our shadow. In destructive groups, denial becomes a way of life and *collective panic* can start a war, murder abortion clinic doctors, or demonize immigrants.

Depth psychology suggests that we "host" our wounds, look through them, see them as metaphors for a soul-making process. Symptoms and maladies are ways the unconscious gets our attention. For example, anxiety's gift is to pull us into our bodies through physical symptoms. In a group environment, fanaticism, fundamentalism, obsession, violence, war, oppression, indifference, cruelty, depression, addiction, in fact, any form of extremism, negative or positive, all indicate immense collectively induced repression and subsequent projection of massive quantities of shadow energy; we are in the midst of a collective Jekyll-and-Hyde dynamic.

"Phobia," an intense abnormal fear, comes from the Greek *phobos*, meaning "fear, fright." The god Phobos was the "god of fright," a child of the union *between love and war* in mythology. Well-known collective phobias like homophobia flourish in the crowd mentality. Groups tend to have phobic reactions to outsiders particularly when they represent their own unacknowledged shadow side.

Dissociation, the splitting of the personality, results from complete identification with a group or system. This splitting enables the group mind to assume control of the individual. Such splitting activates a serious fragmentation of the psyche; the now fully autonomous collective belief system *controls* the individual. Pushing aside one's former identity and personality, one is in fact dispossessed. One performs on command (internalized) for the group. In this manner, people imprison themselves in the icy-cold "either/or" world of patriarchal absolutism. They are absolutely for their group's cause and absolutely against any perceived opposition. In their split-off, group-mechanized thinking, burning an abortion clinic suddenly becomes part of a "holy mission," slaughtering innocent civilians in Bosnia becomes justified, exterminating millions of Jews becomes racial purification, "smoking" a rival gang member becomes a way to prove one's loyalty, and destroying the rainforests to raise cattle for hamburgers becomes "free enterprise." This uncontrolled (unwilled) form of dissociation contrasts with a "willed" dissociation where one consciously chooses to separate certain aspects of the psyche as occurs in various aspects of meditation.

GANGS: STREET CULTS

You look at me wrong and I'll shoot you!

Los Angeles gang member[66]

An excellent example of a social disease, street gangs are minicults. A gang becomes a replacement family providing structure, authority, and discipline. With its clear system of initiation, reward, and punishment, the gang replaces parents with an absolute totalitarian structure devoid of any trace of humanity. Regard for human life is minimal at best. Like other destructive groups, gang members must forsake all outsiders—family and friends—for the group. In pure totalitarian form, gang members perceive themselves as soldiers defending their territory (turf) against outside enemies.

Eric Noran, age eleven, said after attending the funeral of his classmate Robert Sandifer, killed in a gang shooting in Chicago: "The only way to get out of this is to die."[67] Street gangs provide an extreme example of how the totalitarian grip on individuals makes it nearly impossible to leave once one is "in" the group. The right to existence, dispensed by the gang, confines members to strictly defined boundaries, both physical and psychological. Tribal and territorial, street gangs provide a sense of discipline and structure along with perverted or extreme feelings of grandeur, power, and exclusiveness. Once more, all manner of atrocities are rationalized as a means of *protecting* their "hood." Gang members claim they want "respect," yet they have no respect for others. Guns become instruments to gain respect and power.

Respect, an issue important enough to kill for, becomes a collective demand in gang relationships. Perhaps this "demand for respect," so prevalent among gang members, indicates the shadow of our collective disrespect for ourselves as individuals. We institutionalize disrespect when a society places groups and organizations above individuals. And in our semidemocracy where patriarchal authoritarianism underpins our political milieu, individuals are both devalued and disrespected.

Gangs are the inevitable outgrowth of entropic collective systems, both political and economic. Intact families are rare and a deep feeling of hopelessness pervades the community. Hopelessness sooner or later begets anger; people get angry about things they think they cannot change. And nothing is more dangerous than a young person without hope. Kids who believe they have no future do not care about the present. They will sacrifice themselves, anything, and anyone without compunction. Shadowy, collective inner-city rage fuels and justifies ever-increasing youthful violent crime.

PATRIARCHAL RULES

> Perhaps the manly thing to do nowadays is to try to live without the guidance and structures that defined manliness in the past.
>
> Andrew Samuels[68]

Culturally implanted patriarchal group dynamics are apparent in individuals, families, businesses, religions, and other groups. Patriarchal rules follow fundamentals of totalitarian authority by incorporating

- a demand for blind obedience;

- repression of most emotions;

- destruction of individual will power; and

- repression of individual critical thinking.[69]

John Bradshaw submits that typically patriarchal attitudes of self-righteousness spawn violence. A totalitarian stance in any group creates shaming and polarization among members. Thus a family's spoken and unspoken rules, a religion's "moral code of ethics" (which are often rules in disguise), a business group's "company policies," and most of our nation's laws are all patriarchal in nature. We need patriarchy as much as we need matriarchy, but when patriarchy "rules," it invariably destroys individual freedom and integrity.

SUICIDE AND THE COLLECTIVE

> The death experience is needed to separate from the collective flow of life and to discover individuality.
>
> James Hillman[70]

Thus we find suicide has two sides: psychological death and rebirth, and physical death. We lay the foundation for feeling suicidal by not living an authentic life. Symbolic of exiting our collective bonds, suicide represents one's final declaration of independence, and, as such, is antiestablishment, particularly antitheology. Indeed, our collective viewpoints say we must go to any length to prevent suicide.

The illegality of assisted suicide has exposed the extent to which the state (a political group) controls individual freedom of choice and does in fact consider individuals to be property—one of our chief attributes of destructive group dynamics. Indeed, Hillman maintains "we are being ordered by law to live."[71] Does the state *own* its citizens and require intolerable suffering? Or does each person have the ultimate freedom to die with dignity and by choice when deemed necessary? The assisted suicide debate points out how far the group mind, in this case the state, has eroded our personal freedom and integrity. It also illustrates how ethics become distorted when groups assume such dictatorial control over our lives. The issue of assisted suicide, in collective authoritarian hands, has nothing to do with ethics, but rather it is an issue of rules, regulations, and the exercise of state power over individuals. The state would like to add assisted suicide to its growing list of "consensual crimes"—illegal activities that are freely consented to and harm no other individual or property. Such consensual activities like assisted suicide usually become illegal when they go against some established collective morality that the state wants to impose on others. As such, consensual crime has theological roots and illustrates yet another facet of totalism in groups: the irresistible inclination to more and more *power* over the individual.

Displacement, another basic defense mechanism, enables us to maintain conscious awareness of an experience but displace the feeling. For example, you are angry at your boss, but unable to express that anger without serious consequences. Upon arriving home, you take out your anger on your spouse, dog, or children. With the slightest provocation, volcanic repression erupts. Displacement in a group demands that we repress legitimate feelings in favor of collectively approved behavior, or in order to go along with the group's ideology. This giving up of our authentic self-expression has disastrous consequences. One's psychological, spiritual, and emotional growth stops, regressing to earlier developmental stages where, as children, we depended on adults as role models to confirm our behavior and provide a sense of self. Groups have an inbred infantalizing push on the psyche that is nearly impossible to resist.

Repressed Collective Tension

> We are presently dealing with the accumulation of a whole society that has worshiped its light side and refused the dark, and this residue appears as war, economic chaos, strikes, racial intolerance.
>
> Robert A. Johnson[72]

Repressed tension becomes the lair of the beast, our cultural backside giving birth to demons. The immense energy of all that we collectively repress in order to conform, to fit into some gargantuan cultural machine so that we can "do our part," has produced a dark underground factory generating collective evil.

Whatever we repress eventually *forces* itself back upon us—the ultimate terror of living collectively automated lives. On a collective level, such repression creates a society where certain members feel *compelled* to act out what we have pushed into the unconscious. As Koestler wrote, "I have suggested that the evils of mankind are caused, not by the primary aggressiveness of individuals, but by their self-transcending identification with groups whose common denominator is low intelligence and high emotionality."[73]

COLLECTIVE TENSION PRODUCERS

As groups impose their expanding grid of power on the fabric of our society, the gap between opposites grows to titanic proportions, creating extreme tension. Power and authority become increasingly concentrated in groups. Social unrest, chaos, and discontent mark this dark and dangerous group dynamic as the tension becomes unbearable.

Societal Opposites

Poverty/insecurity	Wealth/security
Unemployment	A good job
No status or respect	Status and respect
Unknown	Fame
Violence/crime	Safe environment
Uneducated	Good education
Minority group member	Majority group member

According to R. Buckminster Fuller, "geodesics (spherical structures held together by tension and compression) represent the most economical relationship between any two events."[74] War, a process of releasing surplus tension, is costly and tragic for everyone. Working through opposing views, holding both simultaneously (holding tension), and producing a synergetic solution result in beneficial change for both sides. Within the human psyche, *tension* provides the "most economical relationship between any two events." Holding tension is a *both/and* dynamic. Compromise with a group temporarily relieves psychic tension, but destroys one's soul and individuality; no tension means we have been flattened, dehumanized. As groups become synergetic, cooperative, solution making, and creativity-based, the less there will be head-on dualistic confrontation between groups and individuals, winners or losers; the whole will act in ways unpredicted by its separate parts *only* when individual human beings are back in control of their own natures.

The dark side of groups is deadly to the individuation process and is anti-Self, or from another perspective, "anti-Christ." Collective aspects of society are cultural necessities and at the same time regressive influences on society as a whole. *Holding the tension* between these two conflicting forces is a key to maintaining one's integrity and freedom. Breaking free of collective influences and our dysfunctional relationships with groups will be our most important task as we approach the millennium. Giving in to group authority in our society means losing touch with the soul—the extraordinary uniqueness and creative potential inherent in each person; it means the destruction of all that is sacred, human, and of lasting value. No wonder millions flock to psychotherapists, our twentieth-century shamans, trying to make some sense and meaning out of lives that have become void of purpose—empty role-playing for collective agencies.

The fact that a totalistic superior-to-the-individual collective ideology is outmoded and no longer a viable approach to life on planet Earth would appear to be obvious, but the dark side of groups remains alive and well in our society, in our institutions, school systems, religious groups, businesses, and even in our interpersonal relationships where one individual dominates another.

Like a toxic substance, the *mass* mind implants itself within the human psyche. And a *mass-minded* society perpetuates our collective hypnosis, psychologically culturing individuals to follow the common herd over the cliff of an illusory common existence.

5

Systems: Mega Groups

⊡⊏⊏⊏⊏⊏⊏⊏⊏⊏⊏⊏⊏⊏⊏⊏⊏⊏⊏⊏⊏⊏⊏⊏⊏⊏⊏⊏⊏⊏⊏⊏⊏⊏⊏⊡

The willingness to obey the "authorities," to do what the boss tells us, not to question the orders of our superiors, to surrender private conscience to the goals of the group is a part of the job description. Evil has become a by-product of duty, an unfortunate consequence of loyalty.

Sam Keen[1]

Progress is our most important product.

Advertising slogan[2]

In angling to have myself fired, I had begun the duplicitous behavior familiar to those on welfare—to get what we need, it becomes necessary to play the game in a system that is set up pretty much on an all-or-nothing basis. I didn't need very much help, but in order to get any at all, I had to turn my back on my work ethic.

Beth Lovern[3]

All the present bureaucracies of political governments, great religious organizations, and all big businesses find that physical success for all humanity would be devastating to the perpetuation of their ongoing activities. This is because all of them are founded on the premise of ameliorating individual cases while generally exploiting on behalf of their respective political, religious, or business organizations the condition of nowhere-enough-life-support-for-all and its resultant great human suffering and discontent.

R. Buckminster Fuller[4]

121

The Serpent in Our Free Market Paradise

The market's power includes the power to *seduce*. If the expansion of the System's empire requires the rechanneling of human needs, the System has the power to engineer the necessary restructuring of the human psyche.
Andrew Bard Schmookler[5]

It is said that every paradise contains a serpent. The market system's *dehumanizing bite* on our common humanity—the snake in our free market paradise—may well be its utter lack of conscience. As I drive through the Pacific Northwest, I frequently see areas of denuded mountains, stripped of every tree. Homes that once looked out on forested vistas now are surrounded by wastelands of tangled stumps and eroding hills. And, in another all-too-common scene, housing suburbs, concrete, and strip malls cover what was once pristine forest. The collision between modern capitalism and our environment continues to devour not only our planet's natural resources, but part of our humanity as well. How has this one-sided market dominance over our environment happened? What have we lost by allowing a system that sees board feet of lumber or toothpicks instead of a tree—a system that places profits ahead of human beings?

A market system devoid of conscience breeds predators—hunters stalking consumers with high-tech cunning and stealth. And we become shark bait thrashing around in deadly waters.

Something seems to be widening the gap between rich and poor. According to a recent report, the number of working poor in the United States increased 50 percent over the last 13 years (1981–1994).[6] Since 1970 the number of children living in poverty has increased 40 percent—one child out of every five in the United States.[7] At the same, wealth in the United States has increased dramatically. A recent Federal Reserve study found that "a surprisingly large percentage of all U. S. families (4 percent) were estimated to have a net worth of more than $500,000.[8] The same study found that nearly 2 percent (1,310,000) of all families had reached net worths over $1 million.[9]

The system readily provides anything, guns or flowers, cocaine or aspirin, provided we have money. To some extent we all participate in what has become a global market system. Money is its deity, consumerism its discipline, "more" its mantra. As consumers, every choice we make, no matter how insignificant, stirs the great economic sea and attracts the intent eye of the beast.

We need a *free* market system, but *with a conscience—with a soul*. Without a conscience, the market system's "invisible hand" does not acknowledge anyone or anything not producing a profit; and if left to itself, it would catch the last fish in the ocean, execute the last elephant, cut down the last tree, and completely poison our environment. The remarkable benefits of free markets are beyond dispute. I am writing this book using a technological miracle of sorts—a desktop computer—and, with a few keystrokes, I can log on the Internet and browse through an immense, global network of information and knowledge. The home I live in, the car I drive, the books I love to read are all readily available and inexpensive because of capitalism's "invisible hand": the almost magical effects of individuals conducting their affairs as they see fit, to their individual economic advantage. Out of seeming chaos, a vast universe of goods and services emerges without any centralized planning or control. Indeed, capitalism, if truly left alone—and by "alone" I mean not interfered with by endless governmental regulations, taxes, and political manipulations— would bring about gradually decreasing prices and gradually increasing real wage rates. In other words, capitalism's natural bent is toward a steadily rising standard of living, increasing efficiency and declining prices. So what has gone wrong? I suggest that destructive group dynamics within government agencies, political groups, and business groups play a major role in the decline and deterioration of the natural progression of free markets throughout the world. Moreover, destructive group dynamics are responsible for the increasing alienation of individuals from the consequences of their decisions and choices in our market system and the resultant devastation of our environment.

What appears to be conscious involvement with market processes often reveals programmed behavior resulting from powerful group dynamics that distort the system and nullify the individual's conscience. In this chapter we will examine many of the ways group dynamics impact our market system; we will expose aspects of this "serpent" or dark side, and look at some potential remedies.

The word "conscience" comes from the Latin *conscientia,* from *conscire,* meaning *"to be conscious."* The market system's *unconsciousness*— its inability to distinguish between right and wrong—depends upon individuals, who act *without consciousness of consequences.* Our choices in the marketplace must be governed by conscience and consciousness, to impart a sense of conscience to the system.

A system does not have a soul or a conscience in and of itself. According to the renowned economist Adam Smith, the individual contemplating "only his own gain . . . is led by an invisible hand to promote an end which was no part of his intentions."[10] *Unconscious* participation in the market system by billions of individuals reinforces the system's conscienceless "invisible hand." Conscience requires consciousness, being awake. It means one has a sensitivity to others based on feelings and emotions; it means being in touch with the feminine side of one's nature. Only with consciousness can we be aware of the consequences of our individual participation in the market system. A lack of sensitivity and the capacity for deep feeling mark the individual who has lost touch with both conscience and soul. The market system, with mechanical indifference, reflects this loss of soul in individuals. Thus the market system's loss of soul and lack of conscience ultimately come from widespread individual *unconscious participation* in the system.

The system's total lack of conscience and its efficient replication of *any* desire has a numbing effect on our individual sense of *relationship.* We are not remotely aware (conscious) of the impact on the earth's resources to make even one car. There is little or no relationship between consumers and the system's immense machinery sucking raw materials from a finite earth to produce the endless stream of goods we buy. Modern supermarkets and packaging more often than not conceal the true relationships between products and those who made them. Business groups have a way of "laundering labor," so that consumers have no idea how or who made a particular product, or how a product impacts other people and our environment. The market system's patriarchal, either/or, totalistic structure makes it oblivious to any relationships other than money-based exchanges of goods and services. Such efficient indifference toward the human side of life gives the system a nonhuman intelligence. Computerlike, it functions as "on" or "off," as "either/or." Either there are profits to be made or there are not. Permeating Western civilization, this either/or, black-and-white mindset has proven to be a political, economic, and environmental disaster. Only a shift in consciousness to a soul-based, conscience-filled, *both/and* approach to life will move the human spirit forward, out of the present social chaos and self-destruction. Without a functioning soul and conscience, we face an inner and outer holocaust, consumed by collective systems of our own creation.

In his book, *We've Had a Hundred Years of Psychotherapy and the World's Getting Worse,* James Hillman alludes to this lack of soul in our systems: "By removing the soul from the world and not recognizing that the soul is also *in* the world, psychotherapy can't do its job anymore. The buildings are sick, the institutions are sick, the banking system's sick, the schools, the streets—the sickness is out *there*"[11] (emphasis added).

Without a conscience, the market system is pure patriarchy: authoritarian power and control through the medium of cash. Modeled after a totalistic hierarchy, the market system defines self-worth according to one's position in the system: the more money and power, the greater one's value to the system. Unfortunately, self-worth derived from an outside system can never define even one individual. And the instant one awakens from the system's hypnosis, one is confronted with a gaping hole—a deep, crushing blackness without any sense of who one really is. This is our greatest tragedy: that in playing the system's games, we lose our integrity, freedom, identity, and uniqueness as individuals.

Free markets with private and corporate ownership of the means of production and distribution characterize capitalism, what we commonly refer to as the market system. European mercantilism, which was a politically based, colony-establishing system designed to attain a favorable balance of trade, still forms the basis of our present market economy. For the most part, we remain stuck in a mercantile mythology with multinational business groups creating worldwide economic colonial systems. Large corporations are gradually replacing nation-states as centers of power and wealth, becoming modern equivalents of colonialism.

The market system spawns thousands of subgroups that operate like parasites. Political, legal, union, and other groups feed off the behemoth, the market system. What, at first glance, gives the appearance of control and manipulation of the market is actually a feeding frenzy of smaller groups living off the system. But this relationship is a two-way street. The system needs its parasites. For example, in order to buy the things I am supposed to buy, I have to get to a store. So I get in my car and use the *road system*. Or I use the electronic *highway system* by phone and computer.

Slavery American Style

> We are trapped in the terrible jaws of something shaking the life out of us, something . . . deep-down bad.
>
> John Edgar Wideman[12]

I suggest that the "something shaking the life out of us" is the group mind: the notion that groups can somehow solve society's complex problems.

Our fascination with "how the economy is doing" is the market system's way of looking at itself as a system. Are *we* growing fast enough, is employment up, are *we* shopping enough to maintain what has become a gargantuan dysfunctional economic system? Such group introspection does not reflect the human quality of life, as evidenced by our staggering market wealth in the United States alongside the widening gap between rich and poor and the ever-growing discontent, violence, and social chaos. In fact, the "free" in "free market" is itself a misnomer because it is the *system* that has the freedom while individuals find themselves caught in a never-ending round of highly addictive consumerism that perpetuates the system. No wonder closet space in new homes and apartments has become such a big deal, and storage space is a booming industry. We have all noticed, usually while looking for a house or apartment, how small closets were just a few decades ago and the incredible amount of stuff we manage to accumulate between moves.

What appears to be individual freedom is *conditional.* It depends upon our role-playing as buyers and sellers of those goods and services the system produces. Capitalism operates with varying degrees of freedom depending on the political climate in particular countries. However, this apparent freedom centers itself in the system, not in its participants. Even capitalism remains essentially unfree, operating within a tangled web of governmental regulations and laws. Requiring ever-flowing cash, market forces manipulate and control consumers possessed by the process of consuming. In turn, our market-programmed behavior perpetuates the system.

Always alert for new ways to convert the unenlightened masses, religions quickly succumbed to the market's siren call. Becoming efficient marketing organizations, religious groups sell their particular brand of spirituality to ever-thirsty customers—hawking an invisible product to cure invisible ailments. Pat Robertson, when not saving souls, travels the globe checking up on his business investments.

In order to benefit from the market system, we must participate by following the system's rules. This can hardly be called freedom. The market system parents us with a complete set of "thou shalts" and "thou shalt nots." And it provides a limitless selection of "how-to" books that help us "work the system," and profit from it. The "pursuit of happiness" has been neatly defined, packaged, and sold to the masses. Before we are born, the system has already defined us. And all we can do is "measure up." If we don't measure up, we somehow feel shamed, put down, a failure.

The market, with its voracious appetite for cash, shapes and molds individuals and society in its image. But don't we as consumers shape the system through the choices we make and what we decide to buy? This is a valid point and partially true, but the system uses powerful techniques of psychological persuasion via the media in order to convince us fulfillment and happiness means getting *more:* more money, more things, more of what the system produces. John Watson, a psychologist and founder of modern behaviorism, was a former advertising executive. He believed in "shaping" a person, and that we must throw out all references to consciousness. But without *consciousness,* there can be no *conscience and no soul.* This Pavlovian manipulation of people without *consciousness* permeates our market ideology. Like rats in a maze, we hungrily search for the system corridor that leads to the cheese.

Cash flows to our popular obsessions—sports, movies, drugs, and celebrities—pouring billions into the pockets of cultural icons and media superstars—not because of their integrity or character, but instead due to the *profitability* of an image. Like sheep led to the slaughter, *we have to buy* those shoes because some Madison-Avenue-created image jumps around in them. So we spend our money *exactly where we're directed to spend it;* we buy into the system, making choices that are anything but free. A recent "life-style" ad began with this profound blurb: "Never let your expenditures drop too low or people will start to question your conceptual package."

Such *systemese*—group speak—saturates our system-shaped media, which attempt to make us feel like we're doing something wrong if we're not consuming at optimum speed, not behaving like the system says we "should," not enjoying the "good life."

Turning the Heart Into Stone

> Gold is the soul of all civil life, that can resolve all things into itself, and turn itself into all things.
>
> Samuel Butler[13]

A market system devoid of soul transforms everyone and everything into a dehumanized "it." Thus people become expendable *things* instead of human beings. We have allowed the system's machinery to replace the human heart, resulting in a psyche mechanized and trained to *service* the system.

In the TV series "Star Trek: The Next Generation," the "Borg" is a nearly indestructible, collective mechanized life form whose members are each wired in to a cold unfeeling group intelligence. The Borg live by assimilating other life forms into their collective mind, announcing to their captives, "From this time forward you will service us"—a perfect analogy for any group or system devoid of soul. Borglike, the market system wires consumers into its collective brain.

In California, the system's invisible hand, concerned for agri-profits, sprays people along with medflies. From the system's *profit-first* perspective, killing medflies is more important than human life. Los Angeles psychoanalyst and clinical psychologist Robert Goodwin maintains that purposeful manipulation has a lot to do with magnifying the market's dark side. Writing in the *Journal of Psychohistory,* Goodwin points out: "Because it has become politically incorrect to ask that the free market bear on any higher purpose, it has easily been hijacked by elites who wish to use it for a lower one. Thus, the system has generated a bell curve of increasing inequality, with one extreme possessing more than it will ever need, a shadow side needing more than it will ever possess."[14] Goodwin aptly illustrates the destructive effects of large groups and institutionalized systems that operate in permanent self-preservation modes. Totalistic and inhuman, they require clearly defined outside enemies to survive.

In the credit card business, instead of people, market share is referred to as "share of wallet." The system classifies and labels people, not in human terms, but as potential markets to be exploited.

A potent and ancient collective symbol, money has been made into a god in our times. In most parts of the world, money defines success and failure, accomplishment, meaning and value, and, like a god, bequeaths power and control. Our twentieth-century saints are listed in the "Fortune 500." We measure intelligence and leadership in billion-dollar increments. If so and so has made $4 billion, he/she must be equally wise and more knowledgeable than the rest of us. The Bill Gateses and the Rupert Murdochs of the world have become our tribal elders. We are ecstatic when shaking hands with the president, the corporate hero—the modern equivalent to "touching the hem of Jesus' garment."

Money gathers around our collective icons. In 1994, there were 262 baseball players who make over one million dollars per year. One basketball player may sign a $90 million contract! Like old King Midas, the *system* turns everything into gold. We have monitized life, and in the process we look down on anything or anyone who does not "make a good living." Certainly, money gives people the *appearance* of control over certain aspects of their lives. But, in the relentless pursuit of our golden gods, we pour our lifeblood into the ever-deepening pit of a group-defined "more."

The *monetary system* has become more important than human beings. People serve the system, are enslaved by it, are consumed in the pursuit of its Promised Land, and *spend* their lives disconnected from who they really are, and from their own creativity, which, when expressed, provides the only genuine justification and meaning for life.

In the Shadows: Black Markets

Auschwitz was efficient. And the sun still shone on the woods. It did not matter that what this factory produced was death, the death of innocents. The earth did not crack open to swallow the showers and the ovens and those who ran them.

Andrew Bard Schmookler[15]

Like a downsizing corporate America—replacing older workers with less expensive younger workers—efficiency without humanity removes the gold teeth from its victims. The market system's lack of conscience produces an increasingly ominous dark side that blindly responds to blood in the water—the smell of profits. Our fascination with sharks and their innate nature as predators may well be the reason that they are a perfect metaphor for the market system as brutal, conscienceless feeding machines. Perhaps the great white shark is our system's totem. This dark shadow of the market system spawns crime, violence, and people whose interpersonal and inter-group relationships are governed by greed. What's more, this dark side *depends upon illegality,* which insures greater profitability for the legion of back-street, black-market entrepreneurs. Black markets immediately respond to laws attempting to stop what are popularly termed "victimless crimes," by creating lucrative new business enterprises. According to the Justice Department, overall crime has increased 300 percent in the last thirty-three years (1960–93). According to the FBI, our total crime rate increased from 188.7 per 10,000 in 1960, to 566.0 per 10,000 in 1992. This is in spite of a proliferation of laws supposedly intended to discourage crime, further indicating a seriously diseased system not only impervious to traditional legal remedies, but perhaps exacerbated by them.

Society labels any economic activities operating outside the law or crossing boundaries of socially acceptable behavior as "black markets." All socially unacceptable enterprises and all that the market system ignores or is unconscious of become part of its shadow, its steel-like brutality, its soulless inhumanity. All that society abhors flourishes in this teeming dark side of the market system: greed, mercilessness, violence, pornography, illicit drugs, prostitution, weapons, pollution, poverty, and homelessness. A reporter on the radio program "All Things Considered" declared, "Crack is a capitalism problem."[16] Traffic in street drugs especially flourishes in our inner cities where people see little or no opportunity to get into the legally sanctioned side of the market system.

Much to our dismay, the end of the Cold War seems to have precipitated a flourishing black market in nuclear materials and technology. To build an atomic bomb, you need four things: (1) a design, (2) skilled technicians, (3) hardware and equipment, and (4) fuel, commonly uranium or plutonium.[17] The nuclear underground or black market derives its dark labeling from its illegality for those outside officially sanctioned state agencies. Of course, it is not illegal for the state to use nuclear materials if it so desires. Groups like the Department of Energy, because they are cultlike closed systems, do not answer to anyone, least of all the citizen who, finding it more comfortable to let "others" take care of such matters, unwittingly becomes the enabler of increasingly vast and ruthless corruption.

According to a January 26, 1994 ABC News report, 60 percent of the 925,000 prisoners in the U.S. prison system are drug offenders. The cost of housing these prisoners is staggering. Criminalizing drugs is an example of how you and I subsidize the market system's dark side. By supporting politicians who criminalize victimless crimes, we must pay for the inevitable and continuing imprisonment of those who operate lucrative black markets. Worldwide, the U.S. State Department estimates that the illegal drug industry has $300 billion in sales and about $240 billion in profits.[18]

By now you're thinking I advocate abolishing free markets. No, their benefits and even the sprinkling of freedom they provide have transformed the world and made available uncountable advantages, which I also enjoy, to masses of people. Completely eliminating something is a totalistic, one-sided reaction to a problem. The alternatives to free markets have proven to be social disasters. Any economic system, no matter how well it works, has a dark side that *cannot* be suppressed or legislated out of existence because it reflects a *necessary* part of human nature. Only when we fail to *engage* this dark side do we find ourselves in deep trouble.

THE RELIGION OF ORGANIZED GAMBLING

An estimated 10 to 12 million persons are addicted to gambling in the U.S., and the numbers are rapidly increasing.

ABC News[19]

In most of the industrialized world, where money has become a deity and a symbol of heaven on earth, the gambling industry then is really another form of organized religion complete with elaborate gaming rituals, and filled with superstition, lucky numbers, and so on—the *jackpot consciousness.*

As part of a rapidly growing hi-tech theologically based industry, gambling seduces its victims with the promise of paradise, an earthly paradise provided by its reigning god, cash. Consequently, many are addicted to the pursuit of gambling's paradise, for the epiphany of winning. Gambling casinos become the "way" to paradise, and like patriarchal religions, allow individuals little glimpses of heaven—economic Nirvana—small winnings, just enough to keep their loyal flock working the system. And not unlike many religious groups, gambling often consumes all of a person's financial resources. Legalizing what was once illegal, like gambling, usually amounts to a transfer of power and money to different entities, either big business or the state.

The fact that in many areas gambling is still illegal creates many of the problems with legalized gambling. By licensing certain business firms in certain areas, states create monopolistic business entities (groups), which tends to concentrate wealth in the hands of those who own the casinos. In contrast, if gambling were legalized everywhere, the consumer would benefit from the natural competition, creativity, and innovation that freedom always creates. However, if one wants to gamble, he/she should be free to do so.

Many cities are now turning to gambling revenues to offset decreasing tax revenues. The town of Chelsea, Massachusetts, is bankrupt and in receivership. Yet each citizen spends an average of $572 each year on the lottery.[20] State-run lotteries (a $36 billion business) are Robin Hoods in reverse, using millions in advertising to fleece the poor and give to the state.

Capitalist Heaven and Hell

And the people bowed and prayed, to the neon god they'd made.
Simon and Garfunkel[21]

Obedient to our marketplace gods, we worship the golden calf, the almighty dollar. In the system, people search for the Holy Grail: the perfect investment, the idea that will make them rich, the jackpot, the winning lottery number. The market system translates the inner human drive for greater consciousness (the hero's journey) into an outer quest for more money. As in all groups, individuals empower (unconsciously) the market system by giving up their individuality, freedom, autonomy, and integrity.

Money is a powerful drug, and once addicted to it, one's behavior follows typical patterns of drug abuse. We need ever-increasing quantities to feel secure, to feel in control, to experience the same high. The system always has *more* available: something bigger, more expensive, more luxurious. No wonder the government controls the money supply, the drug of choice in our nearly omnipotent market system.

Paradoxically, within the market system, we can purchase the illusion of freedom and autonomy and buy our way into capitalist nirvana *if* we make enough money. Salvation, in the market system, means having plenty of cash so that one does not have to worry about everyday concerns of living: food, clothing, and shelter. Purity equals economic success, while impurity and sin equal economic failure. In fact, the mythical hero's journey has been nicely incorporated into the market system as rags-to-riches, climbing the corporate ladder, or failure to success. When we achieve "success" in the system, we feel heroic. But system-defined success is without doubt the most ephemeral, non-soul-sustaining, fleeting illusion we will ever encounter. The instant one no longer *fits* the system's image, it drops one into a pitiless chasm of icy obscurity.

Market salvation often equates to selling one's soul in order to adapt to the *system*, as Douglas LaBier, author of *Modern Madness*, describes: "the working wounded, healthy people adjusted at great emotional cost due to conditions that are good for the advancement of career but not of spirit."[22]

Consistent with other totalistic systems, the market has its rewards and punishments:

HEAVEN

Illusion of superiority and exclusiveness
Illusion of independence, freedom
Respect from others
Security, protection
Power, influence, control
Position, status, fame
Privilege
Success
Worship and adoration from those still climbing the ladder
System-defined self-esteem
Wealth, luxury, credit

Hell

No credit
Economic failure, bankruptcy
Homelessness
Poverty
Unemployment
No retirement plan
No health insurance
Working for minimum wage

Penalties (punishment) for not belonging to the system include the stigma of failure, low self-esteem, shunning by successful members of the system, and the *feeling* of poverty if not actual poverty. In case we're not sure if we should feel "poor," the system defines poverty for us in terms of how much money we make. By labeling a particular wage as "minimum," we automatically mark persons working for such wages as inferior, uneducated failures. We are embarrassed and ashamed to work for "minimum wage."

The system has its built-in alarms, electronic subsystems that reverberate throughout thousands of computer databases whenever we stray from our collective roles: credit ratings, economic failure, bankruptcy, and unemployment.

We believe we are in masterful control when in actuality we are but economic pawns shackled to the almighty dollar. One could say that individuals are free to play the system or not, but choosing not to play has serious consequences in the varied forms of economic discrimination: homelessness, poverty, ostracism, and low-income housing. When the system has trouble with people, it throws them out.

To get back into the system, we have fleets of state-licensed therapists, thousands of self-help groups and motivational courses to help us return to the system or achieve greater success in the system. Of course, the system's survival requires its own *educational system* that teaches us how to play the game and how to adapt to the group's rules.

Putting a Conscience in the Machine

That capacity to create from suffering was epitomized by Gandhi, whose tough-minded protean transformations began with himself as he made himself into a nonplayer for the existing system—one who plays another game, refusing to be either a player or a counter-player.

Robert Jay Lifton[23]

The renowned mythologist Joseph Campbell said, "The threat is that we live in relation to a system instead of our humanity."[24] We desperately need a new sort of *relationship between the system and individuals*—a relationship that places people first, and profits and progress second. Money becomes cloaked in evil when we make it more important than people and life. Indeed, money itself is not "the root of all evil," but the systems that elevate money above human beings are definitely evil. We have to dethrone the god of the system—money. This will mark the beginning of returning *human-heartedness* to the market system.

The paramount question becomes, how do we put a conscience in the machine before it's too late? How can you and I begin this conscience-instilling process? First, we must stop playing the system's games without an active conscience in the process. We need to be aware of the full spectrum of relationships impacted by the choices we make. We need to know that the dollar going into a slot machine does so at the expense of something else, and that we are perpetuating a system that impacts society in profound ways. You and I need to be aware that a great price on that oriental carpet may be due to the slave labor of about twenty-thousand children who work in the mafia-controlled East Indian carpet industry.[25] Suddenly buying a rug becomes child abuse by proxy. On the other hand, maybe a distant child's labor will save their family from starvation. Not so simple a problem, but the "invisible hand's" unfeeling, efficient selection of cheap labor markets, particularly children, is a sad fact of late twentieth-century life.

We can begin simply by distinguishing between the system's needs and wants and our own individual needs. This requires what Jung called "a new process of self-reflection."[26] When the urge to splurge comes over us, we can *hold the tension*—stop, wait, and reflect: is this something I need, or is it something the system has trained me to want? If I buy this something, will I be a better human being and will the earth be a better place for all life? Is the product or service I am considering life-enhancing or life-destructive? Of course, there are gray areas, like ice cream.

When we participate in any collective system without weighing the consequences of our actions and without considering the human element *first,* we become enslaved and dehumanized. Faced with such collective brutality, it becomes the individual's overwhelming task to think, reason, and feel *independently of the system.*

CORPORATE MURDER

According to an ABC News report, two million middle-management jobs were eliminated during the recent recession.[27] While business firms appear to behave logically, laying off workers when sales and profits decline, they exemplify people caught in a group dynamic where money and profit are deified and considered to be more important than human beings. A business organization that places profits before people becomes a callous, unfeeling authoritarian machine, never hesitating to dump long-term employees provided it helps the bottom line—profits. In fact, such companies will often target their highest-salaried people, replacing them, if necessary, with younger lower-paid employees.

Companies pressured by shareholders and investors to produce short-term profits weigh every business decision on the basis of whether it makes money or not. It's the "either/or," no imagination, divisive mentality. Obviously one cannot survive in a market economy without the element of profitability. However, just as companies build reserves to replace worn-out equipment, business firms ought to build reserves to protect human resources in the inevitable ups and downs of economic cycles. But in a culture that has made money a god and turned people into "things," business groups rid themselves of people with a chilling, conscienceless contempt. Those who suddenly find themselves cast-offs soon realize that business associates they believed were friends now have nothing to do with them. The anger and frustration from realizing that one has been "used" and then discarded like unwanted junk can be devastating. A "profits first" business ideology breeds unconcerned, self-centered, "what's in it for me" workers. When a business organization puts human beings first, it will find that it attracts uncommonly talented individuals who are loyal, creative, and hardworking.

Closing plant facilities in one area to open up again in another with lower wage scales and fewer regulations is a corporate practice that has become alarmingly common. Many firms move their manufacturing plants out of the country in order to save money and supposedly stay competitive in an increasingly global marketplace. Americans are understandably upset about jobs going to other countries, but when Mercedes Benz built a plant in rural Kentucky, where wages and fringe benefits for most workers are substantially less than prevailing German rates, were we concerned for German workers who could have worked in a new German plant? In working with such dilemmas, we have to be careful not to get caught in our own group-think dynamic, setting up adversarial groups: workers against owners, American workers against Asian workers. Our thesis suggests that employees and business owners, whether sole proprietors or shareholders, would place human values and quality of life ahead of profits. This does not necessarily imply making less profit. Instead, it means making people an integral part of the decision-making process.

Difficult decisions require creativity, innovation, and flexibility. Part of the solution involves empowering citizens so that both sides to a dispute can come together with the goal of integrating new business growth with individual quality-of-life concerns—concerns that are frequently unique to each community. For example, in Eugene, Oregon, a city well known for its tenacious environmental, antibusiness stance, business promoters and environmentalists (two opposites) sit down with each other and struggle through the complex and difficult issues that arise when large companies want to build plants in their community. Interestingly, unlike most other cities, residents of Eugene do not compromise what they call "aspects of livability," which include "clean water, public spaces, wilderness."[28] These quality-of-life issues come first and recent new arrivals like Symantec, Sony, and Hyundai had to integrate their operations into Eugene's "aspects of livability."

Paradoxically, we can use the market system's self-correcting, "invisible hand" to remove the profit motive from destructive enterprises such as drug trafficking by legalizing drugs, and at the same time making the penalties for crimes committed under their influence extraordinarily severe. Individual irresponsibility must add to the consequences of criminal behavior and not excuse it.

Widely acclaimed author Andrew B. Schmookler is a senior policy advisor to Search for Common Ground in Washington, D.C., and a research associate for the Center for Psychological Studies in the Nuclear Age at Harvard University. In his excellent book *The Illusion of Choice,* Schmookler suggests that we begin by changing corporate law so that directors must submit major decisions to individual shareholders, who are the actual owners.[29] Responsibility would then shift from the present one-sided board-of-director power center to shareholders, who would then vote on issues after being notified of the pros and cons and the consequences of a particular choice, not only for the corporation and its employees, but for the environment as well. Such a plan would empower the individual and disempower legally empowered big business totalism.

We can demand that our government stop subsidizing destructive commercial enterprises through tax loopholes, farm subsidies, price controls, and uncountable other programs that perpetuate destructive organizations. Recently, ABC News reported that Americans spend $6 billion each year on cigarette-related health problems, while taxpayers subsidize the tobacco industry to the tune of $1 billion annually.[30] Religious institutions and most nonprofit groups, because of their tax-exempt status, are supported by every taxpayer who must make up the difference in state and local tax revenues. Whether we belong to a church or not, we are supporting religious systems, which supposedly are "separated" from the state. Logically, true separation would mean no special tax treatment by the state. Systems and groups become economically destructive when subsidized by the state because of lost tax revenue and the resultant increased taxes on all citizens.

Only individuals can suffuse the market system with integrity and soul, but only when they are *free* of the heart-deadening influences of what is now essentially a money-ruled, *heartless* system. We need to recognize and nourish meaningful relationships between a product and the environment, between a product and society, and between a product and the quality of life. The more we instill a sense of relationship with life in the system, the greater will be the system's integrity. The next time you make a choice in the system, stop and ask yourself, "Am I on a leash held by the 'invisible hand,' or am I acting out of my inner integrity and conscience?" The responsibility rests with you and me. When the desire to make money dominates, we become slaves to the system.

MONOTHEISTIC CAPITALISM

> Modern totalitarianism in America works in subtle ways. It has no flag,
> but the company logotype, and no weapons but paychecks, promotions,
> and the promise of happiness.
>
> Earl Shorris[31]

Business enterprise has for centuries derived its ownership and organizational structure from the mythical idea of a one-god authoritarian, patriarchal mind-set. Traditional business management with its strict authoritarian hierarchy stands in contrast to highly autonomous team project-centered groups with decentralized management, empowered employees, and scattered authority. A business revolution is underway with companies restructuring themselves into a *polytheistic capitalism* with shared responsibility and authority among employees and owners. Indeed, our time-honored traditions of ownership may have to undergo drastic change. Ultimately, what we like to call "employee empowerment" will mean shared ownership. We see this beginning to happen in the corporate world as more groups of employees buy their companies. However, we are in a dangerous transition. Since the fall of communism, the market system has taken on an air of infallibility; it is now *the* solution for every country. We are close to enshrining capitalism as the religion of the twenty-first century. However, a one-sided economic position that rules the globe would be a disaster, both for humanity and for our planet.

Educational Systems

> [M]any of the nation's school systems have become entrenched, self-perpetuating, tax-supported bureaucracies that sometimes lose sight of their mandate.
>
> *Business Week*[32]

Our public educational system is designed to perpetuate itself. That means the *system* has become more important than individual students. The *system* clearly no longer works, as entrenched bureaucracies eat up more and more of our tax dollars while doing less. An August 1993 CBS News report stated that three-fifths of high school graduates in our public school system function at or below a seventh-grade skill level.[33]

When we are taught to respect the system, which means obeying the system's authority figures, teachers and administrators, regardless of whether they are right or wrong, we condition our children *not to think for themselves.* This group conditioning prepares children for collectively acceptable roles where they will not question authority figures, whether a priest, doctor, teacher, or cult leader—a dangerous naiveté for any adult. We let the "system" parent our children, educate them, baby-sit them, and brainwash them.

Western education has deteriorated into a system designed to teach collective goals and values instead of promoting individual creativity and skill development; this teaching stresses group values, not individual worth. Hence, individuals are worthwhile only when they become "socially acceptable," reaching a state of collective normality and dead equality with the masses. Thus we have *system-centered* education, not *student-centered* education. One is no longer an individual with unlimited potential, but part of a predefined group that has already dictated what is acceptable and what is not. Furthermore, James Hillman maintains, "An education that in any way neglects imagination is an education into psychopathy. It is an education that results in a sociopathic society of manipulations. We learn how to deal with others and become a society of dealers."[34]

Most education now trains people to "make money." Money has become a global obsession particularly in the West. We have a collective *money complex.* A teenage Los Angeles gang member said, "Money is power."[35] The quest for power motivates most groups' intense drive to "make money." Recent studies have shown that one of our children's primary concerns is to make enough money when they grow up. Children are victims of our collective money complex. Money equates to "making it."

THE NEW INQUISITION AND THE RELIGIOUS RIGHT

> This isn't a sprint, it's a marathon. Years from now we'll be hugging each other on *our* night of the big victory. Someone, perhaps even Huckabee, will lead America back to biblical values.
> Ralph Reed, Director of Pat Robertson's Christian Coalition[36]

A well-organized and dangerous group, the religious right is gradually infiltrating the educational system by gaining control of local school boards. The religious right establishes front organizations like "Focus on Family" that hide behind popular social issues such as "family values" and better education while they really promote their particular religious views in direct opposition to the separation of church and state guaranteed by the Constitution.

Robert Simonds, president of "Citizens for Excellence in Education," insists that educational censorship by school officials and teachers is healthy. "It doesn't mean they can't teach with freedom. It just means freedom has certain limits."[37]

Using an already dysfunctional school system, religious fundamentalists quickly work to control channels of communication, a fundamental part of thought reform in destructive groups. They erect mental barbed wire by banning unacceptable curriculums, books, films, journal writing (inner communication), and even exercises requiring the use of one's imagination. This censorship results in a debilitating cultural illiteracy, a lethal absence of essential knowledge in an increasingly global high-tech society.

An excellent example of what Robert Lifton calls "ideological totalism," the religious right exudes elitism, superiority, judgmental behavior, and smugness. Following a literalized, patriarchal dogma, religious fundamentalists search out "impurities," creating what Lifton refers to as a "guilty milieu and a shaming milieu." With their "doctrine" superior to any individual, they dehumanize both teachers and students. This superiority of doctrine over individuals tragically diverts the educational process from developing individual human potential into the "totalist dynamic of controlling people's behavior," as Lifton articulates: "the demand that character and identity be reshaped, not in accordance with one's special nature or potentialities, but rather to fit the rigid contours of the doctrinal mold. The human is thus subjugated to the ahuman."[38]

The ominous loss of freedom and liberty accompanied by authoritarian mind-control techniques threatens to plunge a disintegrating educational system into a dark quagmire of medievalism where opposing teachers' reputations are burned at the stake of religious fundamentalism and prejudice, along with any literature that threatens their belief system. Kevin Teeley, president of the Lake Washington Education Association (Washington State) said, "People from the far right will do things like print up fliers that say, 'Do you know you have a pervert teaching around your neighborhoods?' This is what these teachers are faced with."[39]

Such cult-style milieu control isolates our children from themselves and the rest of the world; they are *involuntarily* subjected to an education that further reinforces the primary social ills of our century: separateness, prejudice, bigotry, intolerance, and racism. Kevin Teely cautions:

> What we will never be able to measure is how many books were not taught, how many topics were not discussed, how many newspaper articles were not brought into the classroom that would have been very valuable for kids to have read and learned about because of the fear that teacher had that they might become the object of another challenge.[40]

The Industrialized Psyche

> Things are in the saddle,
> And ride mankind.
>
> Ralph Waldo Emerson[41]

The industrialization of America was in full swing especially in the three decades following the Civil War. Prior to the Civil War, farmers accounted for 60 percent of U.S. workers.[42] Linking the country by railroad in the early 1900s vastly sped up business growth by creating a national market. In 1892 there were four thousand millionaires,[43] a significant number for a time in which a single dollar bill could still purchase something of value. This booming *industrial system* revolutionized life in every way. In particular, it imprinted a "rags-to-riches" capitalist hero mythology on our collective American psyche. Images of "success" were inexorably tied to the industrial system; to be successful, one followed the system's rules, essentially buying into a way of life defined from top to bottom by the Industrial Revolution and its modus operandi, capitalism.

Indeed, the Industrial Revolution had enormous benefits for the world, but its patriarchal structure coupled with a widely embraced "Protestant work ethic" engendered a one-sided blindness toward our environment, and toward other *living systems*. In the system, profits and power came before people, making the system's dark side a destructive force of unimaginable ferocity—a force that still wreaks havoc around the globe.

The market system, in typical patriarchal mode, split a world into two classes: owners and workers, the "haves" and the "have nots." Ironically, our mushrooming technology, in large part the offspring of the Industrial Revolution, now empowers citizens to become both owner and worker. The boom in home-based businesses, often with a single entrepreneur doing a variety of tasks, is the equivalent of Gandhi's "spinning wheel in every home" economy of self-sufficiency, which he used to help overthrow the tyranny of British rule. Hence, the hope for a bright and creative individually empowered economic future rests not so much in lofty towers of big business, but rather in the hands of those turning out "homespun" gold.

As victims of a mechanizing, patriarchal culture, we have allowed ourselves to be machine-fed like livestock. Factories replace gardening while we obediently buy the system's manufactured, artificial foods. It comes as no surprise that our patriarchal, antifeminine collective machinery so easily and swiftly disconnects us from our relationship with our environment. When we buy a product, we usually have no idea where it came from or who produced it. Media-programmed dehumanized *reactions* replace meaningful relationships with the food we eat. Some unknown company or conglomerate pulls our strings and puppetlike we dance to the system's music.

In business groups, totalism fosters attitudes of arrogance, which reinforces isolation from workers and customers. Arrogance characterizes patriarchy—a hierarchal, entrenched bureaucracy. The chief defect in the marketplace of such totalistic top-heavy structures is a dysfunctional *relationship* between the company and its customers, between management and workers, and between products and the environment; relationships on all levels break down and become competitive and confrontational.

Perceiving customers as *things* to be persuaded and manipulated typifies a totalistic approach to marketing where customers become more like an ignorant enemy to be outwitted and conquered. In such systems, instead of useful, quality, life-enhancing products, companies produce unnecessary gadgetry, gizmos, and hype. On the other hand, a soul-based relationship with customers and co-workers means that emphasis centers upon integrity and empathy; the market system now has a *conscience* derived out of *holding all relationships sacred*, including the environment. A business with soul operates in a holographic manner, knowing that the whole appears in every part: that no matter how insignificant something may appear, it matters, is important, and affects everything and everyone.

In the late seventies and early eighties, "reindustrialization" resulted in U. S. auto makers like General Motors (GM) highly automating their assembly plants. They came to rely more on *things* (machines) than people. In destructive business groups, there are powerful inclinations to over-mechanize everything. Mechanization allows management to remain in absolute control. In the GM example, this one-sided overautomation contributed to a marketing disaster. In some GM plants, the new automation allowed for little or no flexibility; automakers often were able to build only one model. In contrast, Japanese automakers relied more on people, resulting in teams and cooperative flexible plants that produced much higher quality products along with multiple styles and models in the same plant.

Municipal water systems still use outmoded technologies of which people are naively unaware. Again, we have lost our relationship even to the water we drink, separated by a state-owned *system,* which we are obliged to attach ourselves to through archaic piping systems which keep us dependent on the state.

The inability of employees to think independently and critically about a company indicates that they have lost the ability to see both sides of an issue. Ask yourself, "Can you name three things seriously wrong with your company?" If not, you are caught in a polarized position within your company or group. Of course, dysfunctional management lives in this one-sided dynamic, looking at problems through the either/or, black-and-white totalistic lens. In the scientific establishment, scientists are effortlessly swept up into popular viewpoints. Established and accepted theories by establishment gurus take on a sacrosanct quality. Individuals worship and enshrine popular theories. Differing opinions are attacked. New concepts are mocked.

Chi roughly translates as "bio energy," or the "force of life." The Chinese scientists hold to an alchemical view of the human body, which sees energies, elements, and the interaction between different organs; they see *relationships.* Western science has compartmentalized the body, dividing it up into pieces, while in reality, the mind and body are inextricably bound up in complex patterns of interconnectedness and relationship. Dividing everything into bits and pieces is a patriarchal approach to healing instead of a holistic approach. Caught in a scientific dualism, Western traditional medicine is often blind to the synergy of relationships involved in the healing process.

CHARACTERISTICS OF BUSINESS TOTALISM

Destructive business organizations, following the largely unconscious totalistic bent inherent in all groups, develop features characterized by:

- Distinct levels of authority, each reporting to superiors;

- Management separated from employees physically, empathically, and ideologically;

- Excessive responsibility in only a few individuals;

- Lots of secrecy within company, employees kept in the dark about company plans and activities;

- Poor delegation, employees not trusted with responsibility;

- Overworked, top-heavy autocratic management;

- A "win-lose" mentality;

- Profits more important than people;

- Competition encouraged between employees and departments within the company;

- Criticism about company policies is not tolerated, or at least discouraged;

- Gender- or race-related salary-pay discrimination;

- Enormous compensation gaps between entry-level workers and management;

- Exclusive areas off limits to "ordinary" employees;

- Results-oriented management instead of process-oriented;

- A we/they competitive worldview; and

- Public reprimands/criticism of employees.

Cultism in Politics

This is one of the paradoxes of the democratic movement—that it loves a crowd and fears the individuals who compose it—that the religion of humanity should have no faith in human beings.

Walter Lippmann[44]

Major systems spawn numerous parasitical subgroups and splinter groups that *use* and feed on larger systems. Our political system proliferates with thousands of such groups: lobbyists, special interest groups, public relation firms, and uncountable federal and state agencies/programs whose existence depends on a larger system. To survive, each subgroup must perpetuate the status quo, promoting and protecting the parent system.

As a nation, we are problem avoiders, experts at dodging confrontational issues. Or we allow ourselves to get caught in extreme political views that often result in violent confrontation—polarization that simply perpetuates political and social warfare between immovable factions and special interest groups. In order to get elected, candidates for office must please the electorate. If politicians base their campaigns on unpopular sentiments, confronting difficult issues directly and honestly, the voters get uncomfortable and they lose the election.

Americans are still stuck in the collective premise of "something for nothing" when it comes to politics, a variation on *salvation theology,* which depends on someone else to "die for our sins." We want the social ills fixed, but not by our effort or at our expense. So, we elect individuals who are expected to solve all our problems but who end up solving little or nothing.

In the United States we have the appearance of a democracy, but in actuality, the politicians we elect are themselves firmly in the grip of the "system," which has its own life. In the majority of situations, the political system totally controls its members. Our government, with all its various departments, programs, and agencies, is an excellent example of a cultic political system: government by group. For example, gun manufacturers lobbied to be excluded from the Consumer Safety Act. As a result, *no one* checks manufacturers of guns or any weapon for product safety. We check toys but not guns? This is an example of government by special interest *groups,* and is anything but democratic. No group should be allowed to intervene in the democratic process. The moment any group influences legislation, we lose our individual voices in our representative democracy. Democracy supposedly means people have a voice. James Madison, one of the founders of our republic, cautioned, "If a majority be united by a common interest, the rights of the minority will be insecure."[45] Even though our democracy has built-in safeguards designed to protect individual rights, the concentration of power in the hands of those who represent 51 percent of the voters divides our nation into two distinct groups: winners and losers, a totalistic political dynamic that inevitably results in the exclusion of many voices. One simple way to make our "representative democracy" more representative would be to have proportional representation like many European democracies. In 1992 Bill Clinton was elected president with only 43 percent of the vote in a three-way split. This is not "majority rule."

In politics, power rules. Most decisions are designed to influence the reelection process. Governors frequently pardon battered women who have been convicted of killing their partners because it is *politically popular* to champion the cause of abused women. This is not "equal justice," but rather a justice *system* heavily controlled and manipulated by political groups determined to stay in power.

In developing countries ("developing" implying they are following our collective standards), governmental food aid is distributed along political lines; food goes to groups of people who are needed to keep the local politicians in power. Food exported to these countries by the United States at below-market prices undermines their farmers' ability to get fair prices for farming. Instead of encouraging self-sufficiency and independence, politically based groups like the U. S. Department of Agriculture, along with giant grain brokerage firms that benefit from our government's largess, oppose encouraging self-sufficiency. Again, the group mind aborts individual innovation and forestalls constructive change. At their best these agencies operate on a subhuman level, reduced to their lowest common denominator by their abstract embodiment of group perpetuation at any expense.

We have a crucial need for political leaders to sit down with those who oppose their views and respectfully work out a solution. This working with and through the other's point of view is the only way to unlock gridlock and to initiate meaningful creative change. Political leaders need to learn what philosophers and other great thinkers have known for generations: that we grow as a nation and as individuals when we face problems, admit our mistakes, and take steps to rectify the damage done.

A large portion of our national distrust of politicians and the anger and frustration we experience originate in the dynamic of displaced anger at ourselves for tolerating a politics of expedience, corruption, extravagance, and waste for so long.

Nonprofit medical insurance groups like Blue Cross/Blue Shield have no board of directors or shareholders. Operating as economically powerful autonomous organizations, they are known for having top-heavy bureaucracies of highly paid executives. Some have become so influential that even high government officials bow before their lobbying might. In fact, insurance industry lobbyists are among the most influential and powerful on Capitol Hill.

Lobbyists represent groups, not individuals. They subvert a representative democracy by turning it into a plutocracy, government by special interest groups with lots of money. The millions that lobbyists spend are provided by loyal policy holders, obedient consumers, dutiful members, and not very discriminating shareholders. In this manner we all participate to some degree in a system that directly undermines our freedom and subsidizes the profits of entrenched commercial enterprises at taxpayer expense. Many lobbying groups provide valuable information and help prevent legislation that would be harmful to individual citizens, but their destructive side emerges when they influence new legislation that provides economic or political advantages to specific organizations at the expense of individual citizens.

Our group-influenced political system eats away at individual liberty and freedom. It smacks of corporate welfare where big business obtains government concessions (really taxpayer subsidies), which insure immense profits for a *select group* of owners and shareholders. Thus we see Mercedes Benz receiving hundreds of millions in tax concessions in order to altruistically foster greater economic progress in Kentucky. It can be argued that the future tax revenues received from salaries paid to workers will more than compensate for any tax incentives given to entice large companies. However, economically subsidizing powerful corporations, while for the most part ignoring individual small business firms, tends to concentrate more power and control in the hands of a few giant companies, making new competition and innovation increasingly difficult and improbable. Indeed, the notion that *bigness* will solve society's problems runs counter to fostering individual freedom, initiative, and creativity.

With our present high technology, we have the capability to implement a truly representative government. Electronic town meetings and electronic instantaneous voting would *empower individuals and disempower groups*—business, social, and political—that have taken control of our government.

The Feres Doctrine, the inability of individuals to sue the government, prohibits lawsuits if an injury was "incident to government service." With political and legal power at their disposal, the government easily shields itself from charges of negligence and irresponsibility. When a governmental organization manages to disconnect itself from a democratic system of checks and balances, corruption and waste are inevitable. The lack of working relationships between the different agencies in our government facilitates and perpetuates totalitarianism. For example, the U. S. intelligence community, which essentially disregards and ignores Congress, continues to spend billions on satellites to track supposed enemies of the United States. The National Reconnaissance Office (NRO), in particular, operates in its own world. In spite of the end of the Cold War, the NRO is building a new one-million-square-foot headquarters at a cost of $340 million, *without congressional approval.*[46] In the NRO's case, as in all destructive groups, *secrecy* plays an important role—secrecy rationalized by the need to maintain our "national security." Governmental organizations that shield their activities from the public are in fact not part of any representative government, but rather are totalitarian anomalies operating behind the cover of assumed (rationalized) legitimacy, their "right" to existence seemingly justified by the task of "protecting" freedom. In fact, they are the modern-day equivalents of a walled-in aristocracy supported by a heavily taxed populace who, like medieval serfs, labor in the fields of private enterprise. The result is always the same: you and I lose our freedom and end up supporting a bloated, self-sustaining bureaucracy that answers to no one.

Black individuals, or for that matter any so-called minority, ought not to wait or rely on any outside group or government agency to help them, but instead should start their own enterprises and hire whomever is best for the job, regardless of color or group orientation. Starting a business is not easy, but we read over and over about successful enterprises that started in someone's garage or basement with little or no start-up capital. The sense of accomplishment that comes with struggle and hard work builds integrity and solid self-esteem—qualities that are in rapid decline in our society. Racial quotas simply serve to perpetuate racism. When people are hired *because they are a particular color or race* rather than possessing some particular ability or training, this demeans individuals, making them dependent.

For example, the government program Aid to Dependent Children (ADC) has been roundly criticized for breaking up families because of the eligibility rules it imposes. Instead, our collective efforts to help others ought to be directed at providing a safety net for those individuals who really need help, by providing job training or other assistance directed toward supporting and motivating individuals to become self-sufficient. This requires reexamining group dynamics that perpetuate destructive policies in many public agencies entrapping people in socioeconomic groups and destroying individual initiative. We must remove the economic benefits for *remaining* unemployed or unproductive.

THE RELIGION OF POLITICS

> God has marked the American people as His chosen nation to finally lead in the regeneration of the world. This is the divine mission of America, and it holds for us all the profit, all the glory, all the happiness possible to man. We are trustees of the world's progress, guardians of its righteous peace.
>
> Senator Albert J. Beveridge of Indiana[47]

According to the Christian Coalition's director, Ralph Reed, their ultimate goal is to transform the Republican party into a religious-political organization by the year 2000, with the political power to spread the "gospel" according to the Christian fundamentalist viewpoint. To accomplish this ideological infiltration, the Christian Coalition, under Pat Robertson's leadership, can draw on a ten-million-dollar annual budget plus millions of contributing members in over one-hundred-thousand born-again churches.[48]

Madison's concern about a single ideology controlling the majority party is coming closer to reality. At the 1995 Christian Coalition's Washington, D.C., conference, Pat Robertson, its president, reaffirmed, "The Christian Coalition's goal is to gain substantial influence, if not full control, over the Republican party apparatus in all 50 states,"[49] calling for "the legitimate role of God in public life."[50]

On January 1, 1994, CNN news reported that Christian conservatives, who now comprise 15 percent of the electorate, want to "reclaim America."[51] Like a modern ideologically bound Columbus, these morally elite fundamentalists want to exterminate or convert the "heathens," who include all nonbelievers. Toxic religion at its worst, Christian conservatism represents a modern Inquisition intent on stamping out what it considers to be heretical ideas and life styles. This return to a political medievalism centered around a fanatical religious movement would be a gigantic step backward for the human race.

Like faithful church members, we tithe a third or more of our incomes to sustain and perpetuate a power-based, rule-saturated, money-manipulated polity. Royalty of old would be hard pressed to maintain even a semblance of the life style of our average member of Congress, let alone the president. We have empowered a new political aristocracy complete with its kings, queens, princes, and servant classes—that's you and me who still manage to "work" for a living.

Minimum wages are another example of a collective scheme that creates joblessness by attempting to centrally control our economic system. The minimum wage encourages children to start criminal careers and erodes self-esteem on a massive scale. The marketplace should be left alone to determine wage levels. The state, patriarchally governed, proliferates with rules and laws supposedly designed to improve the quality of life. But collective interference in a marginally "free" market system only serves to create complex economic aberrations. Low-paying jobs and marginal business enterprises disappear, kids who could do esteem-building part-time work become socially branded as unemployed; bored, hopeless, and discouraged, they fill the ranks of our growing capitalist shadow.

Economic evidence continues to demonstrate that the minimum wage does indeed cause increased unemployment among those who can least afford it: low-skill, low-productivity workers. In a Michigan State University study of dozens of federal and state minimum wage hikes since the 1970s, David Neumark found that every 10 percent rise in the minimum wage consistently caused a 1 to 2 percent drop in total employment.[52]

When comparing employment data from 1989 and 1992, Texas A&M University economist Finis R. Welch found that teenagers and high school dropouts suffered the worst job losses.[53] We are just beginning to see long-term ironic side effects of the minimum wage. According to Mike McNamee, a *Business Week* writer on social policy, higher minimum wages actually may tempt some teenagers to drop out of school, sacrificing higher education and the better pay that would result over the long term. McNamee points out, "the new entrants push aside less educated working teens—who end up with neither schooling nor jobs."[54] Indeed, research shows that: "Of the $9.7 billion cost of a .75 cent hike, only about one-quarter—$2.7 billion—would go to poor or near-poor households, . . . $3.3 billion would line the pockets of spouses or teenagers in families with incomes above $43,000."[55]

THE WELFARE SYSTEM

No force can defeat the steady revenue stream of checks in the mail for not working. The result is that many of the people in the inner city . . . have changed their normal behavior to satisfy the government's demands.

Martin Gross[56]

The welfare system imposes severe economic restraints on individuals who want to continue receiving their government checks. Again, the expectation that some *group* will solve our problems makes us dependent on the collective, and as with any handout, there are strings attached. It is a rare group that does not demand that individuals compromise their distinctiveness, freedom, and autonomy in exchange for collective help.

Welfare systems represent a collective acting out of one of our most ancient myths: the vision of a paradise on earth, a "Golden Age" where all that we desire is provided by some wise and beneficent being. The problem being that turning this myth into a political system keeps people in a state of perpetual childhood fantasy in addition to trapping individuals in a one-sided, unreal world without a shadow.

All collective systems tend to grow exponentially. The welfare system has grown from 4.4 million recipients in 1965 to over 14 million recipients in 1994.[57] Without drastic change resulting in the complete dismantling of the present system, we are headed for certain economic disaster, as a shrinking taxpayer base strains to provide ever-increasing government handouts. For most people, being on welfare equates to abject failure—a grim set of circumstances that proves to be extremely demeaning. The misguided belief that we can help the poor by subsidizing illegitimacy, scams, and nonwork is alienating generations of people into stigmatized camps of welfare recipients. The *New York Times* reported that an investigation "of 1,800 of Newark's welfare recipients found that 23 percent had been listed with the same names and Social Security numbers in Manhattan at some time between 1991 and 1993. Those 425 cheats have collected more than $1 million illegally since 1991."[58] Ultimately we will have to decide what the state's proper role is, who legitimately needs assistance, who can best provide that assistance—the public or private sectors—and how we will pay for it.

Up to 70 percent of inner-city births are to single or unwed mothers; about one out of three, nationwide, and two out of three in our inner cities.[59] The state pays *only* if no man is there. So the welfare system provides powerful incentive for men to abandon women and break up families. In a market-driven economy, babies born out of wedlock produce substantial economic benefits; "they," in this example, the welfare system, will take care of the problem. Hence, we have a social system that promotes broken families, irresponsibility, low self-esteem, and loss of human dignity while draining diminishing resources from every sector of society.

Ironically, in a system that purports to help people, the welfare system destroys the essential ingredients of a free democracy: individual freedom, dignity, integrity, and self-esteem. Indeed, those on welfare become employees of the "system." Their jobs are to do nothing, to stay as they are. Welfare recipients are to the system what sinners are to the priesthood—job security. Like a highly addictive social drug, state handouts to individuals who are able to work create a seductive market for indolence, apathy, and laziness. The long-term social costs are enormous and if unchecked, will certainly complete the financial ruin of the U. S. economy. Welfare systems in their present form support and perpetuate institutionalized poverty. As a highly addictive collective system, it degrades and disempowers individuals, trapping recipients in an economic caste system that is extremely difficult to escape.

The welfare system as it presently exists ought to be completely abolished because it has deteriorated into an extremely destructive group. An enormous bureaucratic political system, welfare discourages local community volunteer help and encourages a detached, dispassionate, "let someone else take care of it" heartlessness. We no longer care about our neighbors. In fact, neighborhoods are turning into "hoods." Never has there been such a glaring public failure of a government system. Yet, even a mention of tampering with its gargantuan totalistic apparatus brings wails of protest from supposedly concerned do-gooders. Any truly concerned government would never have started the welfare system as we know it. The fact that it has evolved into such a destructive system confirms the inexorable grip the group mind exerts on its members to preserve and perpetuate itself. In order to survive, the welfare system must recruit and sustain the disadvantaged masses.

In a nation built by immigrants, with our Statue of Liberty welcoming newcomers, we have placed the onus of our economic and political failings on the backs of new immigrants. Our nation-state has reached a stage that all mass movements eventually encounter. Having attained a degree of prosperity and laboring under the illusion of limited resources which must be divided among more and more people, we unflinchingly adopt the politically popular, scapegoating view that immigrants are responsible for many of our society's problems. Our national scapegoating of immigrants ominously recalls historic parallels where particular ethnic groups were singled out as polluting agents, for example, the supposed genetic pollution of the German race by Jews. Using similar logic in the United States, immigration supposedly damages our economy, polluting it with masses of unskilled laborers who are displacing American workers. Unwilling to look at our own economic shadow—our own failures and mistakes—we project our disowned collective shadow onto others. Anthropologist Bruce Hocking, writing in the *Journal of Occupational Medicine,* alludes to this group dynamic with an analogy from the Middle Ages:

> The choice of a feared pollutant is not made directly but through social processes which lead to the boundary of the group being sharpened. . . . In fourteenth-century Europe water was a persistent health hazard, but only became a public preoccupation when it seemed plausible to accuse Jews of poisoning the wells.[60]

Prior to 1965, there were no limits on immigration from the Western Hemisphere. Our border to the south was wide open. The recent widespread, largely political uproar over illegal immigration has created a badly needed outside enemy responsible for a large chunk of our nation's ills. Virginia Postrel, editor of *Reason* magazine, warns about the dangerous implications of immigration control, which epitomizes governmental group-think and enemy-making: "It [immigration] defies human nature and market forces. It draws a line between willing sellers and willing buyers and enforces that line with guns. It tells workers they must stay where there is no work, seekers of liberty they must endure dictatorship, parents they cannot seek a better life for their children. It is like wage and price controls, taxi medallions, vice laws, rent control, and every other attempt to interpose state power between consenting adults. It creates black markets, corrupts law enforcement, encourages contempt for the law, and at best, works only imperfectly."[61]

In 1921 Congress passed a temporary and later a permanent quota act. Like our present paroxysm of invasionitis, the 1921 Congress, in what must have been a similar fit of group paranoia, justified their actions by warning that "an unprecedented number of filthy and unassimilable Jews were fleeing persecution in Europe."[62] Further establishing immigrants as an undesirable *group,* this act legalized then-prominent Cornell economist Jeremiah Jenk's concept that our immigration policy should change from "an individualistic basis" to one based on "racial characteristics."[63]

History is replete with examples of groups fearing infection from outsiders. Entrenched systems, both political and economic, respond vigorously to perceived outside threats, particularly when some other group appears to embody an alien ideology. As long as we respond to problems from a group context, we will perpetuate prejudice, hatred, war, and bigotry, and we will deteriorate as a civilized society. Freedom means the ability to come and go as one pleases. A free country does not build walls to keep people in or out. The economic/political monkey wrench in our collective machinery is the welfare mentality that rewards people for doing nothing. It doesn't take an economist to realize that the free market system efficiently extends its "invisible hand" to millions of immigrants who see a "profit" in immigrating to the United States.

Not surprisingly, the 700,000 to 800,000 legal immigrants coming to this country each year rarely go on welfare, primarily because they tend to be better educated than native-born Americans. In contrast, political refugees and illegal immigration are a serious drain on state and federal assistance programs. During the last great immigration surge, 1900 to 1910, the only public assistance offered to new immigrants was public education and occasional public health. Today, a multitude of aid programs including food stamps, Aid to Families with Dependent Children, and unemployment insurance act as a powerful magnet luring immigrants who would otherwise stay home. Rice University immigration expert Donald Huddle recently reported that "the 19.3 million legal, illegal, and amnestied aliens accepted into the United States since 1970 utilized $50.8 billion worth of government services last year."[64] This was offset by $20.2 billion in taxes, leaving $30.6 billion to be paid by American taxpayers.[65] Without any changes in the present system, Huddle estimates taxpayers will have to pay an average of $50 billion per year over the next ten years.[66]

To embrace both a free market system and the present welfare system at the same time is a formula for economic disaster. Without government handouts, immigration would sharply decline. As a nation, we would tend to attract self-sufficient individuals looking for a new start, willing to work and to earn their living.

Furthermore, labeling people who immigrate to this country as "illegal" and "undesirable" simply feeds collective hysteria and group enemy-making instead of promoting creative change in a corrupt political agency.

THE FOOD AND DRUG ADMINISTRATION: A POLITICAL CULT

> On February 26, 1987, an armed force of about 25 FDA agents, U. S. marshals, and members of the Hollywood, Florida police department smashed down the glass doors of our store at 2835 Hollywood Boulevard, and stormed into our nearby warehouse with guns drawn. As Bill Feloon, the vice president of the Foundation, was trying to leave the warehouse to find out what was going on at the building, he suddenly found himself staring down the barrel of a .45 caliber pistol, which belonged to a member of a second group of FDA agents, U. S. marshals, and police officers, who were simultaneously attacking the warehouse.
>
> Saul Kant, Director of the Life Extension Institute[67]

The Food and Drug Administration (FDA) was originally established to "protect public health," a valid and important function. However, the FDA has evolved into a large political bureaucracy that often abuses its power, authority, and unlimited legal resources, all paid for by taxpayers. It is this cultlike destructive bent and its effects that we will look at in the FDA. Glenn Lammi of the Washington Legal Foundation, a Washington, D.C., public-interest litigation group, observed, "As with most administrative agencies, the agency [FDA] constantly attempts to expand its jurisdiction and power, straining against the limits the law places upon its actions."[68] As with all destructive groups, the road to hell is paved with good intentions. With increasing raids on private business firms, enforcement has become increasingly one of the FDA's top priorities. In his first two months as FDA commissioner, David Kessler added one hundred criminal investigators.[69]

As the FDA proliferates with new regulations and extends its jurisdiction to ever-widening product categories, its enforcement arm expands while life-saving products are swamped in a maze of paperwork, bureaucratic intimidation, and interminable delays. Alexander Volokh, a Reason Foundation policy analyst, reports that "tens of thousands of Americans die every year" because of the FDA's policies.[70] Volokh's research provides these estimates which clearly document how the FDA, like other destructive groups, makes its agenda more important than the individual:

- Seven thousand people die every year because the FDA hasn't approved the Ambu CardioPump, a CPR device that is available in just about every other industrialized country.

- Nine hundred people die every year because the FDA hasn't approved the OmniCarbon heart valve, which also is in use just about everywhere else.

- From November 1988 to May 1992, about 3,500 kidney-cancer patients died waiting for the FDA to approve the drug Interleukin-2, which was already available in France, Denmark, and seven other European countries.

- In 1988 alone, between 7,500 and 15,000 people died from gastric ulcers caused by aspirin and other nonsteroidal anti-inflammatory drugs, waiting for the FDA to approve misoprostal, which was already available in forty-three countries.

- And 22,000 people died between 1985 and late 1987 waiting for streptokinase, the first drug that could be intravenously administered to reopen the blocked coronary arteries of heart-attack victims.[71]

Whenever a large political group becomes destructive, it creates refugees. The FDA's abuses and delays have created business refugees, companies that move their manufacturing facilities to countries where new drugs and life-saving medical devices can be freely marketed with a minimum of delay and government interference. Medtronic, a large American manufacturer of medical devices, recently (1992–1994) moved twelve new businesses and product lines to Europe, along with its $40 million research and development group.[72] In fact, the *Irish Bio Tech News* reports that "Ireland is now home to more than forty expatriate American medical-device companies, employing 8,500 people, and that ten more American companies are building facilities in Ireland."[73] Called the "number-one jobkiller in America" by Newt Gingrich, the FDA perpetuates itself by waging war on the supposed legions of unscrupulous manufacturers and alternative, natural remedies.

One aspect of freedom, according to the U. S. Constitution, is "life, liberty and the pursuit of happiness." Each time a government agency (a political group) decides to "protect" consumers by intervening in the market place, we lose more of our freedom. The FDA, a cultlike agency, works against individual autonomy and freedom of choice. The FDA's totalitarian formula is: More protection equals less freedom. Case in point: Nutritional supplements represent a movement outside the traditional medical establishment (the state-approved system) in competition with the officially sanctioned drug and pharmaceutical industry. Most FDA practices, like their attempts to make vitamins and herbs prescription drugs, maintain and promote powerful business groups.

Following typical destructive group dynamics, the FDA designates nutritional supplements and the natural food industry as the evil empire, out to trick consumers with snake oil and unproven remedies. Certainly there are unethical manufacturers, but the occasional miscreant becomes an inflated monster to the enemy-creating group mind, which to survive and grow must have an enemy that survives and grows.

The FDA supposedly wants to inform consumers. Then why do their "label extension" laws prevent natural food stores from displaying any literature or books that explain about natural remedies next to the actual products? Even in retail stores, the FDA tries to prevent consumers from finding out about natural, "unapproved" products—remember our destructive group dynamic of controlling communication. The FDA, under pressure from giant pharmaceutical companies, wants to classify natural medications like vitamins and herbs as drugs. Classification as drugs means that consumers will have fewer and much more expensive choices. Common vitamins would become prescription drugs with drastically higher prices, placing many remedies out of reach for persons with lower incomes. Once the FDA labels a particular herb or vitamin a "drug," it must undergo extensive "scientific" testing in order to be approved for sale to the public. This FDA approval process now costs companies several hundred million dollars per drug. Who ultimately pays for this "protection racket"? You and I do through exorbitant prices for medicine. Meanwhile, the medical establishment ignores hundreds and in some cases thousands of years of experience in using natural healing remedies because a natural substance has not undergone "modern" scientific testing. Consequently, one of our most precious freedoms, the ability to make *informed choices* about our own lives, quickly disappears into collective hands in the name of "protection." When a "group" believes they know better than you or I what is best, it implies that we as individuals are not capable of self-determination. Not only is this demeaning, but allowing groups to decide what is best for us also means that we are enabling our own loss of freedom.

In an atmosphere of *group-think,* democratic institutions are transformed into pseudoreligions where the masses look to their godlike government and its evangelizing leaders to solve every human problem—to take care of us from the cradle to the grave. No longer free, we become mechanical parts of the system, trapped by demigods of our own creation in voluntary servitude.

In 1981, the FDA approved aspartame for use in food products. We know it as NutraSweet. Since its approval, there have been nearly seven thousand complaints and five deaths connected with the use of aspartame.[74] Aspartame is but one of thousands of "FDA approved" chemical food additives that are potentially poisoning our collective well. A recent report stated that: "Aspartame is unstable in liquids and breaks down into methyl alcohol (methanol), a cumulative poison which further breaks down into formaldehyde."[75] Ironically, methanol is one of the Environmental Protection Agency's "toxic substances," a "human poison by ingestion and a narcotic."[76] Giant drug companies, potent entrenched groups in their own right, become subtle agents of mass destruction. The FDA, supposedly "protecting" consumers, could better spend its time seeing that foods are properly labeled so that we can make informed choices. Caught in their own scientific ideology, the FDA prevents innovative products from ever being developed. Jonas Salk, the discoverer of Polio vaccine, recently commented that his vaccine could not have been produced under current FDA restrictions.[77]

What's in back of this political evil? Authoritian groups with police power and patriarchal belief systems that assume they have the right to decide what we can or cannot do regarding our own life and safety. This establishes a parental relationship between citizens and their government.

Approval and certification processes differ vastly in other countries. In Canada, they have "post-market notification," which means they can't stop you unless they find something wrong with your product. This gives small and large companies the freedom to market their products while keeping incentive high to avoid having their products pulled from shelves. European companies can get a "CE" (Certified Europe) stamp from an assortment of competing certifying organizations called "notified bodies."[78] With their emphasis on *certification* from competing groups, the process goes much faster than the FDA's. Ultimately the individual should have the freedom of choice and the right to determine the element of risk in taking any medication. This requires clear and informative labeling on all products and it requires including evidence and experience from other countries as well. Perhaps the FDA ought to insure proper labeling and leave purchasing decisions up to individuals.

THE ENVIRONMENTAL PROTECTION AGENCY

> The dead weight of institutions, which have a life of their own, then gradually tames the impetus of the original appeal.
>
> Elias Canetti[79]

While the avowed purpose of the Environmental Protection Agency (EPA) is admirable, like most groups, it preserves itself by creating perpetual devils to eradicate, without which it would have no purpose and no right to exist. Granted, environmental pollution certainly qualifies as a demonic effect of patriarchal attitudes in groups as well as in individuals, but the group self-preservation dynamic constantly redirects such organizations' operations and activities. In the EPA's case, their "cause," which is a legitimate one, gradually becomes the dominant force in the group. This leads to a tribal zeal, which, if unchecked, becomes an obsessive search for the enemy—polluters.

For example, the EPA may be exaggerating the dangers of radon gas, a naturally occurring element in the earth. In fact, scientists tell us that we are all breathing radon, generated by "the decay of trace amounts of uranium found throughout the earth's crust." Citing what are now questionable test results, the EPA claims that radon gas is responsible for between 7,000 and 30,000 deaths from lung cancer each year.[80] As a result, they are calling for nationwide testing and structural alteration of homes and commercial buildings to shield occupants from radon. The EPA's radon program could cost taxpayers $50 billion. The EPA's war against radon clearly illustrates how a large political group, in this case a federal agency, easily and inevitably slips into a cultlike dynamic typical of fanatical religious groups.

THE DEPARTMENT OF ENERGY

> But when no risk is taken there is no freedom. It is thus that, in an industrial society, the plethora of laws made for our personal safety convert the land into a nursery, and policeman hired to protect us become self-serving busybodies.
>
> Alan Watts[81]

The Department of Energy (DOE) certainly qualifies as a megapolitical group that has successfully resisted attempts to reduce its size. With over 165,000 workers and contract employees, an annual budget in 1994 of $18.5 billion, the DOE is one of the largest political cults in existence. Incredibly, in these post-Cold War years, the DOE has 5,000 government bureaucrats being paid substantial salaries to supervise manufacturing of nuclear warheads by 140,000 employees of major industry giants like Westinghouse, General Electric, Dupont, Martin Marietta, and the Flour Corporation even though we no longer make nuclear warheads. U. S. taxpayers are paying over $200 million per year in overtime alone, in spite of zero nuclear warheads being manufactured.[84]

Extremely successful at perpetuating itself, the DOE exemplifies the cult imperative to sustain and perpetuate its power and control. Like many other destructive government agencies, the DOE is a secretive, top-heavy bureaucratic institution that has become masterful at self-preservation, extravagance, and immense waste—an excellent example of a political group not only beyond the control of other government officials, but also far beyond any semblance of control by taxpayers who are its de facto supporters.

Like all destructive groups, federal agencies have a patriarchal pathology, a hierarchal authoritarian structure, and a tyrannical "either/or" mindset; either you support and go along with the party line, or you are an enemy and must be either made to "see the light," be silenced, or be fired.

This is not representative government, but rather institutionalized cultism. I am not saying that there should be no Department of Energy, but instead that any such group ought to be accountable to those who support it. Political power must flow from the individual out, not from groups down to individuals. For those in power, totalistic political groups establish an institutionalized aristocracy far beyond the wildest fantasies of times past. For employees, who must either conform to the status quo or lose their jobs, political cults turn work into political prostitution where individuals give up their integrity for money. The peer pressure to compromise one's values and morals is intense and nearly impossible to overcome. Whistle-blowers make news headlines precisely because of the rare courage required for one solitary individual to stand up to a well-organized mass.

UNIONS: LEGALIZED EXTORTION

> Evil rests on the passionate personal motive to perpetuate oneself.
>
> Ernest Becker[83]

Unions in America began in the eighteenth century as fraternities of shoemakers, bricklayers, craftsmen, printers, and other trades. These first union groups organized to maintain quality standards and prices. In the early 1900s, unions were formed to address serious abuses of primarily industrial workers by employers—a legitimate and necessary response. But unions' "us versus them" patriarchal group dynamic divided managers and workers into two hostile camps. After years of bitter, often violent struggle with business owners, unions managed to get legislation enacted (Wagner Act of 1935) that gave them new political and economic clout in their war against management. Organized labor became a force to be reckoned with. Legally empowered, they set out to win all they could for their members. Collective bargaining soon became more like blackmail-by-group. Strikes shut down entire industries—not to mention police departments, fire fighters, and teachers—with serious economic effects rippling throughout our economy. Meanwhile, the unionization of public employees has created special interest groups dedicated to expanding state bureaucracy; the reason why is obvious: more union jobs.

Barely one in eight American workers now carries a union card. Perhaps as a nation, we are growing tired of management-by-threat—exhausted by endless demands that exceed reasonableness and fairness: Jackie Vaughn of the Chicago Teachers Union says, "It's unreasonable to ask high school teachers to spend more than four hours a day in the classroom." United Auto Workers' Owen Bieber says, "It's not fair to ask auto workers to pay even a small portion of their health-insurance premiums."[84]

More important, unions are *organized groups* that have significantly distorted and abused the free market system, resulting in a very high price tag for all Americans. Winning often exorbitant wage and fringe benefits from business firms, unions have been a major factor in driving up consumer prices and at the same time making large industry segments uncompetitive in the global marketplace. The wreckage of companies that could no longer meet union demands and operate viable businesses litters this century's landscape. From major newspapers to the garment industry to steel mills, unions have in fact decimated American business. In a futile attempt to retaliate against foreign workers who, according to totalistically organized unions, have taken American jobs, the destructive side of the union movement has attempted to demonize anything not "made in America."

Did unions care about the effects of such irrational behavior? Evidently not. In 1977, I. W. Abel, former head of the United Steelworkers of America, was asked whether he felt demands for a guaranteed life income might be too heavy a burden for the steel industry and consumers. Abel replied, "We're not concerned with that side of the question. We must look out for members."[85] By the early eighties, the American steel industry had laid off over 40 percent of its workers.[86] Once more we see the one-sided aspect of destructive groups. The group's agenda justifies any means and those who do not belong to the union must be converted to the cause. Destructive unions need unhappy, disgruntled employees.

Some unions are in fact undergoing rather startling transitions. At General Motor's Saturn Corporation, teams of workers manage themselves with union officials involved at every level of management.[82] Relationships between workers and managers are based on *both* independence and cooperation to create greater efficiency and productivity, which will then justify higher wages. Leaving behind traditional adversarial bargaining, Xerox CEO Paul Allaire said, "If we have a cooperative model, the union movement will be sustained and the industries it's in will be more competitive."[88] In Sweden, management and unions work with each other to achieve *lagom,* a term for fairness that means "just right." In his book *Sweden at the Edge: Lessons for American and Swedish Managers,* Michael Maccoby explains *lagom:* "It is said that the word comes from the Viking drinking horn that was passed around among a circle of villagers. Each person was expected to drink not too much and not too little, but just enough so that the horn would be emptied."[89] Too much or too little is not *lagom,* and Swedish unions insist that wages be *lagom,* fair. This idea of reaching a place between extremes helps to alleviate the destructive groupthink characteristic of taking sides.

We are in the midst of a tremendous shift from factories to service and information, and if unions are to survive at all, they must reinvent themselves, completely dropping the "us versus them" group dynamic that has proven to be so destructive to others and to themselves.

The Medical Establishment

And it is just in the neglected areas of eros and soul, not in rational technique, that modern medicine finds its predicaments: overspecialization, house-calls, fees, hospital administration, medicine in politics, medical education, the doctor-patient relationship—and all those issues which show how the human aspect has fallen into the shadow.

James Hillman[90]

"Modern medicine" has become one of the most entrenched and powerful belief systems in modern times. Backed by powerful lobbying groups like the American Medical Association (AMA), the authoritarian-structured medical establishment preserves itself at the expense of individual freedom and innovation. In order to "protect" you and me from alternative therapies—therapies that do not fit the prevalent belief system—different approaches to healing are labeled as "quackery." By establishing and controlling licensing of medical practitioners, by implication, alternative medicines become outside the "law," and automatically suspect in the establishment-manipulated minds of consumers. It bears repeating that whenever any group tries to "protect" us from some group-perceived danger, we lose some degree of freedom. State licensing of professions creates exclusive (and expensive) groups—a state-empowered monopolistic professionalism. In contrast, emphasis on *certification* of professionals would provide consumers with better information with which to evaluate individual expertise and training. Again, we need to distinguish between *enabling and empowering* individuals instead of *controlling*. Carl Rogers, a past president of the American Psychological Association, believed that state licensing of professionals does not protect against charlatans or guarantee integrity. He wrote: "the first and greatest effect is to freeze the profession in a past image. This is an *inevitable* result. . . . The urge towards professionalism builds up a rigid bureaucracy. Bureaucratic rules become a substitute for sound judgment."[91]

Throughout history those individuals who sought new and different alternatives to established systems have been persecuted by the established order. Socrates and Galileo were put on trial for their "different" ideas. The Inquisition murdered those who held "different beliefs." Several million women were put to death for practicing what the Church saw as pagan practices. Again the label of "witchcraft," like "quackery," was used to mark those people whose beliefs did not fit the system in power. Nazi Germany persecuted anyone who tried to keep a balance between two views; only *one* point of view was tolerated. Authoritarian-structured systems always strive to maintain the status quo at the expense of individuals.

The medical establishment—the American Medical Association with its established, *acceptable* procedures—frowns on alternative therapies that are outside the domain and control of the establishment. Like all destructive organizations, the medical establishment demonizes alternative therapies as "quackery." Granted, there will always be charlatans in any area of human endeavor. But this sort of labeling by groups like the AMA serves to entrench and perpetuate a particular approach to medicine while branding many historically proven alternative medicines as evil. In their rigid adherence to system-approved procedures, which essentially treat the effect of illness rather than the cause, they ignore centuries of empirical data that show many alternative remedies do indeed work and often without the highly toxic side effects of pharmaceutical drugs. For medical doctors to be restricted to one type of medicine is a tragedy for doctors as well as patients. Ironically, some natural remedies do occasionally slip through the system's defenses. Digitalis, a potent heart tonic, comes from the foxglove plant. Aspirin is a chemical imitation of salacin from the bark of the white willow tree. Reserpine, used to control blood pressure, is an ancient Indian remedy derived from an Asian shrub. Ephedrine and pseudoephedrine, used in lots of over-the-counter cold remedies, come from the ephedra plant, which has been used for centuries in China to treat colds and flu. Two successful cancer medicines, vincritisine and vinblastine, are extracts from Madagascar's rosy periwinkle tree, and have saved thousands of victims of childhood leukemia.[92] But natural medicines pose another serious threat to the medical/pharmaceutical establishment: they *can't be patented* as unique chemical formulas and therefore the profits to be made are far less than manufactured drugs. In the end, individuals, with sufficient information provided by doctors or other experts and clear labeling, should have the freedom to choose their own medications. A one-sided medical establishment is not only dangerous, it leaves little room for choice. The major reason for the decline in natural remedies was economic, plus the medical establishment's ban on herbs in the 1930s[93] in favor of drugs. As a result, since the 1930s, doctor-caused illnesses and deaths have soared.[94]

The AMA's numbingly common "either/or" mentality typifies a patriarchal-parental-authoritarian position that demands childlike trust and obedience to the establishment's authority figures. This abdication of individual responsibility and freedom of choice empowers organizations who are dedicated to self-preservation at our expense. We, as individuals, gradually lose more and more freedom, as medical group dogma theologically splits the healing arts into pure and impure, good and evil.

A medical theology that tries to "save us" from all suffering exposes their totalitarian bones beneath the "savior" exterior. Depth psychology has amply illustrated that the human psyche, as well as nature itself, requires resistance, tension, and suffering in order to grow. Dr. Lendon Smith, in his essay "DTP Shots and Infants," explains that our immune system needs "priming," that we each need to experience resistance in life. He writes:

> It appears that the American Academy of Pediatrics, the Centers for Disease Control, and the FDA are not reading and evaluating the vast literature available that indicates that vaccinations to control whooping cough, diptheria, measles, mumps, rubella, and polio are not effective, and worse yet, are hurting the children's immune systems to the point of allowing these same diseases and other devastations to promptly invade their unprotected bodies.[95]

In fact, researchers in Australia and Japan have linked Sudden Infant Death Syndrome (SIDS) to DTP shots. Japan, with one of the lowest infant death rates in the world, in 1979 stopped DTP shots for infants before age two. Confirming the research, they have gone without any cases of SIDS for the last fifteen years.[96]

This is but one of many examples of how we lose a lot more than our freedom when we look to a group to *protect* us or make our lives perfect. Ernest Becker (1924–1974), a University of California professor and Pulitzer Prize-winning author, explains why people so willingly place their lives in collective hands: "It is the politician who promises to engineer the world, to raise man above his natural destiny, and so men put their whole trust in him. We saw how easily men passed from egalitarian into kingship society, and for that very reason: because the central power promised to give them unlimited immunities and prosperities."[97] These are actually patriarchal religious ideas embedded in the medical establishment. Like a healthy psyche, our physical bodies require *tension* and resistance for true "immunity," which in actuality means greater psychological and physical *integrity*—the ability to hold together as a whole person. A feminine, soul-based approach to medicine would be a "both/and" inclusiveness where doctors utilized all known therapies *both* within and without the "system." Of course, even suggesting such an approach raises the medical establishment's defenses. For a totalitarian-based group, acknowledging alternative therapies equates to letting barbarians storm the castle walls; it is unthinkable.

Groups and systems have so distorted life that we've forgotten the value of death. In our collective rush to save lives "at any cost," we no longer know how to let go. As a result, people are robbed of their dignity. Death has turned into a high-tech circus—the ultimate mechanization of the human soul. We cannot even die without being attached to the system's machinery. Totalism, in its propensity to *control* every aspect of life, tries to control death.

Drugs: Putting the Soul to Sleep

America is turning a corner with vast moral, scientific, and medical implications. We may have finally adopted a "National Prescription Drug"—and with it, the idea that drugs are the answer.
Peter R. Breggin[98]

Prozac, while having legitimate use in serious mental illness, becomes an agent of the state, a political tool, when used to simply make one feel better. In this sense, drugs like Prozac enable us to enjoy our collective imprisonment—an example of how a society medicates itself in order to compensate for the inevitable psychological consequences of living collectively ordered and defined lives. Lost in the popular herd, our lives lack uniqueness and potential; purpose and meaning slip under the quicksand of mass-mindedness.

To medicate away our pathologies means losing touch with the soul, the deep down tension-producing stirrings and struggles that insure beneficial transformation for both individuals and groups. A form of soul lobotomy, drugs become the Orwellian collective medication of choice: how we deaden our distinctiveness, and put our dis-ease to sleep, and eliminate *tension.* With our prescription in hand, we obediently take our pills, obliterating any sense of struggle, tension, and frustration. Life flattens out as we become collectively "acceptable" and nondistinctive.

The idea of a drug to enable us to feel "good" and behave in a socially acceptable manner is surely the ultimate horror, keeping the psyche drugged, in a numbed-out state equivalent to anesthetizing the psyche's warning system. Mood altering drugs are the logical extension of a feel-better, obsessed-with-good-times collective.

Upsetting the body's chemistry always has unexpected side effects, no doubt serious ones we do not yet understand. For example, one serious side effect will be the deadening effect on our collective culture from removing some of the natural tension-producers in life. And without tension, we are psychologically and spiritually dead.

Psychiatrist Dr. David Rothman identified the primary drawback with drugs like Prozac: "If we listen to Prozac, we can avoid listening to the patient."[99] Rothman points out a serious dilemma: what can doctor or patient accomplish in a drugged state? Perhaps psychotherapy will disappear, replaced by medications that obliterate symptoms and hence prevent individuals from discovering the real meaning in the symptom. Drugged so that one fits into a socially defined "normality," one can return home, performing one's socially acceptable duties to God and country.

We may even be creating a new form of addiction, *socially addicted* persons who must drug themselves in order to avoid the frustration of leading collectively dictated lives. From the state or any group's perspective, the prospect of chemically cultivating submissive, unquestioning, and obedient followers would be nearly irresistible. In this Orwellian state, all are equalized. Diversity and individual distinctiveness blur. Like the Stepford wives who were scientifically altered to become permanently happy and obedient to their husbands' every whim, drug therapy would enable us to lead false existences, unreal lives, without feeling any frustration or unhappiness.

Prozac, more than any recent antidepressant drug, has sparked a heated debate regarding society's approach to mental illness. Drugs like Prozac raise profound ethical dilemmas that illuminate the age-old conflict between the individual and the collective. Individuals and society thrive on a diversity of temperaments, not sameness. If it were not for a state of *normal tension,* a certain degree of healthy frustration created by the differential between what we are and what we would like to become, there would be no purpose for our existence.

If our social "group" uses some drug and we don't, what are the implications? We must decide whether or not to medicate ourselves in order to alter our personalities so that we fit into acceptable collective standards. If we don't use drugs, and our peer group does, then we make ourselves social outcasts; we feel abnormal, that something must be wrong with us; now we are in the classic trap of "blaming the victim"—ourselves.

Any drugs that medicate away our legitimate feelings of anxiety and tension are also doing away with the process of becoming a whole person with increasing *consciousness.* Being human encompasses the full range of human emotions. It is not abnormal to sometimes feel depressed, any more than it is abnormal to sometimes feel happy. Both are two sides of the coin of life.

Reclaiming Our Economic Integrity

What we have now is democracy without citizens. No one is on the public's side. All the buyers are on the corporation's side. And the bureaucrats in the administration don't think the government belongs to the people.
Ralph Nader[100]

We need to separate government from money and *control* over money similar to the separation of church and state. In order to promote true economic integrity and freedom, the federal government must relinquish any form of manipulation or control of the money supply. This control rightfully belongs in the hands of local community groups who, reversing the power flow, then would contribute funds to the federal government for legitimate functions like the criminal justice system and national defense. In this manner, the power base would shift from an outmoded, centralized, patriarchal bureaucracy to communities, where *individual citizens* would be back in control.

6

The Collective Machine

Power takes as ingratitude the writings of its victims.

Rabindranath Tagore[1]

It's far easier to get your fingers into a machine than it is to get them out.

John W. Davis

Where it is a duty to worship the sun it is pretty sure to be a crime to examine the laws of heat.

Novalis[2]

The collective shadow can take form as mass phenomena in which entire nations can become possessed by the archetypal force of evil. . . . [T]his can mean that people identify with an ideology or leader that gives expression to the fears and inferiorities of the entire society. . . . When a minority carries the projection of that which a society rejects, the potential for great evil is activated.

Jeremiah Abrams[3]

Robotization of the Human Psyche

What has to happen is that human beings have to apply their creative and artistic sides. Those have to be the moving forces, not the mechanical side.

Eric Lloyd Wright[4]

165

Totalism, defined as "a monolithic unity upheld by authoritarian means," is a formidable characteristic of our collective dark side. In a totalitarian group, the belief system is designed to corroborate itself. Totalism is a *mechanizing* force not only in the collective, but in the individual psyche as well. It springs from a primitive instinctual fear of the other as having the potential to destroy us. This survival *mechanism,* while a necessary part of human nature, becomes self-destructive when expressed as part of a group dynamic.

The popular fascination with cyborgs and androids—part human and part machine beings—suggests the pervasiveness of totalistic influences in our society and culture. Our deities have moved into machines; technology has become a perfect home for a totalistic ideology. "Terminators," "replicants," and myriad *semireal* part machine beings become metaphors for the human soul infected by a totalistic ideology. Totalistic group ideologies that have been elevated above the individual are crucifying what James Hillman refers to as "soul-making."[5]

Our collective heroes have become part metal, part computer, invincible machines who use the latest hi-tech destructive machinery (weaponry). This creeping, group-perpetuated ideological totalism has convinced us that strength lies in brute force instead of in the heart. Anything mechanical from autos to guns (hand-held machines) captivates our imaginations, gripping our very souls. Even music has not escaped the mechanistic influences, with groups like Heavy Metal and Metallica. Totalism requires the "other" to conquer, dominate, or destroy. Collective enemy-making is inherent in a totalistic organization or nation-state. As converts to a totalistic theology, instead of God saving the day we look to the Rambos and Terminators who now carry the savior archetypes for our culture.

Throwing off the brute yoke of a totalistic ideology and returning to our humanness as individual human beings is the challenge now before us. But how can a mechanistic collective ideology be humanized? What will give back heart, meaning, and soul to a mechanical, dehumanized psyche? To find solutions, roads leading out of this common morass, we must first explore the inner workings of our collective machinery so that we become more *conscious* of exactly how destructive groups work, and how we unwittingly enable self-destructive ideologies to flourish in the human mind and in our collective institutions, religious groups, business enterprises, and political parties.

William Blake (1757–1827) maintained that hell was the repressed energy from having to live like machines. Blake's insight into the mechanization of the human spirit is profoundly more true today, where we live in a world of machines and technology that constantly intrudes upon the spirit—a world ever more demanding of our time and energy *if we allow it.*

As Data of "Star Trek: The Next Generation" would say in reply to the question, "Who are you?" "I am Data, and I am operating within established parameters." We, like Data, live our lives "within established parameters."

Technology is at once our greatest benefactor and also the greatest threat to life, producing a tremendous tension between cold science and humanity and between masculine and feminine. Science has a cold side that we can think of as masculine-oriented: rational, logical, and mechanical—a cause-and-effect, black-and-white view, in contrast to feminine attributes having to do with the relationship between things, feelings, spontaneity, and creativity. Both are necessary, not only for the individual psyche's health, but for our collective culture as well.

In many ways we are becoming androidlike—part of the collective machinery—controlled by a high-tech world that can beep, fax, phone, or bomb at a moment's notice almost anywhere on earth. Technology intrudes upon once solitary spaces: we listen to tapes or music while walking and now we talk on the phone and drive at the same time. Weaving all over the road used to be a sign of drunkenness, now we can't tell; someone may be on the phone.

Ideological totalism, a fundamental psychology of destructive groups, requires *strict obedience* from individuals, which in a collective context encourages individual *irresponsibility*. As adults, unquestioning obedience to any *outside* authority, whether a god or a philosophy, is an abdication of self-responsibility, an abandonment of one's real self. This abdication of self-responsibility is especially true for the increasingly fanatical religious movements of recent years.

In back of this mechanistic totalism is a black-and-white ideology that says things must be my way or no way, that "difference" creates our enemies. We fear those who are alien, foreign, or appear to act or think differently. They must somehow be converted to be like us. Conformity rules.

Both women and men have fallen victim to this collective mechanization, but men particularly are prey to this mass infection because of the social/cultural roles placed on males in most of the world. The male plays the macho, don't cry, show-no-feelings, lop-sided warrior-hero. Women who mistakenly believe that stepping into male roles in society is a step up, enact an even greater tragedy of self-destruction—a fatal compromise with a deadly patriarchal ideology. I am not saying that women ought to be excluded or ought to exclude themselves from traditional male domains, but that women ought to be alert to stepping into collective personas that perpetuate loss of soul and personal integrity. Rather, it is precisely the feminine that we need so badly—the mother, Sophia, wisdom, passion, and feeling—the soul—in both men and women.

Whoever or whatever has a solution for our life always requires obedience in order to implement the solution. If Jesus is going to save us, then we must be obedient to Jesus' precepts; this is *conditional salvation* and plays right into collective hands that dominate and control people. Indeed, in one's relationship to a destructive group, "surrender," "obedience," and "acceptance" become a relinquishment of individual accountability, when given over to any image, idea, doctrine, religion, or deity that is *authoritatively implanted into the individual psyche from an outside source.*

Psychologist Stanley Milgram tested how individuals react to authority and found that "over 90 percent would obey orders, even if they believed that doing so caused physical suffering to another person."[6] Milgram concluded, "The essence of obedience consists in the fact that a person comes to view himself as the instrument for carrying out another person's wishes, and therefore no longer regards himself as responsible for his own actions."[7] In a group context, the attitude of being an "instrument" or "vessel" is a trap; individuals are manipulated into thinking they are supporting a great savior figure, a company mission, a political cause, when in fact they are being used as slave labor for some collective agenda. History has amply shown that it is the individual's singular experience that influences and changes society in beneficial ways. While there has been mass civil disobedience like the Vietnam protest and China's Tienamen Square, they represent the combined sentiments of *individuals* who happen to share a common ground. Even in these mass movements, one individual often stands out while others become obedient followers. Organized protests can draw attention to abuse and injustice, but, as organized groups, they carry an ever-present destructive potential that is nearly impossible to stop.

In order to demechanize the individual psyche and, in turn, demechanize the collective, the human soul needs resurrecting. Bringing more soul (more humanity) into existence, bringing more consciousness, becomes each individual's challenge. Only in a state of inner and outer freedom from any form of monolithic authority can we achieve this return of soul.

Living and acting from one's individual reality is essential, as opposed to living under external group influences and authoritarian control. Caught in group belief systems, we sell our souls to leviathan, the inhuman beastlike machine that becomes our tyrannical deity, which in this case is not so much a specific group, but a soul-killing ideological motif within groups that permeates the mental fabric and psyche of civilization. In this sense we are all victims of collective trickle-down totalism. In the process of losing touch with soul-based relationships, we become dehumanized, unable to empathize with other human beings.

The burning question becomes: what have we as individuals repressed in order to live a totalistic, machinelike existence? Judging from our society, that repression has taken on monstrous forms of violence, abuse, and, in particular, an increasing lack of feeling (soul) for life. Life is no longer valued; instead *things*—machines, power, and the ability to destroy life— are valued. When things become more important than people, totalism reigns as our master.

Carl Jung, describing the effects of group dynamics on the individual, identified the destructive power and influence of the group mind:

> A group experience takes place on a lower level of consciousness than the experience of an individual. This is due to the fact that, when many people gather together to share one common emotion, the total psyche emerging from the group is below the level of the individual psyche. If it is a very large group, the collective psyche will be more like the psyche of an animal. It does work a change in you, but that change does not last.[8]

A general lowering of consciousness in destructive groups activates primitive, animal-like regressive instincts. We can begin to understand why individuals in a gang commit atrocities that they would never consider on their own. A "lynch mob" mentality is but one aspect of the group-mind dark side in action. And the mob need only be present in one's mind to effect barbaric changes in behavior. In the 1994 Florida murder trial of Michael Griffin, charged with killing abortion doctor David Gunn, Melinda Beck reported: "Griffin is now advancing the latest don't-blame-me defense: he claims that anti-abortion propaganda drove him to it. Shooting Gunn 'was the action of a good, decent human being [who] had been fed poison,' Griffin's lawyer, William Eddins, said in court."[9] Griffin's reasoning sounds a lot like "the Devil made me do it," which, paradoxically, is pretty accurate. The Devil in this case being the Christian group's extremist dark side. It's interesting how a religion that supposedly teaches people to "love one another" becomes so caught in its own shadow. Italian dramatist Luigi Pirandello (1867–1936) said, "There is somebody who's living my life. And I know nothing about him."[10] We can substitute "it" for Pirandello's "somebody," with the "it" being a group. This automation by group means enslavement of individuals, which ultimately means a dying society and culture.

Along with this organized mechanization of humanity, our mythologies have been concretized into either nuts-and-bolts historical facts or stories looked upon as foolish nonsense. Consequently, we have lost our stories—our metaphors for living life—our soul guides.

In *Experiences in Groups,* distinguished psychiatrist W. R. Bion synthesized the approaches of psychoanalysis and group dynamics. Bion describes what he calls a group's "basic assumption," roughly equivalent to a collective complex that "operates outside the domain of thought, and is formed by intense emotions of primitive origin within the individual. These primordial [archetypal] emotions kindle the innate readiness in humans . . . to seek containment in a group mentality."[11] For example, "The basic assumption of *dependency* involves the conviction of a fantasied 'perfect object' that could fulfill all the needs and desires of the group . . . an omnipotent group-fantasy about how to resolve certain emotional problems endemic to the human situation"[12] (emphasis added).

Salvation constitutes one of Christianity's basic assumptions, another version of the hero's journey adapted to a particular religious belief system. Enlightenment forms the basic assumption of many religious groups. Other groups' basic assumptions involve accumulating material wealth, economic or political power and control, perfect love, and eternal youth. Like Jung's projected unconscious contents, a "fantasied perfect object" becomes the elusive carrot that groups dangle before their eager disciples. Of course, a group's basic assumption must never actually be realized without collective collapse.

Once realized, the ever-present feeling of hope that sustains and energizes group members would evaporate, along with the group's cohesiveness and purpose, since, in Bion's words, "Only by remaining a hope does hope persist."[13] Hope of an ever-rising standard of living keeps our country fired with purpose and meaning. Even the suggestion that we've attained this or any other ideal leaves one with a certain sense of hopelessness, of nothing to look forward to; a certain vitality seeps out of our collective psyche. If the Christian Messiah were to show up next Saturday and fix everything, what then? In groups, it becomes essential to maintain hopeful expectations that are *never actually attained.* This requires creating a high degree of dissatisfaction with one's present circumstances, and, of course, destructive groups are adept at stirring up intense dissatisfaction. Dedicating one's life to some future event that never occurs demeans the present moment, making one uncreative, ineffectual, and useless. In 1640, John Milton (1608–1674), a bright young poet, spent twenty unproductive years writing pamphlets, deeply caught up in the Puritan Revolution. When the revolution died, he found himself disgraced. He then wrote *Paradise Lost.*

Robert Godwin, a psychoanalyst and a clinical psychologist, writing about the "law and order mentality," points out how our criminal justice system spends over "50 billion dollars per year to apprehend and jail the four million consensual criminals."[14] They have incarcerated over 350,000 people for "consensual crimes"—activities of adults that do not harm other people or property. Regarding the "war on drugs," Godwin observes: "At the bottom of this pointless and ineffectual drug war is the deep fantasy of an external agent seeping through our boundaries and poisoning us from within, and that if we can eliminate the agent, all will be well. Like so many basic assumptions, the drug war is designed not to solve a problem but to locate an enemy. Thus, it has been a stunning success, since it has created a tidal wave of criminality but done absolutely nothing to stem the flow of drugs into this country."[15]

EXTROVERTS, INTROVERTS, AND GROUPS

> The extrovert's philosophy of life and his ethics are as a rule of a highly collective nature with a strong streak of altruism, and his conscience is in large measure dependent on public opinion.
>
> Carl Jung[16]

Most of us express a mixture of extroverted and introverted characteristics, with one or the other predominating. In our Western society, extroverted persons are more socially acceptable and consequently collectively reinforced. Extroverted persons, relating externally to the world and to others, are particularly vulnerable to groups. The extrovert objectifies everyone and everything. According to Jung, extroversion means "a ready acceptance of external happenings, a desire to influence and be influenced by events, a need to join in and 'get with it,' the capacity to endure bustle and noise of every kind, and actually find them enjoyable, constant attention to the surrounding world, the cultivation of friends and acquaintances, none too carefully selected, and finally by the great importance attached to the figure one cuts."[17]

Thus extroversion powerfully orients one toward collective living. Extroverts trust outside experience instead of their own inner experience, which they rarely admit to or examine. As Jung pointed out, "He [the extrovert] lives in and through others; all self-communings give him the creeps. . . . If he should ever have a 'complex,' he finds refuge in the social whirl, and allows himself to be assured several times a day that everything is in order."[18]

Extroverts are perennial optimists, carefully guarding against anything that runs counter to a positive outlook. The individual unconscious remains just that, unconscious. Relying almost exclusively on outside data and influences, extroverts easily fall under the spell of collective forces whether expressed in a particular mass movement, a group, a crowd, or a mob.

Extroverted persons quickly adapt and change according to popular views. This means that being "normal" for the extrovert requires fitting into the established order—being something that one is not, assuming a collective persona. Were it not for the outwardly influenced, obediently complying extrovert, collective power structures would be in dire straits.

Extroverts do what groups expect; they conform to outside values and images in order to be acceptable to others. Introverts have all, at one time or another, envied the extrovert's considerable social skills and easy adjustment to social and cultural expectations. But when extroversion becomes too one-sided, one sacrifices living one's own life. Contrary to appearances, the extrovert lives a life of *real social cowardice.* This destructive form of self-sacrifice happens all too often, especially in groups. People give their lives to a popular "cause"—a business, a religion, a guru, a political movement, a spouse—while repressing their own unique expression and therefore losing the meaning and purpose of life. This flies in direct opposition to an inwardly-outwardly balanced individual where inner and outer worlds are allowed to collide, creating tension, fire, and illumination. Here, in a landscape of balanced forces, we discover the source of creative consciousness—the place where, often with great struggle, we bring something unique from the inner *into* the outer world.

Those who live authentic lives live from the inside out, relying first on their own hearts, enriching the collective in remarkable and unforeseen ways.

To restate a biblical saying, we must "lose our collective lives in order to find our authentic lives." In fact, most Scriptures contain stories about the necessity for individuals to escape the collective: the state, Herod's soldiers, Pharoah's army. Jung, explaining the vulnerability of extroversion, said, "He [the extrovert] gets sucked into objects and completely loses himself in them."[19]

Our dreadfully extroverted Western society collectively sucks up those individuals expressing this one-sided aspect of the human psyche. People readily join popular movements, give their lives to a corporate ideal, dedicate their existence to sports or to a religious mythology, vow to exterminate a different race or nationality.

Ironically, the self-sacrificing attitude of the extrovert creates the opposite shadow of profuse egotism and self-absorption. Extreme extroversion, like all extreme one-sided positions, results in a proportional unconscious opposite—a shadow that Jung described: "The more complete the conscious attitude of extroversion is, the more infantile and archaic the unconscious attitude will be. The egotism which characterizes the extrovert's unconscious attitude goes far beyond mere childish selfishness; it verges on the ruthless and brutal."[20]

As with all repressed material, the extrovert's repressed inner life results in a self-centered unconscious attitude that ultimately erupts into conscious life. Thus we see the apparently selfless "good" person who always thinks of others first, suddenly becoming cold, abusive, indifferent, and even dangerous.

Conscious Attitude	Unconscious Shadow
Eros, love	Will to power
Extroversion	Egotistical, self-centered, ruthless, morbid intensification of fantasy

In a group situation, extroverts often express constant needs to appear interesting and to impress others. To accomplish these ends, extroverts become highly suggestible, impressionable, and imitative of their surroundings. This exaggerated adaptability in groups adds to their victimization by collective forces.

In contrast to extroverts, introverts' psyche gravitates toward the inner world, relying more on their own beliefs and convictions as opposed to the ideas of others. Unlike the extrovert, for whom mass movements seem to be irresistible, introverts are likely to find themselves equally vulnerable to groups, but preferring solitary, secretive organizations and in particular groups that promote so-called solitary practices such as meditation. Introverts keep their group affiliation private and only close friends are aware of their involvement. Introverts are particularly vulnerable to spiritual groups, where the novitiate's mental processes are gradually taken over by the group's belief system and rituals. For introverts, group rituals become addictive, a way of escaping a difficult outer world. Jung explained that introverts are basically antisocial:

> In a large gathering, he feels lonely and lost. The more crowded it is, the greater becomes his resistance. He is not in the least "with it," and has no love of enthusiastic get-togethers. . . . Under normal conditions he is pessimistic and worried, because the world and human beings are not in the least good but crush him. . . . His own world is a safe harbor, a carefully tended and walled-in garden, closed to the public and hidden from prying eyes.[21]

Extreme introversion produces a curious opposite: "an *unconscious* reinforcement of the object's influence."[22] Hence introverts, supposedly depending on their own inner guidance, unwittingly empower others' influence over their lives. Additionally, they become paranoid about the opinions of others. Being loved deteriorates into pathetic yearnings, and lousy relationships become commonplace occurrences. In Jung's words, "It is now the unconscious that takes care of the relation to the object, and it does so in a way that is calculated to bring the illusion of power and the fantasy of superiority to utter ruin."[23] And, "It [the object] continually imposes itself on him against his will, it arouses in him the most disagreeable and intractable affects and persecutes him at every step. A tremendous inner struggle is needed all the time in order to 'keep going' . . . a malady characterized on the one hand by extreme sensitivity and on the other by great proneness to exhaustion and chronic fatigue."[24]

Accordingly, we readily see how introverts, caught in groups, suffer in the worst possible way, constantly struggling to live life from an inner orientation while a group's dogma constantly overpowers their own innate sense of right and wrong. The introvert in a collective organization feels perpetually compromised and devoid of integrity. Ultimately this leads to a sense of utter futility, deep frustration, and suicidal feelings.

Healthy introversion finds its expression in persons who value solitude, who find their creativity in singular activities, and who rely on and trust their own inspiration and judgment. They are self-reliant without ego-inflation, preferring the company of their close friends in a familiar environment. "His retreat into himself is not a final renunciation of the world, but a search for quietude, where alone it is possible for him to make his contribution to the life of the community."[25]

Mind Control and Thought Reform in Groups

How do you find a lion that has swallowed you?

Carl Jung[26]

I am your brain.

Rev. Sun Myung Moon, Unification church[27]

Steven Hassan, a psychologist who spent several years in the Unification church (headed by Sun Myung Moon), describes mind control as "systems that seek to undermine an individual's integrity in making his own decisions. . . . [I]t [mind control] encourages dependence and conformity, and discourages autonomy and individuality."[28] Certain types of twelve-step groups, recovery groups, and scientific research such as biofeedback actually use mind-control techniques to help persons recover from serious addictions or illnesses. Although mind control has some potentially positive uses, its damaging aspects are so destructive that one must carefully question such methods, especially techniques that eliminate or break down a person's old persona, which may then leave the individual with a new identity (existential) crisis.

Robert Lifton's extensive research into the dynamics of group mind control provides a basic framework for looking at groups from a depth psychology perspective. He identifies eight primary themes common to thought reform: "milieu control, mystical manipulation, the demand for purity, the cult of confession, sacred science, loading the language, doctrine over person, and the dispensing of existence."[29] Lifton calls these eight aspects of thought reform "Ideological Totalism,"[30] which he describes as "an extremist meeting ground between people and ideas." In his landmark book *Thought Reform and the Psychology of Totalism,* he explains:

> Some potential for this form of all-or-nothing emotional alignment exists within everyone. Similarly, any ideology—that is, any set of emotionally charged convictions about man and his relationship to the natural or supernatural world—may be carried by its adherents in a totalistic direction. . . . And where totalism exists, a religion, a political movement, or even a scientific organization becomes little more than an exclusive cult.[31]

How do we find the beast that has swallowed us? Logically, people who are under mind control do not consciously realize that they are. But they can and do suffer from a myriad of physical, emotional, and psychological consequences that may be rationalized away as some personal fault or weakness, or a test of their faith, loyalty, dedication, and endurance. A group-implanted "truth" or "conscience" complicates this dynamic as David Norton, author of *Personal Destinies: A Philosophy of Ethical Individualism,* observed, "Conscience means a voice within the individual that belongs to an authority outside him."[32]

From my own experience in a religious cult, I found that breaking free of a group using mind-control techniques often requires some sort of psychological or emotional shock to snap one out of the mass hypnosis. In some cases, one eventually gets overloaded with contradictions and cannot push anything else into an already overflowing unconscious. Or, in other cases, members' projections begin to rattle and the tension between their sense of reality and the group's artificial reality becomes unbearable. This rattling of projected idealism often begins when the recipients of our projections fail to live up to our expectations; one's priest is found sexually molesting children, or a media hero is exposed as being less than perfect.

A "complex" is defined, in the Jungian perspective, as "an emotionally charged group of ideas or images . . . that over the years accumulate around certain archetypes, for instance *mother* and *father*"[33] (emphasis added). Saturated with compelling, culturally implanted ideas and images surrounding a particular deity, idea, idealism, or concept, we become vulnerable to any group that appears to embody this complex of ideas and images. Joining such a group gives our complexes an outer-world home, a resting place. We actually feel that we have come home, been *reborn,* and there is generally a great relief and satisfaction, even euphoria. In fact, one's complex has taken over. It now possesses us. Succumbing to a complex relieves the immediate tension, but stops cold any further spiritual development. We find ourselves imprisoned in the complex, living life through the complex; and groups perpetuate and empower group-sustaining complexes, maintaining a state of collective psychosis.

For example, a complex of ideas might cluster around making money, which makes persons easy prey for any get-rich-quick scheme or for any education, degree, career, or investment that promises greater wealth. Money takes on a mystical quality, and anything to do with money becomes an all-consuming passion. I remember, as a young ambitious entrepreneur, every so often withdrawing large amounts of cash from my savings account, taking it home and stacking it up on the floor so I could look at it. The bigger the pile, the safer and more secure I felt. Money was better than any god. I could control it, accumulate it, make it—or so it seemed at the time. As a young man, I choose a career that would make a lot of money, and it was not a profession that really interested me. Actually I was stuck—possessed by my complex. To this day, I struggle with my money complex. I feel more secure when I have it and I get anxious when I don't have enough of it, or when my wife spends it.

We want that M.B.A., not so much to further our knowledge, but to get a prestigious position, power, and money—all of which, in turn, perpetuate the system, its images and ideals. In this manner, we once again willingly participate in the sacrifice of our individuality. And in our willing participation, we become the genetic material used by groups to clone obedient servants for their collective ideologies.

Another complex may center around a father image, which makes one particularly vulnerable to religious groups, as Jung explained: "In men, a positive father-complex very often produces a certain credulity with regard to authority and a distinct willingness to bow down before all spiritual dogmas and values; while in women, it induces the liveliest spiritual aspirations and interests."[34]

Our culture places so much value on money, not having any is like being excommunicated. In a market-oriented society, being without money equates to being the ultimate failure. Homelessness and welfare, the market system's version of hell, have become the modern-day equivalents of leprosy. And we, as a society, place these system dropouts in special places: at best, in ghettos and housing projects, at worst, on the streets—hopefully out of our sight and far away from our neighborhood. The system's "invisible hand" penalizes "good citizens" for living too close to social outcasts; it lowers their property's market value.

The market system is adept at attaching a price tag to every aspect of life, so much so that it is increasingly difficult to exist without ample cash. Our institutionalized educational system trains children for collective roles that will perpetuate this system. The bottom line is that groups—political, religious, and economic—dictate our collective roles from the womb to the grave. Thus totalism reigns supreme in the collective psyche where the dominant groups control, direct, and manipulate individuals.

Alcoholics Anonymous is an *either/or* group; if you're not *in* AA, you are *labeled,* you're an outsider, "white-knuckling it." Labeling persons who do not follow "our" group's way of doing things illustrates one way peer pressure persuades and affects even those who do not belong to a particular group. Hence we feel guilty for expressing self-responsibility, for simply choosing self-rehabilitation. In this manner we are each affected by peer pressure even when we do not belong or subscribe to a group doctrine or system. One of the most obvious examples is our market system, which exerts vast economic control over billions of persons, many of whom do not subscribe to its principles. Labeling individuals as "atheists" simply because they do not belong to a culturally sanctioned religious group provides another example of outside peer pressure. This is merely another way of demonizing outsiders, whether they be non-Catholics, noncapitalists, or just unique, having views that don't fit neatly into some collective container. Therapists label individuals as being "in denial" when they do not fit the popular therapeutic agendas.

Placing people into categories with antisocial connotations pressures us to conform to collective standards and morals. In this manner, groups destroy individual distinctiveness and originality, which are always in opposition to the status quo. Language becomes the collective weapon of choice. By naming the enemy, we infer they are guilty, judged and sentenced without a trial.

False assumptions about people result from labeling: So and so could not have done such a thing because he or she is a "Christian"; "heterosexual" implies one is "normal" or "straight"; "gay," "fag," and "queer" infer badness; for there to be a "Moral Majority" there must be an immoral minority. Labeling objectifies a group's own shadow, and placing the locus of evil in those outside the group or culture ennobles brute savagery and extinguishes human-heartedness—the group or community becomes a marauding beast.

How Groups Control Inner and Outer Communication

The disciple is unworthy; modestly he sits at the Master's feet and guards against having ideas of his own. Mental laziness becomes a virtue; one can at least bask in the sun of a semi-divine being. He can enjoy the archaism and infantilism of his unconscious fantasies without loss to himself, for all responsibility is laid at the Master's door.

Carl Jung[35]

Influence and control of an individual's *inner* communication and private inner thought processes are insidious aspects of mind control. Lifton explains that this inner control of one's thought processes creates a "disruption of balance between self and the outside world. . . . [T]he individual encounters a profound threat to his personal autonomy."[36] Individual autonomy and a healthy sense of self require input *outside of one's group* and the ability to subject this input to *independent logic and reflection.* James Hillman argues, and experience confirms, "What is unreflected tends to become compulsive, or greedy."[37] In a totalistic collective environment, individual thinking and reflection are seen as a threat to the group doctrine. Consequently, people are taught to suspect their own thinking processes as potential dangers to the system.

Ideological totalism, to survive, must reinforce a *black-and-white* thinking mode—an "either/or," "we/they" dualism. And this dualistic mind-set applies not only to one's inner thought processes, but also to the outside world. Accordingly, thoughts that are critical of a group's ideology are considered to be—in religious groups, for example—inspired by the devil. Those not in the group are looked on as either potential converts or as evil-controlled, contesting the organization's ideology.

Even our intuition easily becomes collectivized. Our thinking process becomes so saturated with collective images and ideas that what appears to be individual spontaneity and intuition are just conditioned, programmed responses. Many religious groups, desirous of expanding their influence, are gaining extensive control of public print and broadcast media.

Any subject one is afraid to talk about indicates entrapment in a group or belief system. When one identifies with a particular belief system, open discussion involving opposing views is either impossible or extremely uncomfortable.

For fundamentalist-oriented Christianity, martyrdom and persecution are seen as proof of their calling—a view that reinforces polarization and projection of good and evil, pure and impure onto outsiders. In this manner, collective systems structured around a totalistic ideology rationalize techniques of mind control and indoctrination as *necessary to protect* some ultimate truth or just cause that has taken possession of the group, which then becomes the rationale for their continued existence. In this group-preservation process, individual thinking, creativity, and potential is sacrificed to preserve a collective "truth," which is usually a complex of archetypal ideas, images, and mythology that has gained absolute control over the masses.

Mystical Control: Calculated Spontaneity

The world wants to be deceived.

Sebastian Brant[38]

A powerful attraction in many religious groups is the idea of being "chosen," called as a special select group to save humanity from their sins. Of course, being chosen is a tremendous ego trip. People feel superior to others and become extremely judgmental of anyone who, according to their group's exclusive wisdom, remains unenlightened.

Mystical manipulation is further enhanced when a particular person is supposedly "chosen" by God. This "chosen" individual is then looked on as a savior figure, an "anointed" preacher, a guru, a mediator for God, or an illumined teacher. Once we *accept* a "chosen" leader's special status, we are sunk—trapped in the viselike grip of *someone else's interpretation* of a particular religious doctrine. Whatever doctrine is being promulgated is automatically accepted without question because of the supposed divine source. Anything our chosen guide does, good or evil, must be okay because he or she is "God directed." According to Lifton, "mystical manipulation" in groups is characterized this way:

> Included in this mystique is a sense of a "higher purpose," of having "directly perceived some immanent law of social development," and of being themselves the vanguard of this development. By thus becoming the instruments of their own mystique, they create a mystical aura around the manipulating institutions—the Party, the Government, the Organization. They are the agents "chosen" (by history, by God, or by some other supernatural force) to carry out the "mystical imperative."[39]

Lifton goes on to explain that individuals react to this manipulation by a process of "adaptation" to collective forces as a defense against the deeply painful movement against and away from one's own reality. He calls this the "psychology of the pawn."[40] Basically individuals are conditioned, in a Pavlovian sense, to play a collective game of rewards and punishments—to go with the societal flow—to merge with the crowd, which is at the same time a profound betrayal of one's own reality and autonomy. One survives at the expense of losing one's soul. The "pawn" is rewarded by the *illusion* of acceptance and love from the group. One is a "good" citizen, according to the popular definition of what "good" is. We are good *provided* we follow group dictates and ideology.

Rationalizing Evil

When one has once given Evil a lodging, it no longer demands that one believes it.

Franz Kafka[41]

The numinous quality of a group and its leadership is a seductive influence that results in individuals becoming adept at rationalizing anything the group does, no matter how cruel or unethical it may actually be, and no matter how abhorrent it may be to one's individual conscience. Learned *rationalizing into-the-collective* is an insidious process that kills individual critical thinking. Anything a group does is *accepted and defended* because it is for "the big picture," "the company mission," "a higher purpose," "saving souls," or "for Jesus." Thus propaganda, manipulation, lying, violence, and even murder become defenses of a just cause. War comes from people who are polarized inwardly and outwardly into good and evil camps—people who are unconscious of their inner evil camp. Sam Keen, in *Faces of the Enemy,* calls warfare "applied theology," explaining that outside enemies make groups feel solidarity and purpose. Keen concludes, "We create surplus evil because we need to belong."[42]

Greed becomes "God's blessing of prosperity for the group's leaders," or necessary compensation for the Godlike person who founded the firm. Human slavery translates into "giving oneself to a higher purpose—to something bigger than the individual." "Something bigger" in any type of group-embodied ideal or cause is ultimately destructive for individuals and consequently for society as well.

Leon Festinger, a social psychologist, theorized that "cognitive dissonance"[43] provides an explanation of how persons rationalize different types of behavior. According to Festinger, cognitive dissonance occurs when a person is caught by two conflicting ideas, and tries to hold both as true. For example, a group I belong to tells me that Jesus is the *only way* to God. But, I happen to read the life of Krishna, Buddha, or Lao Tzu, and realize that they also seem to be quite Godlike. This contradiction creates tension (dissonance). Becoming terribly uncomfortable, and to eliminate the tension, I change one of my cognitions so that everything fits together in a manner that does not threaten my group's viewpoint.

For example, in the religious group I belonged to, we explained this problem of multiple world saviors by assigning a totalistic hierarchy, a spiritual rank to each individual. Jesus was number one—a four-star general; Buddha was close, but ranked as number two in the spiritual pecking order. Other mystics and saints of various religions were well thought of, but were in differing states of evolvement. Of course, the most spiritually advanced souls were those who most closely emulated the life of Jesus. Many New Age groups obliterate this dichotomy by claiming that former world saviors were actually past incarnations of the same evolving savior.

In the end, such rationalizing simply stops legitimate inquiry dead in its tracks. We miss exploring the inevitable mystery of existence, grouping different approaches to life into one amorphous mass of collective non-thought. Anthony Pratkanis, in his book *Age of Propaganda,* wrote, "In these circumstances [cognitive dissonance], individuals will go to great lengths of distortion, denial, and self-persuasion in order to justify their past behavior. When our self-esteem has been threatened by our own past behavior, we all have a powerful tendency to become rationalizing animals."[44] Tragedy strikes us all when this rationalizing involves cruelty and violence to others, either psychological or physical. Destructive groups depend heavily upon rationalizing-out-of-existence all conflicting ideologies and viewpoints. Right to Life groups, who justify violence and the murder of doctors who perform abortions, are excellent examples of the destructive side of rationalizing. Murder, paradoxically becomes the "Christian" thing to do, when, in fact, Christianity teaches "thou shalt not kill."

Totalistically organized groups always assume they have the right to control individual freedom of choice and autonomy. The Inquisition made the same assumptions that many religious and political groups make in modern times.

Fanatical Separation of Pure and Impure

Violent men reel from one extremity to another.

Thomas Fuller[45]

With what pleasure we read newspaper reports of crime! A true criminal becomes a popular figure because he unburdens in no small degree the consciences of his fellow men, for now they know once more where evil is to be found.

Carl Jung[46]

One-sidedness is a foremost characteristic of neurosis. In fact, Jung explained that: "Neurosis is self-division. . . . [T]he conscious mind wants to hang on to its moral ideal, while the unconscious strives after its . . . unmoral ideal which the conscious mind tries to deny."[47] Groups encourage a one-sided aspect of consciousness, resulting in a build-up of surplus tension. To survive in a group, we must repress one side in favor of the other, splitting the psyche, forcing the soul into a pathologizing role. Ideological totalism, whether in a group or in an individual, is a dualistic system dividing everything and everybody into two parts, as Lifton explains, "[into] the pure and the impure, into the absolutely good and the absolutely evil. . . . All 'taints' and 'poisons' which contribute to the existing state of impurity must be searched out and eliminated."[48] Shades of gray are too complicated and take thought, which is the last thing groups want their members to do. Groups also don't like shades of gray because it becomes much more difficult to set limits and control members.

The increasing occurrence of eating disorders like bulimia and anorexia indicate how powerful opposites are when reinforced by a collective culture that is itself split. In the binge-purge process of bulimia, the opposites of complete control and total lack of control are estranged from each other. The part trying to be perfect holds the opposite prisoner, the "prisoner self" becomes filled with out-of-control intense energy. Hence, our widespread eating disorders are another example of social diseases—conditions caused more by collective influences than by individuals.

Destructive groups redefine individual morality and ethics to be anything that conforms to their belief system; all conflicting opposing ideas and behavior become—through the totalistic view—immoral, unethical, or illegal. Difference is outlawed, diversity is perceived as threatening. The social system establishes its own rules that become moral imperatives forcing individuals to conform, be cast out, or be ostracized. In spiritual groups, people "confess their sins," which consist of whatever the belief system determines to be impure and immoral. Or one repeats certain prayers and mantras to erase one's "bad karma." Bad karma becomes anything or anybody not supportive of and conforming to the group's dogma.

Theological totalism, the group-implanted mind-set of separating the pure from the impure, "us" from "them," is a root cause of fanaticism, perversion, violence, and war on every level of society from nation-states to street gangs. Political groups, and special interest groups war with one another, using their power and influence to eliminate opposing views. *Difference* becomes a threat—an impurity in the social order. Other political, cultural, and social systems that are labeled as "primitive," "heathen," "Godless," "not as spiritually evolved," or having a "lower standard of living" are eliminated through *assimilation* into our group, which is a form of ideological imperialism. Others (those outside our collective ideology) are made to conform to our system under the guise of altruism. Describing collective paranoia, Sam Keen wrote:

> The process begins with a splitting of the "good" self, with which we consciously identify and which is celebrated by myth and media, from the "bad" self, which remains unconscious so long as it may be projected

onto an enemy. Paranoia reduces anxiety and guilt by transferring to the other all the characteristics one does not want to recognize in oneself.[49]

Underdeveloped countries—countries that by definition do not "measure up" to our standards—are "helped" to improve themselves, which from the totalistic perspective means that they are taught how to conform to a collective political, religious, or economic doctrine. In a similar manner, many fundamentalist Christian groups eliminate impure ideas by converting persons to the Christian ideology, which is simply inquisition-based theology masquerading as missionary zeal.

Meanwhile, our humanity burns at the stake of twentieth-century totalistic philosophies. The *missionary consciousness* is alive and well throughout the world. In effect, the missionary consciousness says that all other gods are devils and that *my* god is the god all must embrace. The penalty is eternal damnation, life in hell. If this sounds like prejudice, bigotry, racism, egotism, and judging others—it is.

Similarly, business enterprises (operating under a totalistic structure) eliminate evil (competition) by accumulating monopolistic (or political) power and control within a particular industry, thus imposing not only their products, but also their economic ideology upon others and stifling *difference*. Economic purity means that others must conform to our particular economic system. In a truly "free" economy, *difference* provides individuals with increasing choices over a broad range of price and quality.

Additionally, Lifton explains how a "demand for purity" creates guilt and shame:

> At the level of the relationship between individual and environment, the demand for purity creates what we may term a *guilty milieu* and a *shaming milieu*. Since each man's impurities are deemed sinful and potentially harmful to himself and to others, he is, so to speak, expected to expect punishment—which results in a relationship of guilt with his environment. Similarly, when he fails to meet the prevailing standards in casting out such impurities, he is expected to expect humiliation and ostracism—thus establishing a relationship of shame with his milieu.[50]

This shame-based relationship with one's environment also applies to one's thought processes. In religious groups, and in many "pop psychology" groups, one becomes guilty for thinking a "negative thought," for a "lustful image," for having a selfish idea or desire; these must be confessed, or they must be blocked, by repeating a prayer or mantra, which has the effect of preventing the individual from thinking—hypnotically lulling one back into a collective mind-set.

Prayers and mantras, when directed toward authoritarian inner control of psychic processes, become techniques of self-hypnosis instead of spiritual exercises. One then must ask, "Whose god and what ideology does this particular mantra or prayer implant in my mind?" Avoiding this dilemma suggests that one choose spiritual techniques that are not preformatted or doctrinally specific. We ought to be as concerned about what we put into our psyches as we are about what goes into our stomach. Unpolluted (doctrine-free) spiritual practices help keep us on our own pathways.

Separating the pure from the impure, an aspect of ideological totalism thoroughly inbred in the Christian myth, prevents one from any semblance of soul-making, which requires *imaginative* depth—a movement into oneself, *holding both pure and impure, light and shadow*—a working through of images and thought processes as opposed to killing a demonized (doctrinally impure) imagination.

Even though this splitting process is highly internalized in the individual, one begins to rationalize interior impure thoughts or images as emanating from evil outside sources. Because of this splitting, inner and outer satanic forces assault the Christian; devilishly unscrupulous competitors attack the company; those extremists attack a just and righteous political group.

A monocratic state where we are *all the same* and all others are automatically wrong or evil ultimately results from a dividing collective mindset that says, "You are either with me or against me." Such ideological separateness promotes mass projections of evil, hatred, and prejudice onto others. Religious groups wage "holy wars," nation-states eliminate "evil empires." Economic groups and special interest groups incite "trade wars" using propaganda as psychological warfare to promote profits, exclusiveness, and isolation. Slogans and catch-words such as "Buy American" become our collective mantras preventing any original thought or idea, and insuring a *mindless* totalistic conformity to collective agendas. If we don't "buy American," we "should" feel guilty and disloyal to our national group. Totalistic psychology is filled with "shoulds."

Depth psychology has shown that the "shadow" in human nature is responsible for the unconscious tendency to see in the other person or group those traits we most abhor, the repressed aspects of our own nature. And this shadow increases as a response to one's one-sided adherence to the "light," which may be a religious viewpoint, a cure-all health product, a particular psychotherapy, a twelve-step program, a political party, environmentalism, or a self-improvement movement. Caught in this shadow dynamic, we are absolutely convinced that the "other" is the cause of our difficulties—the enemy who must be eliminated, the spouse who must be divorced, the gang member who must be "smoked."

The shadow side becomes dangerous only when unacknowledged, and according to Carl Jung, contains hidden treasure—revitalizing qualities that are needed by the conscious personality. Unconscious, unacknowledged and ever-more dangerous, the collective shadow becomes a Jekyll-and-Hyde drama, where demonic Mr. Hydes are lurking in our inner cities, full of brutish energy, with no conscience (no consciousness), preying on their victims.

Control Through Confession

The common excuse of those who bring misfortune on others is that they desire their good.

Vauvenargues[51]

Confession, in a destructive group milieu, implies forgiveness, which means the core authority in an organization becomes the judge and jury over one's existence. This existential control gives groups limitless power and control over individuals who *surrender* themselves to popular deities, whether persons, ideas, or images. And, as Lifton explains, "The individual . . . tends to imbue certain aspects of himself with excessive virtue, and condemn even more excessively other personal qualities—all according to their ideological standing. In totalistic hands, confession becomes a means of exploiting, rather than offering solace for, these vulnerabilities."[52]

Thus the human propensity for confession, the innate need to expiate one's perceived wrongdoing, becomes an ideological hook. Along with confession, there is the notion of a purging of evil, an emptying out of one's burdens. However, destructive groups pervert this innate human need for unburdening. The act of confession implies guilt and shame, which groups use to further polarize the psyche into extremes: one centered around feelings of self-reproach and self-hatred, and the other caught into feelings of superiority and self-righteousness. Collective appropriation of the individual's confession dynamic places a significant chunk of one's mental and emotional functioning in the hands of collective authority.

Regarding confession, Albert Camus wrote, "[I] . . . practice the profession of penitent to be able to end up as a judge . . . the more I accuse myself, the more I have a right to judge you."[53] This "right to judge" is particularly evident in religious groups, especially where confession is practiced frequently and in public. A "right to judge" attitude means a group is constantly seeking to expose individual errors and sins. And the entire religious notion of "original sin" presupposes some eternal guilt and shame, which such dualistic and judgmental organizations are ever ready to capitalize upon, thus gaining a position of implied superiority and control over the individual.

The Quicksand of Knowing

Only the shallow know themselves.

Oscar Wilde[54]

An explanation for everything translates as "Don't think for yourself." When one clings to material objective factual information transmitted by the senses, the resultant projection gives a mystical, emotional resonance to mere facts. What Lifton calls "sacred science"[55] has a lot to do with language, and putting a doctrinal, numinous spin on a word or concept. Sacred science means that a group's ideas become absolutes, fixed, immovable, "universal," "ultimate truths," which, of course, cannot be questioned. Such collective images and concepts become objects of worship. The Jungian perspective would call this worship of absolutes a form of possession by one side of an archetype—an example of being caught by one side of a pair of opposites. In this sense, a person can be trapped in the "wise old man (or woman)" archetype and surrender to a group or group leader who appears to embody this image. Consequently people give their lives to Jesus, or Divine Mother, or a company president.

Many popular spiritual groups try to blend science, philosophy, and religion into an eclectic ideology that attempts to make rational science a confirming participant in a religion of precise absolutes. Lifton clarifies how this inclusion of the scientific realm actually works to intimidate and suppress critical thinking:

> Thus the ultimate moral vision becomes an ultimate science; and the man who dares to criticize it, or to harbor even unspoken alternative ideas, becomes not only immoral and irreverent, but also "unscientific." . . . The assumption here is . . . that an absolute science of ideas (and implicitly, an absolute science of man) exists, or is at least very close to being attained; that this science can be combined with an equally absolute body of moral principles; and that the resulting doctrine is true for all men at all times.[56]

In spite of the enlistment of a confirming science, the group ideology maintains a position of supremacy over the scientific establishment by acknowledgments such as, "They're (the scientific community) just now discovering what we knew all along," or "Our insight and special wisdom explains this phenomenon, which scientists are just now trying to figure out." Additionally, Lifton argues, "Since the distinction between the logical and the mystical is, to begin with, artificial and man-made, an opportunity for transcending it can create an extremely intense feeling of truth."[57]

When "sacred science" becomes part of a group's dogma, even more pressure is exerted on individuals to not admit any contradicting ideas into their minds. The system demands that we maintain *unquestioning faith,* which is antiself and totally destructive to individual autonomy. In essence, one cannot allow oneself to think or to reason except within the precisely defined boundaries of the group's belief system. Guilt and fear result from the slightest whisper of a critical thought or idea. Of course, censoring one's own thoughts according to a group ideology is the ultimate compromise, and in this state of *no-mind,* a state of *collectively induced emptiness,* one has no relationship to soul, no empathy, and *zero* integrity.

7

Going Backward:
Developmental Regression
in Groups

Westerners bring so much baggage into the ashram. The spiritual search coexists with the inner child's search for belonging.

Jean Callahan[1]

And the word "courage" should be reserved to characterize the man or woman who leaves the infantile sanctuary of the mass mind.

Sam Keen[2]

Groups behave at a much lower emotional level than do individuals so that group behavior is less psychologically mature. Thus, in group situations, affect emerges as an expression of group-induced regression.

Jerrold Atlas and Laura Porzio[3]

Survival Mode

The situation [in groups] is not unlike that observed in children and undifferentiated adults where the lack of a distinct individuality leaves the mind without guards against the intrusion of influences from without.

Eric Hoffer[4]

Adult developmental regression in groups, a state of self-helplessness, results from the individual's attempt to survive and adapt to the group ideology. An outside authority keeps one in a dependent state, whether the FDA, a religious leader, a politician, some deity, or an advertising campaign. Joseph Campbell described this dependent state:

189

Now if there's a way or a path, it's someone else's way; and the guru has a path for you. He knows where you are on it. He knows where he is on it, namely, way ahead. And all you can do is get to be as great as he is. This is a continuation of the dependency of childhood; maturity consists in outgrowing that and *becoming your own authority* [emphasis added] in life.[5]

In destructive groups, leaders become abusive parental figures while the members become ever more dependent and incapable of independent decision-making. The propensity toward developmental regression within such groups is so powerful that most people find it nearly impossible to not modify their behavior in some fashion in order to be accepted by the group's leader(s) and by their peers.

A child wants to be bliss-filled, taken care of, and unconditionally loved. A needy inner child, when unacknowledged, forms an unconscious complex producing an outer longing for a nurturing, mothering, blissful environment. When this needy child gets in control of our life, we find ourselves being parented, mothered, fathered, loved, and *controlled* in a dysfunctional one-sided relationship or in some group that appears to fill these needs.

The dark side of groups initiates a process of developmental regression, which takes place on two primary levels: cognitive and emotional. Emotionally, one is drawn into a supportive group of friends and associates who become a replacement family. A social codependence quickly develops that is extremely difficult to walk away from. Cognitively, the group dynamic slowly changes one's thinking and thought processes with the subsequent behavioral changes. As the group message, agenda, belief system, and rules gradually take over, all outside and inner events are interpreted through the group mind-set. One's viewpoint becomes a collective viewpoint. One alters reality to suit newly acquired concepts and ideology. Anything that challenges that new reality is rationalized away, suppressed, or transformed into an enemy of the group's purpose. The actual reversal of the individual's normal growth and development is a distinctive feature of destructive groups.

The Cult Awareness Network's extensive research has shown that destructive groups cause these specific harmful effects in adults:

1. Development of dependency and return to childlike behavior.
2. Loss of free will and control over one's life.
3. Loss of spontaneity or sense of humor.
4. Psychological deterioration (including hallucinations, anxiety, paranoia, disorientation, and dissociation).
5. Inability to form intimate friendships outside the group or enjoy flexible relationships.

6. Physical deterioration and abuse.
7. Involuntary, de facto servitude or exploitation.[6]

In addition, according to the Cult Awareness Network, destructive groups generally have some or all of these characteristics:

1. *Mind control(undue influence)*: The group manipulates by the use of coercive persuasion or behavior modification techniques without the informed consent of the individual.
2. *Charismatic leadership*: A leader or small core of leaders with power and special privileges demand unquestioning obedience.
3. *Alienation*: The group encourages and sometimes enforces separation from family, friends, and society, a change in values and substitution of the group as the new family—there is evidence of subtle or abrupt personality changes as members conform to the group's social and belief system.
4. A *totalitarian worldview*: The group has a *we/they* outlook: reinforcing dependence, promoting goals of the group *over the individual* and approving unethical behavior while claiming moral superiority, goodness, righteousness, or enlightenment.
5. *Exploitation*: This can be financial, physical, and psychological—pressure to give money, work long hours, to buy courses, to give excessive time to special projects, and in some cases, to engage in inappropriate sexual activities.[7]

Peer pressure in such a group is a formidable psychological weapon. When one first enters the group, one is commonly fawned over and made to feel very special and loved—a process often referred to as "love bombing." This threshold experience of being accepted and loved feeds a deep, instinctual, childlike longing in human nature. Most persons want to belong, feel accepted, be needed, and be loved by others. However, this apparent acceptance and love from a group is *conditional*, which the new member quickly learns. In order to continue to receive this familial-style nourishment, new members must conform to and accept the group ideology. In fact, one soon discovers that increasing dedication to the group's belief system results in proportionate increases of loving acceptance from the group.

The group takes on a monolithic, parental, authoritarian role while the individual must play a childlike role in order to survive. As a reward, people receive love, acceptance, the *illusion* of belonging to something special, and the illusion of being special because of *identification with the group's mission or cause*. Hence one no longer functions as an adult but regresses to an infantile state of survival-adaptation.

Recent studies have found an increasing incidence of *dwarfism* among the estimated 300,000 Amish living in the United States because of inbreeding.[8] We are just beginning to realize the potential damage, both psychological and physical, for persons living within a restrictive group ideology. Inhibiting one's life experience to one particular cultural view is cultural and psychological incest—a breeding ground for a *devolving* species. Destructive groups tend to isolate members from the outside world. Isolation makes it difficult to verify the reality and accurateness of information dispensed by the group. This isolation is often subtle and usually goes unnoticed by the individual members. Because of constant meetings, activities, and group projects, members commonly have little free time for outside activities such as visiting family and socializing with friends. Lack of sufficient rest and sensory overload contribute to the inability of the individual to have time to *think* about the validity of information being received.

Some groups discourage close family ties because anyone not in the group is perceived as a threat to their collective mission. Any activities or influences from the group's leadership or other members that tend to discourage free participation and socialization with persons outside the group is a destructive and regressive characteristic. A mature adult does not tell another adult whom they may or may not socialize with. Indeed, separating and isolating group influences reinforce a parent-child relationship and thus add to the regressive push on the individual psyche. In religious groups, spiritual disciplines often become a reprogramming process— mental pacifiers to bring a doubting member back down to a group mind level of consciousness. Thus group spiritual practices become thought-blocking, mind-altering techniques that promote a regressive deterioration of rational intellectual and social functioning.

Childlike roles are further reinforced by encouraging some form of public confession. A group's need to perpetuate itself by instilling feelings of guilt and fear in individual members requires confession, or some form of public testimonial where people admit their shortcomings. Thus, confession, a valid human need, becomes an entrapment technique. Public confessions create an atmosphere of emotional vulnerability where one is subject to punishment from one's peers or the group leader(s). Of course, confession in a group also reinforces a powerful parent-child relationship; and once one enters into this dynamic, absolute control is automatically given over to the group and the group hierarchy. Plus, through confession in a group context, one activates the punishment-reward syndrome which is a basic behavior modification method used by parents in disciplining their children.

Confession-induced fear and guilt are based on adhering to collective rules and formats that reinforce a collective reality one can belong to only by playing the collective game—a deadly game. Individuals are caught in a double bind: in seeking love and a sense of belonging, they lose their own uniqueness, regressing back to childhood. One's group becomes, in essence, a large dysfunctional replacement family.

Trapping the Inner Child

The training for addiction is abuse.

John Bradshaw[9]

Renowned poet, editor, and translator Robert Bly wrote: "In child abuse the rule is: every act of cruelty, conscious or unconscious, that our parents take, we interpret as an act of love. So the moral intelligence redefines gross human behavior as an act of love."[10]

Once a group has an individual firmly in the child's role, the group leaders have unrestricted power to do whatever they want. And whatever they do is rationalized by the child in the adult as something *for their own good*—love in disguise. This regressive childlike position in a group makes one again developmentally vulnerable in the same way small children are vulnerable to their real parents.

John Bradshaw, in his Inner Child workshops, points out that, as an adult, our inner child is a powerful, often hidden, factor in life. In a sense, we can picture one aspect of our inner child as a vulnerable, innocent, and trusting part of the psyche. Healthy rules learned in early childhood can rescue one from group-think and simultaneously expose the vulnerabilities that destructive groups exploit. Bradshaw's childhood rules include:

- Trust what you see and hear;
- It's okay to think what you think;
- You have a right to feel and express your feelings;
- It's okay to want what you want; and
- It's okay to play and have fun.[11]

As children, we naturally trust parental authority figures who we depend upon for our survival. As adults, the mystique of a group under authoritarian leadership easily traps one's inner trusting child. When a charismatic leader appears to be sincere, the naive inner child quickly succumbs to the group's structure and ideology. Naiveté in an adult might be endearing at times, but it can also be dangerous if unchecked by critical thinking. My own naiveté played a large role in getting me into a religious cult. It is naive to think one can control life. Overly naive persons are particularly vulnerable to idealistic groups that appear to embody a worthy cause, a great mission of global importance. One-sided, such individuals have no bite on reality and are hazardous to themselves and to others.

Unfortunately, an atmosphere of patriarchal authority quickly suppresses healthy childlikeness, whether in a family, church, or a corporation. We learn to suppress the healthy aspects of our inner child—banishing the child in us to some dark, locked attic room. In a destructive group, it's *not* always okay to think your own thoughts, to express your ideas and feelings, to want what *you* want, and it's often not okay to play. Saint Paul's admonishment to "put away childish things" becomes a new patriarchal rule that means playfulness, humor, and spontaneity are bad. In this manner, so-called religious dogma slays the divine child in each of us—our twentieth-century "slaughter of the innocents."

DEVELOPMENTAL STAGES

Erik Erikson's[12] developmental stages (see table) are excellent reference points for regressive behavior within a collective context: Erikson described the core pathology of adolescence as "exclusivity,"[13] which especially attracts individuals to groups that believe they have some exclusive wisdom and knowledge.

Table of Developmental Stages

Stage	Psychosocial Crisis	Strength
I. Infancy	Basic Trust vs. Basic Mistrust	Hope
II. Early Childhood	Autonomy vs. Shame, Doubt	Will
III. Play Age	Initiative vs. Guilt	Purpose
IV. School Age	Industry vs. Inferiority	Competence
V. Adolescence	Identity vs. Identity Confusion	Fidelity
VI. Young Adulthood	Intimacy vs. Isolation	Love
VII. Adulthood	Generativity vs. Stagnation	Care
VIII. Old Age	Integrity vs. Despair, Disgust	Wisdom

Exclusiveness has a strong appeal to a young adult ego. According to Erikson, the rituals associated with this developmental stage are "affiliative and elitist."[14] All groups have their sacred (often secret) rituals whether in religious, commercial, economic, or political settings. Group rituals are a strong inducement for young adults to join groups. The rituals become like a security blanket, promising a special providence or protection from the ills of the world. And people feel they belong to *the unique group* that has all the answers.

In research at the University of Chicago's Pritzker School of Medicine, psychiatrist Sherman Feinstein[15] examined adolescent attraction to cults, and found that most young people attracted to cults are not psychologically ill but are *developmentally vulnerable* to the life that cults and religions appear to offer. In another study at the Cornell Medical Center in White Plains, New York, Dr. Otto Kernberg researched regressive behavior in organizations using a systems approach. He identified three organizational situations that result in regressive behavior: "Dependency groups in which members perceive their leader(s) as being omnipotent; pairings, or situations in which group members attach symbolic meanings to interrelations between two selected members; and the fight-or-flight situation, in which group members either unite in fending off perceived external threats or splinter into warring subgroups."[16]

Persons caught in destructive group environments reenter a highly structured family-like system, which is another way of delaying growing up, of leaving *home*. The group, like a good family, provides protection and security from having to face an often cruel and hostile world. One reconstructs what seems to be a safe place—a new home complete with parental structure, rules, love, and friends. This newfound home can be a temporary safe haven, a halfway house of sorts.

Because of group influences, regression in the young adult pushes back behavior to Erickson's first three developmental stages; individuals revert to infantile early childhood, play-age emotions and thinking. Basic trust and mistrust characterize one's attitudes—the *we/they* syndrome described earlier takes over: you can only trust the group and its leaders, everyone outside is suspect.

Early childhood psychosocial crises such as "autonomy versus shame and doubt" reappear. A destructive group discourages individual autonomy, creating feelings of selfishness, guilt, and shame for even thinking of one's own desires and needs. Early core behaviors of withdrawal, compulsion, and law and order are reinforced by the group: you follow the group dictates and rules or you are ostracized (punished). Beginning rituals (infancy and early childhood) of cosmic order, numinosity, and idol worship are reinforced by any destructive group's totalistic orientation.

Erikson also pointed out a regression to "infantile needs" in our present culture exemplified by the "clinicians who, besides a powerful technique, partake in a professional movement, with a founder's picture on the wall and a heroic prehistory as ideological guide."[17] However, he goes on to explain that it is not so simplistic and we cannot automatically lay all the blame on a particular group for the regression, but have to also look at other possible explanations for this type of human behavior. Destructive groups may simply be a marketing phenomenon—opportunist religious, commercial, and political entrepreneurs profiting from developmental vulnerabilities of the times—free enterprise on another level.

Erikson describes "rejectivism" as a core pathology of adulthood and explains:

> Rejectivity, furthermore, periodically finds a vast area for collective manifestation—such as in wars against (often neighboring) states who once more appear to be a threat to one's own kind, and this is not only by dint of conflicting territorialities or markets, but simply by seeming *dangerously different*—and who, of course, are apt to reciprocate this sentiment. The conflict between generativity and rejection, thus, is the strongest ontogenetic anchor of the universal human propensity that I have called *pseudospeciation*. That is, the conviction (and the impulses and actions based on it) that another type or group of persons are, by nature, history, or divine will, a species different from one's own—and dangerous to mankind itself. It is a prime human dilemma that pseudospeciation can bring out the truest and best in loyalty and heroism, cooperation and inventiveness, while committing different human kinds to a history of reciprocal enmity and destruction.[18]

Every adult has a built-in propensity to revert to the childlike behavior of distrust of the "other," which divisive collective forces in society especially promote. Thus, joining any group carries with it potential psychological triggers for our innate regressive tendencies, resulting in a devolution of consciousness. In essence, the natural traits that one expresses as a young adult and as a maturing adult also make one vulnerable to joining a group, which at first may feel just like an ideal home. Lita Schwartz, in an article for the *Cultic Studies Journal*, wrote: "Essential components of cult indoctrination are *depersonalization, deindividualization,* and an appeal to the individual's desire for happiness"[19] (emphasis added).

Homelessness, real or imagined, becomes a metaphor for loss of soul, loss of meaning in one's life. But unfortunately, the collective solution soon fades under the ominous shadow of mind control and other coercive techniques practiced by many groups. The basic adult individuation processes of growing integrity and integration are either totally blocked, or considerably diminished in a group setting.

8

Creating Gods

All religion is the creation of the human mind.

George Santayana[1]

The Ethiopians say that their gods are snub-nosed and black, the Thracians that theirs have light blue eyes and red hair.

Xenophanes[2]

Kill a man, and you are a murderer. Kill millions of men, and you are a conqueror. Kill everyone, and you are a god.

Jean Rostrand[3]

Gods are metaphors of archetypal behaviors and myths are archetypal enactments.

Critical Dictionary of Jungian Analysis[4]

Escaping Life Through Religion

I could only believe in a God who dances.

Friedrich Nietzsche[5]

The constant desire to escape reality—to avoid life's necessary tension—places one in the trap of one-sidedness, possessed by one polarity of consciousness. Religion is one way people escape the tension inherent within the human psyche. Religion offers the hope of transcending

197

existence, overcoming death as in the resurrection, which could be viewed as the Christian model for escaping from life's burdens. In the Buddhist tradition, the goal is to reach Nirvana.

Spiritual ecstasy, as one extreme of consciousness, is a perfumed trap, a sweet poison in the soul, an infection of *light possession*—all air with no feet on the ground. Imprisoned in a childlike world, individuals caught by this ecstasy-of-light experience are unable to deal realistically with life's existential issues and conflicts. Frequent dreams of flying or levitating off the ground are an indication that this escape-life-mode-of-consciousness that characterizes many popular spiritual disciplines has assumed control of one's psyche. We humans have a built-in propensity to leave the earth, to escape the weighty side of living—a sort of innate suicidal impulse. We create the conditions for suicide by not living our *own* lives. Thus, groups that emphasize spiritual escapism reinforce suicidal impulses. Members of such groups begin to think nothing of death, particularly their own death; both death and life are devalued by ideologies that split life into opposites of good and bad, light and dark, while repressing the dark. This sort of one-sided neurosis results from any obsessive idea dominating consciousness. Being caught in a religious cult was a significant death experience for me. It enabled me to substantially differentiate my thinking processes from the collective. As James Hillman maintains, "the death experience is needed to separate from the collective flow of life and to discover individuality."[6]

Dualistic monotheism, so embedded in our Western culture, effectively frustrates the cultural shift into our third space of the relationship between things. This three-dimensional shift requires a dismantling of our two-thousand-year-old, religious mind-set, and a reimagining and re-mythologizing of inner and outer psychological space.

Christianity provides an excellent example of the ideological predicament that results from identifying with one side of a pair of opposites, creating a dualistic religion, which then is a model for a dualistic society and culture. In a speech intended for Unification church members only, the Reverend Moon (1973) said, "When it comes to our age, we must have an automatic theocracy to rule the world. So we cannot separate the political field from the religious. . . . Separation between religion and politics is what Satan likes most."[7] Moon's goal of an "automatic theocracy" demonstrates the natural evolution of a destructive group's sphere of influence to ultimately reach a position of *divinely sanctioned rulership* over masses of people—government by a god. Ominously, Christian fundamentalists have thoroughly infiltrated the Republican party and many local school boards, substantially increasing their ideological grasp on our collective necks. Christian or not, I now must consider the effects on my life of a potential theocracy.

Women, separated from their instinctual natures, are tragic victims of a patriarchal collective milieu. Masculinized by powerful totalistic impulses, they become indentured servants to systems, empowering the status quo through their assumed roles. Thus the dominant aspects of our mass culture are advantaged at the expense of both men and women who split themselves into "acceptable" and repressed "unacceptable" fragments. Additionally, feminine subservience is built into our culture in our marriage rituals where the woman drops her last name in favor of her husband's name.

Interestingly, "female" and "woman" contain both male and female elements: fe-male and wo-man. It's as if we've linguistically impregnated the feminine with patriarchy. Starting with *mann,* the Anglo-Saxon word for "human being," *wif* ("wife") was prefixed for "female." *Wifman* eventually became *wimman* and currently *women.* We have split male and female by concretizing gender, by *grouping* individuals, versus looking at gender as an inner, female-male, yin-yang, soft-hard play of opposites. Cultures tend to be gender specific. In the West we are under the patriarchal side, while much of the East is under the matriarchal. Hence our affinity to a male father-God, and the East's affinity with Divine Mother.

Bewitchment: Projection and Groups

> Another dangerous form of addiction is ideological possession, which can make the individual just as "drunk," puffed up, and dissociated as a drug, and in addition misleads him into wanting to impose his ideas on society through force.
>
> Marie-Louise Von Franz[8]

Projection is a significant factor in group dynamics, most notably in religious organizations. Carl Jung describes the effects of projection when we are unconscious of who we are as unique individuals:

> When you are in the condition of the beginning of life, in an adolescent condition of mind, you are not in possession of the animus, or the anima, in a man's case—and you have no consciousness of the Self, because they are both projected. You are then liable to become possessed by somebody who seems to contain these values; you get under the influence of the apparent proprietors of your treasure, and that is of course a sort of magical influence. Now the more you get under that fascination, the more you become immovable . . . you are in prison, you are utterly unfree. . . . It frequently happens that the object offers a hook to the projection, even lures it out.[9]

Jung described how one projects specific qualities onto another person who in actuality does not possess those qualities at all, but unconsciously encourages it. For example, several years after my religious cult experience, I bumped into one of the group's ministers at a local theater, who I had idealized while in the group. I was immediately struck by the fact that he seemed to be at least six inches shorter than my memory. For an instant I thought I was standing on a higher step, but we were on the same level. I later realized that I had taken back my projections and for the first time was seeing him as he really appeared. My projections had actually made him appear physically taller than he actually was. We commonly experience this type of "reality check" when seeing a movie star for the first time in public, and are shocked to realize our image of the person did not match reality. It is much more comfortable to live in the fantasy of our projections, but in so doing, we live in an unreal world.

A would-be teacher, priest, leader, or guru accepts the projections of a group of persons and relishes the subsequent ego-inflation and adoration from people who are convinced that they see before them a true prophet, a divine being, an anointed minister, a prominent leader, an enlightened guru. What's more, once one is "hooked" on positive attributes in another person, one often projects "all sorts of other positive qualities onto that person," which is called the "halo effect."[10] In a group context, mass projections of this sort take on awesome potency, making it extremely difficult for any individual not to be drawn into a collective hypnosis and hysteria. Each person's individual illusions reinforce the collective illusions. The projection of one's own inner demons (shadow) onto those persons not in one's group is the other side of this projective illusory coin. Robert Godwin explains how projection also enables people to "transform private anxieties into shared ones,"[11] which is one of the reasons we join groups. The group's collective anxieties are then projected on outsiders who are perceived as enemies, or at least threatening to the collective purity. Depth psychology has shown that enemy-making is a process emanating from repressed aspects of oneself. The other side of projection, enemy-making helps to alleviate our own anxiety and guilt. We feel better when the enemy is *out there* somewhere as opposed to right *in here,* a part of our own nature.

The point is that these needy, hungry projections place everything in an illusory state, and one then sees an ordinary person in the role of a god-like being or teacher in *both* the waking state and in dreams. However, most persons (those doing the projecting) eventually see behavior that does not match their projected ideal, resulting in disillusionment and doubt. The unconscious, compensating for the erroneous and inflated views, ultimatcly reacts to the compromised state of affairs with dreams that show the teacher or guru in not-so-good roles or in dream dramas unbecoming to the teacher. We can postulate that the soul, having had its fill of unreal projected experiences, wants to move on—to "get real!"

Contained within the innate desire to belong is the desire to derive value and a sense of worth for our own life from our belonging. In a totalistic group, it is automatic that a person's self-worth and self-esteem are based in large part upon the fact of belonging to it; we place our self-image in collective hands.

The dynamic of projection applies to inanimate objects as well, even to the printed word. Books, articles, and video and audiocassettes take on a numinous quality. One is enthralled by a celebrity's book, by a guru's poetry. Whether a particular piece of writing is good or bad is not the issue, rather it is the fact that the individual's projections place a mystique on the words, imbuing them with an *inflated* sense of authority, divinity, and wisdom. And even more, the one-sided aspect of projection makes it impossible for an individual to objectively compare what is seen, read, and heard with relevant outside information and contrasting viewpoints. Poetry and other writings by my spiritual teacher deeply inspired me while I was in the group, but after leaving, I found the same words to be at best mediocre and the poetry nothing special at all; I had taken back my projections.

Are these projections easily removed? Certainly not! In fact, we hold on to them with a tenacity that is beyond reason or logic because letting go of them means we have to face in ourselves the tremendous error of our group-centered illusory existence. And because our own ego has also been inflated along with the recipient of our projections, our group-engineered self-image shatters and suddenly we don't know who we are at all! This inflationary aspect of projection is self-destructive, as Jung explained: "Many fathomless transformations of personality, like sudden conversions and other far-reaching changes of mind, originate in the attractive power of a collective image, which . . . can cause such a high degree of inflation that the entire personality is disintegrated."[12]

Consequently, letting go of collective projections takes great courage and moral strength. But without collapsing the illusory world created by this process, we will never find or even begin to know ourselves.

Owning our projections means regaining one's integrity and disowned split-off parts of the self that need to be *consciously* reintegrated into the personality; it is a process of becoming *self-responsible*. Our unconscious projected material causes us to see in others what we cannot see in ourselves.

Students of gurus and members of religious organizations make a tremendous effort to maintain collapsing projections, often prolonging the process for years. Eventually, the projected images lose their hold, and like a house of cards, the entire sham collapses. For one whose projected temple has crumbled into ruin, realizing the extent of one's self-delusion comes as a severe shock. Suddenly all one trusted has become untrustworthy. Those we looked to for answers are not only fallible, but probably didn't know in the first place. After a short-lived attempt at Christian love, spiritual forgiveness, or New Age acceptance of our karma, a deep, justifiably furious, "I'd like to smash so-and-so" anger sets in. In fact, a lack of anger indicates that one is still in a state of denial, caught in group propaganda and holding on to projected illusions. Modern psychotherapy has shown that suppressing our feelings is a serious mistake, putting us back into a collective mind-set, where, to survive in a family or any group, we became adept at shutting down legitimate feelings.

Interestingly, a support group comprised of former members of a destructive group can be extremely helpful *provided the support group has no authority figures,* each member has equal status, and everyone is free to express their feelings and opinions without fear of reprisals. In such a group, simply sharing experiences that one had while in a destructive group is a tremendous help in working through the inevitable feelings of guilt, resentment, loss, and anger that follow any negative group experience.

The politician, god, goddess, cause, or image that triggers the projecting-out of our inner gods must ultimately fail us, and in failing us they paradoxically do us a profound service. By taking back our projected good and evil, we become self-responsible, reentering our own life and unique path. In fact, the issue of self-responsibility hits at the heart of how groups and individuals blame someone, something, or another group for their problems. The individual's *outward-directed* search for an inner reality or godlikeness is, to begin with, an abandonment of the self—a spiritual and psychological irresponsibility—an outer objectification of an inner dynamic. And this quest for something outside of ourselves is both a symptom of and a chief perpetuator of *ideological totalism,* as Robert Lifton explains: "Behind ideological totalism lies the ever-present human quest for the omnipotent guide—for the supernatural force, political party, philosophical ideas, great leader, or precise science—that will bring ultimate solidarity to all men and eliminate the terror of death and nothingness."[13]

Millions of persons carry multitudes of projections to their grave. Most live in an illusory world of their own creation, designed to fit the mass ideology of the time. For a fortunate few, these projections eventually fall apart: they find out their priest committed adultery; their guru is obsessed with sex, money, and power; their politicians are corrupt; their police are career criminals; and their media heroes turn out to be disappointingly normal, if not altogether ignorant. Disillusionment is the tragic consequence of projecting light and wisdom onto others, creating a one-sided, perfect, pure, loving God. The more individuals try to be *good,* the more darkness and evil accumulates.

Identification: Unconscious Conformity

> The shoe that fits one person pinches another; there is no recipe for living that suits all cases.
>
> Carl Jung[14]

Closely related to the process of projection is *identification.* Individuals unconsciously identify with a group ideology, adopting the behavior and attitudes embodied by a collective doctrine. Identification, while beneficial in facilitating a child's adaptation to an adult world, becomes a regressive infantalizing of consciousness for an adult. The fact that identification is an *unconscious conformity* makes it an important group dynamic, for through identification combined with projection, *a group's images and belief system gradually replace the individual's original identity.* One then becomes an articulate and apparently sincere spokesman for a group, often recruiting many new members or followers. The psyche utilizes all our experiences, even when we go "where angels fear to tread." Jung wrote, "Anyone who identifies with the collective psyche—or, in mythological terms, lets himself be devoured by the monster—and vanishes in it, attains the treasure that the dragon guards, but he does so in spite of himself and to his own greatest harm."[15] "[Identification] is also responsible for the almost universal desire to correct in others what most needs correcting in oneself. It has a dissociative effect, splitting the individual into two mutually estranged personalities."[16] This "splitting" of the individual in two parts proves to be terribly damaging and difficult to recover from after leaving a group. Once this splitting occurs, the individual becomes his or her own worst enemy; the group ideology is now firmly transplanted into the individual psyche in a manner that prevents *conscious* tension between the two split-off parts. Because of the *lack of consciousness between the two personalities,* individuals who are zealous promoters of a particular religion, product, or ideology are virtually impossible to reason with.

The split individual, when threatened by a conflicting idea, unconsciously switches to the collective mind-set role, becoming completely impenetrable to any new idea, logic, or reasoning. Due to this splitting, to reach any person so trapped in a collective system, one must attempt to reach the *pregroup* personality, for attempting to reason with the new group-implanted personality is a futile task. The collective personality, like a recorded message, replies with programmed responses for everything. Jung maintained there are major implications for individual psychological development as well: "A conscious process of differentiation, or individuation, is needed to bring the individuality to consciousness, i.e., to raise it out of identity with the object. A man cannot get rid of himself in favor of an artificial personality without punishment. Even the attempt to do so brings on . . . unconscious reactions in the form of bad moods, affects, phobias, obsessive ideas, backsliding vices."[17]

Identification, in contrast to projection, indicates a "psychological process in which the personality is partially or totally dissimilated. . . . [Identification] denoting an unconscious conformity between subject and object, oneself and others."[18]

A subtle and *unconscious* process, identification enables one to hold to a collective doctrine or idea as applying to all others regardless of their beliefs. Psychologically, individuals who identify with a group's agenda believe that "what's good for us must be good for everyone else." Their own blind conformity and one-sidedness extends itself to any and all situations. Exemplifying the *missionary consciousness,* they will not rest until all others outside their group are "saved" or enlightened as to the obvious benefits of their program. Identification then becomes a necessary prerequisite for the transition from an individual soul to a collective robot; one becomes a "dedicated" member, a loyal supporter, a "true believer," a "follower." *Followers* are one of the most essential ingredients in creating god stew. Certainly many roots of our dysfunctional identification as adults have their origins in our childhood: parents who never encouraged independent thinking and who ridiculed their children's ideas, creativity, imagination, or choice of vocation—parents who put down the hopeful idealism and wonder inherent in a child's heart.

Proselytizing and the desire to convert others to one's way of thinking and to one's moral system all indicate persons who have lost their own identity and assumed a collective persona; they represent not an individual, but a "system." This psychological situation can only endure with tremendous effort, relentlessly repressing conflicting inner parts. Such individuals become something else, live someone else's life.

While identification facilitates adaptation to the outside world in childhood, as an adult it becomes a psychological trap leading to a dead-end, empty, group-approved life. Additionally, when other opportunities outside one's group present themselves, the insidious character of identification will assert its deadly grip on the individual, often becoming a critical, fear-producing inner voice that destroys all possibilities of escape from the collective position. The group mind has wired itself into the identified psyche, and detaching from its Orwellian implant requires superhuman effort. Indeed, Jung found that identification with an idea or belief system has disastrous consequences:

> However, the necessary insight is made exceedingly difficult, not by one's social and political leaders alone, but also by one's religious men-

tors. They all want decision in favor of one thing, and therefore the utter identification of the individual with a necessarily one-sided "truth." Even if it were a question of some great truth, identification with it would still be a catastrophe, as it arrests all further spiritual development.[19]

Jung explained how the unconscious responds to such one-sided identification: "the unconscious usually responds with violent emotions, irritability, lack of control, arrogance, feelings of inferiority, moods, depressions, outbursts of rage, etc., coupled with lack of self-criticism and the misjudgments, mistakes, and delusions which this entails."[20] We can infer that much of our Western culture's violence and abuse has its roots in psychic frustration from masses of people living collectively identified lives—lives that are in fact unreal, mechanized, uncreative, and unfulfilled, with the real half of the personality forced to survive in an unconscious state. Basing one's life on collective values through identification while suppressing one's true nature is analogous to living in a childlike state, never growing up. This is why so many individuals, including myself, explain that they feel like they have "grown up" after leaving a destructive group. One-sided identification with a group's mission or belief system—be it political, religious, or economic—activates a silent agony of existential despair, which, through the psyche's compensatory nature, must eventually burst into outer consciousness as rage against what we have done to ourselves. Rage turned inward produces depression, a modern epidemic.

The remedy for such one-sided identification depends upon bringing the repressed side of the personality to consciousness; it means undertaking a conscious process of "individuation" in order to lift the psyche out of a state of identification with some idea or leader. This requires a confrontation and collision of opposites, which one must patiently tolerate as a necessary part of a birthing process to greater self-awareness and greater consciousness.

When individuals are under the spell of identification within a group, they commonly experience their individuality through another person. They "worship" or excessively admire the group's leader(s). Again, the psyche eventually attempts to compensate for this suppression of one's true identity, as Jung explained: "this . . . frequently gives rise in dreams to the symbol of psychic pregnancy, a symbol that goes back to the primordial image of the hero's birth. The child that is yet to be born signifies the individuality, which, though present, is not yet conscious."[21]

Organized religion is intrinsically antidiversity. Paradoxically, Jesus admonishes Christians to "Love your enemies." Who is the enemy? Perhaps our most feared enemies are, as Gandhi said, "within the human heart."

CULTURAL CLOAKING

When individuals immerse themselves in a group ideology such as the Christian myth and its accompanying symbolism, the unconscious speaks through that myth. One dreams of Mary and Jesus; the saints inspire us. For those persons immersed in the Hindu myth, the self appears as Krishna or other Eastern deities. For spiritual leaders who have dissolved their egos by *identification* with and possession by the self, a grossly inflated super-ego—an immense, exaggerated, Olympian loftiness—and superiority become their hallmark. Identification plays a major role in creating the all-knowing guru, the anointed evangelist, the spiritual teacher; all are examples of this hyperinflation of the human ego. One becomes puffed-up, conceited, self-centered, and extraordinarily narcissistic. What appears to be great wisdom is in actuality a mental disorder, a disease of one-sidedness.

What Is This Thing Called "Self"?

> People often say that this or that person has not yet found himself. But the self is not something one finds, it is something one creates.
>
> Thomas Szasz[22]

Jung submitted that the self cannot be completely described: "The self designates the whole range of psychic phenomena in man. It expresses the unity of the personality as a whole. It is a transcendental concept, for it presupposes the existence of unconscious factors on empirical grounds and thus characterizes an entity that can be described only in part."[23] Some idea of my meaning in using the word *self* is important because the concept of the individual and of what the individual psyche is comprised of is a principal player in our conflict between the collective and the individual. I will rely on Jung's definition as a starting point:

> The self is not only the center but also the whole circumference which embraces both conscious and unconscious; it is the center of this totality, just as the ego is the center of consciousness. . . . [T]he self is our life's goal, for it is the completest expression of that fateful combination we call individuality. It might equally be called "the God within us."[24]

Jung stressed the importance of a relationship to the Self: "because relationship to the Self is at once relationship to our fellow man, and no one can be related to the latter until he is related to himself."[25]

In contrast, James Hillman believes the concept of the self to be a problem, stating, "For to be about the Self is not to be about the Gods. I would not encourage Titanism, a menace far greater than Narcissism, which presents only a pensive pretty-boy compared with the titanic grandiosity of Self."[26] The danger of identification with and subsequent possession by the self, which Hillman identified as "Titanism," is a common event especially among group leaders who consider themselves to be gods, infallible, all-knowing, and exercising complete control over other individuals. In this view, identification with the self causes, as Jung maintained, a tremendous ego-inflation.

Marie-Louise Von Franz, a prominent Jungian analyst and writer, observed that some individuals become "possessed by the Self instead of being realized and related to the archetype of the Self." She further states, "These people cannot relate to their material but get possessed by it. They speak 'out of the archetype' and 'announce' archetypal material like an old medicine man, but they do not link up with their modern level of consciousness, and they never ask themselves about it."[27] Jung described the images of the self, which appear "in dreams, myths, and fairytales in the figure of the 'supraordinate personality,' such as a king, hero, prophet, savior, etc., or in the form of a totality symbol, such as the circle, square, cross, etc."[28] Hence, our vast assortment of speaking-in-tongues preachers, New Age channelers, evangelists, religious zealots, gurus, and other self-appointed demigods may be more examples of symbolic (image) possession than wisdom.

These seeming contradictory notions of what the self is give us a healthy way to think about words. The impulse to make language conform to a particular ideology kills the soul—the vitality in words. In *The Human Province,* Nobel Prize-winning author Elias Canetti wrote, "The smashers of language are looking for a new justice among words. It does not exist. Words are unequal and unjust."[29] Somewhere in the tension, the relationship in between our own reality and that of Jung and Hillman, we can find a deeper significance to the meaning of "self."

Writing in the *American Psychologist,* Philip Cushman, professor of psychology at the California School of Professional Psychology, believes the self to be more culturally specific. He writes, "By the *self* I mean the concept of the individual as articulated by the indigenous psychology of a particular cultural group, the shared understandings within a culture of what it is to be human."[30] Cushman's concept of the self enters murky waters in describing what is in effect a group or cultural self, a self derived not from the individual, but from the collective. While the self necessarily must reflect our cultural ground, it is vital that we think of the self as a unique representation of one's individual spirit, first and foremost distinct yet also interconnected, an integral part of the human spirit.

From these definitions, you can appreciate the considerable difficulty in defining the self. Such definitions can be deceptive, particularly when a certain culture or social system unduly influences one's perceptions. Suffice it to say that defining the self, like our attempts to conceptualize anything of a transcendent order, is like trying to trap the wind. But this mystery makes life a true adventure.

THE EMPTY SELF

> [The empty self] may also take the form of an absence of personal meaning. This can manifest as a hunger for spiritual guidance, which sometimes takes the form of a wish to be filled up by the spirit of God, by religious "truth," or the power and personality of a leader or guru. The wish to be spiritually filled up and guided can make the individual vulnerable to the deceptive practices of restrictive religious cults, charismatic political leaders, unethical psychotherapists, or even highly authoritarian and controlling romantic partners.
>
> Phillip Cushman[31]

Harville Hendrix, author and director of the Institute for Relationship Therapy, distinguishes between three aspects of the self:

1. Your "lost self," those parts of your being that you had to repress because of the demands of society.
2. Your "false self," the facade that you erected in order to fill the void created by this repression and by a lack of adequate nurturing.
3. Your "disowned self," the negative parts of your false self that met with disapproval and were therefore denied.[32]

A world dominated by groups, institutions, and systems steals the individual's sense of a real self, which is uniquely an individual reality—one's "God(s) within." This "disowned" self wreaks havoc, not only within the individual, but in society as well. Groups, because of their deindividualizing characteristics, reinforce what Hendrix calls the "disowned" aspects of the self. And these disowned parts of the self create our enemies, both inner and outer.

As a society we rush to fill our emptiness with "meaning-full" relationships, with food, with endless activity, with psychotherapy, with more and bigger things. Yet this existential pit seems to be unfillable. Perhaps we are looking for meaning and for fulfillment in all the wrong places. Outside groups will never fill the void of our own self-abandonment.

The "invisible hand" of our capitalistic system abhors a vacuum. We can depend on our market system's invisible hand, legal and illegal, to pour goods and services, pleasures and vices, pop religion and pop psychology without end into our collective emptiness. Sadly, no quantity of *things* can fill this void.

In this light, the promises of the advertising industry become the market economy's brand of salvation. We will feel better if we own that house, buy a certain car, take a romantic cruise. And we often do feel better, temporarily, as we find ourselves suddenly relieved of a particular desire— something was filled for a moment. But then there is next year's model with all its indispensable improvements; suddenly, we are not as filled up as we imagined.

Thus we *allow* the groups we are embedded within to construct false selves. The more we follow the dictates of the collective, the emptier and more alienated we become from our real selves. Consequently we split our psyches in two: one outer false shell-self, a group construct, and the real self, deeply hidden and suppressed. In this sense, many social skills become learned behavior expressed by the false self in order to survive in a social system or group.

Unfortunately, this false self has no real concern for community. Its only concern is survival, whether deciding how one *should* dress or killing a rival gang member; the group that survives wins. In an era where *self-help* is epidemic, we find that much of what is termed "self-help" is in reality another how-to-adapt-to-group survival course, teaching us how to be like our cultural icons and celebrities and how to be better actors on the collective stage.

In fact, our mythological heroes have been replaced by *celebrities*. The difference in meaning is significant. The word "hero" refers to "one noted for feats of courage or nobility of purpose," while "celebrity" comes from the Latin root *celebritas* meaning "a multitude, fame." A celebrity is a creation of the masses, of groups, and a hero is a creation and an expression of the self—very different concepts with profound implications for those who try to emulate "celebrity" images instead of drawing forth their own inner heroism, character, and integrity. Renowned psychoanalyst Heinz Kohut believed that "disorders of the self produce a powerful wish to psychologically merge with admired figures, to take them into the empty self."[33]

Obediently, we have played the roles that we have been *cultured* (taught) to play: get a good education, work hard, make money, shop, get married, raise a family, get more things, retire. Caught in a self-perpetuating group-structured world, we find ourselves in a totalistic dilemma, an *either/or* system that dictates what is legitimate and what is not legitimate, according to our social group's ideology. We find ourselves living an "approved-by-others" life. Either we are with the system or we are against it. The *middle ground*—the place of soul, of individual uniqueness and freedom, of human relationships—has been devastated like a nuclear bomb dropped in the citadel of the human spirit.

Erik Erikson explains that the individual's task is to attain a sense of identity, a sense of the real self. In a group setting where individual autonomy is perceived as a threat, and the group leadership takes on authoritarian parenting roles, the task of finding one's true self is not only thwarted but, even worse, moves backward, resulting in the fabrication of a *false self.*

An instability of one's self-image coupled with extremes of overidealization and devaluation in interpersonal relationships characterize "borderline" personality types.[34] A group milieu intensifies and encourages borderline personalities, particularly when a leader(s) exercises authoritarian control and also receives (and believes) mass projections from individuals who are convinced they see before them a godlike being. Aspects of the Self, unconsciously projected, result in self-alienation and self-hatred in addition to zero self-esteem.

Margaret Singer, professor of psychology at the University of California at Berkeley, explains, "Attacking the stability and quality of evaluations of self-concepts is the principle effective technique used in the conduct of a coercive thought reform and behavior control programs."[35] Thus a destructive group directly erodes the individual's self-esteem and sense of worth while at the same time paradoxically maintaining the illusion of elitism and superiority.

A process of dissimilation occurs in dysfunctional groups. Dissimilation means that the group belief system becomes a "self object," resulting in self-alienation. Persons trapped in this dynamic derive their self-worth and sense of identity from a group and their position in the group. Instead of positively integrating outside information as autonomous, critically thinking beings, they make the group ideology (or leader) the predominant object in their psyches. For example, one joins a certain political party because the group's ideas and purpose supposedly approximate one's political beliefs. But in order to completely assume the party's position, we must alienate ourselves to some degree in favor of a political agenda, repressing certain ideas that "bother" us. Most commonly, the political agenda becomes the individual's "self object," displacing and masking over the authentic self. As a result we have those who participate in political movements as fanatics and zealots, trapped in a one-sided view. Any attempt to criticize the political viewpoint is interpreted as "gridlock" or "politics." When someone criticizes an "idea" and we feel personally attacked, we have allowed our "self" to identify with an external object—the "idea." It is always more comfortable to repress one of the opposing views in any conflict. When repression of one side of a conflict is successful, the personality splits. A disassociation from one's authenticity accompanied by a breakdown in one's integrity occurs. Tragically, this compromise with one's inner values and authenticity collapses integrity.

One of the most influential psychoanalysts after Freud, Karen Horney pioneered the concepts of alienation, self-realization, and the "idealized image." Horney distinguished between three aspects of the self.[36] The "despised real self" she described as a "false self" made up of false assumptions based on the evaluations of others. In groups, we essentially build a false self, which ultimately results in self-hatred because we lose self-respect. We lose our vital sense of self-worth, and we lose our *dignity*. Horney's[37] third aspect of the self is the "real self," which is the individual's authentic, true self. It is this "real self" that group dynamics pushes aside.

While a group can temporarily provide the illusion of self-worth and self-respect, such illusory images are fleeting and can never be sustained outside the group. The Latin root of the word "dignity" is *dignitas*, meaning "worth, merit." Our sense of self-worth gives us dignity and our dignity inspires the respect of others. Building a false, idealized collective self means we are voluntary participants in destroying our own essential character, integrity, and dignity.

Horney explained that the "ideal self" is characterized by a "striving for perfection" in order to compensate for inadequacies, and a struggle with what she calls "the tyranny of the shoulds."[38] Hence, there is a constant battle between one's own self-direction and one's perception of what others think one *should* do.

In a group, the emphasis centers on building an "idealized false self," which fits a collective ideal. Social pressure from one's peers is a potent and persuasive molder of this false, collectively reflected self-image. Of course, this idealized self can never quite be attained, resulting in a continuing state of self-hatred—a guarantee of continuing failure and unhappiness. Idealizing others, while a necessary developmental task for children, becomes self-destructive for adults. As a result, one's life becomes more and more false and empty—a collective iron mask.

The ultimate effect of all this "false self-building" are people who, in spite of being close friends or in the same group, do not actually know each other. Poet and writer William Stafford poetically clarifies the consequences of self-ignorance: "If you don't know the kind of person I am and I don't know the kind of person you are, a pattern that others made may prevail in the world and following the wrong god home we may miss our star."[39]

Archetypal Paralysis

Who says I am not under the special protection of God?

Adolf Hitler[40]

Von Franz also explains that "archetypal patterns are so meaningful and exert such an emotional grip that such people talk like a book and are drowned in the material instead of understanding it. . . . [T]hey identify with the archetype of the Self and adopt the pose of the Wise Old Man or the Great Mother."[41] I like to call this transfixed state of affairs *archetypal paralysis.* When we listen to individuals under this archetypal spell, they appear to be totally sincere, 100 percent dedicated, and incredibly knowledgeable. Charisma and charm ooze from these people, and others are literally *captivated* by their message because it circles around a potent universal motif deeply embedded in human nature, such as the hero's journey. Such persons do in fact come up with occasional profound bits of wisdom, but along with a sprinkling of truth comes a whole lot of junk. Unfortunately for the unwary, spell-bound listener, the junk gets absorbed also. We think: "That's certainly true, so everything else must be true." Jung referred to this as contamination of the ego and the archetype of the Self—a sort of identity blurring.

Introjection, where one projects archetypal images on oneself, results in the ultimate of self-delusions; we believe we are the chosen leader, the anointed teacher, the incarnation of god or goddess. Jung said this all-too-common form of archetypal possession makes "human relationships impossible. . . . The mistake he makes in both cases [projection and introjection] comes from attributing to a *person* the contents of the collective unconscious. In this way he makes himself or his partner either god or devil. Here we see the characteristic effect of the archetype: it seizes hold of the psyche with a kind of primeval force and compels it to transgress the bounds of humanity."[42] Of course, in the situation where a group's ideology dominates individuals, archetypes are in possession of the masses. When a particular archetypal image or idea has tremendous emotional influence, groups have greater coherence, more archetypal glue. This archetypal possession means that collectively we are fated to run into the opposite. The rational, ordered society inevitably encounters irrational devastation. Through an acute one-sidedness a culture loses its equilibrium, its balance.

Since archetypal images make up the basic content of mythology and religions, we can readily appreciate the powerful attraction persons develop for groups that base their ideology on archetypal ideas and images. It is as though a switch is thrown in the psyche; one's inner hero/heroine projects itself onto a group or a particular leader. The group activates an archetypal image in the collective unconscious, which for the individual then becomes objectified in the form of an outer person. We see this sort of archetypal projection everyday in irrational worship and adulation of gurus, celebrities, sports heroes, preachers, politicians, and so forth.

Archetypes express themselves as metaphors. When they are interpreted literally, as historical fact, they become psychological tyrants enslaving the masses. For example, if we think of Jesus as representing a savior archetype, then he becomes a potent hook in our psyche. Religious groups purporting to represent Jesus and his gospel become imbued with an archetypal fascination and what Jungian analyst Daryl Sharp describes as "descriptive of persons, things, or situations having a deep emotional resonance, psychologically associated with the self."[43] However, looking at such an archetype as a metaphor we have to ask, what is the savior archetype a metaphor for?

One obvious metaphor is the hero's journey: Jesus as the hero who transforms himself. A god, he descends into matter, experiences life with all its bliss and suffering, and overcomes the world. Jesus is credited with saying "The Kingdom of God is within you" (Luke 17:21), referring to the symbolic meaning of "God" as an innate aspect of one's nature—what the mystic Kabir called "the Guest."

To be sure, this archetypal marketing of hero images comes with dangerous implications for you and me. Group literalization of mythology turns a valuable psychological lesson into a totalitarian trap. As a result, we have a proliferation of dogma-ridden groups totally controlling people who have irresponsibly given up their own critical thinking process to a "belief system." One cannot *fit* an archetypal motif or mythology into a system or formula for *mass* enlightenment as so many groups try to do, without killing meaning for individuals. Archetypal images like Jesus, Buddha, Krishna, Mary, and others lose their transformative value and spiritual potential when they are "adapted" to or organized as a particular system.

The self appears often in dreams and our imagination. For example, the continent of Africa began to come up repeatedly in my imagination as a place of cruelty and oppression for the black race. Soon I had this dream: I was seeing the African continent, looking down as though from a plane. Then I saw a tremendous black African elephant with enormous white tusks. He was supposedly dead, but I knew he was only sleeping. Standing beside this elephant were two dark, shadowy figures who were pulling at the elephant as if the elephant were the rope in a tug of war. This struggle awakened the elephant. He stood up (much to their surprise) and with great strength and power strode off across the plain. It is an awakening of the Self that we put to sleep.

Africa is a land of cultural upheaval revealing the emergence of a group of people out of bondage and enslavement by another culture. Here is an example of how one is enslaved by a culture and surrenders to the roles culture and society dictate. It is interesting that the elephant has no natural enemies, but is so vulnerable to destruction by cultures that place a higher value on ivory carvings and trophies than they place on the great dignity and spirit of such a beautiful creature. Similarly, the collective does not value the individual Self—the great spirit of the elephant. The symbol of the elephant contains interesting opposites of great strength combined with gentleness.

The elephant gives me courage and strength and reminds me to be watchful over that side of my nature that would destroy or shoot down the elephant: the critic and the cultural imperatives that are filled with "shoulds" and artificial role playing, valuing *things* more than life. Now, when I enter the dark forest of my unconscious, I am riding on my Elephant Self and I am fortified for what awaits me on the journey ahead. I now have embodied this symbol and carry it with me as an inner helper and guide.

We have been bewitched by the culture we live in. A spell has been cast over us and we have become actors playing our assigned roles—the great elephant is sleeping, the inner child is starved, we wait for someone or some event to break the spell, to awaken the sleeping giant within.

> One night I watched the Great Elephant
> awaken from a long sleep,
> and now he carries me into the ancient forest
> where it is darkest,
> where no one has ever been before.

Certain music seems to penetrate into the very depths of one's being, awakening something if even for a moment. Beautiful music is considered by some to be itself a symbol of the Self, especially when occurring in dreams. Interestingly, we often say a particular piece of music was "moving," as if to acknowledge some inner movement that takes us into a greater depth of soul experience.

Perhaps the Self, the unconscious, life, the soul, or whatever we choose to call the *Beingness* that transcends physical consciousness is a *co-creative* dynamic that requires our cooperation in the processes of self-creation. Our participation, *holding the tension,* enables life to express itself through us in a way that is totally unique for each individual. Possibly, even what we think of as transcendental does not know what lies ahead. The present and future may be more of our own creation than we dare to imagine. Our real work is to *participate* in the evolution of consciousness, with knowledge and truth being the ever-moving still point of balance between opposites—the third dimension beyond the push-pull of duality—*creative integrity.*

9

The Neurotic Side of Religion

A so-called good to which we succumb loses its ethical character. Every form of addiction is bad, no matter whether the narcotic be alcohol or morphine or idealism.

Carl Jung[1]

[Jung] told me that he once met a distinguished man, a Quaker, who could not imagine that he had ever done anything wrong in his life. "And do you know what happened to his children?" Jung asked. "The son became a thief, and the daughter a prostitute. Because the father would not take on his shadow, his share in the imperfection of human nature, his children were compelled to live out the dark side which he had ignored."

John Conger, *The Body as Shadow*[2]

Self-sacrifice enables us to sacrifice other people without blushing.

Bernard Shaw[3]

When we refuse to face the shadow or try to fight it with willpower alone, saying, "Get thee behind me, Satan," we merely relegate this energy to the unconscious, and from there it exerts its power in a negative, compulsive projected form. We become increasingly isolated; instead of a real relation to the surrounding world there is only an illusory one. . . . The most dangerous times, both collectively and individually, are those in which we assume that we have eliminated [our shadows].

Edward C. Whitmont[4]

The Shadow of Christianity

> We tend to get trapped in the idea of a static perfection that leads to rigid
> perfectionism. Abstract speculation can create an image of God that is
> foreign to the human heart. On the level of religious doctrine, it's a God
> that is totally purged of anything that we call dark. Then we try to live up
> to the standards of a God that is pure light and love and we can't handle
> the darkness within us; and because we can't handle it, we suppress it.
> But the more we suppress it, the more it leads its own life, because it's
> not integrated. Before we know it, we are in serious trouble.
>
> Brother David Steindle-Rast[5]

Repression, our most basic defense mechanism according to Freud, means preventing a thought or feeling from coming into consciousness. For example, in the Christian tradition, undesirable thoughts, feelings, and images are repressed as intrusions from the Devil. In New Age thinking, "negative thoughts" are repressed by "positive affirmations." The question becomes: what happens to the repressed psychic energy? A big chunk of this repressed material is projected onto our supposed enemies. Christianity has historically labeled non-Christian nation-states as "Christ killers." Christianity labels its enemies and sees them as in league with the Devil. Christians who cannot see their own shadow are a plague far more deadly than any disease. Repressed energy accumulates in the unconscious, ultimately gaining enough strength to take possession of the conscious ego—what Jung calls a complex takes over. Because we are not aware of our unconscious repression-driven complexes, we act under their control, while at the same time believing *we* are in control of our lives. Christianity, in its quest for supreme power and authority, modeled itself after the Roman Empire and "developed the institution of an absolute leader and used every means to absorb all existent elements of life and power."[6] Monotheism has repressed the gods and goddesses of polytheism, which, pushed underground, have now become our collective complexes, pricking at our social fabric through all manner of rampant ills. Christianity's separation of matter and spirit turned our environment into a *thing* to be controlled, used, and abused.

If Christians followed Jesus' admonition to "love your enemies," they would *never* convert others to their belief system. Instead, they would respect and "love" others' religious views.

Jesus perpetuated a patriarchal hierarchy by referring to a male deity, "our Father." Indeed, Christianity is an excellent example of what Joseph Campbell calls a "corrupting myth."[7] The Church demonized pagan rituals, particularly goddess rituals, by labeling them "witchcraft" and making the label official church doctrine. The word "pagan" comes from the Latin *paganus,* meaning "country dweller." Our present usage of the word as indicating "one who has no religion," shows the awesome power of organized religion to demonize different belief systems, and actually subvert language. Eric Hoffer wrote of Christianity's shadow, "Thus it seems that the more sublime the faith the more virulent the hatred it breeds."[8] After all, Christianity became a world religion by waging "holy war." The sword spread "the Faith" throughout Europe.

By persecuting women, the Church destroyed a major threat to its patriarchal authority. By eradicating "witches," who took part in "pagan" rituals and healing traditions, the Church eliminated the goddess spirit, which is just now beginning to resurface. Tragically, this methodical and deadly theological genocide also wiped out the Church's feminine side.

As individuals, we need to distinguish between spirituality, which is an individual relationship to the transcendental, and institutional, organized religion, which is really nothing more than a particular group's adaptation and concretization of a specific mythological theme. All religious traditions necessarily have their dark side, and in a group context, this shadow side is all the more ominous because of the mass repression and denial required to maintain the group's dogma. Religion has the greatest value when it is *unorganized,* and when viewed metaphorically.

Traditional religions, particularly in the West, consider personal inspiration a defect, where only the official institutionalized leaders are acknowledged and mimicked. Because of this institutionalized orthodoxy, individuals cannot be initiated into a group path mythologically. But they can be and are consumed by a group's ideology at the expense of their own souls. Ironically, being "saved," in a collective context, equates to being destroyed as a distinct, creative individual.

In our Western society, we are under heavy cultural and social influences of a patriarchal Judeo-Christian concretized morality and belief system, which, for the most part, rejects the sensual body-nature, and at the same time represses human sexuality into a shadowy theological underground. Similarly, good and evil are split into opposing forces, dividing God in two: darkness and light. The ethical and moral are against the evil and morally bankrupt; this group is against that group. A partitioned world with a proliferation of opposing groups from street gangs to nation-states, each acting out against a perceived enemy or threat to their moral position, is the disastrous consequence of collectively induced splitting.

Both Eastern and Western religious traditions have fallen under the spell of collective images, and consequently spiritual devotees follow, en masse, another's path, forsaking their own authentic journey. The pull from collective ideologies on the individual psyche is hard to resist, especially when groups center their belief system around archetypal figures with numinous qualities, and only by incorporating their belief system can we enter their collective sacred ground. The group dogma becomes the only "way" to salvation.

Surely as light and perfection are followed by shadow and imperfection, twentieth-century Christianity and other religions as well are haunted by their own shadow of evil, perversion, slavery, tyranny, and coercion—the inevitable result when one side of anything rules the psyche. Marie-Louise Von Franz observed, "As soon as you enter the human herd you deteriorate and your own shadow is constellated. . . . People get lured into attitudes which are not theirs, and when they have time to think they wonder what happened to them."[9]

Dragging an enormous sexual shadow, not surprisingly, Christians removed the erect penises from statues, tombs, and monuments of Osiris in Egypt—an example of the long-standing Christian bias against the human body, particularly the sexual organs. Sexuality must be hidden and repressed. Of course, the result of this repression is inevitable: an immense shadow of sexual perversion—sexuality pushed to the extreme inside the Church, its ministers, priests, and officials. Frequently we hear stories of priests, ministers, and evangelists, many of whom are prominent and well known, caught in scandal after scandal, trapped by their own as well as their group's sexual shadow. This is but one example of how a one-sided obsession with light and purity ensnares persons; they fall victim to whatever they have turned their backs on.

Many of the world's major organized religions essentially follow the maxim, "All other gods are devils." This attitude of intolerance and judgment has built a formidable, demonic shadow of exclusiveness and separateness. Traditional religions either *exclude* or try to convert those who do not follow their particular ideology. For the Christian, this attitude of exclusiveness goes against the savior figure, Jesus, who said, "Judge not, that ye be not judged" (Matthew 7:1). If Christians actually followed this wise counsel, they would never even consider converting anyone to their belief system, for we must judge others as *inferior* before we can "save" them.

A "let us make *man* in our image" theology requires the destruction of any image that appears to be different. Another culture's gods and goddesses become feared and hated objects, idols to be obliterated. Other images, other beliefs, must be converted to the acceptable doctrine. As an example, in mythology, the original Holy Grail was a green emerald bowl made from Lucifer's crown. Christians later adapted the story to fit their ideology.

COLLECTIVE COMPULSIONS

> The spirit of religious totalitarianism is abroad in the world; it is in the very air we breathe today in this land. Everywhere are those who claim to have a corner on righteousness, on direct access to God. . . . The bigots of the world are having a heyday.
>
> Sonia Johnson[10]

In destructive religious organizations, *compulsion* rules, instead of reason. Following a group's dogma often requires irrational behavior. With revealing totalistic jargon a spokesperson for the International Churches of Christ said, "Good Christians are *compelled* to spread the word"[11] (emphasis added). Compulsion from outside sources means one has lost self-control and free choice. This earth is filled with the graves of those who were on the receiving end of religious *compulsion.* It took the Church two hundred years of torture and executions to convert paganism to devil worship.[12] Women became the scapegoats for the Church. All social evils now had a cause: witchcraft. And, of course, another infamous woman, Eve, was responsible for the Fall and the expulsion from Eden.

Paradoxically, many religious groups curb their members' desire to participate in community work, to provide a meaningful contribution to society. Because groups, by definition, set boundaries and attempt to define individual human beings in terms of mass ideologies, they thwart constructive social change, effecting an immoral collective stagnation and regression.

Like all destructive groups, ideologically inspired mass compulsions are rationalized as necessary to preserve and increase collective influence and control. Of course, many subtle compulsions emanate from collective sources in our society and culture. We are psychologically medicated with collective implants far more than we realize. Even our own families inculcate us with their own implanted dogma. Nathaniel Brandon, a close colleague of Ayn Rand and an advocate of objectivism, explains that "Parents who accept the teachings of religion are very likely to infect their children with the disastrous notion that there are such things as 'evil thoughts' or 'evil emotions'—and thus fill the child with moral terror of his inner life."[13] This inner programming's destructive effect is compounded as the group replays its doctrine through inner voices that constantly struggle to control our behavior so that we conform to the group pattern. Therefore, we disown vast areas of our true nature, effectively destroying our own integrity and distinctness. Thus, introjected collective voices profoundly affect each of us. Christianity excels at what we call "blaming the victim." If members fall short and do not live up to church expectations, it is their fault. In this way vast areas of legitimate human experience are labeled as "sins," "evil," or "bad."

These essentially invisible influences are in fact more threatening to our survival than actual physical abuse. Indeed, it is precisely subtle collective manipulation and influence that quietly direct human endeavor in predetermined directions—avenues that lead to increasing empowerment of the status quo, the establishment, our group culture. Individual creativity and innovation are diverted, redirected, and immersed in the crowd; we are enslaved as surely as Pharaoh enslaved those who built the pyramids.

Christianity has become a religion of escapism: to escape hell, poverty, damnation, sexuality, matter (Mother Earth). An escapist theology results in a repressed and lost feminine. No wonder we abuse women, pollute, and destroy our environment! As we recover more and more of our Earth Mother nature in both men and women, we will be less inclined to persecute and desecrate our environment. The masculine without the feminine opposite becomes a conscienceless destroyer of matter. The *balance* of male and female gives birth to a sense of sacredness, a soul relationship with heaven and earth, light and dark.

Jungian experience has shown that repression of one side of a pair of opposites prolongs and worsens conflict, eventually leading to neurosis.

To counterbalance political mass ideologies, people typically turn to the religious perspective. Religious groups can provide opportunities for individual spiritual experience, which would be a way out of the collective. But, unfortunately, most persons find themselves again caught in the collective where they worship group-defined gods.

Once more the same dynamic ensnares people; individuals switch from a state- or political-based system to a religious-based system. While a religious viewpoint may offer temporary relief, it often serves only to deepen our estrangement from ourselves.

Until our search is redirected experientially within the individual psyche, our seeking will consist of an outside-implanted group path leading to nowhere, accompanied by a tragic loss of personal freedom, integrity, and a relinquishment of self-responsibility. In this manner people sacrifice themselves to the same many-headed beast with a new name and a different costume.

The individual's relationship to the transcendental cannot be replicated or mass produced; it is a personal and unique relationship—a one-on-one experience. Jung explains: "The Churches stand for traditional and collective convictions which in the case of many of their adherents are no longer based on their own inner experience but on *unreflecting belief* [emphasis added], which is notoriously apt to disappear as soon as one begins thinking about it."[14]

Everywhere we see so-called religious leaders caught in acting out the sexual shadow side of Christianity. Behind a seeming purity is a boiling repressed sexuality. In other cases, Christianity has developed a sadistic cruelty that while professing divine love has led to the inquisition responsible for the torture and murder of uncountable individuals accused of deviation from the religious dogma of the times. Many persons who are considered saints by the church exhibited behavior that can only be described as extremely neurotic, often brutalizing themselves with a variety of self-inflicted torments, all the while claiming to be living a religious life. Saint Francis of Assisi tortured himself on many occasions, including throwing himself into thorn bushes, in an attempt to punish his body for its sexual nature. In more recent times, Jean-Marie-Baptiste Vianney, the Curé d'Ars (1786–1859), a parish priest in the rural French village of Ars who was later designated the patron saint of parochial clergy, spent the greater part of his life scourging himself. This account by Vianney's biographer, Abbé Francis Trochu, graphically portrays what can only be a serious religious psychosis:

> [H]e subjected his body to a yet more severe punishment. Armed with a discipline [a scourge], the effectiveness of which had been increased by sharp iron points, he mercilessly struck his "corpse," "this old Adam," as he used to call his poor body. On certain nights a woman of Lyons . . . heard him thus punishing himself for the space of an hour or more; now and again he would pause for a moment, only to resume with renewed energy. He made his own instruments of penance, or, at least, he repaired and improved them. The person who did his room in the morning used to find under the furniture fragments of chains, small keys, and bits of iron or lead which had come off his disciplines. It was pitiful to see the left sleeve of his shirt all cut up and dyed with blood.[15]

We now know that individuals derive sexual pleasure from sado-masochism, whether inflicted on others or on oneself. In fact, such so-called saints were unknowingly caught in the dynamic of opposites, acting out repressed shadow material on themselves and others while one-sidedly clinging to a two-dimensional, one-sided, human-created, flat God who has no back side. The back side of God is split off as the Devil. The Devil becomes the carrier of all that we refuse to acknowledge in ourselves, both the bad and the good. It logically follows that the angels of a split God are also split into legions of good and evil. We have dark fallen angels and angels of light at war in two kingdoms, heaven and hell. Interestingly, religious fanatics like the Curé d'Ars always encountered devilish phenomena, which, psychologically, would indicate unleashed immense shadow energy from such titanic efforts at repressing one half of one's nature.

As such, all paradises are doomed to failure because of their one-sidedness. And all collective paradises necessarily contain a serpent, who awakens our innate oppositeness—our shadow.

SALEM REVISITED: MASS PARANOIA

> [T]hese accounts are essentially screen memories for other traumatic events whose contents are derived from internally generated fantasy influenced by the satanic stories and images which have permeated the mass market media. MPD [multiple personality disorder] and other dissociative patients would then create an entire world of cult figures who in turn manufacture pseudomemories of ritual cult abuse which feel like real memories to the main parts of the personality.
>
> David J. Lotto[16]

Repressed Memory Syndrome is rapidly becoming a twentieth-century witch hunt. If we are to believe the reports of substantial numbers of counselors and therapists, a phenomenal number of people have been abused and molested in horrific fashion and have repressed these memories because of their unacceptable horror. Children are taken away without any real proof of such allegations. Like the witch hunts of medieval times, parents are presumed guilty without a trial, reputations are burned alive. Individuals and families are destroyed as surely and swiftly as by the executioner's blade.

No doubt children are and have been seriously abused, but competent research reveals that most individuals cannot separate reality from imagination when it comes to early childhood memories. Perhaps more importantly, dreams or imaginings of childhood incest and molestation may point to a collective malady of infantile regression caused by the deeply regressive forces inherent in a society oriented toward group solutions for everything. A preponderance of collectively ordained living creates a form of *cultural incest* in which we are all victims to some degree. Hence, the rising tide of ritual abuse and child molestation may well be a warning about what we are allowing our collective parents to do to us; we prostitute the Self to the crowd mind.

The power of suggestion, especially when coming from supposed experts (therapists) is awesome. Brainwashing by images may be closer to reality than repeated satanic ritual abuse. Repetitious suggestion combined with a religious-induced repression of our own shadow side and an ideology based on blaming others (in this case Satan) turn imagination into reality. Indeed, the idea of satanic abuse, whether real or imagined, suggests a religious collective shadow erupting from ages of fanatical puritanism—

the inevitable opposite of Christianity's collective one-sidedness. That such abuse finds children as its victims follows a Christian mythology whose archetypal stories and images tell about the forces of darkness attacking the Christ child. The proliferation of repressed memories of ritual and satanic abuse indicate that we are in the throes of a collective nightmare of our own making, warning that we are killing our own inner hopefulness, meaning, purpose, creativity, and childlike authenticity.

In a literalized and hence fanatical Christianity, the dark side splits off from the conscious personality and goes underground. The collective eruption of these mythological images indicates the extent to which a dogmatic one-sided religiosity builds a culture of repression and guilt—a shadow of ominous and monstrous proportions. Like Herod, this dark beast is once more after our inner child. Whether or not we call ourselves Christian, we cannot escape the collective imprinting of two thousand years of Christian ideology. We unwittingly enable this collective shadow-making by leaping on the popular bandwagon, joining cultural witch hunts, believing that we alone protect the flame of truth and that all darkness must reside in someone else's heart.

We have to ask, "What exactly are Satanists trying to kill?" What characteristics in the human psyche reflect our innocence? Satanists go after what most symbolizes God. Herod killed the innocents because he was afraid of the competition to rule his kingdom. Perhaps, satanic ritual abuse, with its reported abuse of small animals, newborns, and young children, is a metaphor for how individuals under the spell of fundamentalist religions slaughter their own innocence and crucify the child within. Intense commitment to a particular belief system or ideology builds a powerful and dangerous opposite. One's shadow becomes satanic and self-destructive—one of Herod's soldiers wielding the collective sword. Satanism constitutes the logical and inevitable collective compensation for "pure" Christians, an example of our collective unconscious attempting to keep itself in balance.

For example, devout Christians, intoxicated with cult-style religious fervor, have empowered an imagined satanic opposite—the result of tremendous collective repression of their own shadow material. Psychotherapy opens the imaginary realm, which clients can mistakenly perceive as reality, particularly if images are from early childhood. Thus most memories of satanic ritual abuse may really be imaginal representations of repressed collective shadow material pushed underground by a one-sided, completely split puritanical ideology. Indeed, the increasing phenomenology of Satanism indicates a serious collective neurosis, one of the many inevitable consequences of the destructive power of the group mentality. Such collective hysteria—wandering cultural wounds—points to the urgent necessity of looking at what we are doing to ourselves by living group-ordained lives split off from our own reality.

Rigid and repetitious ritual easily becomes little more than *spiritual masturbation,* pleasurable and reassuring to the infantile, unquestioning, obedient part of one's psyche that feels more secure when following collective "shoulds."

STIGMATA: OUR COLLECTIVE HYSTERIA

> Hysteria. A state of mind marked by an exaggerated rapport with persons in the immediate environment and an adjustment to surrounding conditions that amounts to imitation.
>
> Daryl Sharp[17]

Perhaps religious mystics' stigmata are further evidence of collective religious hysteria, "wandering wounds." Interestingly, stigmata usually appear in the wrong places on the physical body—hands instead of wrists in Jesus' example. But they do match paintings (images) in particular churches where instances of stigmata occur. This would suggest that the mind is somehow projecting an image onto the physical body. Hence, religious stigmata may be more a testimony to the awesome power of the mass mind than to religious miracles. We tend to classify as miraculous anything we do not yet understand.

The Savior Business

> The Mormon Church alone collects at least $4.3 billion a year from its members and another $400 million from its many business enterprises purchased with tax-exempt donated money. The churches own $81 billion dollars' worth of tax-exempt real estate in Texas and $1.3 billion in Los Angeles County alone. They [churches] now own 20 to 25 percent of all real estate in America.
>
> Austin Miles[18]

A powerful motif in our collective unconscious, the savior archetype easily infects not only individuals but groups as well. Numerous examples of activated savior archetypes are found in those who see themselves as *the* bearers of special wisdom that will save the world. Symbolic of the Self, the savior metaphor turns destructive when individuals either project their inner self onto leaders, or, identifying with the archetype, they become possessed by it, believing themselves to be "chosen" by God or by destiny to lead others.

The psychological purpose of the savior archetype, as adapted to Christianity, is that one "saves" oneself, protecting one's inner divine child from Herod, who represents the state, the collective authority. The Herods of the world work to make us conform to tradition and to collective standards and beliefs; they seek to destroy our singular identity, killing our ability to live as unique individuals.

Religious groups want to convert others to their belief systems because they fear difference, because of a misguided judgmental do-gooder mentality, because they themselves are split, and because a fantasy cannot stand the light of opposing views. This missionary zeal is so blatantly judgmental of different gods and others' religious freedom, that it flies in the face of most spiritual teachings. Jesus said, "Judge not, lest ye be judged" (Matthew 7:1). In a talk about work and creativity, John Bradshaw observed, "When I judge you, you become responsible for my discomfort."[19] Judgment, in group hands, then becomes a form of denial and irresponsibility.

The moment individuals follow the specific spiritual rules and techniques of another person or group, they abandon their own unique journey. Each must find their own path to what Jung called the "inner transcendent experience."[20] Granted, another's experience with their god(s) can inspire us and give much-needed encouragement, but to attempt to duplicate another's journey is to lose our way rather than finding it. The important question is not whether or not to use a specific practice or ritual, but rather, does someone else's experience pollute it, does any outside doctrine or ideology color it? One's journey is just that—it is singular. No group can make the journey for the individual.

THE BORN AGAIN PHENOMENON

> But make our fundamental convictions your own, join our brotherhood, give yourself up to us, let yourself be guided, and you will at once feel yourself, as I have felt myself, a part of that vast invisible chain the beginning of which is hidden in heaven.
>
> Leo Tolstoy[21]

The religious "born again" experience happens when one accepts something supposedly larger, beyond the "I" or ego. In surrendering one's small self to a larger self, a psychological shift in consciousness occurs. Whether we call this larger self Jesus, or Buddha, or Allah, or whatever, does not matter. A significant movement in thinking and outlook has occurred: the individual, possibly for the first time in his/her life, realizes they are not completely self-sufficient. Consequently, a substantial inner transformative shift in consciousness takes place. However, as commonly experienced in the traditional religious life, persons objectify this inner change, projecting it onto some outer cultural object of worship. Projected outside onto a collective, exterior deity, this larger self within the individual then acts as a restrictive *censor* for the individual's Self-expression. Real spiritual conversion takes place when we discover our own life's passion and meaning, which necessarily incorporates the transition from living a collectively ordained life to living our own unique life—a continuing psychological process of death and rebirth.

Mistakenly objectifying this necessary developmental, inner growth process, we confine our own transcendental, unrestricted, unique wisdom to a culturally sanctioned and defined deity or guru. We put Christian, Hindu, Moslem, or someone else's clothes on the Self. In effect, we cripple a numinous and potent attribute of the psyche. In this manner the "group" robs us of our reality and authenticity. And now there is a great danger of becoming possessed by a collective motif/image that is culturally specific, such as Jesus. This really amounts to one being directed by a group implant, as opposed to individual autonomy and increasing awareness of one's true inner and outer reality, which, of course will always be totally unique for each person.

All religions contain some version of a rebirth motif. Christians are "born again" or "resurrected." Eastern religions teach reincarnation. Psychology expresses rebirth through notions of "individuation," personal growth, self-realization/actualization, "re-birthing," and so on. Religious groups, in order to be successful, must incorporate these universal motifs or ideas into their systems. In fact, what Jung refers to as "universal archetypal images"[22] in the collective unconscious make up the nucleus of all religious movements.

ELECTRONIC HYPNOSIS: THE CULT OF EVANGELISM IN AMERICA

> Two hundred-fifty Christian stations in the United States bring in an estimated $500,000,000 in revenue each year, with at least 15 million people viewing once every week.[23]

Once traveling tent revival meetings, American evangelism with its zealous preaching and strict adherence to the Christian Gospel has become BIG business. Modern marketing combined with TV enables evangelists to reach into millions of homes. Following typical patterns of destructive groups, contemporary evangelists sell a benefits package designed to appeal to the masses in a market economy. Peddling their prosperity theology, followers are admonished to "send money and Jesus will prosper you."

The hypnotic effect of religious fervor is contagious, and even on television, one can be drawn into a collective mind-set—converted, saved, and gratefully mailing that check for Jesus. Perhaps this electronic witchcraft is not entirely negative. Stirring up religious passion in others may be an improvement over an otherwise passionless life. However, this wasted passion flows into the pockets of slick businessmen and perpetuates a mass ideology with a medieval mind-set dead set on their agenda and theirs alone. Patriarchally organized, their anti-abortion hysteria exposes their true inquisitional nature as antifreedom and antifeminine.

Possessed by a *missionary consciousness* with community outreach programs including schools, clinics, and well-organized recruitment programs, evangelism is a growing religious cultic system intent on infiltrating our educational and political infrastructure and imposing its moral value system on everyone.

Dogma-Free Meditation

> The *imitatio Christi* has this disadvantage: in the long run we worship as a divine example a man who embodied the deepest meaning of life, and then, out of sheer imitation, we forget to make real our own deepest meaning—self realization.
>
> Carl Jung[24]

After an inspiring and eloquent lecture, someone asked Joseph Campbell, "So Joe, what do you do for meditation?" He replied, "I underline words." Each must find their own unique way to tap the unconscious. No one can say what is best for another individual. We ought to avoid like a plague any spiritual practice that is infected with a particular religious doctrine. If people want to brainwash themselves into thinking through a group mind, that is their choice, but there should be no illusion about the consequences of trying to duplicate another's path and another's concept of God; we become a subhuman part of the herd.

The human mind is remarkably powerful, and if you want to make yourself into someone else's image, you will find endless groups ready and willing to take you in to their religious clutches. Granted, various spiritual techniques can help one relax and improve one's concentration, however, neither Eastern or Western meditative practices/spiritual exercises aid in the integration of the personality. Indeed they "shield consciousness from the unconscious and suppress it."[25] Such practices throttle individual development, which requires that unconscious contents be brought into conscious awareness, facilitating a tension between opposites. Ironically, most so-called "consciousness raising" techniques are in fact putting people to sleep, deadening individual awareness, and shutting down the individuation process. Indeed, group prayer and meditation is not unlike marching in the army, a psychological marching in formation killing individuality.

Whatever conscious attitudes we have, our unconscious contains their opposites. Hence our increasing self-realization depends upon first becoming aware of our oppositeness and then *holding the tension in between;* the alternative means stagnation and death as we suppress more and more unconscious energy. In fact, Jung maintained that "when an inner situation is not made conscious, it happens outside, as fate."[26] Group dynamics reinforce unconsciousness by demanding that we suppress unacceptable qualities—a continuation of childhood.

Meditation is an individual process. Inherently hypnotic, group meditations are a potent form of mind control. Mantras and prayers easily become obsessive habits disguised as spiritual rituals. Obsessive-compulsive individuals are often extremely "spiritual," obsessed with the rituals and disciplines of religious life. Because repetitive ritual so easily become compulsive behavior, what began as sincere searching deteriorates into a psychological prison—an effective end to soul-making. Additionally, many group rituals are highly addictive. In my own experience, after leaving a religious group, I found it exceedingly difficult to stop numerous daily rituals without feeling guilty. Individual spiritual experiences, although valid even in a group setting, acquire real significance only when we separate collective influences from our experience. When groups use rituals and spiritual practices that trigger transcendental mystical experiences, collective interpretation typically follows that validates the group's belief system instead of individual reality. Religious groups interpret spiritual experiences as confirming the group's unique knowledge, when in fact, spiritual experiences usually happen *in spite of* collective influences. However, most institutionalized religions look down on individual experience with the divine. Instead, they prefer to establish a spiritual hierarchy, a priestly parental authority as mediators between individuals and God.

Chapters 11 and 12 of this book elaborate on different techniques that aid in overcoming the influence of destructive groups, which include, but are certainly not limited to, the following meditations beyond dogma:

- Active imagination, dream therapy;
- Poetry: reading, writing;
- Creative (uncensored) writing, journal work;
- Art, tensional art, music;

- Movement, dance; and

- Walking, "walkabouts," meditative walking.

In the West we are culturally programmed to associate goodness and spirituality with church attendance, repetitious rituals, and worship formats. Such collective cultural programming is simply no longer a viable socializing format for the world. In fact, Christianity has become our cultural "self object," without which most of us feel somehow bereft of a moral base, guilty and abnormal. Most Christians think all other religions are evil or inferior, and most other religious groups believe their way is the only way to *their god.* Biblical absolutes such as Jesus' statement, "I am the way, the truth and the life; no man cometh unto the Father, but by me" (John 14:6), established an authoritarian theology of superiority and judgment that has driven inquisitions, crusades, and holy wars for centuries—a bloody patriarchal religious dogma that still permeates the individual and collective unconscious. Unbelievably, this Dark Age religious mind-set is alive and well in our present era: Randall Terry, founder of the fundamentalist Christian-based "Operation Rescue," said, "What this is coming down to is who runs the country. It's us against them. It's the good guys versus the bad guys. It's the God-fearing people against the pagans, and some of the pagans are going to church."[27] Such attitudes foster separation, prejudice, war, and hatred, which are opposites of what society expects the religious community to provide for mere mortals. We are particularly influenced by the Christian myth, whether or not we belong to a specific religious tradition. This group-implanted totalitarian attitude prompts us to divide the world into opposite camps; in the Christian example, good or evil, Jesus or the Devil.

Persons who equate "spirituality" with a "higher" consciousness are primed to be victims of groups masquerading as religious movements, which in actuality are sophisticated, usually tax-exempt, lucrative business enterprises selling an invisible product. Moreover, the Christian belief system, in its obsession with perfection and purity, collectively indoctrinates the individual with this one-sided equating of spirituality with "light" and a higher consciousness.

Within such a splitting-of-consciousness perspective, a meditator's or prayer's "high" becomes an extreme one-sided psychological and emotional reaction, which insures inevitable movement to the opposite extreme of depression and moodiness, placing the so-called spiritual devotee in a continuing state of being bounced back and forth between opposites: one a collective hypnosis, and the other a moody withdrawn bottoming out; thus begins the impetus for continuing religious addiction.

Meditation with a *predetermined agenda* to become "one" (identification with *one side* of an archetype) with Light (God) and goodness tends to further split the psyche in two, inevitably repressing the shadow side of the personality more and more until one is overcome with a darkness turned demonic. As the conscious ego is less and less able to keep the lid on these ignored repressed energies, all sorts of abnormal behavior erupts from the shadow. Indeed, we have ample evidence of this dark side manifesting itself in the lives of so-called gurus and spiritual leaders whose erratic behavior and sexual perversions eventually bring about their downfall. Jung stated it well when he said, "I would rather be whole than good."[28]

Marion Woodman, a prominent Jungian analyst and author of several books on addictive behavior, suggests that addicts are trying to escape their humanity, anesthetizing the shadow side of the personality. Woodman explains that "every time an addict wants a substance, he/she faces the shadow. Eventually the shadow becomes a monster."[29] Living an authentic life requires a conscious working relationship with our shadow side. No shadow means no wholeness and no humanity.

As more people ignore their own darkness, the more out of balance life becomes. When an entire culture strives only to identify with the light, that culture will automatically (unconsciously) project onto others their own disowned evil and darkness. Just as our guru, minister, or savior becomes the center for all light, others must carry the polar opposite of ultimate evil. Devils and scapegoats pop up everywhere—other races, other nations, other groups who believe in a different God, the local gang who is trespassing on our turf.

Integrity and Evil

> There is no doubt that healthy-mindedness is inadequate as a philosophical doctrine, because the evil facts which it positively refuses to account for are a genuine portion of reality; and they may after all be the best key to life's significance, and possibly the only openers of our eyes to the deepest levels of truth.
>
> William James[30]

The existence of evil gives good its value through its oppositeness. Would goodness exist without evil? No. This at first appears to be an impossible paradox, a verbal trap. But it points out a fundamental given: all life is subject to the play of opposites—a sort of *conflict continuum* where the only true relief requires becoming more aware, to expand one's awareness using both sides as a *tension engine* of consciousness. A long time ago, Lao-Tzu said:

Under heaven all can see beauty as beauty
only because there is ugliness.
All can know good as good only because there is evil.
Therefore having and not having arise together.
Difficult and easy complement each other.
Long and short contrast each other;
High and low rest upon each other;
Voice and sound harmonize each other;
Front and back follow one another.[31]

A Hasidim saying also points out this paradox of opposites: "Without evil, the chickens would not lay eggs." And without some degree of suffering, we would be totally lacking in empathy for others. Being "creatively centered" equates to being in Jung's "transcendent function," which comes out of the collision and union of opposites.

A large part of what we call "evil" is culturally specific. We can divide evil into two basic segments: natural disasters, what insurance groups curiously call "acts of God"—tornadoes, earthquakes, fires, and floods—those events that seem to originate out of some godly wrath. Second, we have the evil that originates in the human being: what we do to each other. Recalling my philosophy 101 class, the Golden Rule is supposedly the only moral view that seems to be outside any particular belief system. In other words, it is difficult to find any morality or definition of good and evil beyond the confines of some ideology or cultural system. One thing we can be sure of: we are in the hands of the Devil (evil) when we take any extreme position.

Psychologically, the message in Jesus' suffering implies that we must accept suffering, work through it, and face it. Then we are healed, psychologically resurrected. As long as we resist our suffering, we are avoiding life and are living in a state of denial. Possibly Jesus meant this when he spoke of those who "deny him." The Pharisees were the governing patriarchal order, which in Jesus' time encompassed both religion and politics. People either abided by the prevailing rules or they were cast out, or put to death.

WHEN OBEDIENCE IS EVIL

The pope gives in to denial when, standing in Mexico City, surrounded by three million people destroying the environment and their own children, he says that birth control is wrong. Each of us has the pope's brain defect, which is perfectly compatible with nobility, intelligence, courage, education.

Robert Bly[32]

In a group, obedience means following the explicit dogma of a particular system. Each religion has its rules, its "thou shalts," and its "thou shalt nots." In the collective sense, obedience then becomes evil when allegiance to the group's doctrine is more important than individual human relationships. Self-discipline, when formulated and dictated by a group, turns into self-inflicted evil, as novelist Arthur Koestler relates: "The inner censor in the mind of the true believer completes the work of the public censor; his self-discipline is as tyrannical as the obedience imposed by the regime; he terrorizes his own conscience into submission; he carries his private Iron Curtain inside his skull, to protect his illusions against the intrusion of reality."[33] The Devil (evil) has us when we do not follow our own path, when we listen to a collective voice that *lures* us into cultural role-playing where our lives conform to popular expectations.

"Empathy" comes from the Greek *em*, "in," and *pathos*, "feeling"—"an *in* feeling." Empathy pertains to our ability to comprehend and experientially feel others' thoughts and feelings. When we cut ourselves off from our own feelings through repression and other self-denial mechanisms because of some group, we tragically lose the ability to empathize with ourselves and with others. Our largely theological collective doctrine labels healthy self-concern as selfishness, self-centeredness, and egotism, while our *intentional suffering* and self-flagellation become saintly acts for which we are duly praised. This moral inversion, so common in Western theology and many Eastern ideologies, rewards self-torture, legitimizing evil when directed at one's self.

Indeed, in commercial organizations structured by totalitarian ideas, there is no concern (empathy) at all for employees who have given their lives to a particular company, group or cause. Psychiatrist and author of *People of the Lie*, M. Scott Peck describes as "evil" those seemingly good persons: "Utterly dedicated, preserving their self-image of perfection, they are unceasingly engaged in the effort to maintain the appearance of moral purity. They are acutely sensitive to social norms and what others might think of them. They dress well, go to work on time, pay their taxes, and outwardly seem to live lives that are above reproach."[34] Peck's "evil" moral purity alludes to those who become expert at collective adaptation while remaining unconscious of their own reality, both dark and light.

FUNDAMENTALISM: A SOCIAL PLAGUE

> Fundamentalism is, moreover, always on the edge of violence because it ever mobilizes for an absolute confrontation with designated evil, thereby justifying any actions taken to eliminate that evil. Fundamentalism thus creates a thwarted self, never free of actual or potential fragmentation.
>
> Robert Lifton[35]

In Sri Lanka, a militant antigovernment group known as the Tamil Tigers train their members as suicide forces. Members believe death is honorable for their cause. The idea of martyrdom replaces heaven or paradise as a goal. Like the Second World War's kamikaze suicide pilots, self-sacrifice for a group's cause becomes virtuous. In modern Islam, the *jihad* keeps the patriarchal, concretized ideology of holy war alive. Death in battle means instant arrival in paradise. What is actually a metaphor for an inner psychological struggle becomes real warfare and terrorism. To give one's life for some great purpose is considered noble and courageous. This innate desire to attach great and significant meaning to one's life fuels the martyr complex found so often in destructive fundamentalist organizations. But when individuals sacrifice their lives for a *group cause,* one instead becomes a lamentable victim caught in someone else's purpose. The real meaning of self-sacrifice is to give oneself over to one's inner potential, which must always be unique and distinct from the masses. This is one's real "treasure hard to attain," which requires that we leave the comfortable, but deadly security of living a socially acceptable life. The fact that conformity-producing collective ideas have been culturally implanted in our psyches for countless eons makes one's inner journey a formidable quest indeed. And the collective beast lies within, guarding the threshold, waiting for our first attempt to find our long-buried gold.

The Reverend Mel White, a Christian fundamentalist, was secretly gay. Since going public, he is heading a war *against* the fundamentalist antigay position represented by Jerry Falwell and Pat Robertson. Fundamentalist Christians use "Christian" psychotherapy and electric shock treatment to "cure" the sin of homosexuality.[36] Fundamentalists, in their extreme and literal interpretation of mythology, use a particular ideology as a religious snake-oil cure-all. The therapeutic solution becomes a matter of conversion to *one particular viewpoint* accompanied by the consequent repression of all other viewpoints. This releases one from holding the tension between opposites, which produces a temporary feeling of euphoria, of having escaped adult self-responsibility.

Extremist attitudes are found in all types of groups and institutions. Fundamentalism quite effectively "kills the souls" of its adherents, replacing the human heart with an icy cold mechanical either/or reasoning that guarantees repression and violence. Violence begins when we *violate* our own integrity and our innate obligation to live an authentic, distinctive life.

Finding Values Outside the Religious Community

[A] morality based *solely* upon the tenuous thread of religious mythology is only effective for a comparatively primitive mind, through which God is invested with magical parental powers of punishment and reward. As people in general become emotionally healthier, more able to individuate from their parents, the gods become divested of their power to control.

Robert Godwin[37]

A common complaint from people who leave religious communities is that they no longer have a clear set of values. Life suddenly becomes quite muddled and confusing. No longer mechanically performing collective rituals, they undergo *ritual withdrawal,* frantically searching for another group, ritual, or system to fill their apparent spiritual void. Brainwashed into believing that spirituality can be formatted and packaged, recent immigrants from organized religions soon fall prey to another system, perhaps seeming more benign, but none the less deadly to their integrity and individuality. True ritual is a meaningful, numinous enactment of a particular mythology, personal or collective. In a collective organization, where most rituals have become stale and rigid over many centuries, they represent nothing more than an indoctrination process, keeping one dependent on a group.

Each individual must find their own way of relating to the unnameable mystery that interpenetrates and permeates both the seen and the unseen, the knowable and the unknowable. As Sam Keen so aptly states:

Any effort to discover a purpose that transcends eating, drinking, and making money must begin with a leap of faith. But where religion requires a broad-jump into the arms of authority, the spiritual quest requires only this basic assumption: My life is the text within which I must find the revelation of the sacred.

Sam Keen[38]

THE DARK SIDE OF ILLUMINATION

I think one has fallen to the archetype of the spirit.

James Hillman[39]

James Hillman, in his book *A Blue Fire,* relates his experience when a student of Transcendental Meditation (TM) told him that the political world didn't matter and that, "Computers can run the political world, the whole country . . . and that frees us to pursue enlightenment with meditation."[40] Shocked by the student's remarks, Hillman writes: "Do you see the complete harmony between central dictatorship, fascism, political callousness, and the self-centeredness of the spiritual point of view? . . . I saw the present cults of meditation not so gentle, not so harmless as they like to be, but a vicious bunch of totalitarians."[41] Ideas of enlightenment, illumination, and self-mastery can be an addictive psychological trap, luring egocentric and hyperinflated persons.

The continuum of self-knowledge, in its constant changing and shifting, provides life with mystery, adventure, and challenges. In contrast, notions of illumination and mastery imply an ending, a state of obtainable perfection, a remarkably potent marketing concept religions and many self-help groups use to snag new members. There could be no worse state of affairs than to be finished with one's life, to be a "master." Such would be the end of living and the beginning of dying. Granted, most of us strive to "master" different aspects of our lives, but individual mastery makes sense only within a context of a continuing *process* rather than an ultimate goal to be achieved.

Perfection, a totalitarian-rooted idea, can never be attained and is in reality a state of death. Perfection, once achieved, would mean the end of all further development. To disengage from the collective consciousness, we must let go of such *absolutes*.

Dualism in Religion

> Since 1985, the Catholic Church has paid out over $350 million in damages related to sexual abuse.
>
> Jason Berry[42]

Christianity has rejected physical sensation as sinful, lustful, materialistic, and worldly. This separation of the world matter ("matter" or mother from the Latin *materia*) as something distinct from a *moral* life has nearly destroyed our planet and has fostered a disastrous splitting off of the feminine side of our natures, for both men and women. The results have been a patriarchal hardening of the heart for women, a brute mentality in men, and a lethal collective shadow of perverted sexuality and inhuman cruelty. Hardness and brutishness result from a deeply rooted masculine one-sidedness. A *tension between masculine and feminine polarities* will return a sense of equilibrium—a way of being that is not too soft and not too hard—compassion tempered with wisdom and strength filled with gentleness.

A quick look at the different world religions and philosophies reveals God to be an adept gender-switcher. Christians have their "Father-Jehovah" God while the Hindus have their Divine Mother. Wherever we find the female aspect of God, we are likely to find a people with strong ties to the earth—for mother (*mater*). Cultures with emphasis on the patriarchal are more often empire-building and militaristic, wanting land that does not belong to them. Male gods want to own and conquer while female gods want to plant and harvest. To be caught in either of these two collective perspectives destroys our capacity to live whole and complete lives.

In the West, after thousands of years of patriarchal oppression, we have a terribly wounded feminine side, and this applies to both men and women. We see a resurgence of men's groups where men struggle to get in touch with long-lost and suppressed feelings—feelings crushed beneath the weight of the macho Jehovah, warrior-god-image, the *he*-man. What the world so desperately needs are *he-she* men and *she-he* women—individuals who are unique blends. Instead we have she-women bashing all males—the dark, terrible mother pitted against the negative, terrible father. This struggle takes place not only in interpersonal relationships, but within each individual as well. The he-man searches for a female to conquer and possess while the she-woman tries to conquer a male-dominated culture.

Joseph Campbell said, "I don't have to have faith. I have experience."[43] Religious ideas have important meaning and value metaphorically. Because of the West's patriarchal devaluation of myth and dream, we have lost our inner road maps for living. Myths give us a way of relating to the transcendental. They fill the *spaces in between* the physical and spiritual realms, and consequently are antidualistic. When we literalize myth and legend, as organized religions tend to do, we kill the soul-life of our culture and we sever the linkage sacred places and rituals provide between the gods and humankind. Psychologically, we disconnect from our own inner reality, repressing our imaginal and creative side.

10

The Color of the Dream

The American workplace is based on the myth of money. Money is the bottom line. No value can supersede the value of money. The value that you stand for is your life. And if money is the final term, that's your mythology, and I'm afraid that's what's working. To what society do you belong? Do you belong to this little in-group? Do you belong to the United States? Or do you belong to the planet, to mankind?

Joseph Campbell[1]

You should aim to be independent of any one vote, of any one fashion, of any one century.

Gracian[2]

All too many people do not live their own lives, and generally they know next to nothing about their real nature. They make convulsive efforts to "adapt," not to stand out in any way, to do exactly what the opinions, rules, regulations, and habits of the environment demand as being "right." They are the slaves of "what people think," "what people do," etc.

Jolande Jacobi[3]

The American Dream

John, I want to say one word to you—just one word—money.

The collective voice of the American Dream[4]

237

Therefore profit comes from what is there,
Usefulness from what is not there.

Lao-Tzu[5]

The smell of profit is clean and sweet, whatever the source.

Juvenal[6]

This is the paradox: The usefulness of the individual to the community and culture depends upon the individual *differentiating from the community.* Only when one is *not caught* in a community can one become useful to it.

For most people there is a tremendous gap between reality and the so-called American Dream, a dream primarily created by Madison Avenue. Commercial groups, especially the media, which in turn are driven by money and profits, commerce and consumption, profoundly direct and shape the American Dream. We feed this dream culture through our system-directed life styles. In this regard, the collective American Dream is self-perpetuating. Following our group-implanted images, we try to replicate life styles that supposedly represent success and achievement, and in doing so, we contribute to that aspect of the collective machinery represented by the American Dream. We are at once driven by this dream and at the same time provide fuel for its collective engines—a never-ending merry-go-round. Real dreams are brought into the fabric of life when one has the courage and strength of character to differentiate from popular ideologies—to step into one's own space and live an authentic life.

This dream-shaping by collective forces in our culture points out a serious dilemma: that of distinguishing media-created *dream-introject*s from, an authentic American Dream, if one exists. We need to ask ourselves, whose dream is it? Where does it come from? What role am I playing in the dream? Whose morality/value hoop am I trained to jump through in order to have my part of the dream?

Who or what creates and defines our American Dream, something deep within us, or the outside collective machinery of our culture? Perhaps the real American Dream has long ago been buried under a collective dream that has been force fed to us; and, fattened like cattle, we are led into the collective slaughterhouses of Madison Avenue dreamscapes where we sell our souls to obtain the latest toys.

Our popular American Dream is bought and sold in the marketplace—a dream with hideous contrasts and theological underpinnings that obscures and pushes underground individual dreams that hold the promise of enlarging the human spirit and bringing forth greater integrity and human relatedness. Our Western culture has written a vast, complex Dream Bible, and this collective scripture is filled with potent images, with "shoulds" and "should nots." Its message: "conform and survive, lose your-*Self* (soul) and be accepted into the masses."

Pre-Packaged Dreams

> Success and me,
>   we became partners—made a blood pact,
>   accumulating, growing, empire building.
> Success and me,
>   we had a rule:
> Things come first, people second.
> But just as the palace was complete,
> I realized I'd lost my soul
>   and living in that empty room
>   would be my certain fate.
>
>   John D. Goldhammer

Most of us, myself included, dream of ways to get some portion of the media-packaged American Dream. But the availability of the dream is definitely related to one's socioeconomic status. This means that our relentlessly pursued American Dream is in reality a trickle-down dream, where money and status determine one's place in the dream. One person's portion of the dream may be simple food and shelter and not starving to death, while another's dream may be a still bigger mansion, another million or billion socked away, another mega deal consummated. Individuals who do not fit the collective dream image and those who are *different*— are ostracized with limited possibilities of experiencing the American Dream. They are the dreamless, those of other races, of different sexual persuasions. They are denied admission to our dream and, as a result, are frustrated and enraged by a dream that is perpetually just out of reach. The Dream, like any destructive group, has its rules, its qualifications, its admission requirements, its standards. It does not admit the homeless or the uneducated—our modern-day lepers who have the disease of *being different*. We keep our societal rejects economically banished just as effectively as we isolated leper colonies in former times.

Many black Africans see their community as something to be ashamed of and they reject their particular culture's dreams. Does a black person, or member of any other race, discard his/her dream by stepping outside of their collective community and joining the white culture? Can we change dreams so easily? Does the dream change when our viewing point changes—from inside a particular group's dream to outside looking in?

How does one with a different cultural background contend with an American Dream that is filled with "perfect 10s," prejudice, greed, and bigotry? We have but three choices: (1) remain within a community or culture that is set apart—a sub-dream culture, (2) put on the American Dream costume and play the game, or (3) step into an apparently dreamless landscape where reliance must be on one's own unique dream that springs from within one's soul and heart. In this manner the collective dream is impacted by the authentic dreams of the awakened persons who are no longer mesmerized by the illusion of a media-driven dream. We need to awaken from the collective dream in order to see it for what it is. Perhaps a major aspect of the American twentieth-century hero's journey will be to awaken from our collective dream and slay the collective dream-shaper. We buy (pun intended) into collective dream images while forfeiting our own souls, ending our hero's journey and falling from grace.

The degree to which the collective forces in our society and culture influence our imaginations is beyond calculation. For example, the mass media have so thoroughly implanted ideas and pictures in our minds of how life *should* be lived that we find it difficult to imagine how we could possibly be happy (or fit in) without a proper house with the right furniture; the right car (or cars); enough insurance; a great career; clothing that is "in style;" a good retirement plan; the right soap, deodorant, toothpaste, mouthwash, and breath mints; a perfect figure and weight while at the same time eating the most savory foods.

In addition, we are immersed in the moral and ethical views of mainstream religions. It becomes difficult to find an original thought or idea that is not colored, *culturized,* and *socialized* by some group doctrine. Our minds are culturally active, busy imagining how we can afford the latest hi-tech (adult toy) automobile or a bigger house, or how we can *save* all of China by converting them to our religious, cultural, or economic belief system. The prospect of stopping this addictive pursuit of a culturally sanctioned life style and stepping into the inner journey to find out who we really are is both frightening and dangerous. Our real nature is at home where we are free to express our innate uniqueness, but in the collective this is extremely difficult if not impossible. Our own fears of being different from collective cultural images and dictates are a major obstacle to overcome.

Those who succumb to the collective feel threatened by individuals who do not play by society's rules. In effect, we put on the mask of compromise between the individual and the collective. We are not real, but role playing. When we submit to collective forces, life loses its deeper meaning and purpose. This submission and compromise with the collective produces an "existential crisis" of major proportions for the individual.

And what happens when the media-profit-driven dreams overwhelm our authentic collective and unique individual dreams? How does it affect the world we live in when millions of individuals are placing the priceless wealth of creative, imaginative, and physical resources into a collective Dream Game whose slogan-mantras repeat: "Get your piece of the pie," "Life is short, play hard," "Sacrifice nothing," "Buy now, pay later," "Don't leave home without it," or "More is better"? The message is clear: *Things* are more important than people! In other words, group values make *lifeless* objects more important than living ones. Anything or anybody that does not fit the accepted dream images is expendable, excluded, or ignored.

The American Dream is a collective creature with a life of its own—its shadow side driven by the dark underground factories whose workers have never seen the light of day. The collective dream we have all coauthored profoundly shapes our reality. Is this our pact, our bargain with the Devil? Does some dark god have our souls locked away in deep vaults beneath Madison Avenue and Wall Street?

The American Dream is predominantly a white, Judeo-Christian Dream, hence, an assimilating dream, imaged or clothed in a cultural persona that requires people to relinquish their particular community or cultural dream in order to adopt our acceptable American Dream. To be "successful" we must fit the Dream image. Yet to some extent, we need a collective dream. The challenge is to walk in the dream without being possessed by it. And herein lies the crucial point of tension: between our individual dreams and the collective dream. It is vital that we *hold this tension,* remaining consciously aware of *both dreams,* for both are necessary. The individual dream, usually at odds and conflicting with the collective, nourishes and enriches the collective *because of its difference.*

Our American Dream has become institutionalized—a socializing instrument of economic, religious, and cultural elitism, where we *assimilate* differences instead of *integrating* differences—and it has a very low tolerance for differences. Our own institutions reflect the Dream through policies and agendas that perpetuate the status quo and resist change. We who live in the American Dreamscape have become comfortable with institutions and political leaders who promise to keep the dream intact, to save us all from the consequences of our dream games. Thus we empower groups that keep us politically, economically and culturally medicated to lessen the danger of waking up from the sleep of an unreal collective American Dream. Of course, this cultural hypnosis is not always all-pervasive; in the sixties and seventies, some people did attempt to drop out of the Dream. And now the X generation claims that the American Dream is unattainable and perhaps even undesirable.

As children we receive society's dream implants in the form of parental and other modeling of adult social values, norms, rules, directives, and expectations. We have been hypnotized by collective dream suggestibles for many years, so that as adults, we continue to perpetuate the dream by playing our roles, and the Dream Mantle is passed on from generation to generation. If we strike out as individuals against the American Dream, society punishes or ostracizes us in some way. The hero who escapes the collective dream is always subject to some critical attack by those still caught in the dream.

Dream Eaters

> Battle is the corporate ordeal through which the heroic nation justifies its claim, to be the chosen people of God, the bearers of an historical destiny, the representatives of the sacred.
>
> Sam Keen[7]

The American Dream is a conquering dream. The Americas were *conquered* by the conquistadors. There was no peaceful settlement and integration of native cultures. We shattered and destroyed their dreams, replacing them with our dream. We physically removed African Americans from their dreamscape and left them dreamless—or so we thought. What does it mean to be a race or culture whose collective or community dream has been destroyed? What dream and whose dream replaces it, and can it be replaced? Or does it go underground only to surface later when our false dreams ultimately self-destruct?

The horror wrought by the "discovery" of the Americas typifies the power of collective rationalization, justification, and denial of evil. Glamorizing genocide by turning murderers into heroes is a far too common characteristic of the body politic. Such twisted values can only occur within a collective context where individuals are turned into expendable things. Add to this mob mentality a cruel and inquisitional religious ideology and you have a deadly mixture—a guaranteed holocaust.

In addition to converting the "heathens" to their enlightened theology, the Spaniards, under Columbus, forced Native Americans to look for gold, or their hands were cut off. Historians estimate that as many as six million Native Americans were killed.[8] The Native Americans could not comprehend European greed and brutality. The Indian Wars were cultural genocide.

In his book, *Faces of the Enemy,* Sam Keen illustrates the deadly effect of our "Puritan ethic," which still pervades our collective psyche's air of superiority: "Holy war was continued in the 'new Canaan' by the New Israelites, the Puritans who believed themselves to have a 'manifest destiny' to inhabit America the beautiful, from sea to shining sea, and who, therefore, considered the Native Americans 'the bond slaves of Satan,' 'snares of the Devil,' 'the Devil's instruments.' "[9]

In the 1830s, under President Andrew Jackson's Removal Act, tens of thousands of Indians were forcibly "removed" from their homes and moved to what was then west of the supposed "Permanent Indian Frontier."[10] This border proved to be temporary, as the Indians were gradually removed from all their lands and placed in what were geographic concentration camps, desolate forbidden lands that the "white man" did not want. Only a highly organized militaristic state could have driven the Native Americans out of their homeland. It is ironic that settlers who were fleeing European persecution would themselves become so expert at persecution and terror, further illustrating the fact that the group mind has no conscience and certainly is no respecter of human rights.

The modern American Dream is *exclusive*. It requires conformity and rejects nonconformity. Paradoxically the American Dream is narcissistic and self-centered in the extreme. It believes *It*, the Dream, is the only way. Accordingly, we export our dream culture, our political and economic agendas to *different*, "underdeveloped" countries that do not yet fit our American Dream. We neatly package the American Dream and sell it to whomever will buy into it. This attitude of *one way*—totalitarian dreaming—destroys other dreams like a gigantic mechanical dream-eater consuming the soul life of planet earth—a form of *ego imperialism* or mind control on a global scale.

The American Dream seeks to grab control of the Cosmos, attain perfection, but the Dream is fated to self-destruct because the Cosmos cannot be controlled. In attempting to eradicate what the Dream sees as imperfection and evil, we become possessed by evil.

Can any dream be eliminated from the human spirit? I think not; we are surely trespassers on foreign soil. The Native-American dreams are in the very earth we walk upon—in the winds, the trees, the waters. And possibly we each carry a portion of their dream which moves in us and stirs us to return to a simpler, less complicated life—a dream that values and respects the earth, the environment, and all life instead of selling domination and destruction. The unexpected paradox may be that the different dreams we have attempted to wipe out may in the end be the dreams that save us from self-destruction.

Ultimately, we have more to fear from our collective dreams than from any nuclear war. The dark side of the American Dream threatens to extinguish the creative spirit, the spark of genius, the spiritual mystery of life, the very heart of living. Herein lies each individual's greatest challenge: to succumb to the masses or to live one's own authentic life, and in so doing add a work of real value to one's community and culture.

Group-Induced Racism

Prejudice is never easy unless it can pass itself off for reason.
                                                    Henry Hazlitt[11]

In the West, we have established a hierarchy of races based on color with white as the supreme race. This hierarchy of "color" has its roots in our one-sided religious traditions that are possessed only with notions of goodness, purity, and "light," which are all attributes associated with the color white. The notion of a leader being defined by color, as in a "black leader," sustains racism. Leaders who speak for others through the collective mask of color or any other collective label, destroy and dehumanize those idealists who mistakenly ally themselves with a popular cause. Both blacks and whites, through their militant anticolor viewpoints, have fallen into the mass-mind trap, losing the *only* characteristic that can make a difference in any society: the uniqueness and creativity of the individual.

Black power (militant) groups have made *color* (whiteness) the enemy, projecting the anger and frustration of prejudice onto another group. This mass projection of hatred onto another race is paradoxically exactly what many whites do to the black race. Through a militant stance, the black race, as well as militant white extremists, become what they each hate most. This is the tragic result for any group caught in a one-sided, extreme viewpoint, which necessarily requires an enemy who occupies an opposing position fueling their imagined persecution by another race or group. Groups do not recognize the individual. Instead groups prejudge others based on color, belief, race, culture, or other collective (group) characteristics.

Racial hate groups have a vested interest in supporting leaders who keep whites or blacks "on the hook." This collective shame perpetuates racial separateness. In the case of African Americans, "black" leaders keep the white race full of guilt so that they will continue to assuage their assumed (original sin) guilt with government aid programs and beneficial legislation. However, government aid directed at specific groups empowers and sustains those groups, cultivating more resentment and anger on both sides. In this manner, one group extorts benefits from another group, instead of working to empower themselves as individuals through better education and fostering individual entrepreneurship.

Racial groups (blacks are no exception) tend to make their greatest progress when they are most oppressed. The exodus of oppressed Europeans to the United States, and the end of slavery in the South are but two examples of how tension and conflict produce significant cultural shifts and change. This is not to advocate oppression, but to point out that when nation-states attempt to alleviate all discomfort for a "group" or particular race, they also remove their chief catalyst for change—the tremendous potential contained in tension and adversity to lift, transform, and empower individuals or even an entire race. The best moral aid a state can undertake for the sake of any group is to guarantee authentic freedom and liberty to each and every citizen.

Black Conservatives correctly maintain that dependence on government (systems) has been their downfall and that blacks need to be self-responsible. Interestingly, black Conservatives are against affirmative action programs. Affirmative action programs, while putting forth the pretense of legislating racial equality, actually perpetuate and institutionalize racism and prejudice. Based on color and ethnicity, such programs doom society to a never-ending conflict between collectively defined groups. To be hired because of one's skin color instead of one's ability reinforces interracial hatred and resentment on both sides.

The Japanese rapidly lifted themselves out of defeat into their new role as a major world economic power. Often our greatest potential exists when we are utterly beaten down, filled with anger and rage at some injustice. If we succumb to our rage, or worse, identify with a collective rage, we become what we hate most; and possessed by a collective rage, we strike out in violence and retaliation at our perceived oppressors.

Only when we become self-responsible, that is, take back and own our problems and take responsibility for our own lives, is there hope for renewal, change, and growth. The *awful* tension of being oppressed, as an individual or as a member of a racial group, is exactly what provides the needed soul-intensity fueling transformation. When we find ourselves being persecuted by someone, or by some other race, we are in one sense fortunate because therein is the source of our transformation, our soul-making.

Thus the tension between where we are (and what we are) and what (where) we want to be opens the way to the hidden treasure—the gold in our suffering, our passport to a new land. As the old cliché says, "Necessity is the mother of invention." I would suggest that "tension" is the mother and father of transformation, both physical and spiritual, both individual and collective.

A real individual cannot be defined by a stereotype, which represents a collective composite, a group-generated image. Some of the more common group stereotypes in our culture include: baby boomers, generation x, feminists, yuppies, wasps, gay/straight, black/white, and poor white trash. Stereotypical images tend to entice us into labeling and judging other individuals because of our perception of their social group.

The Cult of Color in America

I have a dream that my four little children will one day live in a nation where they will not be judged by the color of their skin but by the content of their character.

Martin Luther King, Jr.[12]

By trying to live up to collective expectations, we become our own oppressors. Whites and blacks, as well as many other groups, are caught in a collective mystique of "color." Thus we have the ludicrous examples of blacks cosmetically lightening their skin color, straightening their hair, changing the shapes of their noses and lips in order to ascend the hierarchy of color, to look like a white Anglo-Saxon. As a nation, we have so instilled a collective image of smug superiority that even other races alter their physical appearance. Asians change the shape of their eyes to look more "American." People alter hair styles to fit acceptable, usually "white" images.

It comes as no revelation that color plays a major role in fragmenting our world into often hostile, separated camps. Whatever the reason, our reaction to skin color has become a deeply ingrained, nearly unconscious reflex in our collective culture. Charisse Jones, a black reporter for the *New York Times*, says, "A racist encounter hurts badly. But it does not equal the pain of 'colorism'—being rejected by your own people because your skin is colored cocoa and not cream, ebony and not olive. On our scale of beauty, it is often the high yellows—in the lexicon of black America, those with light skin—whose looks reap the most attention."[13]

Blacks who identify with their color instead of their individuality are themselves perpetuating racism and at the same time empowering a group stereotype based on skin color. Placing color as a dominant characteristic, color-identified individuals adopt a collective exclusiveness and arrogance combined with a sense of persecution from groups who are "different"; meanwhile, individual autonomy and sense of self must be repressed. This dynamic holds true for ethnicity, too; a particular ethnic group, as in Hispanic, Asian, or Native American, carries powerful images—many of which are propaganda-based—related to our perceptions of a "group," which do not tell us anything about an individual.

Relying on others, particularly groups, fosters irresponsibility and helplessness. Allowing others to do what we are quite able to do for ourselves breeds a society of seeming victims—dehumanized, frustrated, angry people.

We have fallen into a culture of having "someone else" do everything for us: package and cook our food, make our clothes, decide what medicines we are "allowed" to take, and so on. As a result we enshrine comfort, and perpetuate a childlike dependency and lethargy. The vital lifeblood of independence and self-sufficiency drains from our society. I do not mean to imply that we should return to a preindustrialized way of life, but that we ought to carefully choose what we allow others to do for us, especially if it means giving up any degree of freedom and our ability to make intelligent choices.

What groups are doing to individuals now is not unlike what we did as a nation-state to Africans brought to this country as slaves. They were "seasoned." Seasoning referred to a period of time for newly arrived slaves to adapt to our Western culture. Part of this seasoning or aculturation process meant they were forbidden to speak their own language—a form of verbal ethnic cleansing. Added to the fact that they were not allowed to learn to read or write was the prohibition against practicing their native religion. By destroying their language and religion, we effectively destroyed their culture. As a result, a tremendous *gap* was created between what they were and what they were being seasoned to become. Black Africans filled this gap with their version of "white" Christianity and a newly formed "black English."

Their process of becoming Christians created another immense conflict, one *between appearance and reality.* African Americans found themselves worshiping a white man's Jesus who espoused love for all, yet the blacks found themselves persecuted by an offensive white Christianity. How do you worship a white god who is the god of your oppressors? Out of this tension "irony," song, and a great sense of humor were born. Thus the African Americans' songs and humor became their collective soul-therapy—a poignant commentary on the impossible circumstances they found themselves in. In this way, they found their voice once more, a voice that had been taken from them in the dehumanizing *seasoning* of an entire race. In this manner, black Africans were *assimilated* into our culture, or at least we made the attempt at assimilation—to make them like *us,* but inferior. Hence the collective need for strong black heroes to compensate for their enforced cultural inferiority. This is not to say that blacks should survive as a collective entity, but that any group that has been stripped of their self-esteem, both as individuals and as a race, desperately needs mentors, real people who mirror back hope, potential, and sense of self-worth as human beings. However, such mentors need not be black or any particular color. Insisting on only black mentors serves to perpetuate racial separateness and enmity.

A big portion of the black community's anger and rage exemplifies the stages one goes through as part of the deprogramming process—deprogramming from the established collective status quo. In leaving their imposed collective identity, a natural rage develops from the dawning realization of what has really happened. Paradoxically, the only way for

African Americans to differentiate from their persecutors is to *drop all connection with color* because it is precisely *color* that keeps them identified with an ethnic group which carries their own projected hatred and that of generations of whites.

We forced an entire culture to wear a false face, to live inauthentic lives, to be something they were not.

Elija Mohammed's group, the Nation of Islam, maintains that all white people are "devils." They believe in separation of the black and white races, and that whites must make reparations to the black race. The Nation of Islam's identification with *color* instead of individual character maintains and guarantees racial hatred between two groups who, when labeled by skin color, drag others into unwilling membership in one or the other. Such are the underpinnings of fanatical mass movements, which must create devils in order to grow and survive. Mass movements thrive by perpetuating identification with a cause, whose outcome is usually far removed from the reality of everyday life into some distant "paradise."

Fanatical mass movements like the Nation of Islam claim to have a doctrine "to heal the ills of the Nations."[14] The promise of an imminent earthly or nonearthly paradise, whether religious, political, or economic, is a fundamental psychological carrot such organizations permanently dangle in front of their members. By placing "paradise" out of reach in some distant future, groups depreciate the present making self-sacrifice and violence justifiable because it involves a life that is imperfect and flawed in a world perceived as persecutory.

Not surprising then, Louis Farrakhan, a prominent Nation of Islam minister, believes drugs are part of a government conspiracy to subjugate and possibly destroy blacks. Like all destructive groups, they must create another group or system to carry their own growing and virulent shadow. Without a devil to fight, such groups lapse into stagnant institutions or eventually collapse entirely. Leaders like Farrakhan perpetuate what they claim to hate most, racism and prejudice. Sadly becoming just like their persecutors, they infect millions with the virus of separatism and fragmentation. Black leaders like Farrakhan help to maintain the spirit of racism and prejudice in the world. What they call "black rage" keeps "black" individuals trapped in labels and attitudes, segregated by color, and identified with a collective rage that must find another group to blame and to hate. Thus Farrakhan's ministry of hate serves the darkest side of human nature—collective rage.

Our Collective Costumes

> No man, for any considerable period, can wear one face to himself, and another to the multitude, without finally getting bewildered as to which may be the true.
>
> Nathaniel Hawthorne[15]

When we step out of our cultural costumes, we are at a loss as to know who is what. Lacking tribal reference points such as dress and fashion, we find it difficult to classify or label others. Perhaps that is one reason why we're so uncomfortable around those who dress in unorthodox ways. In this sense, the clothes we wear to enable us to fit into our peer group, to be accepted or rejected, define who and what we are within a collective context. Clothes do talk, make a statement, tell others about who we are.

As our collective bonds tighten their grip, we instinctively feel the need to remove our clothes, get rid of our cultural costumes, and find out who we really are. Hence we dream of being naked or half-clothed. In the1990s we cut flesh (cosmetic surgery) instead of cloth. We tattoo our bodies. Our fashion is getting closer and closer to our skins, as if we are trying to see ourselves stripped of our collective garb and get a sense of our real identity. The human body becomes a political battleground, a dialogue between the unseen self and our collective culture.

The persona is our way of adapting to the collective, the way we compromise who we are. Of course, we need a certain degree of collective compromise to survive, but far too often we come to believe that our collective garb—both psychological and physical—is who we are. Indeed, we find after much self-introspection and inner work that we have forgotten the authentic self, that we are playing a role that has become our reality, and that we have voluntarily enslaved ourselves. In this way the persona can become a formidable prison, particularly when we find ourselves stuck in a totalistic collective system of reward and punishment as in money, fame, or prestige, which come to those who obediently and single-mindedly fulfill their social roles. Thus we find it difficult to really know a person, especially when all we are exposed to is the individual's public persona.

Similarly, our careers become a major part of this collective costume. Many of us have the nagging feeling that we are really living someone else's life. Susan Wittig Albert concluded, "We must free ourselves from the career culture's definition of what constitutes praiseworthy human endeavor, for if we continue to be held hostage by our careers, there will be nothing left of our families and our communities, not to speak of our souls."[16]

II

Breaking Free

The monster stands also for the crowd within, . . . the crowd soul of man, against which one can only stand *if one does not sell one's soul to an organization and has the courage to stand completely alone.* [Emphasis added]

Marie-Louise Von Franz, *Dreams* (1991)

Today no meaning is in the group—none in the world: all is in the individual. But there the meaning is absolutely unconscious. The lines of communication between the conscious and the unconscious zones of the human psyche have all been cut, and we have been split in two.

Joseph Campbell, *The Hero with a Thousand Faces* (1949)

11

Slaying the Collective Dragon

Piece by piece I seem to re-enter the world.

Adrienne Rich[1]

A god can do it. But tell me, how can a man follow his narrow road
through the strings? A man is split. And where two roads intersect inside
us, no one has built the Singer's Temple.

Rainer Maria Rilke[2]

I said to this wanting-creature inside me:
What is this river you want to cross?
There are no travelers on the river-road, and no road.
Do you see anyone moving about on that bank,
     or resting?
There is no river at all, and no boat, and no boatman.
There is no towrope either, and no one to pull it.
There is no ground, no sky, no time,
     no bank, no ford!
And there is no body, and no mind!
Do you believe there is someplace
     that will make the soul less thirsty?
In that great absence you will find nothing.

Kabir[3]

253

Collective Deprogramming

> One defeats the fanatic precisely by *not* being a fanatic oneself, but on the contrary by using one's intelligence.
>
> George Orwell[4]

Perhaps our modern mythical journey will be to slay the collective dragon, a far more ominous monster than the one Saint George faced. Joseph Campbell, in his book *The Power of Myth,* explains how mythology clarifies the tension between individuals and the collective: "Star Wars has a valid mythological perspective. It shows the state as a machine and asks, 'Is the machine going to crush humanity or serve humanity?' . . . When Luke Skywalker unmasks his father, he is taking off the machine role that the father has played. The father was the uniform. That is power, the state role."[5]

THE HERO'S ADVENTURE

> The self lies hidden in the shadow; he is the keeper of the gate, the guardian of the threshold. The way to the self lies through him; behind the dark aspect that he represents there stands the aspect of wholeness, and only by making friends with the shadow do we gain the friendship of the self.
>
> Erich Neumann[6]

There are two basic adventures: following the crowd or following your own path. Entering a group in one's search for meaning and purpose is a contradiction, a blunder with dire consequences, an *unwilling initiation* that most people never recover from until it's too late.

The darkness or monster that the hero must overcome is first one's own state of unconsciousness. Second, the hero/heroine must extricate him/herself from collective entanglements and influence. From a psychological perspective, becoming more conscious—integrating unconscious contents—is the hero's task. One's own unique individuality and creative potential is the sacred treasure sought by the hero. Blocking the pathway to this inner treasure, we encounter a collective implanted mind-set—a formidable beast indeed! This collective mind tells us what we "should" do in order to conform to our social group; this beast is our inner patriarchal authority—an inner tyrant overflowing with rules, dogma, and tradition. "He" is the establishment, the "Old King" in our psyche, and he wants to stay in total control of his kingdom. Our *cultural unconscious* challenges those who attempt to cross the boundaries of what is "acceptable." In essence, a collective "threshold guardian" who represents our tribal taboos challenges anyone attempting to extricate themselves from the collective.

Going against our inner collective voice results in deep feelings of guilt and fear, for in trying to find our own lives, we must confront nearly invincible collective currents. A collective umbilical cord keeps us attached to group consciousness. Only by severing this collective cord are we free to live our own lives. When we attempt to leave any collective authority, a group or the state—Pharoah's armies disguised as the Internal Revenue Service, the church, families, mental health institutions, flag-waving patriots, tradition, the educational system, the market system, the legal system—pursue us, intent upon either destroying us or returning us to our "proper place." The single most used word in their vocabulary is "should." I once heard about a therapist who had this sign on her office wall: "I promise not to *should* on myself today."

We abort our own journey when living vicariously (projecting our inner hero-self) through others who become our heroes: those individuals who have found and used their treasure and who have slain the inner dragon of "should." One of our major mythological motifs, the hero's main task is to "overcome the monster of darkness: it is the long-hoped-for and expected triumph of consciousness over the unconscious."[7] Since our greatest enemy, collective implants, lurks in the unconscious, we are most often unaware of the tremendous significance of the life-and-death struggle going on. Instead, encountering all manner of fear and doubt thanks to the collective beast, we return to Egypt and give up the battle. For many, the security and comfort of collective bondage is preferable to the self-responsibility that true freedom requires. We self-medicate our existential frustration—that nagging feeling that something is missing—with food, endless activities, travel, drugs, and alcohol in an attempt to make group-directed life bearable. "They" will continue to take care of us, solve our problems, plan our future, tell us when we "should" retire. Voting occasionally will make me feel important, a serious contributor to the democratic process.

ACTIVE IMAGINATION: ANIMATING OUR SYMBOLIC WORLD

> One does not become enlightened by imagining figures of light, but by making the darkness conscious. Philemon and other fantasy figures brought me the decisive knowledge that there are things in the psyche that I do not produce, but that produce themselves and have their own life.
>
> Carl Jung[8]

Active imagination is an important depth psychology tool to help individuals differentiate from groups as well as a way to integrate conscious and unconscious elements of the individual psyche. To differentiate from any group means to act, think, and reason as a distinct individual without the influence of collective ideas and images. Undifferentiated individuals cannot think independently because they cannot separate what is uniquely their own conscience, and authenticity from group ideals, fantasies, and images; they do not know themselves. A Jungian technique, active imagination provides a way to begin one's own journey into the unconscious, the inner, in between realms of the psyche, and in so doing, begin the process of extricating oneself from group-implanted images and doctrine. As a spiritual/psychological technique, active imagination is *pathless* in that it offers one the singular adventure of entering the unconscious in an *undirected* and unplanned way, without preconceived collective images and ideologies. Because it does not have an orientation to any dogma, group, or organized religion, active imagination moves into unique soul domains, accessing and acknowledging one's inner community of gods, goddesses, daimons, and angels—the ultimate hero's journey. This unprogrammed inner movement directly opposes our outer collective entanglements. Hence, if used without premeditation, active imagination does not reinforce cultural or collective values, but instead marks a singular quest, and, as such, is *antigroup* and a collective deprogramming self-therapy that places the individual human soul first.

Many groups perceive depth psychology as a real threat because it empowers individuals and encourages individual integrity devoid of ideological programming. Active imagination is a potent depth psychology tool to help individuals differentiate themselves from the masses as well as a way to integrate the conscious and unconscious elements of the individual psyche. Differentiation from groups does not mean absolute separation, but rather a *continuing relatedness* centered in an *autonomous holding of multiple viewpoints.* Robert Johnson, a noted lecturer and Jungian analyst, in his book *Owning Your Own Shadow,* explains how active imagination works:

> The unconscious is not something to be manipulated to suit the purposes of the conscious mind, but an equal partner to engage in dialogue that leads to fuller maturity. Active imagination consists in going to the images that rise up in one's imagination and making a dialogue with them. It involves an encounter with the images. This often means a spoken conversation with the figures who present themselves, but it also involves entering into the action, the adventure or conflict that is spinning its story out of one's imagination. It is this awareness, this conscious participation in the imaginal event, that transforms it from mere passive fantasy to Active Imagination. When we experience the images, we also directly experience the inner parts of ourselves that are clothed in the images.[9]

There is tension (opposition) between the use of active imagination as applied in depth psychology to open the unconscious and the collective influences in one's culture. Because active imagination helps to differentiate individual consciousness from the mass mind, the mass mind-set (both within and outside the individual psyche) tries to suppress individual imagination and creativity, if not overtly, then covertly.

Unfortunately, religious doctrine has impressed upon individuals the necessity of excluding "blasphemous" or "sinful" thoughts and images. Such mental repression becomes a serious form of mind control. Many New Age metaphysical movements stress the need to think only positive, loving thoughts—a *one-sided* attitude that automatically represses the full range of human feelings and emotions.

As with any form of repression, the potential always exists the for violent acting out of repressed feelings as a direct result of not dealing with them at the time of their occurrence. Trying to keep only loving thoughts in one's mind and still live in the real world means we must suppress gigantic amounts of legitimate emotion and feeling. Any one-sided obsession becomes food for inner demons of hate and rage, which sooner or later grow to overwhelming proportions.

The human soul instinctively struggles to break free of collective influences in order to live a free, authentic life. Just as there are developmental stages in a family, there are stages of differentiation that mark one's emergence from the masses and one's existence as a unique individual. In essence, we are not mature spiritually, psychologically, or emotionally until we have separated from the infantalizing group mind.

As an adult, emergence from collective isms brings about a powerful spiritual and psychological rebirthing experience. An important symbolic aspect of the inner child is one's inner potential that has been pressed out of existence by the group mind. In our collective culture, ideological totalism has driven the divine child from the human psyche. The established order always sees the appearance of this inner divinity (spark of soul) in the individual as a threat. Marie-Louise Von Franz, in her book *Projection and Re-Collection in Jungian Psychology*, describes this process: "As in Egyptian theology and mythology, the king in alchemy represents a dominant of collective consciousness. When the birth of a divine child is prophesied, the old king trembles, fearing to lose his position."[10] Our inner child, like the infant Jesus, is run out of town. We each must face our inner "old king," who would put to death our innocence, hope, and soul-passion for living our own lives. Achieving a greater state of wholeness and *integrity* is a fundamental goal of depth psychology. Each person has a spiritual gradient toward wholeness and integration, which creates a David-and-Goliath style conflict with societal forces that work on *deindividuation* and mechanizing the individual.

We are programmed to live in a *collective pleasure principle.* Finding an original thought or idea that is not polluted, colored, *culturized,* and *socialized* by the media or by some group doctrine is a formidable endeavor. We have to psychologically step outside group landscapes and see through different eyes—eyes that retain their memory of seeing a mythology from within a particular group's viewpoint, but are not caught by that viewpoint. By stepping outside, our viewpoint shifts and a sort of psychological distancing occurs. Thus we can best see a group or an entire culture for what it really is by removing ourselves from it. Distance gives us a new way of seeing, increasing knowledge in the same way that viewing the Earth from space gives us new understanding and appreciation for this little corner of the galaxy.

Jung described how collective forces threaten to stifle the differentiation process, and in so doing, suffocate the precise uniqueness and individual creativity that society so desperately needs:

> Collective thinking and feeling and collective effort are far less of a strain than individual functioning and effort; hence there is always a great temptation to allow collective functioning to take the place of individual differentiation of the personality. For the development of personality, then, strict differentiation from the collective psyche is absolutely necessary, since partial or blurred differentiation leads to an immediate melting away of the individual in the collective. As a result, the one source of moral and spiritual progress for society is choked up. Naturally, the only thing that can thrive in such an atmosphere is sociality and whatever is collective in the individual. Everything individual in him goes under, i.e., is doomed to repression.[11]

When the emergence of one aspect of my own abandoned child actually began, at first I did not understand what was happening. Using active imagination, I found myself continually seeing images of black African children who were starving. One particular small boy with bones protruding came up repeatedly in my imagination. It didn't occur to me at the time that my unconscious was attempting to show me my own deeply wounded and emotionally starved inner child. In the beginning I began praying for starving children in Africa; I spoke to this child, trying to acknowledge his hardship and to comfort him in some way. This dream soon followed: I found myself standing in the desert, holding this small child in my arms. He was looking up at me with giant, deep-set eyes, and those eyes were saying "thank you" in a way that no words could ever articulate.

At the time, I thought this dream was showing me that I was actually helping some distant starving children (the common mistake of concretizing a dream experience). But it soon dawned on me that this starved child was actually a long neglected part of my own psyche. I had emotionally starved myself for many years. By suppressing my feelings as a small boy, especially after my father's death, I denied myself the inner nourishment of the grieving process, starving and almost killing a vital part of my psyche. I had created my own inner wasteland, a desert with no tears, no feeling, no sorrows—no soul. After all, "Big boys don't cry."

To say that I was both moved and stunned by this realization would be an understatement. I was playing the *culturally acceptable* role of the macho male who does not cry or show any emotions. I was acting out my savior complex, concerned for those who were not acceptable in my collective system. The fact that this child was near death and black is certainly symbolic. Black, in the West, is a symbol of death, mourning, grief, sadness, and also the unseen or unconscious. Black Africans suffer tremendous oppression and repression by a white puritanical and prejudiced culture. This oppressive white culture had become a mechanistic part of my psyche; I *was* my own oppressor! Alchemically, black is dissolution and fermentation. This symbolic inner black child from Africa, the *Dark* Continent, is a living, growing part of my psyche that needs the nourishment of tears and of deep feeling.

Symbols point the way to something in the process of becoming. Because of this, creating a dialogue with a symbol opens the ancient gate to our "Secret Garden." A sacred inner journey begins in which the symbolic soul-language of the unconscious becomes, through our direct experience, a part of our conscious life. This process of incorporating symbols into our lives produces a deep, profound sense of meaning and sacredness—an honoring and celebration of who we really are as individual human beings.

For example, we can inquire of a symbol, "What are you trying to become in me?" What metaphor does this symbol represent? Jung maintained that we must live out what the unconscious sends. So living a soul-full life means that it is of paramount importance to incorporate each symbolic experience into our conscious awareness and everyday life, whether from dreams or active imagination.

As a result of reawakening this long abandoned child, I sense a deep validation somehow—that it is okay to feel deeply, to cry, to grieve deeply. This symbolic experience also helped to release me from the expectations of our culture and macho male role playing. It is now all right to acknowledge this long abandoned inner child, which was near death from my own neglect. From such experiences we learn how vital it is to allow ourselves to feel and *experience* grief and to work *through* life instead of burying it or locking some inner child in the cellar without food or water so that we can put on a culturally sanctioned mask of strength, which is actually cowardice in disguise perpetuating a collective codependency.

Such is the pervasiveness of collective influences in one's life and the devastating effect on one's real nature, which is most often submerged in some group ideology. Our emotionally starved inner child can often be touched or moved by art and music, which is another way to link up with the conscious world. Certain music can have a deep effect on one's inner child and on other unconscious aspects of one's nature as well. Whenever we have the desire to hear a particular song over and over, perhaps we are hearing a cry from a lost part of ourselves—a message from deep within wanting acknowledgment and to find expression in our life. This is the value of honoring and genuinely examining the feelings associated with music, symbols, art, moods, and imaginings.

There is a wonderful story about King Arthur's knights: The knights were all seated for dinner, but Arthur would not let the meal begin until an adventure had been decided upon. The knights decided to go in pursuit of the Holy Grail, but "They thought it would be a disgrace to go forth in a group. Each entered the forest that 'he' had chosen where there was no path and where it was darkest."[12] Active imagination is one way to "enter the forest at its darkest point."[13] Accessing the unconscious is a singular journey that each person must undertake. We will find no path to follow and no road map through this inner world. That many individuals have made this journey reassures us that we also can make it. But each individual's experience and journey is unique. Individual difference and uniqueness are precisely what group forces threaten to kill.

There are uncountable techniques of meditation, elaborate formulas, rituals, prayers, groups, priests, and gurus for connecting one with the divine or the transcendent, but most of these mean we are following another's path and not our own. Maturity includes extricating oneself from collective influences, and a consciousness differentiated from one's cultural group indicates true adulthood. Nietzsche said the mature individual "is a wheel rolling out of its center."[14] Old wisdom seems to slip easily from the grasp of our collectively automated hands. An epitaph on a tombstone in Boothill Cemetery admonishes: "Be what you is, cuz if you be what you ain't, then you ain't what you is."[15] The prominent Indian philosopher Krishnamurti, who rejected Theosophy's plans to appoint him the world's "new Messiah," said, "Truth is a pathless land. Man cannot come to it through any organization, through any creed, through any dogma, priest or ritual."[16] Breaking free of group influences means achieving a deeper understanding of who you and I really are as unique individuals.

THIRTEEN STEPS FOR RECOVERY FROM THE GROUP MIND

Disengaging from the group mind requires the courage and integrity to think for oneself. A radical shift of emphasis from the influences of the external world is the first step in slaying the collective dragon. The following guidelines support and protect the natural development of the self, free of destructive collective influences:

(1) Responsible self-interest: Make sure *your interests come first*, before the *group's* agenda and their doctrine.

(2) Always question collective authority. Examine their motives and the consequences of their actions: do they increase or decrease individual freedom and autonomy, and are the group's actions *harmless* both to individuals and to our environment?

(3) Have self-responsibility: refuse to participate in demonizing any other group or ideology. Dividing the world into good and evil camps is a patriarchal disease.

(4) Allow *no censorship* of any conflicting opinions or written material from within or outside your group.

(5) Never allow peer pressure to influence your decisions or choices. Follow *your* heart, not a collective illusion.

(6) Stop collective idolatry. Take back your projections. See and respect individuals for who they really are, not cloaked in the collective mystique of fame, guruship, or celebrity.

(7) Debug your vocabulary: Remove "groupese" from your language (see chapter 3). Speak for yourself and your unique authenticity and distinctiveness.

(8) Don't label others. Refuse to categorize others by group characteristics such as color, ethnicity, nationality, or economic status.

(9) Make *independent critical thinking* your mainstay. Protect the freedom and autonomy of your own mind.

(10) Stop being an "enabler": beware of any *public* testimonials or sharings that support a group's ideology. Be sure you are not trapped into supporting something you do not believe in or have doubts about, just to feel "accepted."

(11) Suspect anything called "sacred" by the collective: groups frequently cloak their agenda in an aura of sacredness. The unspoken implication is that any criticism of what the collective deems to be "sacred" is sacrilegious and a moral sin.

(12) Maintaining friendships outside one's group helps to mitigate one-sided collective influence and promotes fresh and different viewpoints.

(13) Discover your own mythology.* Begin by writing/painting/drawing

---

*By "mythology" I refer to those stories, legends, and symbolic images—both personal and collective—that Joseph Campbell describes as "metaphorical of the possibilities and fulfillment in a given culture in a given time. Mythology is a metaphor. God, angels, purgatory, these are metaphors." (From a *New York Times* interview, February 1985.)

your story, creating your *life totem*. Record and work with your dreams; invite the dream world into your life—let these two realms collide and resonate.

Becoming Your Own Soul Therapist

> [The serious purpose of genuine art] is not merely to translate the human being into a momentary dream of freedom, but actually to *make* him free. It accomplishes this by awakening a power within him, by using and developing this power to remove to a distance of objectivity the sensory world, which otherwise only weighs us down as raw material and oppresses us as a blind force.
>
> Friedrich Schiller[17]

Psychological adaptation means becoming aware of the *middle ground* between one's own unique psyche and the collective, and making this middle ground a creative place—a unique way in which one contributes to one's community and culture. Vital for both individual integrity and a healthy society, holding this psychological/spiritual space in between protects one from compromise and one-sided, soul-deadening conformity.

Practical examples of this middle ground can be found in any creative process. For example, the architect's creativity arises out of the conflict between a physical environment, building codes, and a design idea or image.

CREATING YOUR PERSONAL TOTEM

> Don't be satisfied with stories, how things have gone with others. Unfold your own myth.
>
> Rumi[17]

Discovering one's own myth means finding your unique story, which, as Joseph Campbell points out, is crucial in connecting the individual to the collective world: "The mythogenetic zone today is the individual in contact with his own interior life, communicating through his art with those 'out there.' "[19] Creating a *personal totem* or *life totem* is a way to go deeply into your own authenticity—your sorrows and suffering, and your joys and ecstasies—to find out more about who you really are. A life totem tells the story of your life from birth to the present time. It helps you discover your unique mythology, the psychological motif by which you live your life. Sam Keen, a colleague of Joseph Campbell, points out that contrary to popular notions of myth as a "fabrication" or "lie," "*myth* refers to an intricate set of interlocking stories, rituals, rites, and customs that inform and give the pivotal sense of meaning and direction to a person, family, community, or culture."[20] Constructing your own totem is a profound experience and you should be prepared for unearthing many powerful feelings and emotions that perhaps have been long forgotten. The process of creating a personal totem is a potent self-therapy. You become your own *soul-therapist.*

To begin the process, you will need to write down the major events and experiences in your life; these pivotal events will form the divisions on your totem. As an example, I will describe my own totem (see illustration, p. 266). I built my totem out of two cardboard mailing tubes that together provided a six-foot pole about four inches in diameter. Your totem could also be a long drawing or any other form you decide on. My totem begins with birth at the bottom and ends with the present time on top. It includes poetry, jewelry, pictures, photos, and my Elephant Self—the animal I feel closest to from certain dreams and spiritual experiences.

The totem tells my life story whose major events include themes of great loss, struggle, death, grief, escape, renewal, and spiritual awakening. This process evokes strong emotions, memories, passions, joys, and sorrows. A totem reveals collective and cultural influences, the belief systems that shape and impact our lives. I grappled with many obstacles in myself during the process, but found out more about myself in a rich and insightful manner, adding meaning and a sense of inner direction and purpose. My totem has a prominent place in our home, and when I am tempted to slip into some work or place that is not right, it reminds and encourages me to stay with who I really am—my authentic self.

The "Talking Staff Council," a story-telling, imaginative exercise, can be done in a small group of five to ten persons. A staff or totem is passed around the circle. Beginning with a spontaneous story, each person tells their moment/part in the story, but the stick or staff speaks, not the person. One begins by saying, "I am . . . " This exercise provides insight into both individual and group unconscious material, which helps clarify how individuals affect a group.

POLYTHEISM: CONNECTING WITH OUR INNER COMMUNITY

How many natures lie in human nature!

Blaise Pascal[21]

What James Hillman calls "personifying" provides another way to access one's inner community while retaining one's autonomy free of any internal or external domination. Hillman suggests that "we are each a field of internal personal relationships." Personifying gives us a way to deprogram a collectively implanted "One God," hierarchal consciousness. Hillman wrote:

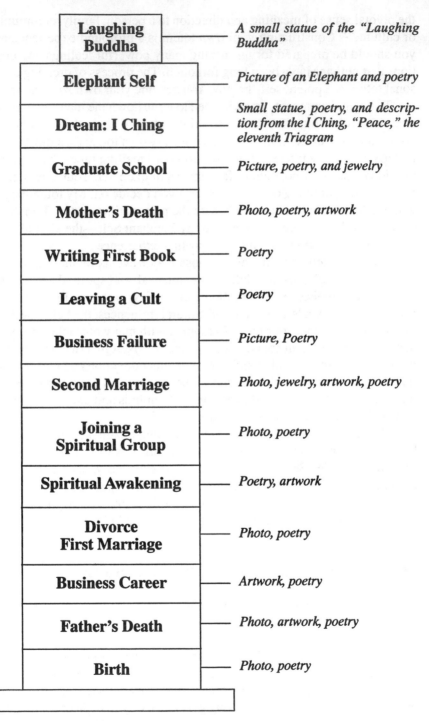

Laughing Buddha	*A small statue of the "Laughing Buddha"*
Elephant Self	*Picture of an Elephant and poetry*
Dream: I Ching	*Small statue, poetry, and description from the I Ching, "Peace," the eleventh Triagram*
Graduate School	*Picture, poetry, and jewelry*
Mother's Death	*Photo, poetry, artwork*
Writing First Book	*Poetry*
Leaving a Cult	*Poetry*
Business Failure	*Picture, Poetry*
Second Marriage	*Photo, jewelry, artwork, poetry*
Joining a Spiritual Group	*Photo, poetry*
Spiritual Awakening	*Poetry, artwork*
Divorce First Marriage	*Photo, poetry*
Business Career	*Artwork, poetry*
Father's Death	*Photo, artwork, poetry*
Birth	*Photo, poetry*

Author's Life Totem

[Personification] implies a human being who creates gods in human like-ness much as an author creates characters out of his own personality. These gods depict his own needs; they are his projections. . . . [Personifying's] purpose is . . . to save the diversity and autonomy of the psyche from dom-ination by any single power; whether this domination be by a figure of ar-chetypal awe in one's surroundings or by one's own egomania.[22]

Hillman's insistence on preserving the "diversity and autonomy of the psyche" is profoundly pertinent to our process of collective deprogram-ming. By dismantling an *inner, collectively implanted* single authority structure, which amounts to no less than a monotheistic possession of the psyche, one begins the process of interconnecting one's *inner* autonomous parts (personalization).

Thus a deepening, widening consciousness embraces an autonomous multiplicity of personas and images, which have a psychic life of their own. Thomas Moore summarizes this concept, "A polytheistic position *holds ten-sion* [emphasis added] so that 'all parties concerned' find a way to coexist."[23] Of course coexistence between all parties concerned applies both to individ-uals and to the collective. Coexistence is a "both/and" approach as opposed to a patriarchal "either/or" doctrine. The former allows working through, the latter only permits taking sides—one of our destructive group dynamics.

Personifying approaches the *mid-point,* our in between soul-making place. Imagining our inner conflicting elements as psychic personalities, whether gods, imps, tricksters, lovers, gurus, or enemies, provides an at-mosphere of self-involved conflict—a gestalt, animating and giving life to inner relationships. Animating relationships *in between* the inner parts of the psyche gets one out of a concrete one-sided point of view, which is a collective infectious disease. One becomes a player on the stage of one's own psyche. For insightful inner communication, one must hold the chaos (tension) between the gods in one's psyche *without taking sides.*

Moreover, Hillman maintains, "A variety of gods and goddesses are to be honored, the *tensions* among them sustained and enjoyed"[24] (emphasis added). From personifying, surprising unexpected insights emerge. Once we put a face on an enemy and know that it belongs to us, hostilities di-minish, consciousness and empathy increase, and our own shadow side be-comes less threatening. For this reason, *naming* our inner personalities is important. Naming gives them more autonomy and more humanity, which also helps to differentiate one from collective authoritarian systems.

Hillman refers to personifying as a "polytheistic psychology" with the "location of consciousness in multiple figures and centers."[25] Discon-necting from a culturally implanted monolithic system is necessary to get into the space of the in-between—into a soul-making perspective.

The Christian inclination to demonize these inner members of the psyche is an ongoing tragedy with ominous implications for our psychological and spiritual well-being. Demonizing one's inner soul life perpetuates our authoritarian collective monotheism which is inherently one-sided, extremist, and certain to be fanatical in its holy war against itself. Additionally, this book postulates that much of our extreme social violence is a result of outwardly projected inner demonized (one-sided) contents of the psyche acted out by *group-influenced* persons who are unconscious of relationships in between.

Extending our inner community imaginative work out into the collective enables us to look at social ills as metaphors. Gang violence, religious and political fanaticism, terrorist organizations, and group brutality when seen as metaphors can lead to creative soul-based solutions. For example, a gang protecting its territory becomes a band of medieval knights defending their castle (king), revealing the need for individuals to protect their autonomy and sense of self. Or perhaps gang members are acting out the repressed mythological violence our Disneyesque, in-denial metaphysics has nicely edited out of our fairy-tales and folklore. Lacking any exposure as children to the shadow side in our culture's stories, they live under the spell of this edited-out dark side.

THE INNER SHAMAN

> This be my pilgrimage and goal
> Daily to march and find
> The secret phrases of the soul
> The evangels of the mind.
>
> John Drinkwater[26]

The shaman might be thought of as one of the guides of our inner journey. Carl Jung dialogued with his inner shaman, "Philemon," who "represented superior insight: "He was a mysterious figure to me. At times he seemed to me quite real, as if he were a living personality. I went walking up and down the garden with him, and to me he was what the Indians call a guru."[27] We each need to find our *inner insight* that provides the way out of collective entrapments and that becomes a guide for our journey. But we must also be careful to remember that we have innumerable parts, perhaps multiple shamans, and that no single individual aspect of one's psyche must be in charge, for this would set up an inner authority figure, a totalitarian religious establishment emulating an outer church with its priests as patriarchal intermediaries.

DREAMS AND GROUPS

> One can understand every dream as a drama in which we ourselves are *everything*, that is, the author, director, actors, and prompter, as well as the spectators. If one tries to understand a dream in this way, the result is a startling realization for the dreamer of what is happening in him psychically, "behind his back," so to speak.
>
> Marie-Louise Von Franz[28]

Dream work is an important intervention between the individual and groups, particularly due to the fact that dreaming provides access to an in between space in consciousness, between the conscious and unconscious realms. In fact, we can think of the dream world as a symbolic mixture of two worlds: conscious and unconscious. However, imbedded in these two worlds is another element, *the relationship between the individual and the collective*—what Andrew Samuels, a training analyst of the Society of Analytical Psychology in London and author of *The Political Psyche,* calls "the political." Indeed, Samuels maintains that this relationship "constitutes a further transcendent function, a further statement about another crucial property of imagery."[29] In other words, dream imagery, on another level, reveals collective psychic infection—ailments of the human spirit transmitted from destructive collective agencies—a sort of pollution by group. The implication is that we can work with our relationship to our community and to any group through dream symbology and imagery. Our dreams reveal that we are each implicated in our institutions and systems, both inwardly and outwardly, whether we are aware of it or not.

When we subject the soul to an outer or inner tyranny, such as involvement in some group, our dreams inevitably communicate an inner dynamic of compensation from the unconscious. The self-regulating nature of the psyche seeks to maintain a balance between consciousness and unconsciousness, as well as a balance between who we really are as individuals and our collective personas.

All messages from the unconscious are profoundly important, especially dreams. Keeping a dream journal is a prerequisite to accessing and working with crucial parts of the psyche that we have repressed or refuse to look at. The psyche invariably tries to alert us to this one-sidedness through dreams, some physical problem, psychological distress, or through the behavior of others around us.

Jungian dream work begins with a subjective standpoint: "The whole dream-work is essentially subjective, and a dream is a theatre in which the dreamer is himself the scene, the player, the prompter, the producer, the author, the public, and the critic."[30]

Dreams, by virtue of their essentially autonomous functioning in the human psyche, often create considerable tension. With an obvious life of their own, they routinely portray dramas that stand in stark contrast to our conscious ego and personality. Dreams span a mysterious world from terror-producing nightmares to the most profound transformative experiences. We find ourselves doing improbable and unbelievable things, caught in the worst possible predicaments, escaping dangerous beasts, or sublimely flying through space. Jung maintained that, "[Dreams] are invariably seeking to express something that the ego does not know and does not understand."[31] This formerly "unknown" psychic material always produces some degree of tension that has profound creative potential to increase self-understanding and insight.

Jung observed that dreaming usually followed three basic formats:[32]

1. Dreams attempt to compensate for any one-sidedness in our outer lives by expressing the opposite side.

2. If the conscious ego has taken an approximate "middle" position, dreams do not move into opposition.

3. If one's conscious attitude is appropriate, according to one's unique expression in life, then dreams confirm and amplify that perspective.

For those who work with their dreams, dreaming then becomes a profound and vital guidance system particularly helping one avoid entrapment in groups. When we are caught in any collective system that is alien to self-expression, dreams inevitably reveal the danger of repressing parts of ourselves in order to maintain a collective position. For example, in her book *Projection and Re-Collection in Jungian Psychology,* Marie-Louise Von Franz relates this dream from one of her analysands:

> The dream was an anxiety dream that had been recurrent for many years until the man's (a pastor's son) late forties. He dreamed that he was walking through a vast wasteland. He heard steps behind him. Anxiously he walked faster, but the steps too became more rapid. He began to run, the terror still behind him. Then he came to the edge of a deep abyss and had to stand still. He looked down; deep, deep down, thousands of miles below he saw hell-fire burning. He looked around him and saw—or rather sensed in the dark—a demonic face. Later on, the dream recurred exactly as before, except that instead of a demon, the dreamer saw the face of God. And when he was almost fifty years old he had the same dream for the last time [after several years of therapy]. But this time panicky fear drove him and he jumped over the edge of the abyss into the depths below. As he fell, thousands of little square white cards floated downward with him from above. On each card, in black and white, a different mandala had been drawn. The cards floated together into a kind of floor, so that he did not fall into hell but found a firm landing about

halfway down. Then he looked back, upward to the edge of the abyss; there he saw—his own face![33]

This dream clearly illustrates the interior splitting of the psyche resulting from the dreamer's religious upbringing. Such a dream points to the many faces of God, both dark and light, and to the difficulty in trying to separate a god image from the psyche through one's belief system. Attempts to conform to any type of absolutism results in a demonization of one's psyche with the dark aspects commonly split off, unacknowledged, and projected onto others. As one-sided attitudes persist, the more powerful unconscious opposites become. Eventually this growing dark unconscious opposition breaks through into consciousness, and we see cultural heroes beating or killing their wives, supposedly religious persons shooting abortion doctors, victims of racism becoming racists themselves. We lose control as the unconscious opposite takes over. A close friend of mine had a recurring dream while he was in a destructive group: he found himself watching the group's leader chop off people's heads. His unconscious was vividly showing him that the collective authority, symbolized by the group's leader, was severing his mind and his ability to think for himself.

On the collective level, unconscious opposites take on lethal proportions; groups wage war with their supposed enemies, and gangs kill those who are disrespectful. In this manner dark, unseen forces explode into conscious life, assuming control of people and events. We have "crimes of passion," crimes due to "temporary insanity," "ethnic cleansing." What we really have are out-of-control personal and collective unconscious complexes assuming control of our lives.

By living a group-imposed life, we contribute to the collective unconscious shadow. In this sense, we are each responsible for the daily terror infecting our planet. Only by becoming more *conscious* can we even begin to alleviate the ominous growing darkness that promises to wreak ever-increasing havoc on us all. Greater consciousness means doing our best to live our own lives. It means *being who we are*, a unique human soul independent of any collective organization or impulse, yet at the same time, remaining *creatively involved* in society. Becoming more conscious means that we must work on ourselves by being responsible for our lives and the choices we make. Self-responsibility means resurrecting our innate *integrity*, our wholeness. It means including our inner life as well as our outer life.

Our dreams immediately inform us of any *interior totalism* resulting from collective implants. Unfortunately, most people dismiss their dreams as nonsense and fantasy, shutting off their primary relationship to the unconscious. In this manner, one leads an *unconscious* existence, the apparent victim of circumstance.

Interpreting dream symbols places one in slippery territory. But there are broad motifs that indicate one is living a collectively driven life. When one is carried along by popular impulses, dream symbols occur such as buses, the mafia or gangsters, uniformed soldiers or police, political figures, snake-filled pits, drowning, wastelands, or marching in formation. Marie-Louise Von Franz found that dreams of officials and civil servants often related to collective adaptation.[34] Jung, from his extensive dream work, found that monsters and, in one example, a monstrous snake in a dream symbolized the "dark crowd-soul within."[35]

A lot of bugs or a swarm of insects can symbolize group action. When we encounter insects, especially in great numbers, they stop us in our tracks. We know that a swarm (a group) of bees can be deadly. When we are enmeshed in a group mind-set, insects can reveal group-implanted parts of our nature that are predatory, creepy, spiderlike, lying in wait to snare unwary victims. James Hillman observed that exterminating bugs in a dream may mean getting rid of something uncontrollable. He says, "If a bug is an underworld creature, then pesticides are a theological agent, a chemical Christ."[36] But dream symbols find their deepest meaning within the context of an individual life, and generalizing interpretations is fraught with exceptions.

By watching dreams, one can be alerted to situations that are in reality collective snake pits, provided we do not objectify the dream images by literalizing them and attributing the images to outside events. Depth soul-therapy requires that one become self-responsible for all images in the dream, allowing each symbol, personality, and event, good or bad, to exist on its own, to have its own autonomy, and to work on and in the dreamer. This subjective approach to dreams reinforces the soul-making process and places us in the midpoint, the battlefield where the creation of consciousness takes place.

According to the Jungian perspective, one must begin to *dialogue* with the imagination, the soul images, the dream figures, holding the tension between where we are and where the images beckon us to go and letting oneself fall *inward* into deeper depths of understanding and meaning.

Moreover, this polytheistic inner dreamscape strikes at the root defect of the collective: its monotheistic totalitarian structure. Hillman also cautions against directing or loading our imaginative process with any alien ideology: "Our approach to imagining is predetermined by our idea of it. Disciplines of the imagination turn into a disciplining of the images. Active imagination becomes subverted into mind control, gaining knowledge, strength, and wisdom at the expense of the images of the soul,"[37] thus the necessity to engage the imagination *without any predetermination.* There is tremendous collective pressure on the individual to make the inner dream world conform to collective images and ideals. Therefore we must not place any *agenda* on our dream images, which would be internalizing a patriarchal group dynamic.

Our market-oriented collective psyche exerts overwhelming influence on us, resulting in a bargaining approach to spiritual practices: we want specific *things* or results in return for our efforts. We want answers or solutions from dreams. From meditation I expect peace, enlightenment, profound experiences. A common example of the market system applied to spiritual practices is the repeating of "affirmations" which are designed to *get* specific things or create specific states of consciousness—religious entrepreneurship. Any preplanned agenda means we are not doing spiritual work, but instead are simply perpetuating the collective system's needs at the expense of our souls.

Jungians purport that floating in a dream means one is not grounded. Instead, dreams of floating and levitation may symbolize a splitting of the psyche as an escape from collective forces. For example, in one dream I became bored with the slow-moving crowds, levitated high in the air, and traveled much faster. Living a life dragging the weight of commonality and sameness and of lost passion will show up in our dream world, where the psyche attempts to compensate for our one-sided involvement in the masses. As group ideology increasingly becomes our "outer garment," no wonder dreams of being unclothed or naked are so common. Perhaps the unconscious is telling us that we need to remove our costumes, to see ourselves as we really are.

Psychotherapy: Mind Control or Soul Work?

> A social order that studies war, rewards competitiveness, restricts resources, promotes isolation and punishes those who are colored, female or poor [requires therapists to] stop using our sessions to fix up the people so the system works better and start fixing up the system so the people work better.
>
> Thelma Jean Goodrich[38]

So how does modern therapy fit into this dilemma? Psychotherapy, in order to encourage the separation, individuation, and differentiation processes, must consider the individual's collective entanglements and the influences from collective sources on the psyche. Freud understood the potential of psychoanalysis to treat the collective: "To throw light on the origins of our great cultural institutions—on religion, morality, justice, and philosophy. . . . Our knowledge of the neurotic illnesses of individuals has been of much assistance to our understanding of the great social institutions."[39] We must bear in mind that *individuals* provide the moral and ethical foundation for our collective agencies; the flow of consciousness must be from the individual outward, not as we commonly find in the example of groups spoon-feeding an assumed mentally inferior populace.

Consideration of group influences in the individual requires that psychologists have no prejudgments, and certainly no therapeutic agenda other than facilitating each client's unique process. Furthermore, a soul-honoring therapeutic stance assumes that the psychologist or therapist has achieved a significant degree of differentiation from collective influences, and that she or he have no group "hang-ups" or preconceived ideas as to what a client should or should not do.

The healing function of therapy is not to make one "well adjusted" to society, but to further one's relationship to the Self, one's true identity and distinctiveness. To be "well adjusted" implies that one fits the collective mold, performs one's "duty," follows established patterns and ideology. We become *institutionalized,* walled in by our conformity. Such therapy operates as an arm of a police state.

Psychotherapy comes from the Greek *psychē,* meaning "breath, life, soul," and *therapeia,* meaning "service." Hence psychotherapy means "in service of the soul." One cannot tend the soul without creating and working with *tension,* the vital consciousness-producing ingredient. In fact, the tension in between opposites or polarities *comprises* the very ground of the soul, the place of soul-making. Because of this necessity to work with and even create tension, psychotherapists and groups that promote a one-sided, tensionless viewpoint abort awakening to greater consciousness and integrity. Real therapy begins with the tension in between things.

Erich Neumann wrote about the "moral courage not to want to be either worse or *better* than [one] actually is."[40] As Neuman points out, self-acceptance requires considerable courage. Groups that promise to make us into someone else's image have a nearly irresistible pull on one's legitimate desire to improve one's lot in life. But modeling our life after a collective image does not "improve" our life. Instead, it destroys it.

A collective deprogramming psychotherapy gives high priority to the attitude of *respect* for a client's autonomy. However, respect for the client's individuality and autonomy would also suggest that the psychologist facilitate the client's process of identifying the difference between group ideologies and uniquely individual images and ideals.

Collective deprogramming would indicate the importance of image work, active imagination, story telling, discovering the client's unique mythology, and digging up the origins of images and clarifying individual ideals versus group ideals. Additionally, a depth psychology perspective would suggest that clients explore creative ways to hold tension between the self and the collective, especially concentrating on areas of conflict.

For example, there is the quite common conflict between creative expression and our market system's imperative to "make money," which often aborts individual creativity; to make money, a writer writes in a manner that is profitable. The collective images of wealth, success, and power dominate the individual psyche as people prostitute their talents, killing their authentic voice. Monetary income becomes the motive and measure of success instead of value added to human life. One becomes an employee of the system, a "performer" perpetuating collective images.

On the other hand, the psychotherapist would have to be on guard not to unconsciously encourage a continuance of collectively inspired totalism in clients. Any agenda on the part of the psychotherapist would reinforce methodologies found in destructive groups, as would any lack of respect for a client's unique perspective and process. Following our thesis, the therapist would encourage clients to respect their autonomous inner parts—their polytheistic natures—thus reinforcing self-respect, self-esteem, and wholeness.

In the final analysis (pun intended), a collective deprogramming psychotherapeutic approach suggests the importance of a deep personal regard, honoring and valuing each client; this means "being" with the client in a manner that honors and holds sacred the individual human soul. There can be no plan or particular expectation on the part of the therapist other than facilitating the client's process of self-discovery and self-understanding, *apart from any group, institution, or system,* including psychotherapy.

Differentiating from the group mind requires a deepened understanding of how group influences affect the individual psyche, for we cannot escape from something that we are unconscious of. Thus the Jungian process of becoming more conscious implies, stressing the collective element, that clients must become more aware (conscious) of how groups operate and how group influences automate the individual psyche. And it follows that the psychologist must also be "conscious" of the collective machinery and its modus operandi in each individual, to avoid becoming a "tool of the establishment."

But the question arises, how does psychology treat a group mind? Where does the psychologist set up office? And who, whom, or what is the patient? Only individuals can dethrone the group mind by reclaiming their lost humanity, their soul autonomy, and by living their *own* lives. When we no longer support a collective agency, it must collapse. In the end, it is our *willing support* that perpetuates the status quo, empowers group-think, and makes us participants in the collective dance of death.

CHARACTERISTICS OF DESTRUCTIVE PSYCHOTHERAPY

While dealing with the dynamic between psychotherapist and client, the following therapeutic processes can also be practiced in any interpersonal relationship.

Therapist has an "agenda." The therapist "knows" what's wrong and attempts to "enlighten" the client, or a therapist uses a certain "technique" and imposes this technique on the client.

Hero/rescuer. The therapist takes on the role of an expert or authority. Also disempowering for clients, the therapist becomes an *outside authority,* reinforcing a totalitarian alignment between client and therapist of master and slave. The only legitimate quest for therapist and client is the genuine expression of one's own life.

Ideological judgment. The therapist's religious or ideological viewpoint influences the process. For example, so called "Christian therapy" is not therapy, but mind control, a marketing and recruitment technique for a particular religion in the guise of psychotherapy. Also called "moralizing," judgmental attitudes demean individual self-worth by telling clients they are right or wrong, or that they "should" do something that reflects the therapist's personal morals and value system.

Giving advice, lecturing, or teaching a client. Advice-giving immediately sets up the therapist as an authority figure, again reinforcing a totalitarian mind-set in clients and keeping them in a helpless state of affairs and dependent on others.

Problem solving, repairing damage. Therapists who solve problems assume clients are helpless, inferior, and incompetent—attitudes that are anything but therapeutic. In constructive therapy, problems are solved creatively and unexpectedly, as a result of holding the natural tension inherent in the relationship between client and therapist, and between the many parts of a client's psyche.

Labeling and classifying. Labeling and classifying clients is a function of patriarchy within a group context. The moment a therapist labels a client as being a certain type or having a certain mental illness, that client is demeaned, boxed in, or trapped within the confines of a name, which often has enormous implications. To say that one "has" a specific mental disorder logically calls for a specific remedy, usually drugs, which are intended to remove or suppress socially unacceptable symptoms.

Such therapies strengthen collective implants in clients, which say, "You are *abnormal.* Only by denying a part of yourself, are you able to be 'OK.' " To be sure, if we are depressed, we are depressed, and I am in no way implying that one ought to deny the fact that *something* is out of order. But I am saying that conventional therapies are overwhelmingly intent upon removing a client's discomfort, which then deadens one's ability to change, evolve, and transform his/her consciousness. Such totalitarian-based techniques abort "soul-making" while both therapist and client become Orwellian-like subjects of collective tyranny.

Distracting. Therapists enable clients to avoid painful or uncomfortable areas by agreeing or joking to *remove and avoid tension.* This particular form of therapeutic avoidance keeps clients' shadow material hidden, exactly what destructive groups attempt to do. By distracting a client away from tension-producing areas of life, the therapist plays a parental role while regressing the client into a childlike dependency.

Reassurance. Like distraction, reassurance reduces tension, disagreeing with a client's negative self-evaluation or agreeing that a client is "all right." Indeed, as tension builds, the often unconscious mechanical defenses by both client and therapist take over the session, thereby quickly eliminating conflict, tension, and any chance for a constructive therapeutic environment.

CHARACTERISTICS OF CONSTRUCTIVE PSYCHOTHERAPY

Constructive psychotherapy is first and foremost client-empowering, facilitating integration and integrity. Moreover, healthy psychotherapy must not be entangled in any manner with collective power structures, political, cultural, or social. Instead, therapists must help to clarify culturally implanted ideas and constructs so that individuals can realize unique meaning and purpose in their lives.

The client is the expert about his/her life, not the therapist. Client-centered psychotherapy does not mean therapists cannot take active roles in the therapeutic process. It does mean, however, that insights and "Ah has"* are not planned or engineered by therapists. Indeed, the *interaction between* client and therapist—the intersubjective and the interobjective—serve to facilitate *mutual* insight and understanding for both client and therapist.

Authenticity. Being oneself in a therapeutic context means being able to share one's thoughts and feelings openly and honestly with a client. This builds the trust and respect which are so essential in any relationship. Authenticity on the part of the therapist reinforces clients' ability to be themselves as opposed to being what society says they "should" be. Obviously, to be effective, such "authenticity" must be devoid of any collective programming on the part of the therapist. In other words, authenticity becomes phony the instant we pollute the psyche with collective thinking and ideological formats. This points once more to the necessity for effective psychotherapists to have attained a significant degree of differentiation from the collective. Without their own substantial differentiation from the mass mind, therapists become unwitting agents for the state or for some particular collective dogma.

Sadly, with the current widespread practice of requiring state licensing for all sorts of therapists, we are destroying the potential of psychotherapy

---

*An "Ah ha" experience refers to a sudden flash of insight—something "clicks," and one suddenly realizes new information, has new understanding.

to "tend the soul" and to empower creative and unique individual distinctiveness. In a "licensed," state-controlled environment, therapists become little more than social police forces sustaining conformity and empowering psychological totalitarianism. Alternatives to state licensing such as certification can insure that consumers are well informed as well as documenting professional training and experience.

Empathy. Empathy relates to a therapist's ability to intimately understand a client's thoughts, feelings, and motives, and reflect this understanding back to a client. Part of an ongoing objective of *mutual* understanding, empathy comes from the ability to enter the *space in between client and therapist,* creating what the Tao philosophy calls a "mutuality of arising." This mutuality of arising results from *holding the tension* between client and therapist—staying with feelings, images, and moods, even when they are uncomfortable.

Respect. Respect means to feel and show esteem and genuine regard for clients and to treat clients as equals. Healing therapy must respect the other's freedom, autonomy, and difference. Of course, such freedom and autonomy can never be genuinely respected in others unless we first respect these attributes in ourselves. This essential self-respect results from our own differentiation from collective forces that seek to automate, define, and control individuals.

Confrontation. Confrontation is the therapist's use of feedback to enable clients to more clearly see their reality. Confrontation helps to create therapeutic tension necessary for the evolution of consciousness. Diametrically opposed to group constructs of expected blind agreement regardless of one's individual opinion, confrontation not only promotes individual awareness but helps those caught in the collective mind-set to disengage through open and direct exploration of heated issues. Thus critical thinking and self-observation are restored to their proper place.

While psychotherapy can facilitate the process of slaying our collective dragons, ultimately individuals must assume this responsibility and begin the journey toward true freedom and independence. Erich Fromm maintained that a "mentally healthy person is the productive and unalienated person; the person who relates himself to the world lovingly, and who uses his reason to grasp reality objectively; who experiences himself as a unique individual entity, and at the same time feels one with his fellow man; who is not subject to irrational authority; and accepts willingly the rational authority of conscience and reason; who is in the process of being born as long as he is alive."[41] Certainly we live in a time when it has become crucial that we recognize and refuse to participate in the extremely self-destructive aspects of the group mind.

12

Putting Soul into Relationships

Between us and events, between the doer and the deed, there is a reflective moment—and soul-making means differentiating this middle ground.

James Hillman[1]

There are so many fine and substantial things in the world at any one time, but they are not in touch with each other.

Goethe[2]

He who knows only his own side of the case knows little of that.

John Stuart Mill[3]

When you lose your imagination, you lose your soul.

John Bradshaw[4]

Holding Tension Between the Individual and the Collective

Social pressure is the enemy! How in heaven's name are you going to find your own track if are always doing what society tells you to do?

Joseph Campbell[5]

The Sufi mystic Inayat Khan (1882–1927) maintained, "The fulfillment of every activity is in its balance."[6] Life is a dance of relation-

277

ships and opposing forces and events, producing *tension*—an indispensable component for both individual and collective consciousness. Opposites create tension in consciousness, in one's psyche. From the moment of birth we begin moving toward death. We cannot lift a finger without tensing a muscle. Tension between opposites is omnipresent as a part of our feeling and emotional experiencing through opposing views, events, experiences, and contradictions.

The widespread breakdown of relationships in marriages and families and between races, nations, and ideologies indicates the pervasiveness of our loss of soul and alienation from each other. Along with the breakdown of relationships between people and between groups, and within the human psyche, we find ourselves alienated from our own souls. Carl Jung, in *Aspects of the Feminine,* explained:

> Loss of soul amounts to a tearing loose of parts of one's nature; it is the disappearance and emancipation of a complex, which thereupon becomes a tyrannical usurper of consciousness, oppressing the whole man. It throws him off course and drives him to actions whose blind one-sidedness inevitably leads to self-destruction.[7]

LIFE'S OPPOSITENESS

Holding the tension *in between acting out and repression* is a primary challenge in the struggle with oneself and with groups. In the collective, this struggle often takes on monstrous proportions. *Acting out* and *repression* are extreme opposites. If I'm angry and slug someone, I have acted out my anger. I may feel better temporarily, but in actuality I become a puppet manipulated by anger—a captive of my emotions. Someone pushes our buttons and robotlike, we *react*, becoming part human and part machine in the process. On the other hand, suppressed anger and rage add to a warehouse of potentially explosive emotions, which eventually reach a critical mass; we react in ways totally out of proportion to some triggering event. So herein is the dilemma: how does one find the space *in between* dangerous repression and smashing a perceived enemy, in between individual autonomy and mass impulses?

In this book, we have explored the dynamic in the relationship *between the individual and the collective.* In particular, how we can *hold* this individual versus collective tension in a constructive manner without being manipulated by destructive group influences, movements, and ideologies. Accordingly, the dynamic of opposites and the *relationship in between* opposites holds particular significance.

Holding tension is an organic approach to life that emphasizes *rela-*

tionships in between people and things. This space of relationship is both a place of tension and interconnectedness. For example, when I lived in Los Angeles, there were earthquake aftershocks every few days. Many structures that are inflexible and rigid had been seriously damaged, while buildings that flex such as wood-frame homes and steel-reinforced skyscrapers, designed to sway and roll with the earth, remained undamaged.

This flexibility in our lives is analogous to holding the tension between the earth and a building. Where we are totalistically rigid and inflexible, natural forces break us apart like dead trees. Just as immovable buildings collapse in a quake, an immovable human psyche loses its ability to remain intact when threatened by difficult circumstances. We fall apart, become unglued, and lose our integrity.

Even too much optimism can deteriorate into a one-sided attitude that makes the inevitable ups and downs of life unbearable and depressive. It is better to maintain an attitude of *guarded* optimism that realizes the dual nature of life's circumstances—optimism with a little tension attached.

Only when we learn to work with relationships (holding tension) between opposing forces do we have a chance to resolve life's inevitable disasters. The Chinese philosopher Lao-Tzu explained, "It is in yielding that we are preserved whole."[8]

In the same sense, we can nourish a working relationship with the earth and our environment just as we nourish a *relationship* with another human being. Unfortunately, most groups destroy relationships on any terms other than within group-defined parameters. The local building department has its rules and codes, for the most part inflexible and totalitarian, to supposedly protect citizens but which actually stifle innovation and endanger masses of people. The market system's "invisible hand" gives the lowest bidder responsibility for human life. Profits, not human beings, determine our fate. The relationships are between profits, construction methods, and building codes; no doubt an excellent tension producer, but very dangerous for us humans when conscienceless groups and systems are the dominant players.

Jungian psychology stresses the importance of the *relationship between opposites,* and how this in-between space relates to the *integrity* of consciousness. According to Jung, "The ego keeps its integrity only if it does not identify with one of the opposites, and if it understands how to hold the balance between them. This is possible only if it remains conscious of both at once."[9] Remaining conscious of opposites sounds easy but actually is a formidable task. However, remaining conscious of opposites holds a pivotal key to maintaining constructive relationships, whether between two people or between individuals and groups.

How often we hear of "irreconcilable differences" being the cause of divorce. In other words, there is a pair of opposites (a relationship) frozen into immovable positions with the inevitable result being separation and es- trangement. We miss the potential, the soul work of exploring the *space of the in between,* the reconciliation of opposites. Not working with this dy- namic removes the adventure and mystery from life; spiritual and psycho- logical growth stops. We are dead while yet living—dead in the water with no wind (tension) in our sails. Our relationships with each other and the en- vironment then become totalitarian: one-sided, parasitical, combative, de- structive, avoidant, judgmental, puritanical, obsessive, fanatical, prejudicial.

We live necessarily with a culturally induced tension, caught between social and group expectations and demands and the freedom to express our individual creative uniqueness. Our Western culture gives us impossible images to strive for. Popular media have many women driven to the pur- suit of unattainable perfection in every aspect of life while at the same time our Judeo-Christian theology compels men to repress their feelings and women to repress incredible quantities of sexual and witch energy. By witch energy, I refer to a kind of wildness, qualities that embody the op- posite of group-dictated roles as obedient wives—qualities that have been most repressed by our predominately patriarchal society. Women in par- ticular are victims of repression from organized religions that portray fem- ininity as dangerous or seductive. In Christian mythology, women have been the spell-casters, the herbalists turned into witches, the seducers of a pious priesthood, as biblical power structures sought to eliminate the com- petition from other religious groups. The terms "witch" and "witchcraft" have different meanings, *both good and bad,* in different cultures. In the West, an evil connotation still surrounds these words as a result of church indoctrination during the Renaissance, which defined witchcraft as "evil magic, heresy, and devil worship."[10] At the start of the thirteenth century, Christianity began a methodical campaign to eliminate heretics. The In- quisition concentrated on witches, who were hunted down and executed. Most modern historians estimate that 150,000 to 200,000 women were burned over a 150-year period.[11]

For men, our culture produces androids—part machine, part human— who cope with societal expectations by acting out culturally implanted roles as macho providers. We have the women's movement and the men's movement, both attempts to help persons reclaim their real natures, a soul- based authenticity. Unfortunately, the fanatical side in both the men's move- ment and the feminist movement traps many people in one-sided extremes where they become possessed by a particular group's viewpoint.

By repressing one side of our nature while playing out the roles soci- ety expects of us, we become *things* instead of human beings. Life becomes expendable, losing its value and its soul. Is it any wonder that we are killing each other, abusing ourselves and others at alarming rates; that gangs war with each other in our cities; and anyone who is *different* from our in-group is persecuted, ostracized, or looked down upon as inferior?

Far too often we attempt to medicate our existential emptiness, acting out extremes through addictions, self-destructive behavior, and dysfunctional relationships and reacting from one side of a pair of opposites while repressing or ignoring the other. Instead of working through, we split or separate. We grow apart instead of coming together. Nations, races, and other groups commonly react from separatist, elitist, one-sided points of view, resulting in war, hatred, bigotry, and prejudice. Our culture desperately needs to shift from a striving for goodness and perfection to a striving for wholeness and integrity, which is the coming together of opposites to create a third aspect in one's consciousness: a triangulation of opposites and integration instead of separateness and division.

How does "character" relate to integrity? Character means the "combination of qualities or features that distinguishes one person, group, or thing from another."[12] This "combination of qualities" speaks to the manner in which the individual combines the diverse qualities or parts of the psyche. Having character is another way of saying that one has integrity, that one *holds together* as a human being *in a unique way.*

Relationship: Finding the Space of the In-Between

> At the still point of the turning world.
> Neither flesh nor fleshless;
> Neither from nor towards;
> At the still point, there the dance is,
> But neither arrest nor movement.
>
> T. S. Eliot[13]

> A collision of opposites:
>   success and failure,
>   top and bottom,
>   the height and the depth,
>   sitting pretty and striking out,
>   triumph and destruction.
> But the space in-between
>   became something else—
>   now I sense some deep failure in success,
>   and some deep success in failure.

This book's basic thesis holds that one's innate integrity, freedom, evolving consciousness, and self-understanding are grounded in the dynamic of *holding the tension between opposites*. A vital individual self-therapy, *maintaining the tension between opposites within one's nature as well as between oneself and collective imperatives* is an indispensable prerequisite to living one's own life and making a constructive contribution to the collective.

Similar to the concept of "balance," holding tension is like an astronaut's weightlessness in space, which results from a precise balance between the gravitational inward pull of earth and the outward centrifugal force generated by an orbiting spacecraft traveling at a certain velocity. The spacecraft "holds" the tension between these two forces just as the tension between lightness and strength builds the bones in a bird's wings making flight possible.

Within the human psyche, a state of balance between opposing forces is a rare occurrence, a Zen-like instant of transcendence (weightlessness) where one's consciousness undergoes a state of heightened awareness.

We all have instinctive inclinations to eliminate or repress anything uncomfortable. Therefore, in order to get into a *tension-holding* state of mind, we need to think of the process as one of *holding the tension in between repression and acting out*. The following chart shows this relationship between opposites. The space in between repression is analogous to Jung's "transcendent function," which is activated when we hold both sides in conscious awareness at the same time.

Extreme	Space In Between	Extreme
Repression	Holding the Tension	Acting Out
Unconsciousness	Awareness of both	Violence
	Patience, waiting	Rage
	Tolerating ambiguity	Impulsiveness
	Talking through	Blaming others
	Creativity	Fanatical
	Uncertainty	Absolutism
	Shadow work	Perversion
		Addiction

Nicholas of Cusa described a "wall of paradise" concealing God from mortal sight, comprised of a "coincidence of opposites," with its gate guarded by "the highest spirit of reason, who bars the way until he has been overcome."[14] Joseph Campbell compares this realm in between opposites to "the clashing rocks (Symplegades) that crush the traveler, but between which the heroes always pass."[15]

Jung wrote about the overriding direction of his personal journey to be one of "leading back to a single point—namely, to the *mid-point* . . . the path to the center, to individuation" (emphasis added).[16] Jung's psychology emphasized returning to this "mid-point," this in between place in the human psyche that seems to be so difficult to enter, yet is of such central importance in the individuation process. It is precisely *this mysterious midpoint place* in the psyche that holds an important key to resolving the serious world problems stemming from a collective totalistic mentality gone mad, obsessed with and utterly caught in a dualistic world of opposites. The rapidly increasing problems of extreme violence, gangs, warlords, and racial hatred are ripe for a cultural depth psychology—a soul-centered approach that addresses intergroup and intercollective relationships. James Hillman relates soul-making to an in-between place, writing, "By soul I mean, first of all, a perspective rather than a substance, a viewpoint toward things rather than a thing itself. This perspective is reflective; it mediates events and makes differences between ourselves and everything that happens. We have lost the third, middle position which earlier in our tradition, and in others too, was the place of soul."[17]

In a group context, the question arises, How does one go about differentiating a "middle ground" in between the individual and a group? The dilemma at the heart of our task is how to resolve, reconcile, mediate—hold the tension *in between* the collective and the individual, and in so doing, extricate oneself from the clutches of the collective. Hillman's "soul-making" parallels Edward Edinger's "Creation of Consciousness,"[18] which postulates that conscious and unconscious react upon and shape each other—that what we call God may actually be a cooperative process, a paradoxical ever-changing changelessness, a supernatural codependency. Hence consciousness is an individual process that no collective agency can assume. It is exactly the individual's process of becoming more conscious that ignites the fire illuminating the community.

Historical parallels to this in-between place are found in the Gnostic *krater* (mixing vessel), a spirit-filled vessel sent down to earth from God to baptize those who were seeking enlightenment. And there was the alchemical *vas* in which the process of transformation took place, similar to Jung's process of individuation. In the *I Ching or Book of Changes,* we find a *caldron* or *ting,* a ritual vessel containing food, which is often a symbol of spiritual nourishment. The alchemists' *Philosopher's Stone,* which results from the ability to experience opposite viewpoints simultaneously (a union of opposites),[19] correlates to the creation of consciousness, with the soul being the thrashing ground in the middle. In Novalis we find this passage: "The seat of the soul is there where the inner and the outer worlds meet."[20] In the writings of the third-century B.C. Chinese philosopher

Chuang Tzu we find this statement: "There is a point of correspondency between two views which is called the pivot of the Tao. As soon as one finds this point, he stands in the center of the ring of thought where he can respond without end to the changing views; without end to those affirming, and without end to those denying."[21]

This midpoint space is essentially feminine in nature, womblike, a vessel wherein pain and birth occur—a place of soul-making, a place of relatedness to oneself and to life. It is Robert Frost's "Stopping by Woods on a Snowy Evening." It is the "still point" in Zen Buddhism, and Kabir's "swing between the conscious and the unconscious." Edward Edinger, a Jungian analyst, author, and teacher at the C.G. Jung Institute of Los Angeles, describes a similar vessel image found in the *Kabbalah of Isaac Luria:* "at the beginning of creation God poured his divine light into bowls or vessels, but some of the vessels could not stand the impact of the light. They broke and the light was spilled. Salvation of the world requires recollection of the light and restitution of the broken vessels."[22]

A polarized society trapped into popular points of view cannot see this soul-making place of the in-between; the blinded collective leads subservient, blinded individuals. We have a totalitarian group dynamic problem that allows no place for the human soul.

Jung found that the individual is not necessarily the cause of what might at first appear to be a personal problem. He wrote: "A collective problem, if not recognized as such, always appears as a personal problem, and in individual cases may give the impression that something is out of order in the realm of the personal psyche. . . . The cause of the disturbance is, therefore, not to be sought in the personal surroundings, but rather in the collective situation."[23] Here Jung pointed out the importance of considering group influences in the individual psyche. Accordingly, a soul-oriented depth psychology now has a remarkable opportunity to bring greater understanding to the problem of the individual's relationship to the collective, in a manner that will free the creative potential in masses of persons who are yet under the control of addictive, often brutal, and at times overwhelming group impulses. Thus, resolving destructive group dynamics, "collective situations," holds the potential for removing the cause of many apparently personal neuroses.

Depth psychology offers a way to return the experience-based lost soul to the human spirit. The implication of this *return of soul* marks a significant transition in civilization, in culture, and in how individuals relate to life, to each other, and especially to groups. This shift means that individuals will no longer be *subservient* to collective ideologies.

The Jungian perspective maintains that when one succumbs to anything at all, good or evil, one suffers a loss of integrity. Therefore, the attitude of surrender, which is commonly believed to be a virtue, becomes a compromise of one's integrity *when one surrenders to a group's doctrine.* In a group context, surrender aligns one with one side of a pair of opposites—the first step toward becoming a victim.

The danger rests in thinking of opposites as absolutes, when in fact opposites complement each other, making relationships vital and meaningful. Just as the moon requires the backdrop of night to be clearly seen, we require the other, the opposite as a catalyst for the creation of consciousness—for soul making. Conflict and tension, which provide the fuel for the individuation process, originate in this dynamic of relationships. Opposites are, as Jung said, "halves of a paradoxical whole."[24]

For example, *peace* comes from facing fear and conflict. We lose our peace the moment we *resist* going into a problem. True peace is not a state of rest or passivity, but instead exemplifies a state of healthy tension necessary to sustain psychological and spiritual understanding. In this setting, we can better understand peace as more a *state of balance* or equilibrium between extremes (opposing forces) and not denial or avoidance of any kind.

London Jungian psychologist Anthony Storr, writing in the *Journal of Analytical Psychology,* describes how the self-regulating nature of the psyche tries to avoid extremes, relating this to a "middle course": "The life of the body is thus conceived of as proceeding along a middle course between pairs of opposites; neither too hot nor too cold; neither osteoporotic nor calcified; neither hypertensive nor hypotensive. A self-regulating system, in fact, in which excesses in any direction are barred; or if not barred, at least dearly paid for in illness, discomfort, or death."[25]

Extricating ourselves from the collective involves holding the tension between one's personal reality and group imperatives. This means *consciously* experiencing the conflict (holding the tension) produced by pressures to conform to group demands on the one hand, and the individual's drive for individuation and differentiation from groups on the other hand. When we allow these two opposing forces to be a problem instead of giving in to one side, a solution inevitably comes out of the alchemy of struggle.

In the West we have a competitive dualistic economic system that does not acknowledge the feminine. As a result, we have lost the ability to relate to each other out of our humanness. Only now is the feminine beginning to return through a reawakening of mythology, the environmental movement, and women's rights. The negative father aspect of the masculine wants to control the feminine—to dictate what women can do with their own bodies. A puritanical, one-sided, male-dominated religious orthodoxy further reinforces these patriarchal attitudes. There is no *middle ground,* no sense of relationship. In such a patriarchal dualism, power is the focus: who controls whom. Destructive groups exploit this dualism to control billions of individuals. Relationships become bartering arrangements: if I do something for you, I expect something in return. We prostitute ourselves, sell our souls, in order to play according to the system's rules. Our relationships with each other become predatory: what can I *get*? How can I *use* someone to my advantage?

The masculine sees concrete opposites while the feminine finds *spaces in between*—relationships between things and persons. Authoritarian dualism, so characteristic of destructive groups, is essentially a masculine trait. In contrast, the *relationship* in between the group and the individual depends upon feminine attributes. Splitting humanity into sects, groups, and classes is a patriarchal function. Blending, combining, finding the meaning in things, and entering into the experience are feminine soul-making functions, which are inherently antigroup. Of course, we find this feminine aspect of the psyche in both women and men. It is altogether humorous and serious (and very healthy besides) that the men's movement is trying to recover the repressed feminine—the ability to express real feelings while feminists are trying to recover their repressed masculine side.

WHERE INNER AND OUTER WORLDS MEET

> Our own healing proceeds from that overlap of what we call good and evil, light and dark. It is not that the light element alone does the healing; the place where light and dark begin to touch is where miracles arise.
> Robert A. Johnson[26]

To create and hold *healthy tension,* we can look for places where inner and outer worlds meet and often overlap. We can name the end and the beginning and let our imagination fill the space in between. Dreams provide the most readily accessible meeting place of our inner and outer worlds. Windows into the unseen landscape of the Self, dreams are a *coincidentia oppositorium,* "coinciding opposites," a resonance between two worlds—conscious and unconscious. True dream work begins when we face the uncomfortable, painful, and often embarrassing aspects of our own nature, which are so often revealed in dreams. Keeping a dream journal immensely helps to clarify our inner and outer journey, which are really two aspects of the same adventure.

Another important overlap of inner and outer worlds occurs during the creative process. This may include writing, poetry, art, music, or any creative expression, particularly one that arouses our passionate interest and involvement. Uncensored journal writing about our experiences and feelings is an excellent way to access the unconscious. There is something about the writing process that draws out unexpected, unconscious content—often much to the writer's surprise.

Overlap can occur in silence, quietude, in times of giving ourselves *space in between* things. Being completely silent and still periodically opens a door to the inner worlds. To keep the mind occupied with *someone else's* prayers or mantras is more sleep-inducing than consciousness-producing—a form of self-medicating behavior that reduces or eliminates tension and does not hold it.

I am not for or against traditional forms of meditation, but we need to understand what we are really doing to ourselves. There are times when mantra/prayer self-medication may be helpful in reducing abnormal anxiety and stress, or for other health reasons. However, I am saying that zero-stress is psychological and spiritual death, while too much stress is likewise injurious to both body and mind. Paradoxically, much of the stress and anxiety we suffer results from trying to avoid it in the first place.

Tension and Integrity

> Greatness is usually the result of a natural equilibrium among opposite qualities.
>
> Diderot[27]

Internalized in the human psyche, the balance of opposing forces *integrates* the structure of consciousness, producing *integrity,* which the dictionary defines as "a state of being unimpaired; soundness, unity," from the Latin *integritas,* meaning "completeness, purity, wholeness," and *integer,* meaning "whole, entire." Thus, consciousness maintains its form or integrity through the mutual coexistence and interdependence of opposites. This means a working relationship with the many aspects of ourselves as well as others.

Tension is "the act of stretching or the condition of being stretched."[28] Tension need not be a negative state, but rather is an ever-changing dynamic potential— a catalyst for increased consciousness. Paradoxically, too much tension, which is destructive physically and emotionally, occurs when we resist and ignore conflict, fighting against opposing views instead of finding solutions: the mixture of opposites that synergetically produces an outcome that is not only unpredictable, but unattainable through *identification* with any singular opposing ideology, attitude, or event.

A balance between the universal forces of attracting or pulling inward, and repelling or pushing outward—the same forces that shape galaxies and hold planets in their orbits—hold together the *tensional-integrity* structure of consciousness. Tensional integrity, then, forms the basis for integrity in groups, for integrity in individuals, and for integrity in the relationship in between a group and the individual. To identify with one side collapses our integrity—we become undependable, fragmented, split, fanatical, and dangerous to ourselves and to others, turning the psyche into a totalistic structure.

Tension, like an invisible superstructure, holds everything together from stars to the individual psyche like a sort of cosmic glue binding together the universe: a *natural connectivity between all things.* R. Buckminster Fuller, in his book *Synergetics,* concluded that: "All structures, properly understood, from the solar system to the atom, are tensegrity structures. Universe is omnitensional integrity."[29] Engineers are now designing earthquake-resistant skyscrapers with what are called "tuned pendulums." The pendulums move in the *opposite* direction of the building's movement. This interplay of *opposite forces* preserves the structure.

Holding tension is analogous to walking the razor's edge of consciousness—a point of *justice* between opposites. Holding tension means *to weigh conflicting views in the mind with equal consideration.* It means becoming more aware of opposing forces, both inner and outer, *without allowing one side to assume control.* Jung wrote, "Nothing so promotes the growth of consciousness as this inner confrontation of opposites."[30] The poet Rainer Maria Rilke (1875–1926) affirmed, "Only in the *double kingdom,* there alone, will voices become undying and tender" (emphasis added).[31] Thus, psychological and spiritual development (greater consciousness), both in the individual and in groups, emerges from the interaction between opposing forces—a natural eternal stress.

Tension and integrity are two sides of the same coin. By holding the tension, one builds a field of integrity, a structure of wholeness and integration that holds the psyche together. When we let go of tension, we lose our integrity; we come apart at the seams psychologically and spiritually. When life becomes too comfortable, growth stops; we become more unconscious and we have less *conscience.* We will not find an ultimate resolution, answer, or solution to this struggle, this tension; it is a continuum of existence—a fundamental, necessary modus operandi in the universe and in each of us.

Holding tension moves one outside of self-imposed and group-imposed boundaries; we create a third space in consciousness. In this context, the struggle between the individual and the collective is a creative one—a hero's journey into the land of the beast, returning (regaining one's autonomy) with the hard-won treasure of our experience. Indeed, Jung equated being truly alive with conflict:

> The self is made manifest in the opposites and in the conflict between them; it is a coincidentia oppositorum (opposites occupying the same position simultaneously). Hence the way to the self begins with conflict.

Just as all energy proceeds from opposition, so the psyche possesses its inner polarity, this being the indispensable prerequisite for its aliveness ... (and) that an ego was possible at all appears to spring from the fact that all opposites seek to achieve a state of balance [holding tension].[32]

A "state of balance" is another way of saying we are *holding tension*. Life then becomes the art of holding and incorporating opposing forces in a manner that is neither self-destructive or other-destructive. Unfortunately, most of us find ourselves caught on one side or the other. Rilke's poetry eloquently illustrates this inner struggle, implying even the gods themselves grow in consciousness through conflict: "Take your well-disciplined strengths and stretch them *between two opposing poles,* because inside human beings is where God learns" and "This life that *faces both ways* has marked the human face from within" (emphasis added).[33] Understanding the danger of one-sidedness, Rilke believed that constant (one-sided) ecstasy, bliss, purity, and enlightenment are meaningless unless we invite the dark to participate.

Life without conflict is death. Consciousness requires conflict, tension, and some degree of anxiety. Increasing consciousness requires new understanding and discernment gained by holding tension between opposites. Tension between opposites lets us know we are alive, energizing the psyche. Indeed, we look for tension in order to *feel* alive; we seek out tension-filled movies, thrill-packed amusement park rides, risky business ventures, and dangerous hobbies. Our culture's fascination with death-defying experiences such as skydiving, bungee jumping, mountain climbing, auto racing, and many other potentially lethal activities illustrates our common thirst to feel more alive by approaching its opposite, death. When a society succumbs to the life-numbing influences of collective agencies and ideas, the individual psyche attempts to compensate by searching out ways to feel more alive; this often compels us to create tension by finding excitement and danger.

Heraclitus is credited with discovering *enantiodromia,* meaning "running counter to," the "regulative function of the opposites."[34] Thus, when we become enamored of one side of a pair of opposites, and in particular when our obsession is unconscious, we set into motion this "regulative function," which means that our one-sidedness creates the inevitable opposite situation: order is balanced by chaos, morality by immorality, the rational by the irrational, love by hatred, good by evil. The only escape from this psychological equation, according to Jung, requires *consciousness* of opposites—awareness of the both sides in all their brightness and in all their terror. We must *hold the tension between opposites*—no small feat! We cannot do away with the other side of the coin; we can only work with both sides, understanding that *both* are an integral and necessary part of life, that the back requires a front to be complete.

Moreover, conflicting forces become the pathway to access who we really are and why we are here. What Jung referred to as the "transcendent function" is the *unforeseen* solution that invariably arises when we hold the tension between opposites *with awareness*. This unforeseen solution transcends the opposites, bringing a feeling of peace and new insight about the situation; our attitude shifts and we gain a new perspective.

While extreme conflict can indicate a neurosis, normal conflict is like gravity, sometimes a drag, but necessary. Jung saw the "stirring up of conflict" as a "Luciferian virtue in the true sense of the word. Conflict engenders fire, the fire of the emotions, and like every other fire it has two aspects, that of combustion and that of creating light."[35] We are all too familiar with conflicted muscles: back pain, sore necks, tension headaches. But there are more subtle conflicts we usually ignore in order to be accepted in our social group; collective expectations frequently collide with individual expectations, ethics, and values. Sadly, the collective routinely crushes our self-expression, integrity, and creativity. Additionally, Jung maintained that conflicts with others are outer projections of internal conflicts. Similarly, in any group that does not *consciously* deal with its own dark side, the group's collective repression of anything that conflicts with their agenda or mission will cause this shadow (unconscious) side to be projected onto outsiders or onto certain members who are perceived as disloyal to their cause; these carriers of the group shadow become scapegoats. Of course, this dynamic of projecting shadow material onto others happens between husband and wife, and in groups and institutions of all sizes.

Holding tension shifts the psyche from a one-sided striving for goodness and perfection to a striving for *wholeness,* which, unlike a state of perfection, refers to a coming together of opposites creating a third aspect of consciousness. Wholeness, in this context, is a triangulation of opposites producing integration and completeness instead of separateness and division.

Author and Jungian therapist Jeremiah Abrams declared, "Shadow work is good medicine! It leads to a practice I refer to as the pursuit of the unhypocritical life, which some might call living with *integrity*" (emphasis added).[36]

Creating Healthy Tension: Soul Work

ACKNOWLEDGMENT

[T]o make a disclosure, sometimes with reluctance or under pressure. . . . to accept responsibility for something one makes known or to

give recognition to someone. . . . to assert openly and boldly and implies the likelihood of opposition.

American Heritage Dictionary[37]

One of the best ways to hold the tension in interpersonal relationships is by
sincere *acknowledgment* of another's feelings. This does not mean that you
have to agree, but that you recognize how someone else feels. A simple acknowledgment provides a way of honoring and respecting another human
being—their beliefs, feelings, sorrows, pains, and joys. Of course, in destructive groups, honest expression of one's feelings or opinions is taboo. Patriarchy is not interested in how others feel, only that they are *obedient* to the
established authority. Acknowledgment can hold tension between different
parts of one's psyche. For example, when I acknowledge a frightened part
of myself instead of repressing it, my fear diminishes because of my *holding* the feeling in my conscious awareness. In this fashion, by holding the tension in between the fearful and the fearless parts, we create a *third aspect* of
consciousness *beyond opposites.* Our fear may turn into healthy respect for
a real danger tempered with a newfound courage, which results in a totally
new attitude and new level of awareness about a situation.

The same dynamic holds true for the full range of human emotions and
feelings. We overcome obstacles not by repressing them, but by squarely
facing them, by *acknowledged* openness to the most unpleasant aspects of
ourselves. This builds integrity and self-responsibility and strikes a death
blow to many collective impulses that seek to control human behavior.

In a therapeutic setting, Jung maintained that, "Unless both doctor
and patient become a problem to each other, no solution is found."[38] In this
manner, the individual must learn to patiently tolerate (with conscious
awareness) conflict between the self and collective impulses in order to
find a solution, and in order to avoid being caught by a one-sided view, either personal or collective. Of course, holding this tension (not taking
sides) takes considerable individual integrity and strength of character. It
requires a *reflective* and not a *reactive* approach to life.

Unfortunately, our comfort-oriented, pleasure-principle, collective society considers tension and conflict something to get rid of. Most people
try to eliminate conflict as soon as possible in the easiest way possible—
a quick-fix approach to life, which only insures falling into a trap of compromising expediency, sacrificing the process of soul-making. Here the
axiom "haste makes waste" becomes paramount. In the Middle Ages there
was a saying, "All haste is of the devil."

India has a custom called "sitting dharma"; one sits on the doorstep of
one's enemy until things are rectified. Another way to look at our idea of
"holding tension," sitting dharma means we don't leave difficult situations.

Whether another person or an inner dilemma, we stay with it, talk it through, and work it out.

We can often unravel the meaning of an experience by considering what it would be like to have the circumstance/problem/energy/the other erased as if it never existed or happened. What does it feel like to utterly remove it from our life?

When relationships get difficult, we automatically go into an escape mode or a rage mode, both instinctive defense mechanisms that keep us in the grip of totalism and a power struggle. Paradoxically, when we hold conflict, staying with problems, situations lose their sting—they become less fearful, more soluble, and more understandable.

Being irritated about something then means we have greater potential for increased understanding and passion in what we do. In this sense, a lack of tension and irritation become the basis for increased ignorance and greater unconsciousness.

Mythology, like the dream world, provides an imaginative bridge *between* the conscious ego and the unconscious. It follows that discovering one's own story—one's unique mythology—is an important aspect of soul work helping us to differentiate from the group mind. James Hillman maintains, "A mythic manner of speaking is fundamental to the soul's way of formulating itself."[39] Jung found that mythology played an "intermediate" part in the individuation process: "Only here, in life on earth, where the opposites clash together, can the general level of consciousness be raised. That seems to be man's metaphysical task—which he cannot accomplish without 'mythologizing.' Myth is the natural and indispensable mediator stage between unconscious and conscious cognition."[40]

When we find our right work, work that provides a gradient for our passion, we will find it always centered in and arising out of opposing forces. Rilke once said, "To find myself cleaned up one day would be to find myself with no prospect for living."[41] We are in effect out of work when we find our lives "cleaned up." Reaching perfection or total comfort amounts to a state of death—a condition of *no tension,* no soul, no consciousness, and no creativity.

We each must find our own unique approach to holding tension. To begin with, one holds tension by *accepting conflict,* and then working through the ensuing struggle. This sounds easy, but in practice it's terribly difficult to maintain the presence of mind required to avoid immediately falling into a reactive mode of behavior, especially in situations involving peer pressure in groups and in close interpersonal relationships. Jung declared, "We must hold our ground [hold the tension],"[42] explaining that tension enables greater consciousness:

The repressed content must be made conscious so as to produce a tension of opposites, without which no forward movement is possible. The conscious mind is on top, the shadow underneath, and just as high always longs for low and hot for cold, so all consciousness, perhaps without being aware of it, seeks its unconscious opposite, lacking which it is doomed to stagnation, congestion, and ossification. Life is born only of the spark of opposites.[43]

Tension, when knowingly held with consciousness, enables creative energy to be released. Thus, tension between opposites is potential creation. Nietzsche understood this dynamic and linked it to the creative process, writing, "The price of fruitfulness is to be rich in *internal opposition*" (emphasis added).[44] When you put fire and water together, you get a third element, steam—energy is released. Just as current flows by connecting the negative and positive (opposite) polarities of a battery, when one moves into the center, incorporating and acknowledging opposites, a spiritual, creative soul current flows—a third synergetic something happens that transcends the push-pull of duality.

To pull up to the shopping mall in a comfortable car with our "Gold Card" and be confronted by a rag-tag family asking to work for food creates tension. When a friend tells me about some dark shadowy side of my personality, I feel tension—tension between my conscious self-image and what I am suddenly being made aware of. It's as though our Western society increasingly mirrors back to us the opposite of our material affluence, which may be the psyche's way of showing us that we are becoming more and more spiritually impoverished. The soul has become homeless, dislodged by our clinging to an unbalanced, one-sided luxury—an *idealized* collective way of life that places bank accounts ahead of human-heartedness and simple empathy for one another.

Why are we so uncomfortable around a homeless person? Could it be that it is painful and distressing to come face-to-face with the long-suppressed oppositeness of how we live our lives? The more we cling to a world possessed by the accumulation of material things, the bigger the shadow world of have-nots becomes, and the more we become spiritually and morally bankrupt—the more soul we lose. Our rapidly increasing inner-city violence and gang warfare is a potent collective message reflecting back to us the danger of repressing anything.

PROCESS OVER RESULTS

Without passion you can't do your work in the single specific way that will give it the best chance of succeeding—that is, you can't stay committed to *process,* as opposed to result. . . . Most important, process is what lets you—and everybody alongside you—be surprised; it lets you discover things you hadn't figured out from the start.

Steven Bocho[45]

The creative process produces surprising and unexpected results that usually frustrate any plans to produce specific results. This frustration, inherent in process-oriented work, is an example of *creative tension.* Our immediate impulse is to relieve the tension by planning every detail, eliminating the unexpected, and controlling everything. But this defeats originality, imagination, creativity, and spontaneity; it removes the soul from life. A process-oriented life is innately more difficult and chaotic. A result-oriented life appears easier, but is actually an escape-from-ourselves mode of living. This is not to say that one cannot expect results. I expect to finish this book. However, this book has a life of its own, which I must follow in a certain sense, in spite of its many twists and turns, complications, and ideas that well up uninvited from some depth and must be inserted in that chapter I thought was finished. The process has me in its clutches; it's in my dreams and in my soul.

Process vs. Results

Process:	Results:
Process over goal	Goal-oriented
Journey-oriented	Destination-oriented
Living in the moment	Concentrating on the end goal
Tolerating the unknown	Ruled by "shoulds"
Chaos is okay	Must be in control
Relationships are important	Relationships ignored
Be flexible	Unbending, rigid
Expecting the unexpected	Fear of change, difference
Respect for the individual	Individual must fit the plan
Improvising	Result more important than individuals
	Meeting deadlines

Most groups are result-centered: they will help you find *their* gods, navigate *their* path to salvation, avoid *their* definition of hell. For religious fundamentalists, the result is to be born again. For twelve-step programs, the result is to become free of something—drugs, alcohol, codependence. For self-help groups, the results run the gamut of culturally defined improvement: from feeling better to getting rich, from starting a business to improving your sex life, from losing weight to gaining the perfect physique. For commercial groups, salvation (heaven) is monetary success; hell is failure or bankruptcy.

CREATING INSIGHT GAPS

> (As I) sit quietly, doing nothing,
> Spring comes and grass grows by itself.
>
> Chuang Tzu[46]

Detached involvement keeps individual autonomy and consciousness intact. This paradox of staying involved while maintaining one's individuality is an example of holding tension and entering the soul space in between opposites. One way to accomplish this is to give yourself *insight gaps*.

We can create an insight gap by giving ourselves space (time) in between a thought and the resultant action. This means no longer mechanically reacting but staying with feelings and images that come out of the gap. Next we try to link the experience from our insight gap to our life by asking, what is this experience a metaphor for? For example, I love ice cream, and whenever I am upset or feeling insecure, something in my psyche takes over and drags me to the freezer section at the local market. I usually feel a mixed bag of emotions afterwards, from euphoria to guilt. Often I say to myself, after realizing I ate three of the 270-calorie, two-ounce servings, "Why did I do that? I don't even like it that much."

So I decided to delay getting ice cream when this impulse overcame me. In the gap in between my urge to indulge and the acting out of my impulse, I thought and wrote about my feelings. A strong association with my father came up; I recalled frequent trips to the neighborhood ice cream shop as a small boy, around three to five years old. For me, my father represented love, security, and comfort. My ice cream impulse became a metaphor for fatherly affection and security. Of course I still love ice cream, but I certainly understand myself in a deeper way, and now I can *acknowledge* and take care of this little kid who wants to be with his daddy. Now when the impulse to get ice cream comes, I can dialogue with this insecure little guy and try to be the father he needs.

The result: I am more in control, not through some patriarchal authority, but through soul empathy for a part of myself—through soul work in the *space in between impulse and action.* I feel more connected with myself. Through such self-empathy, I am more able to extend empathy to others.

A rule of thumb would be to translate particular food into feelings: This ice cream *feels* like ———? And that feeling reminds me of ———? Or, when I want ———, I feel like ———? What need is not being met that this food is compensating for? Every impulse, hunger, emotion, and feeling becomes fertile territory for creating insight gaps—for creating more consciousness and self-understanding. The first empathy we must have is that for our own struggling, suffering, and imperfections. Exploring our feelings about foods that repulse us is just as important. Things that we find repelling and disgusting are equally, if not more significant, to our awakening self—a meaningful part of working with opposites. When I think of canned spinach . . . YUK! You get the idea.

In an example of *holding the tension,* the actor and producer John Cassavettes once said, "Love is the ability to endure the unknown."[47] The unknown creates immediate tension. Holding the "unknown" has to be one of life's most difficult tasks. Faced with the unknown, our patriarchal scientific side tries to figure it out, reduce it to knowable certitude, and eliminate the mystery. Thus the "known" and the "unknown" constitute powerful opposites that when left alone to collide in our psyches become a source of life-transforming synergetic energies.

One way to hold tension is simply to *wait*—wait for the situation, dilemma, problem, or suffering to explain itself. Waiting does not necessarily imply doing nothing, as in a circumstance of serious illness, but rather it means an attitude of cooperation with and even dialogue with the *space of not knowing* how something will turn out. In a practical sense, waiting creates tension, freeing us from compulsive behavior and opening doors to greater insight into what lies behind our unconscious mechanized impulses. As such, waiting demotes patriarchy, reduces group dominance, and incorporates a feminine attitude that helps to insulate us from the crowd and its authoritarian mechanization.

The opposites of life and the inevitableness of death create our most profound experiences with tension. Even while in our youth, the specter of death follows in our footsteps, a shadowy reminder of our common vulnerabilities and humanity. We are born fatally wounded, and time is the ground upon which this dark angel stalks us. Our common woundedness makes life and the necessity to live it authentically a vital task. To waste our time living a group-defined existence is perhaps life's greatest catastrophe—a living death.

SEEING THROUGH FEELINGS

> The one inside moves back, and the hands touch nothing, and are safe.
> Robert Bly[48]

Being able to freely express our feelings and ideas, particularly in a group setting, is indispensable in maintaining a state of healthy tension and dynamic creative relationships. We can't be afraid to enter into controversy, but we need to be alert for the unconscious dynamic in back of the dispute. As an example, when feeling intense anger, we can search for the real cause, which might be a traumatic childhood experience that one is defending against. Or, I'm angry because I feel *entitled* to something, or entitled to be treated like —— because ——. Or my anger may be a completely legitimate reaction to some perceived wrong. Often we displace anger: since I can't speak my mind to my boss at work, my wife, husband, partner, children, and friends receive what I suppress all day long. Then again, I may be furious with myself for living a collectively approved life style instead of living my own life, which, if unacknowledged, will turn into depression and an unnameable sense of tragic loss. Life seems to have no purpose. Situations that really push our buttons call for special attention. Push-button reactions are sure signs of repressed shadow energies that need to be examined.

Similar to my ice cream example, creating insight gaps during the process of becoming angry has exciting potential. Those who study anger tell us that it escalates in definite stages. Some event triggers our anger and we decide, often in a split second, to suppress it, escalate it, or direct it. Stopping to reflect is crucial: what exactly triggers my anger? What was I just thinking? How else might I interpret this situation? What are my hot spots, and what are my hot spots metaphors for? What feelings and memories do they bring up? The moment we stop to reflect on the *process,* we are holding tension *in between repression and acting out;* we are in a soul-making place, and we are back in control.

It is often very refreshing to call shit, "shit." It was Emily Dickinson who wrote, "Anger as soon as fed is dead; 'tis starving makes it fat."[49] Splitting and repression begin the instant we tell ourselves that feelings cannot be acknowledged. The moment some inner voice tells us what we "should" or "should not" do, it's time to ask, who or what taught me to think like this? Church? Parents? School? TV? What do I *think* about the matter? Whose implanted voice is directing my life?

WORDS THAT EXPRESS FEELINGS

> We know too much and feel too little. At least we feel too little of those creative emotions from which a good life springs.
>
> Bertrand Russell[50]

Finding creative ways to express real feelings at the time we are feeling them places us in a state of holding tension. This may include journal-keeping, writing, poetry, humor, art, or some other way that best fits one's needs and temperament. Because so many persons are cut off from their feelings as a result of being dehumanized by the collective, it helps to add to our vocabulary of words that help to clearly articulate how we feel. The following list gives some examples:

Abandoned	Battered	Comfortable	Disappointed
Accepted	Beaten	Comforted	Disconcerted
Accused	Beautiful	Complacent	Disgraced
Aching	Belittled	Complete	Disgruntled
Adventurous	Belligerent	Confident	Disgusted
Affectionate	Bereaved	Conflicted	Distant
Aggressive	Betray	Content	Distressed
Agony	Bitchy	Cool	Distrusted
Alienated	Bitter	Coy	Distrustful
Alive	Bored	Crabby	Dominated
Alluring	Bothered	Cranky	Domineering
Alone	Bound-up	Crappy	Doomed
Aloof	Boxed-in	Crazy	Double-crossed
Amazed	Brave	Criticized	Down
Amused	Breathless	Crushed	
Angry	Bristling	Cuddly	Eager
Anguished	Broken-up	Curious	Ecstatic
Annoyed	Bruised	Cut	Edgy
Anxious	Bubbly		Elated
Apart	Bugged	Damned	Embarrassed
Apologetic	Burdened	Daring	Empty
Appreciative	Burned	Deceived	Enraged
Apprehensive	Burned-up	Deceptive	Enraptured
Approved		Degraded	Enthusiastic
Argumentative	Callous	Demeaned	Enticed
Aroused	Capable	Demoralized	Esteemed
Assertive	Captivated	Dependent	Exasperated
Astonished	Caring	Depressed	Exhilarated
Attached	Carried away	Deprived	Exposed
Attacked	Cautious	Deserted	
Attentive	Certain	Desirable	Fascinated
Attractive	Chased	Desirous	Flattered
Aware	Cheated	Despair	Foolish
Awestruck	Cheerful	Desperate	Forced
	Chokcd (up)	Destroyed	Forceful
Badgered	Close	Different	Fortunate
Baited	Cold	Dirty	Forward

Friendly
Frightened
Frustrated
Full
Funny
Furious

Gay
Generous
Genuine
Giddy
Giving
Grateful
Greedy
Grief
Grim
Grouchy
Grumpy
Guarded

Happy-go-lucky
Hard
Hassled
Hateful
Healthy
Helpful
Helpless
Hesitant
High
Hollow
Hopeful
Horrified
Hostile
Humiliated
Hung up
Hurt
Hyper

Ignorant
Impatient
Important
Impotent

Impressed
Incompetent
Independent
Innocent
Insecure
Insignificant
Insincere
Inspired
Insulted
Intimate
Intolerant
Involved
Irate
Irked
Irresponsible
Irritated

Jealous
Jittery
Joyous

Left out
Lively
Lonely
Loose
Lost
Loving
Low
Lucky
Lustful

Mad
Malicious
Mean
Miserable
Misunderstood
Moody
Mystified

Nasty
Nervous
Numb

Obsessed
Offended
Open
Ornery
Out of control
Overjoyed
Overwhelmed

Pampered
Panicky
Paralyzed
Patient
Peaceful
Peeved
Perceptive
Perturbed
Petrified
Phony
Pleased
Powerless
Pressured
Proud
Pulled apart
Put-down
Puzzled

Quarrelsome
Quiet

Raped
Ravished
Ravishing
Real
Refreshing
Regretful
Rejected
Rejecting
Relaxed
Relieved
Removed
Repulsive
Resentful

Resistant
Responsible
Responsive
Revengeful
Rotten
Ruined

Safe
Satiated
Scared
Scolded
Scorned
Screwed
Secure
Seduced
Seductive
Self-centered
Self-conscious
Selfish
Separated
Shattered
Shocked
Shot-down
Shy
Sickened
Silly
Sincere
Sinking
Smart
Smothered
Smug
Sneaky
Snowed
Soft
Soothed
Sorry
Spiteful
Spontaneous
Squelched
Starved
Stiff
Stifled

Stimulated	Terrific	Unapproachable	Warm
Strangled	Terrified	Unaware	Weak
Strong	Thrilled	Uncertain	Whipped
Stubborn	Ticked	Uncomfortable	Whole
Stunned	Tickled	Under control	Wild
Stupid	Tight	Understanding	Willing
Subdued	Timid	Understood	Wiped-out
Submissive	Tired	Unfriendly	Wishful
Successful	Tormented	Unhappy	Withdrawn
Suffocated	Torn	Unimportant	Wonderful
Sure	Tortured		Worried
Sweet	Trapped	Valuable	Worthy
Sympathy	Tremendous	Valued	Wounded
	Tricked	Violated	
Tainted	Trusted	Violent	Zapped
Tender		Voluptuous	
Tense	Ugly	Vulnerable	

The media shape and mold behavior by manipulating our feelings; we will feel great if we own that car, feel beautiful wearing that outfit. While advertising has a necessary informative role in society, many ads are recreating us in someone else's image and placing impossible burdens on persons to be ultra-thin, to BUY into the "American Dream," which far too often means buying into some housing development and furnishing it to look just like the set on our favorite TV sitcom or like the picture in some magazine.

We build artificial, media-imaged, fit-into-the-collective lives, and then wonder why we feel empty, depressed, and looking for the meaning in life, when all the time what we are searching for is right inside of us— our own unique individuality that we have hidden and suppressed in the socialization process that began the instant we were born and found out that crying (expressing feelings) upset most adults.

Much experience has shown that we can constructively create and utilize tensional energy through various forms of creativity or some mode of creative expression that *we uniquely devise.* Among the many ways to create healthy tension, these stand out as quite effective:

Active imagination;
Acknowledgment;
Art, collage;
Tensional art, combining images representing extreme opposites done
    as a collage;
Delaying gratification, insight gaps;

Dream work;
Expressing feelings;
Humor, including dark humor;
Mythologizing, story telling;
Patience, slowing down;
Ritual;
Shadow work; and
Writing, poetry, journal work.

We can write *without censoring* what we write and make a special effort to write about strong push-button feelings. We can write about what makes us feel angry, passionate, euphoric, or intrigued. Writing, journal work, and art—serious and humorous—are all effective ways to hold and work with tension, creating something new from integrating opposites. Tapping into dynamic, creative tension inevitably results in prodigious bursts of creativity and passion while simultaneously giving unique expression to some inner struggle.

REPRESSION: NURTURING A "POISON TREE"

> I was angry with my friend;
> I told my wrath, my wrath did end.
> I was angry with my foe;
> I told it not, my wrath did grow.
>
> William Blake[51]

Repression reduces tension, and most of us are experts at it. The average person has stuffed so many feelings into some dark hidden closet that to even open it a crack engenders fear and apprehension. Each thing we repress not only does not go away, it grows in secret, eventually becoming one of the demons that torment us. Our dreams will mirror the growing energies of repression; benevolent creatures under our control gradually grow into nightmarish wild beasts, shadowy figures determined to do us in.

We most often repress with our use of language. Our vocabulary is loaded with certain words that we use to diffuse tension, to escape uncomfortable situations, and to avoid painful issues. Collective "shoulds" and "should nots" also play an important role in repression. Cultural clichés abound like "Big boys don't cry." For example, words like "but" and "fine" are popular verbal escape hatches in interpersonal relationships. My wife complains that I left dirty dishes in the sink and I reply, "*But* I was busy." Look for words or word phrases that begin your defense-escape sentences. I've lost count of the times some little boy in me answers my wife with, "I didn't do it," which has the effect of an immediate exit. See how you use words to eliminate tension, which is automatic repression. We are vocabulary quick-draws when it comes to getting out of uncomfortable situations. There is a very alert little kid in all of us who, when accused, says, "I didn't do it."

Another excellent way to avoid repressing feelings is using "I" statements. For example, instead of saying, "This house is a mess," you could say, "This clutter makes me feel really stressed out. I need to talk about it." "I" statements *hold* the feelings in a situation in a least offensive manner. The other person's empathy will likely be aroused, instead of anger and retaliation. "I" statements provide a way to *work through* a conflict instead of repressing it.

EXPLORING OUR BLIND SIDE: SHADOW WORK

> A cultured person is one who has the desired characteristics visible on the right (the righteous side) and the forbidden ones hidden on the left.
> Robert A. Johnson[52]

Escaping the influence of the mass mind requires conscious experience of those attributes that the group abhors. One must reach into the group's unacknowledged shadow, bringing this dark matter into the light of day. For example, part of my own healing process has included the necessity of my owning what my religious group hated most. I had to realize that their unacknowledged spiritual arrogance, exclusiveness, and smugness was indeed a part of my own shadow.

In *Your Mythic Journey,* Sam Keen explains how to access unconscious parts of the psyche by creating tension between the known and unknown: "Assume that you are what you aren't and that you aren't what you are. Flip your story. Take your list of negations and compose convincing arguments to prove that these are your most essential qualities."[53] In an exercise of this sort, it is important to be aware of both opposites at once. For example, if you consider yourself a generous person, hold the feeling of giving and generosity in your awareness *at the same time* you are convincing yourself that you are remarkably greedy and miserly. Holding the tension between two opposites is a difficult but rewarding task. Out of this tension and conflict aspects of the unseen self—the authentic personality—will emerge. This does not mean that our real natures are dark or evil, but rather that what we perceive to be our real self is but a split-off self, a fragment caught in a one-sided dynamic, which means we are living a no-growth or growth-by-disaster-only life.

We often hear about persons accomplishing amazing feats of strength and courage as a result of a traumatic or tragic event in one's life. In other words, when life presents us with a tremendous "bump," the conflict and tension created often produces an unexpected miracle.

Spiritual alchemy transforms base metal into gold, a process requiring integration of one's shadow. This spiritual transformation requires our participation in an adventure into our own kingdom of the Self, where we must ultimately slay the two-headed dragon of *dualism*—a dualism that would destroy our true potential by living half-lives, one-sided fragments of reality.

It is not unusual that most religious texts included the necessity of oppositeness to life as in Genesis: "Male and female created he them . . . " (1:27) and "Then the Lord God said, 'It is not good that man should be alone.' "(2:18). It is apparent also that the authors of many religious texts were caught in a one-sided, patriarchal viewpoint. Christianity is nauseatingly sexist in this regard. When reading any Scripture one must filter out the polarity-bias of its author(s).

A wonderful way to get out of extremes, humor heals by mitigating the deadly one-sided seriousness of life. Humor is an *in-between* soul-invigorating experience. Interestingly, studies have shown that humor is largely involuntary; that we normally cannot make ourselves laugh. But laughter is definitely contagious and even when we don't know what's so funny, others' laughter often starts us laughing.

Humor provides an excellent way to work out one's own shadow. When angry, violent people are able to laugh, especially at themselves, healing begins; this is one form of "shadow work."

CRITERIA FOR A HEALTHY GROUP

> But when a group struggles through to a choice, having heard this need and that demand, this proposal and another that contradicts it, gradually all the data become available and the decision reached is a hard-won harmony of all the ideas, needs, and desires of each and every one.
>
> Carl R. Rogers[54]

Justice, our attempt to balance injustice, comes from placing equal weight—equal value on both sides. If we place all the weight on one side, we have no balance, no justice. Justice means "moral rightness, equity, honor, fairness." Only when we hold both sides with equal value, do we obtain a balanced perspective. Hence, reasonableness requires a mind and heart that can encompass opposing viewpoints and difference.

An effective group needs minimal basic ground rules established by a facilitator or leader. All other rules, if any, ought to be determined by the members. Important ground rules include the following:

- Make tension and conflict natural elements;
- Insure shared information is confidential;
- Establish minimum acceptable attendance guidelines, depending on the group's purpose;
- No verbal or physical abuse; anger is okay but not rage;
- Establish that openness, directness, probing, and emotions are acceptable and necessary;
- Encourage honest feedback and introspection;
- Everyone must know that independent critical thinking is vital;
- Maintain unconditional respect and personal regard for others;
- Make the process more important than the results;
- Establish that chaos is okay; and
- There does not have to be a solution.

Healthy groups depend upon the ability of individuals to weigh both sides of an issue, holding the tension between them. Granted that we must give a piece of ourselves to the collective, the dilemma becomes one of *holding together,* retaining our innate integrity while being meaningfully involved in the world.

13

Life After Group

I am circling around God,
around the ancient tower,
and I have been circling for a thousand years.
And I still don't know if I am a falcon,
or a storm,
or a great song.

> Rainer Maria Rilke[1]

One or two things are all you need
to travel over the blue pond, over the deep
roughage of the trees and through the stiff
flowers of lightning—some deep
memory of pleasure, some cutting
knowledge of pain.

> Mary Oliver[2]

In the huge gap
between the flash
and the thunderstroke
spring has come in
or a deep snow fallen.
Freedom suppressed and again regained bites with keener
fangs than freedom never endangered.

> Cicero[3]

An Archetypal Perspective

> Archetypal psychology implies much more than archetypes and univer-
> sal images. It suggests the infinite range of psychological endeavor,
> rooted in everyday life and culture, but echoing the wisdom, the artful-
> ness, and the beauty of centuries of soulful work, love and play.
>
> Thomas Moore[4]

In the archetypal school of psychology, imagination with its images and musings forms the focus of our attention. Images are autonomous and immediate—existential happenings that beckon us deeper into soul-mak-ing. The archetypal perspective is a *phenomenological** approach to the human psyche and to the collective experience: everyone and everything has meaning, memory, sacredness. It is a soul-centered perspective, not a group-centered perspective.

One lives through *experience* instead of through *interpretation.* A sym-bol or image, once interpreted, dies, shot down so to speak—dead as to deeper *meaning.* However, when viewed from an experiential perspective, an image becomes an unending story, a soul journey, a pathway leading one into deeper and deeper meaning. It is precisely *meaning* that is so utterly lacking in the lives of so many persons—the "existential crisis" of modern times. Through literalization (concretization) of dream, myth, image, and symbol, our culture has surgically removed the soul and the meaning from life.

Through an archetypal phenomenological view of the psyche and the world, we have the opportunity not only to regain meaning in our lives, but also to value and reverence *the soul in things.* It is ultimately meaning that adds sacredness, giving life and value to everything and everyone. Exis-tence becomes paramount and by virtue (the value) of the existence of things, meaning (soul) returns. We regain meaning through the realization of soul in all things, from the individual to a grain of sand to a star. An *in-terconnectivity of being*—a common ground of coexistence and a mutual-ity of arising and ultimate interdependence—somehow link us all.

As such, *all things hold together* and have meaning, value, and *in-tegrity.* Hence, the destruction of things, whether a river or a human being, means a loss of soul for each of us. From the archetypal view, life is sacred, and things are sacred, images are sacred.

---

*As a psychological term, *phenomenological* refers to the inherent meaning and value in both the animate and inanimate. Things as well as people have value and significance, activating memories and feelings that serve as historical records of the human experience; buildings, art, streets, places, forests, streams, oceans—all are part of an intricate *web of life* and we cannot destroy anyone or anything without consequences, without some kind of loss.

How do we hold the tension between the unique and the universal—the ultimate collectivity of things? How does one *exist* as an individual autonomous soul? In between the individual and the universal is an experiential world, a soul-making landscape. Holding the tension between the individual and the universal means that we must enter into a relationship (the space in between) with life, with the soul in all life. That is, we need to create a dialogue with the soul, not only as an inner aspect of individual consciousness, but as soul in all existence. This is an archetypal *eco-phenomenological psychology*—a soul-psychology of relationships. We must find what this soul-in-things wants by doing our own soul-making. Through our own soul work, we enrich ourselves and our communities. On an archetypal level, we share our mythology with all communities. Myth, image, and dream interconnect and unite the human spirit, striking the cord of our common heritage.

For example, an artist creates an inspiring work of art. Everyone who sees this work of art is *moved,* inspired by its feeling, images, and story. The soul of the artist has imparted meaning and significance to a seeming inanimate object (the art piece), and *the soul in the work of art* now moves its phenomenological significance and value out into the observers. Now *more soul* has entered the collective psyche. The community receives a new value. Thus soul-making necessarily means giving space to soul things. Giving space to soul things then builds true culture.

Building a Healthy Community

I do not address myself to nations but only to those few people amongst whom it is taken for granted that our civilization ("Kultur") does not drop from heaven but is, in the end, produced by individuals. If the great cause fails it is because the individuals fail, because I fail. So I must first put myself right. And as authority has lost its spell I need for this purpose knowledge and experience of the most intimate and intrinsic foundations of my subjective being so as to build my base upon the eternal factors of the human soul.

Carl Jung[5]

Considered in a collective context, Jung's "transcendent function" between opposites promotes (the opposites being the tension between the individual and the collective) relatedness, interconnectedness, and a real sense, not only of belonging but of contributing to one's community or group.

Our physical bodies function well when each organ (member) does its unique job. Similarly, a community functions in a healthy manner when each individual is allowed to express their unique individuality. Just as there is a necessary interconnectedness and cooperation among bodily organs, a healthy community requires interconnectedness between its members. Our increasingly fragmented (into groups) society has lost its sense of human connectedness—its indispensable need for relationship. Instead, we use our financial resources to build separate enclosed worlds, removed and insulated from those elements of society that make us feel uncomfortable or unsafe. Walled-in, guarded communities increasingly separate us from each other.

Acknowledging that groups and communities are necessary parts of our social landscape, we can limit their destructive potential by limiting their size. When an organized religion, an IBM, or an Exxon run amuck, the human, economic, and environmental consequences are potentially devastating. In contrast, if the corner market decides to sell outdated fruit, damage is confined to a small area. The noted economist Leopold Kohr (1909–1994) maintained that *bigness* was a major cause of social misery. He believed smaller, more autonomous regions would improve the quality of life and political institutions. Kohr said, "Let us hope the twenty-first century seeks universality at the smallest scale, that it recognizes that the fullness of existence is contained in the smallest of spaces."[6]

The word "autonomy" comes from the Greek *autonomia*, meaning the "condition or quality of being self-governing; self-determination, independence." Autonomy can be thought of as a golden key to overcoming the collective beast, the "tyranny of a totalistic majority."

While individuals require autonomy, the political, economic, and religious aspects of our collective culture become dysfunctional and destructive if given autonomy. Groups must serve the individual. Autonomous groups disempower the individual. Extending the notion of autonomy to our environment means that all life, animate and inanimate, ought to have its own autonomy, an inherent existential "right to be," or at least the right to be left alone as long as *no harm* is done.

OUR NEED FOR COMMUNITY

> With the growth of civilization we have succeeded in subjecting ever larger human groups to the rule of the same morality, without, however, having yet brought the moral code to prevail beyond the social frontiers, that is, *in the free space between mutually independent societies.* (Emphasis added)
>
> Carl Jung[7]

A community's foremost value rests in the linking together of diverse individuals, creating vital relationships, who share a common *ground* or neighborhood. However, the notion that all in a community must be "good citizens" would destroy true diversity and leave a community unchallenged, without the tension needed for constructive social development. A "both/and" approach to community would embrace even difficult opposites, as Andrew Samuels in *The Political Psyche* suggests: "If love and hate do not always have to be linked in so-called normal ambivalence, then there is a place for both community spirit and ruthless selfishness. They do not have to be seen as cancelling each other out."[8] Samuels further suggests the value of constructive tension between groups: "Nor is it unethical to try to subvert the system, to try to out-smart or out-negotiate other people or other groups. Negotiating and bargaining are profound and passionate forms of relating," and, "No clarity exists save in relation to confusion."[9] The value or virtue in a religious community rests in its ability to create a sacred *ritual space* in between two worlds: the physical and the spiritual.

We now have an *electronic neighborhood*. Sitcom and talk-show personalities make up our circle of "friends"—our family. Our collective media world, when excessive, prevents us from living our own lives. Instead, we live vicariously through the media. Indeed, the "mass media" become our electronic group of choice, the shapers of our ideas, desires, and views of the world. We are hypnotically drawn into the daily electronic fare whose images become our most sought-after gods.

Isolating people into economically defined groups, as in welfare communities and housing projects, results from a totalitarian-oriented government bureaucracy that labels and dehumanizes individuals, lumping them into categories, socially branding people like cattle. Such social programs obliterate the social diversity so necessary for a vital creative society.

Suffering evokes our humanity, and therefore is a necessary ingredient in spiritual and psychological development. Discovering that others have been through similar experiences and have survived makes us realize that we are not alone. There is no greater pain than pain suffered alone. In recent research at the Stanford Medical Center in Palo Alto, California, psychotherapy support groups doubled the survival times for terminal cancer patients.[10] We need meaningful connections with other human beings. The ability to express and share our feelings *without fear or guilt* is in itself a potent healer. Groups and community provide a sense of common history, a common humanity, mirroring our underlying interconnectedness. We lose soul stuff when we lose a sense of outer connection with others and inner connection with who we really are as unique citizens.

Community provides an ordering context within which we make sense out of life. Certainly, the community requires a certain degree of compromise. To survive in a community, we must more or less try to follow the community's rules. However, as with any group, the distinction is clear between healthy and destructive communities. A community, in its highest sense, supports and respects individual distinctiveness, freedom, and autonomy. Addressing the conflict between the collective and the individual, Joseph Campbell observed, "There is always a point in your journey where you have to break the rules of the tribe."[11] In order to live one's own life, one must shift from following an outer collective authority to following one's own heart. This shift from an outer-directed life to an inner-directed life creates inevitable conflict between collective powers and individuals. Indeed, we can never step out of collective influences without being ostracized in some manner.

The psyche tends toward wholeness, toward integration, toward greater integrity—a momentum that when acknowledged and used provides one with the energy and will to undertake the journey out of group-think in search of one's authentic individuality. This innate psychic momentum implies that our communities ought to mirror the natural inclinations of the human spirit, meaning laws that try to control and mandate how a community *should* develop prevent real development and keep a community in an infantile state. A prolific writer and philosopher, Alan Watts realized that, "Individuality is inseparable from community. In other words, the order of nature is not a forced order; it is not the result of laws and commandments which beings are compelled to obey by external violence."[12] By not being ourselves, we enable groups and systems to continue their destructiveness.

Endings and Beginnings

> It is not society that is to guide and save the creative hero, but precisely the reverse. And so everyone of us shares the supreme ordeal—carries the cross of the redeemer—not in the bright moments of his tribe's great victories, but in the silences of his personal despair.
>
> Joseph Campbell[13]

There is an immense difference, as Robert Bly said, "between living something and being lived by it";[14] it is the difference between a machine and and a living soul. One is in a neurotic state when something outside oneself is in control. As the English poet, critic, and dramatist John Dryden admonished, "The worst [tyranny] is that which persecutes the mind."[15] New beginnings rest on our shoulders, burn in our hearts, and it is within our capacity to remake our world, but not without first redeeming ourselves in our own *unique image.*

All things are the same,
but I am no longer addicted to any doctrine—
to any "ism."
Therefore all things have changed
because I am changed.
Now something deep and beautiful is growing in me—
the tree of the mid-point is filling with blossoms.
Wonder and mystery have returned.

Appendix

Marks of a Destructive Group

While not all groups exhibit all these traits, destructive groups will have many of these characteristics and attitudes:

Authoritarian hierarchal control;

Black and white thinking: either/or, we/they, us/them;

Centralized power structure;

Child abuse and neglect;

Competition with other members or with outsiders;

Conflicting opinions viewed as moral assaults and disloyalty;

Control of information within group environment;

Criticism of group, system or leaders is discouraged;

Different beliefs or ideas are perceived as threatening;

Discrimination (economic, emotional, and psychological): race, gender, age, religion, politics;

Effusive praise and flattery for leaders;

Enemy making, a common enemy outside the group: other business groups, other religions, other countries, other life styles, other races;

Fear (or feelings of guilt) about the prospect of leaving the group;

Feelings of superiority and exclusiveness;

Gender-based abuse in any form;

Group becomes like a family and is more important than individual's family and outside friends;

Group has the "truth" (the answers), others don't;

Group (system) mission is more important than the individual;

313

Group's doctrine repeated over and over—lots of repetitious lectures and meetings;

Group leader(s) are looked to for answers involving personal choices in life;

Labeling: dissenting members, other groups, and different belief systems are given negative labels/names;

Large pay and power gaps between members and leaders;

Loaded language: the group has its own clichés, jargon, and slogans that become simplistic explanations for complex situations;

Missionary consciousness: converting others to group ideology, product, beliefs, trying to persuade others to be like "us";

Need permission of leader(s) for everything;

Overuse of plural pronouns: we, us, they, them;

Peer pressure: nongroup ideas receive icy silence, ridicule, or condemnation;

Propaganda used to persuade members and internalize group ideas;

Public humiliation or embarrassment in any form;

Public sharings, testimonials, confession, witnessing;

Scapegoating within or outside the group;

Secrecy between members or between different levels of a group's structure;

Selfishness is putting yourself above the group;

Strict dress codes, everyone looks alike;

Suppressing legitimate feelings when they do not fit the group's mindset;

The need to be like leaders or like others in the group;

There is always something to do, excessive business;

There is a group explanation for everything;

Thought control: there are "good" and "bad" thoughts; and

Unquestioning obedience to authority.

Notes

Prologue

1. Marquess of Halifax, *Moral Thoughts and Reflections,* late seventeenth century.
2. Joseph Campbell, *The Hero with a Thousand Faces* (Princeton, N.J.: Princeton University Press, 1949), pp. 245–46.
3. William Morris, ed., *The American Heritage Dictionary of the English Language* (Boston: Houghton Mifflin, 1981), p. 321.
4. "Marks of a Destructive Cult," *Cult Awareness Network* (Chicago: C.A.N., 1988), p. 4.
5. Carl G. Jung, *Psychological Types,* trans. R. F. C. Hull (Princeton, N.J.: Princeton University Press, 1967), p. 67.
6. Joseph Campbell, *The Hero's Journey,* ed. P. Cousineau (New York: HarperCollins, 1990), p. 113.

Chapter 1. Collective Enchantment

1. Andrew B. Schmookler, *Fool's Gold: The Fate of Values in a World of Goods* (New York: HarperCollins, 1993), pp. 31–32.
2. Sam Keen, *Faces of the Enemy: Reflections of the Hostile Imagination* (San Francisco: Harper and Row, 1986), p. 172.
3. William Wordsworth, *Preface to Poems* (1815), Supplementary Essay.
4. Carl G. Jung, *Psychological Reflections: A New Anthology of His Writings,* trans. R. F. C. Hull (Princeton, N.J.: Princeton University Press, 1970), p. 183.
5. Auguste Préault (1809–1889), cited in John Gross, ed., *The Oxford Book of Aphorisms* (New York: Oxford University Press, 1983), p. 83.

6. Dale Dibbley, *From Achilles' Heel to Zeus' Shield* (New York: Ballantine Books, 1993), p. 39.

7. Joseph Campbell, *An Open Life,* ed. John Maher and Dennie Briggs (New York: HarperCollins, 1989), p. 112.

8. Richard Roberts, *Tales for Jung Folk* (San Anselmo, Calif.: Vernal Equinox Press, 1983), pp. 34–41.

9. Carl G. Jung, *Memories, Dreams, Reflections,* ed. Aniela Jaffe, trans. Richard and Clara Winston (New York: Vintage, 1961), p. 342.

10. Erich Fromm, *The Sane Society* (New York: Henry Holt and Company, 1955), p. 360.

11. James Hillman, *A Blue Fire* (New York: HarperCollins, 1989), pp. 37–38. Hillman calls the psyche "polytheistic," referring to the "many gods and goddesses" that make up one's inner nature.

12. Ibid., p. 37.

13. Robert J. Lifton, *Thought Reform and the Psychology of Totalism: A Study of "Brainwashing" in China* (Chapel Hill: University of North Carolina Press, 1989), p. 419.

14. Carl G. Jung, *The Undiscovered Self,* trans. R. F. C. Hull (Princeton, N.J.: Princeton University Press, 1976), p. 31.

15. Ibid., p. 32.

16. David Mayberry-Lewis, "Tribal Wisdom," *Utne Reader* (July/August 1992): 66–93.

17. "The War Against the Indians," Discovery Channel (January 16, 1994).

18. Connie Zweig and Jeremiah Abrams, eds., *Meeting the Shadow: The Hidden Power of the Dark Side of Human Nature* (Los Angeles: Jeremy P. Tarcher, 1991), p. xix.

19. Norman Mailer, *Advertisements for Myself* (1961).

20. Reported by Amnesty International.

21. Joe Klein, "Looking for Enemies," *Journal of Psychohistory* 22, no. 1 (Summer 1994): 29.

22. "Death and Disinterest," episode, "Geraldo," CNBC TV (April 27, 1994).

23. R. Buckminster Fuller, *Critical Path* (New York: St. Martin's Press, 1981), p. 217.

24. Joseph Campbell, *The Hero with a Thousand Faces* (Princeton, N.J.: Princeton, University Press, 1949), p. 390.

25. Carl G. Jung, *The Structure and Dynamics of the Psyche,* trans. R. F. C. Hull (Princeton, N.J.: Princeton University Press, 1969), par. 342.

26. Ibid., par. 325.

27. Carl G. Jung, "Two Essays on Analytical Psychology," in *The Collected Works,* vol. 7 (Princeton, N.J.: Princeton University Press, 1953), p. 37.

28. Log. 30:32, pl. 93. *The Gospel According to Thomas,* trans. A. Guillaumont et al. (Harper and Row, 1959).

29. Jung, "Two Essays on Analytical Psychology," p. 67.

30. Ibid., p. 155.

31. Carl G. Jung, *On the Nature of the Psyche,* trans. R. F. C. Hull (Princeton, N.J.: Princeton University Press, 1954), par. 432.

32. Daryl Sharp, *C. G. Jung Lexicon: A Primer of Terms and Concepts* (Toronto: Inner City Books, 1991), p. 68.

33. Ibid.

34. Alan Watts, *Tao: The Watercourse Way* (New York: Pantheon Books, 1975), p. 51.

35. Carl G. Jung, "Two Essays on Analytical Psychology," in *The Portable Jung* (New York: Penguin, 1982), p. 101.

36. Sam Donaldson, "The Tobacco Industry" on "Prime Time Live," ABC News (December 30, 1993).

37. Louis Rukeyser, *Louis Rukeyser's Business Almanac* (New York: Simon and Schuster, 1988), pp. 141–42.

38. Ibid., p. 145.

39. Martha Brant, "The Alaskan Assault," *Newsweek* (October 2, 1995): 44.

40. Marie-Louise Von Franz, *Psychotherapy* (Boston: Shambhala, 1993), p. 285.

41. Joseph Roux, *Meditations of a Parish Priest*, trans. Isabel F. Hapgood (New York: Thomas Y. Crowell, 1970), p. 122.

42. Carl G. Jung, *Symbols of Transformation*, trans. R. F. C. Hull (Princeton, N.J.: Princeton University Press, 1967), par. 625.

43. Schmookler, *Fool's Gold*, p. 19.

44. Mary K. Blakeley, "Psyched Out," *Los Angeles Times Magazine* (October 3, 1993): 27–28, 46–49.

45. Eric Hoffer, *The True Believer: Thoughts on the Nature of Mass Movements* (New York: Harper and Row, 1951), pp. 14–16.

46. Blakeley, "Psyched Out," p. 28.

47. Viktor E. Frankl, *Man's Search for Meaning: An Introduction to Logotherapy* (New York: Simon and Schuster, 1984), p. 110.

48. Joseph Campbell, "The Hero's Journey," KCET TV, Los Angeles (March 1, 1994).

49. Benjamin Disraeli, *Contarini Fleming* (1832).

50. Campbell, *The Hero with a Thousand Faces*, p. 30.

51. Cited in Von Franz, *Psychotherapy*, p. 285.

Chapter 2. Trapped in Paradise

1. Cited in Connie Zweig and Jeremiah Abrams, eds., *Meeting the Shadow: The Hidden Power of the Dark Side of Human Nature* (Los Angeles: Jeremy P. Tarcher, 1991), p. 137.

2. William James, *Letters* (1896).

3. Cited in Zweig and Abrams, *Meeting the Shadow*, p. 146.

4. Cited in John Gross, ed., *The Oxford Book of Aphorisms* (New York: Oxford University Press, 1983), p. 105.

5. Carl G. Jung, "Two Essays on Analytical Psychology," in *The Portable Jung* (New York: Penguin, 1982), pp. 120–121.

6. "Marks of a Destructive Cult," *Cult Awareness Network* (Chicago: C.A.N., 1988) p. 4.

7. Joseph Campbell, *An Open Life,* ed. John Maher and Dennie Briggs (New York: HarperCollins, 1989), p. 15.

8. William Blake, *The Marriage of Heaven and Hell* (1790–93).

9. Otto T., a Methodist minister. I have used a fictitious name to protect his privacy. From a personal letter.

10. Becky Taylor, from her unpublished article "My Story" (January 1993).

11. Kabir, *The Kabir Book,* trans. Robert Bly (Boston: Beacon Press, 1977), p. 37.

12. Steven Hassan, *Combatting Cult Mind Control* (Rochester, Vt.: Park Street Press, 1988), p. 45.

13. Monica Davis, a former member of the Ann Ree Colton Foundation of Niscience, made this comment to the author several years after leaving the group (1993).

14. Joseph Bottone, from a letter written to Ann Ree Colton's successor and then-minister and spiritual leader of the foundation, Jonathan Murro (1990).

15. Joseph Campbell, *The Hero with a Thousand Faces* (Princeton, N.J.: Princeton University Press, 1949), pp. 30, 245.

16. Caryn Aman, from her personal journal (1993).

17. Viktor E. Frankl, *Man's Search for Meaning: An Introduction to Logotherapy* (New York: Simon and Schuster, 1984), p. 154.

18. Terri Goldhammer, the author's wife. From her personal journal (1973).

19. Carl Sagan, "The Fine Art of Baloney Detection," *Parade* (February 1, 1987): 6.

Chapter 3. Fatal Persuasion

1. Fyodor Dostoyevsky, *The Brothers Karamazov* (1879–80).

2. Anthony Pratkanis and Elliot Aronson, *Age of Propaganda: The Everyday Use and Abuse of Persuasion* (New York: W.H. Freeman and Company, 1992), p. 24.

3. Peter McWilliams, *Life 102: What To Do When Your Guru Sues You* (Los Angeles: Prelude Press, 1994), p. 171.

4. Ibid., p. 67.

5. Heraclitus, *Fragments,* trans. Philip Wheelwright (ca. 500 B.C.). Cited in James Hillman, *A Blue Fire* (New York: HarperCollins, 1989) p. 160.

6. Carl G. Jung, *The Undiscovered Self,* trans. R. F. C. Hull (Princeton, N.J.: Princeton University Press, 1976), p. 31.

7. Carl G. Jung, "Two Essays on Analytical Psychology," in *The Collected Works,* vol. 7 (Princeton, N.J.: Princeton University Press, 1976), p. 289.

8. Ibid., par. 337.

9. T. E. Hulme, *Speculations* (1924).

10. Cited in Hillman, *A Blue Fire,* p. 160.

11. John Seldon, *Table Talk* (mid-seventeenth century).

12. Vauvenargues, *Reflections and Maxims* (1746).

13. Robert J. Lifton, *Thought Reform and the Psychology of Totalism: A*

Study of "Brainwashing" in China (Chapel Hill: University of North Carolina Press, 1989), p. 429.

14. George Orwell, *1984* (New York: New American Library, 1949), p. 246.

15. George Orwell, "Politics and the English Language," in William Lutz, *Doublespeak: From "Revenue Enhancement" to "Terminal Living"* (New York: HarperCollins, 1989), pp. 8–9.

16. Cited in Laurence J. Peter, *Peter's Quotations* (New York: Bantam Books, 1977), p. 71.

17. Ben Johnson, *Timber: or Discoveries* (1640).

18. Carl G. Jung, *The Undiscovered Self,* trans. R. F. C. Hull (Princeton, N.J.: Princeton University Press, 1976), pp. 12–13.

19. Robert Novak, "Political Correctness in the Newsroom," *Imprimis* 23, no. 11 (1994): 1.

20. Lutz, *Doublespeak*, p. 4.

21. John Morley, *Voltaire* (1872).

22. William Morris, ed., *The American Heritage Dictionary of the English Language* (Boston: Houghton Mifflin Company, 1981), p. 1033.

23. Lifton, *Thought Reform and the Psychology of Totalism*, p. 430.

24. Pierre Nicole, *Essais de morale* (1671–78).

25. Anthony Pratkanis and Elliot Aronson, *Age of Propaganda: The Everyday Use and Abuse of Persuasion* (New York: W.H. Freeman and Company, 1992), p. 21.

26. Daryl Sharp, *C.G. Jung Lexicon: A Primer of Terms and Concepts* (Toronto: Inner City Books, 1991), p. 92.

27. Sam Keen and Anne Valley-Fox, *Your Mythic Journey* (Los Angeles: Jeremy P. Tarcher, 1989), p. 74.

28. Sam Keen, *Faces of the Enemy: Reflection of the Hostile Imagination* (San Francisco: Harper and Row, 1986), p. 25.

29. Sir Charles Sherrington, *Man on His Nature* (1940).

30. Carl G. Jung, *Memories, Dreams, Reflections,* ed. Ariela Jaffe, trans. Richard and Clara Winston (New York: Vintage, 1961), p. 91.

31. F. David Peat, *Synchronicity: The Bridge Between Matter and Mind* (New York: Bantam Books, 1987), p. 38.

32. Michael White, "Challenging Specifications of Personhood," *Dulwich Centre* (1992): p. 3.

33. John Bradshaw, "Mystified Love," KCET TV, Los Angeles (December 4, 1993).

34. Elias Canetti, *Crowds and Power* (New York: The Noonday Press, 1962), p. 29.

35. Alice Miller, *Drama of the Gifted Child: The Search for the True Self,* trans. Ruth Ward (New York: Basic Books, 1981), p. 38.

36. Alexander Lowen, *Narcissism* (New York: MacMillan, 1985), p. ix.

37. Andrew B. Schmookler, *Fool's Gold: The Fate of Values in a World of Goods* (New York: HarperCollins, 1993), p. 33.

38. Lifton, *Thought Reform and the Psychology of Totalism*, p. 419.

39. David McClelland, "Is There a Science of Success?" *Atlantic Monthly* (February 1994): 83–98.

Chapter 4. The Dark Side of Groups

1. Carl G. Jung, "Two Essays on Analytical Psychology," in *The Portable Jung* (New York: Penguin, 1982), p. 101.

2. John Babbs, quoted in Connie Zweig and Jeremiah Abrams, eds., *Meeting the Shadow: The Hidden Power of the Dark Side of Human Nature* (Los Angeles: Jeremy P. Tarcher, 1991), p. xix.

3. Thomas Wilson, *Sacra Privata* (early eighteenth century).

4. Eric Hoffer, *The True Believer: Thoughts on the Nature of Mass Movements* (New York: Harper and Row, 1951), p. 62.

5. Blaise Pascal, *Penses* (1670).

6. Thomas Merton, *The Way of Chuang Tzu* (New York: New Directions Books, 1969), p. 43.

7. Rabindranath Tagore, quoted in Maria F. Mahoney, *The Meaning in Dreams and Dreaming* (New Jersey: The Citadel Press, 1966), p. 138.

8. Marion Woodman, *Addiction to Perfection: The Still Unravished Bride* (Toronto: Inner City Books, 1982), p. 15.

9. Carl G. Jung, *Memories, Dreams, Reflections,* ed. Ariela Jaffe, trans. R. and C. Winston (New York: Vintage, 1961), p. 351.

10. Carl G. Jung, *The Structure and Dynamics of the Psyche,* trans. R. F. C. Hull (Princeton, N.J.: Princeton University Press, 1969), par. 61.

11. Stanley Passey, "Theoretical Foundations of Psychotherapy," Lecture at Pacifica Graduate Institute (1991).

12. Carl G. Jung, *The Archetypes and the Collective Unconscious,* trans. R. F. C. Hull (Princeton, N.J.: Princeton University Press, 1969), par. 167.

13. James Hillman, *A Blue Fire* (New York: HarperCollins, 1989), p. 52.

14. Tom Brokaw, "NBC Evening News" (April 4, 1994).

15. Hillman, *A Blue Fire,* p. 153.

16. *The Lost Books of the Bible,* trans. Archbishop Wake (New York: Bell Publishing Co., 1979), p. 144.

17. John Keats, letter (1819), cited in John Gross, ed., *The Oxford Book of Aphorisms* (New York: Oxford University Press, 1983), p. 58.

18. Thomas Moore, quoted in Hillman, *A Blue Fire,* p. 113.

19. Carl G. Jung, *The Undiscovered Self,* trans. R. F. C. Hull (Princeton, N.J.: Princeton University Press, 1976), p. 4.

20. Marie-Louise Von Franz, *Psychotherapy* (Boston: Shambhala, 1993), p. 291.

21. Hillman, *A Blue Fire,* p. 141.

22. Jung, *The Archetypes and the Collective Unconscious,* par. 213f.

23. Ronald M. Enroth, "The Power Abusers: When Follow-the-Leader Becomes a Dangerous Game" (1988), p. 4 (unpublished paper).

24. Joseph Campbell, *The Hero's Journey,* ed. P. Coustineau (New York: HarperCollins, 1990), p. 167.

25. Robert J. Lifton, *Thought Reform and the Psychology of Totalism: A Study of "Brainwashing" in China* (Chapel Hill: University of North Carolina, 1989), p. 433.

26. Ibid., p. 434.

27. Ibid., pp. 434–35.

28. Jerry Falwell, quoted in Peter McWilliams, *Life 102: What To Do When Your Guru Sues You* (Los Angeles: Prelude Press, 1993), p. 322.

29. L. Ron Hubbard, Church of Scientology founder, quoted by Richard Behar, "The Thriving Cult of Greed and Power," *Time* (May 6, 1991): 50–57.

30. Sam Keen, *Faces of the Enemy: Reflections of the Hostile Imagination* (San Francisco: Harper and Row, 1986), p. 90.

31. William James, quoted in ibid., p. 100.

32. Steven Hassan, *Combatting Cult Mind Control* (Rochester, Vt.: Park Street Press, 1988), p. 80.

33. Arthur Schopenhauer, "Counsels and Maxims," *Parerga and Paralipomena* (1851).

34. Guru Maharaj Ji, quoted in Flo Conway and Jim Siegelman, "Information Disease: Have Cults Created a New Mental Illness?" *Science Digest* (January 1992): 86.

35. Lifton, *Thought Reform and the Psychology of Totalism*, p. 421.

36. Jung, "Two Essays on Analytical Psychology," p. 97.

37. Monica Davis, personal interview with the author (1993).

38. Hoffer, *The True Believer*, p. 14.

39. Ibid., p. 15.

40. Carl G. Jung, *Aion: Researches into the Phenomenology of the Self*, trans. R. F. C. Hull (Princeton, N.J.: Princeton University Press, 1969), par. 44.

41. Lifton, *Thought Reform and the Psychology of Totalism*, p. 432.

42. Hoffer, *The True Believer*, pp. 83–84.

43. "Shackled Children," KCET TV, Los Angeles (April 24, 1994).

44. Ibid.

45. Jung, "Two Essays on Analytical Psychology," p. 120.

46. Hassan, *Combatting Cult Mind Control*, p. 54.

47. Viktor E. Frankl, *Man's Search for Meaning: An Introduction to Logotherapy* (New York: Simon and Schuster, 1984), p. 42.

48. Friedrich Nietzsche, *The Gay Science* (1882–87).

49. Hassan, *Combatting Cult Mind Control*, pp. 56–57, 69.

50. Jung, *Aion*, par. 390.

51. Marie-Louise Von Franz, quoted in Zweig and Abrams, *Meeting the Shadow*, p. 7.

52. Joe Berghold, "The Social Trance: Psychological Obstacles to Progress in History," *Journal of Psychohistory* 19, no. 2 (Fall 1991): 221–43.

53. Hassan, *Combatting Cult Mind Control*, p. 44.

54. Ibid.

55. Jung, *The Structure and Dynamics of the Psyche*, par. 253.

56. Carl G. Jung, *The Practice of Psychotherapy*, trans. R. F. C. Hull (Princeton, N.J.: Princeton University Press, 1967), par. 179. 56.

57. Ibid., par. 210.

58. Jung, "Two Essays on Analytical Psychology," p. 99.

58. Montaigne, "Use Makes Perfect," *Essays* (1580–88).

60. Flavil R. Yeakley, *The Discipling Dilemma* (Nashville, Tenn.: Gospel Advocate Press, 1982), p. 191.

61. Jung, "Two Essays on Analytical Psychology," par. 485.

62. Ibid.

63. Jung, *The Undiscovered Self,* par. 540.

64. Arthur Koestler, *The Ghost in the Machine* (New York: Random House, 1976), p. 263.

65. Ibid., pp. 254–55.

66. "Gangs," Public Access TV, Los Angeles (September 25, 1993).

67. Eric Norah, "Perspectives," *Newsweek* (September 19, 1994): 19.

68. Andrew Samuels, *The Political Psyche* (London: Routledge, 1993), p. 191.

69. John Bradshaw, "Mystified Love," KCET TV, Los Angeles (December 4, 1993).

70. James Hillman, *Suicide and the Soul* (Dallas, Tex.: Spring Publications, 1976), p. 64.

71. Ibid., p. 29.

72. Robert Johnson, *Owning Your Own Shadow: Understanding the Dark Side of the Psyche* (San Francisco: Harper, 1991), p. 26.

73. Koestler, *The Ghost in the Machine,* p. 265.

74. R. Buckminster Fuller, *Synergetics: Explorations in the Geometry of Thinking* (New York: Macmillan, 1975), p. 373.

Chapter 5. Systems: Mega Groups

1. Sam Keen, *Faces of the Enemy: Reflections of the Hostile Imagination* (San Francisco: Harper and Row, 1986), p. 109.

2. Advertising slogan used for many years by the General Electric Corporation.

3. Beth Lovern, "Confessions of a Welfare Mom," *Utne Reader* (July/August 1994): 83.

4. R. Buckminster Fuller, *Critical Path* (New York: St. Martin's Press, 1981), p. 217.

5. Andrew B. Schmookler, *Fool's Gold: The Fate of Values in a World of Goods* (New York: HarperCollins, 1993), p. 23.

6. William J. Bennett, *The Index of Leading Cultural Indicators: Facts and Figures on the State of American Society* (New York: Simon and Schuster, 1994), p. 62.

7. Ibid., p. 61.

8. Louis Rukeyser, *Louis Rukeyser's Business Almanac* (New York: Simon and Schuster, 1988), p. 107.

9. Ibid.

10. Adam Smith, *Wealth of Nations* (New York: The Modern Library, 1937), p. 423.

11. James Hillman, "Is Therapy Turning Us Into Children?" *New Age Journal* (May/June 1992): 62.

12. John Edgar Wideman, *Philadelphia Fire* (New York: Vintage Books, 1991), p. 22.

13. Samuel Butler, *Prose Observations* (1660–80).

14. Robert Godwin, "On the Function of Enemies," *Journal of Psychohistory* 22, no. 1 (Summer 1994): 91.

15. Schmookler, *Fool's Gold*, p. 3.

16. From the syndicated radio program, "All Things Considered" (September 15, 1989).

17. "Adam Smith," KCET TV, Los Angeles (July 2, 1994).

18. U.S. Department of Justice, *Drugs and Crime Facts* (Washington, D.C., 1992).

19. "Gambling as an Addiction," ABC News (April 1, 1994).

20. "Legal Gambling: The Dice are Loaded," Discovery Channel (March 21, 1994).

21. "The Sound of Silence," lyrics by Paul Simon and Arthur Garfunkel.

22. Cited in Connie Zweig and Jeremiah Abrams, eds., *Meeting the Shadow: The Hidden Power of the Dark Side of Human Nature* (Los Angeles: Jeremy P. Tarcher, 1991), p. 103.

23. Robert J. Lifton, *The Protean Self: Human Resilience in an Age of Fragmentation* (New York: Basic Books, 1993), p. 217.

24. Joseph Campbell, "The Hero's Journey," KCET TV, Los Angeles (March 1, 1994).

25. "Shackled Children," Discovery Channel (April 24, 1995).

26. Carl G. Jung, *The Undiscovered Self,* trans. R. F. C. Hull (Princeton, N.J.: Princeton University Press, 1976), p. 33.

27. "Now," ABC News report (April 27, 1994).

28. Curt Hopkins and Mark Masse, "Partners and Adversaries," *Oregon Business* (October, 1995): 135–36.

29. Andrew B. Schmookler, *The Illusion of Choice: How the Market Economy Shapes Our Destiny* (Albany: State University of New York Press, 1993), pp. 196–201.

30. "ABC Evening News" (March 9, 1994).

31. Quoted in Schmookler, *The Illusion of Choice,* p. 133.

32. *Business Week* editorial (September 4, 1992).

33. "CBS Evening News" (August, 1993).

34. James Hillman, *A Blue Fire* (New York: HarperCollins, 1989), p. 171.

35. Quote by Los Angeles gang member, "Gangs," KCET TV, Los Angeles (December 31, 1993).

36. Quoted in Howard Fineman, "God and the Grass Roots," *Newsweek* (November 8, 1995): 42.

37. Quoted in Carol Feldman, "Teachers Tread Lightly on Religious Issues," *Los Angeles Times,* September 4, 1994, pp. A10–11.

38. Robert J. Lifton, *Thought Reform and the Psychology of Totalism: A Study of "Brainwashing" in China* (Chapel Hill: University of North Carolina Press, 1989), p. 431.

39. Quoted in Feldman, "Teachers Tread Lightly on Religious Issues," pp. A10–11.

40. Ibid.

41. Ralph Waldo Emerson, *Poems* (1847).

42. "The Rise of Big Business in the Nineteenth-Century United States," KCET TV, Los Angeles (February 2, 1994).

43. Ibid.

44. Walter Lippmann, "Routineer and Inventor," *A Preface to Politics* (1914).

45. Lani Guinier, *The Tyranny of the Majority: Fundamental Fairness in Representative Democracy* (New York: The Free Press, 1994), p. 3.

46. "The Intelligence Community," "Prime Time Live," ABC (September 29, 1994).

47. Albert J. Beveridge, cited in Laurence J. Peter, *Peter's Quotations* (New York: Bantam Books, 1977), p. 215.

48. "Bedevelin the GOP," *Los Angeles Times Magazine* (November 11, 1992): 28–34, 62.

49. Thomas B. Edsal, "Robertson Urges Christian Activists to Take Over GOP State Parties," *Washington Post*, September 10, 1995, p. A24.

50. Ibid.

51. CNN News special report (January 1, 1995).

52. Mike McNamee, "A Minimum Wage Hike Spells Maximum Damage," *Business Week* (January 30, 1995): 36.

53. Ibid.

54. Ibid.

55. Ibid.

56. Martin L. Gross, *A Call for Revolution: How Washington Is Strangling America—And How to Stop It* (New York: Ballantine Books, 1993), p. 91.

57. "The Welfare State," NBC News (April 6, 1994).

58. George F. Will, "Orwell in New Jersey," *Newsweek* (March 21, 1994).

59. "20/20," ABC TV (April 15, 1994).

60. Bruce Hocking, "Anthropological Aspects of Occupational Illness Epidemics," *Journal of Occupational Medicine* 29, no. 6 (June 1987): 526–30.

61. Virginia I. Postrel, "Honest Admission," *Reason* (November 1995). 4–6.

62. Ibid.

63. Ibid.

64. Tom Morganthau, "America: Still a Melting-Pot?" *Newsweek* (August 9, 1993): 16–18.

65. Ibid.

66. Ibid.

67. Cited in Peter McWilliams, *Ain't Nobody's Business If You Do: The Absurdity of Consensual Crimes in a Free Society* (Los Angeles: Prelude Press, 1993), p. 569.

68. Alexander Volokh, "The Agency that Never Loses," *Reason* (May 1995): 23–29.

69. Ibid.

70. Ibid.

71. Ibid.

72. Ibid.

73. Ibid.

74. "Aspartame," *Informed Consent* (May/June 1994): 5–6.

75. Ibid., p. 6.

76. Ibid.

77. Jonas Salk, "Prime Time Live," ABC News special report on the FDA (February 1995).

78. Volokh, "The Agency that Never Loses," pp. 23–29.

79. Elias Canetti, *Crowds and Power* (New York: The Noonday Press, 1962), p. 24.

80. John Horgan, "Radon's Risks," *Scientific American* (August 1994): 14–16.

81. A. Watts, *Tao: The Watercourse Way* (New York: Pantheon Book, 1975), p. 33.

82. "60 Minutes," CBS (July 3, 1994).

83. Ernest Becker, cited in Keen, *Faces of the Enemy*, p. 110.

84. John McCarron, "Unconventional Advice for Unions," *Chicago Tribune*, September 5, 1993, p. 3.

85. Robert B. Carson, *Economic Issues Today: Alternative Approaches* (New York: St. Martin's Press, 1987), p. 135.

86. Ibid.

87. Aaron Bernstein, "Why America Needs Unions But Not the Kind It Has Now," *Business Week* (May 23, 1994): 70–82.

88. Michael Maccoby, "Cooperation Means Common Wealth," *Utne Reader* (March/April 1992): 86.

89. Ibid.

90. James Hillman, *Suicide and the Soul* (Dallas, Tex.: Spring Publications, 1976), p. 125.

91. Carl Rogers, *A Way of Being* (Boston: Houghton Mifflin, 1980), pp. 244–45.

92. Earl Mindell, *Earl Mindell's Herb Bible* (New York: Simon and Schuster, 1992), pp. 12–13.

93. Dick Quinn, *Left for Dead* (Minneapolis, Minn.: Self Health Books, 1992), p. 25.

94. Ibid.

95. Lendon H. Smith, "DTP Shots and Infants," *Total Health* (August 1994): 9.

96. Ibid.

97. Ernest Becker, "The Basic Dynamic of Human Evil," cited in Zweig and Abrams, *Meeting the Shadow*, p. 187.

98. Peter Breggin and Ginger R. Breggin, *Talking Back to Prozac: What*

Doctors Aren't Telling You About Today's Most Controversial Drug (New York: St. Martin's Press, 1994), p. 17.

99. Ibid., p. 33.

100. McWilliams, *Ain't Nobody's Business If You Do,* p. 752.

Chapter 6. The Collective Machine

1. Rabindranath Tagore, *Stray Birds* (1916).

2. John Morley, *Voltaire* (1872).

3. Connie Zweig and Jeremiah Abrams, eds., *Meeting the Shadow: The Hidden Power of the Dark Side of Human Nature* (Los Angeles: Jeremy P. Tarcher, 1991), p. 167.

4. Eric Lloyd Wright, cited in Steve Proffith, "Eric Lloyd Wright: Seeking an Organic Way in Architecture and Life," *Los Angeles Times* (January 23, 1994): p. M3.

5. James Hillman, *A Blue Fire* (New York: HarperCollins, 1989), p. 86.

6. Stanley Milgram, cited in Steven Hassan, *Combatting Cult Mind Control* (Rochester, Vt.: Park Street Press, 1988), pp. 58–59.

7. Stanley Milgram, *Obedience to Authority* (New York: Harper and Row, 1974), pp. xii, 59.

8. Carl G. Jung, *The Archetypes and the Collective Unconscious,* trans. R. F. C. Hull (Princeton, N.J.: Princeton University Press, 1969), par. 225f.

9. Melinda Beck, "Propaganda Made Me Do It," *Newsweek* (February 28, 1994): 34.

10. Cited in Robert J. Lifton, *The Protean Self: Human Resilience in an Age of Fragmentation* (New York: Basic Books, 1993), p. 190.

11. W. R. Bion, *Experiences in Groups and Other Papers* (New York: Routledge, Chapman and Hall, 1961), p. 80.

12. Ibid., pp. 151–52.

13. Ibid.

14. Robert Godwin, "On the Function of Enemies," *Journal of Psychohistory* 22, no.1 (Summer 1994): 91.

15. Ibid.

16. Carl G. Jung, *Psychological Types,* trans. R.F. C. Hull (Princeton, N.J.: Princeton University Press, 1967), par. 972.

17. Ibid.

18. Ibid., par. 974.

19. Ibid., par. 565.

20. Ibid., par. 572.

21. Ibid., par. 976f.

22. Daryl Sharp, *C. G. Jung Lexicon: A Primer of Terms and Concepts* (Toronto: Inner City Books, 1991), p. 76.

23. Jung, *Psychological Types,* par. 626.

24. Ibid.

25. Ibid., par. 979.

26. Cited in Zweig and Abrams, *Meeting the Shadow,* p. 3.

27. Cited in Hassan, *Combatting Cult Mind Control,* p. 118.

28. Ibid., p. 55.

29. Robert J. Lifton, *Thought Reform and the Psychology of Totalism: A Study of "Brainwashing" in China* (Chapel Hill: University of North Carolina Press, 1989), pp. 420–32.

30. Ibid., p. 419.

31. Ibid.

32. Cited in Andrew B. Schmookler, *Fool's Gold: The Fate of Values in a World of Goods* (New York: HarperCollins, 1993) p. 115.

33. Sharp, *C.G. Jung Lexicon,* pp. 37–38.

34. Jung, *The Archetypes and the Collective Unconscious,* par. 396.

35. Carl G. Jung, "Two Essays on Analytical Psychology," in *The Portable Jung* (New York: Penguin, 1982), p. 120.

36. Lifton, *Thought Reform and the Psychology of Totalism,* p. 421.

37. Jame Hillman, *Revisioning Psychology* (New York: HarperCollins, 1976), p. 229.

38. Sebastian Brant, *The Ship of Fools* (1494).

39. Lifton, *Thought Reform and the Psychology of Totalism,* pp. 422–23.

40. Ibid., p. 423.

41. Franz Kafka, "Aphorisms 1917–19," in *The Great Wall of China,* trans. Edwin and Willa Muir (Prague: Schocken Books, 1974), p. 181.

42. Sam Keen, *Faces of the Enemy: Reflections of the Hostile Imagination* (San Francisco: Harper and Row, 1986), p. 27.

43. Cited in A. Pratkanis and E. Aronson, *Age of Propaganda: The Everyday Use and Abuse of Persuasion* (New York: W. H. Freeman and Company, 1992), p. 34.

44. Ibid.

45. Thomas Fuller, *The Holy State and the Profane State* (1642).

46. Carl G. Jung, cited in John Gross, ed., *The Oxford Book of Aphorisms* (New York: Oxford University Press, 1983), p. 182.

47. Ibid., "Two Essays on Analytical Psychology," p. 20.

48. Lifton, *Thought Reform and the Psychology of Totalism,* p. 423.

49. Sam Keen, cited in Zweig and Abrams, *Meeting the Shadow,* p. 200.

50. Lifton, *Thought Reform and the Psychology of Totalism,* p. 424.

51. Vauvenargues, *Reflections and Maxims* (1746).

52. Lifton, *Thought Reform and the Psychology of Totalism,* p. 425.

53. Albert Camus, *The Fall* (New York: Alfred A. Knopf, 1957), p. 120.

54. Oscar Wilde, *Phrases and Philosophies for the Use of the Young* (1894).

55. Lifton, *Thought Reform and the Psychology of Totalism,* p. 426.

56. Ibid., p. 428.

57. Ibid.

Chapter 7. Going Backward: Developmental Regression in Groups

1. Jean Callahan, "Leaving the Ashram," *Common Boundary* (July/August 1992): 32–39.

2. Sam Keen, *Faces of the Enemy: Reflections of the Hostile Imagination* (San Francisco: Harper and Row, 1986), p. 97.

3. Jerrold Atlas and Laura Porzio, "Rage and Anger: Dealing with the Symptoms of Dysfunction in Current American Society," *Journal of Psychohistory* 22, no. 1 (Summer 1994): 109.

4. Eric Hoffer, *The True Believer: Thoughts on the Nature of Mass Movements* (New York: Harper and Row, 1951), p. 102.

5. Joseph Campbell, *An Open Life,* ed. P. Cousineau and S. Brown (New York: HarperCollins, 1989), p. 73.

6. Cult Awareness Network, "Marks of a Destructive Cult" (Chicago: C.A.N., 1988), pp. 4–6.

7. Ibid.

8. "Assignment Discovery," Discovery Channel (November 22, 1994).

9. John Bradshaw, "Mystified Love," KCET TV, Los Angeles (June 15, 1991).

10. Robert Bly, *A Little Book on the Human Shadow* (New York: Harper-Collins, 1988), p. 8.

11. Bradshaw, "Mystified Love."

12. Erik H. Erikson, *The Life Cycle Completed* (New York: W.W. Norton and Company, 1982), pp. 56–57.

13. Ibid., p. 46.

14. Ibid., p. 33.

15. Sherman C. Feinstein, "The Cult Phenomenon: Transition, Repression, and Regression," *University of Chicago Pritzker School of Medicine* 8 (1980): 113–22.

16. Otto F. Kernberg, "Leadership and Organizational Functioning: Organizational Regression," *International Journal of Group Psychotherapy* 28, no. 1 (January 1978): 3–25.

17. Erikson, *The Life Cycle Completed,* p. 46.

18. Ibid., p. 69.

19. Lita L. Schwartz, "The Historical Dimension of Cultic Techniques of Persuasion and Control," *Cultic Studies Journal* 8, no. 1 (1991): 37–45.

Chapter 8. Creating Gods

1. George Santayana, *The Life of Reason* (1953).

2. Xenophanes, Frag. 15, cited in John Gross, *The Oxford Book of Aphorisms* (New York: Oxford University Press, 1983), p. 10.

3. Jean Rostand, *Penses d'un biologiste* (1955).

4. From Andrew Samuels et al., *The Critical Dictionary of Jungian Analysis* (New York: Routledge, 1986).

5. Friedrich Nietzsche, *Beyond Good and Evil* (1886).

6. James Hillman, *Suicide and the Soul* (Dallas, Tex.: Spring Publications, 1976), p. 64.

7. Cited in Steven Hassan, *Combatting Cult Mind Control* (Rochester, Vt.: Park Street Press, 1988), p. 9.

8. Marie-Louise Von Franz, *Psychotherapy* (Boston: Shambhala 1993), p. 303.

9. Carl G. Jung, *The Structure and Dynamics of the Psyche,* trans. R. F. C. Hull (Princeton, N.J.: Princeton University Press, 1969), par. 519.

10. William A. Miller, cited in Connie Zweig and Jeremiah Abrams, eds., *Meeting the Shadow: The Hidden Power of the Dark Side of Human Nature* (Los Angeles: Jeremy P. Tarcher, 1991), pp. 40–41.

11. Robert Godwin, "On the Function of Enemies," *Journal of Psychohistory* 22, no. 1 (Summer 1994): 81.

12. Carl G. Jung, "Two Essays on Analytical Psychology," in *The Portable Jung* (New York: Penguin, 1982), p. 93.

13. Robert J. Lifton, *Thought Reform and the Psychology of Totalism: A Study of "Brainwashing" in China* (Chapel Hill: University of North Carolina Press, 1989), p. 436.

14. Carl G. Jung, cited in Gross, *The Oxford Book of Aphorisms,* p. 51.

15. Jung, "Two Essays on Analytical Psychology," p. 119.

16. Ibid., p. 63.

17. Carl G. Jung, *Psychological Types,* par. 755.

18. Daryl Sharp, *C.G. Jung Lexicon: A Primer of Terms and Concepts* (Toronto: Inner City Books, 1991), p. 62.

19. Carl G. Jung, *Psychological Types,* trans. R. F. C. Hull (Princeton, N.J.: Princeton University Press, 1964), par. 742.

20. Carl G. Jung, *Alchemical Studies,* trans. R. F. C. Hull (Princeton, N.J.: Princeton University Press, 1969), par. 454.

21. Jung, *Psychological Types,* par. 806.

22. Thomas Szasz, *The Second Sin* (c.1930).

23. Jung, *Psychological Types,* par. 789.

24. Jung, "Two Essays on Analytical Psychology," par. 399.

25. Carl G. Jung, *The Practice of Psychotherapy,* trans. R. F. C. Hull (Princeton, N.J.: Princeton University Press, 1969), par. 445.

26. James Hillman, *Revisioning Psychology* (New York: HarperCollins, 1976), p. xii.

27. Marie-Louise Von Franz, *The Psychological Meaning of Redemption Motifs in Fairy Tales* (Toronto: Inner City Books, 1980), p. 78.

28. Jung, *Psychological Types,* par. 790.

29. Elias Canetti, *The Human Province,* trans. Joachim Neugroschl (London: The Seabury Press, 1978), p. 282.

30. Philip Cushman, "Why the Self Is Empty," *American Psychologist* 45, no. 5 (May 1990): 599.

31. Ibid., p. 604.

32. Harville Hendrix, cited in Zweig and Abrams, *Meeting the Shadow,* p. 51.

33. Cited in Cushman, "Why the Self Is Empty," p. 607.

34. Michael B. First, ed., *Diagnostic and Statistical Manual of Mental Disorders,* 4th ed. (Washington, D.C.: American Psychiatric Association, 1994), p. 650.

35. Margaret T. Singer, "Thought Reform Programs and the Production of Psychiatric Casualties," *Psychiatric Annals* 20 (1982): 188.

36. Karen Horney, *Neurosis and Human Growth* (New York: W.W. Norton and Co., 1942), pp. 17–65.

37. Ibid., p. 19.

38. Ibid., pp. 17–65.

39. William Stafford, cited in Robert Bly, James Hillman, and Michael Meade, eds., *The Rag and Bone Shop of the Heart: Poems for Men* (Harper-Collins, 1992), p. 233.

40. Cited in: Peter McWilliams, *Life 102: What to Do When Your Guru Sues You* (Los Angeles: Prelude Press, 1994), p. 173.

41. Von Franz, *The Psychological Meaning of Redemption Motifs in Fairy Tales,* p. 78.

42. Jung, "Two Essays on Analytical Psychology," pp. 70–71.

43. Sharp, *C.G. Jung Lexicon,* p. 92.

Chapter 9. The Neurotic Side of Religion

1. Carl G. Jung, cited in Connie Zweig and Jeremiah Abrams, eds., *Meeting the Shadow: The Hidden Power of the Dark Side of Human Nature* (Los Angeles: Jeremy P. Tarcher, 1991), p. 171.

2. John P. Conger, *Jung and Reich: The Body as Shadow* (Berkeley, Calif.: North Atlantic Books, 1985), p. 104.

3. George Bernard Shaw, "Maxims for Revolutionists," *Man and Superman* (1903).

4. Edward C. Whitmont, cited in Zweig and Abrams, *Meeting the Shadow,* p. 17.

5. Brother David Steindl-Rast, cited in Zweig and Abrams, *Meeting the Shadow,* p. 132.

6. Eric Hoffer, *The True Believer: Thoughts on the Nature of Mass Movements* (New York: Harper and Row, 1951), p. 151.

7. Joseph Campbell, "The Hero's Journey," KCET TV, Los Angeles (March 1, 1994).

8. Hoffer, *The True Believer,* p. 96.

9. Marie-Louise Von Franz, *The Psychological Meaning of Redemption Motifs in Fairy Tales* (Toronto: Inner City Books, 1980), p. 25.

10. Cited in Peter McWilliams, *Life 102: What to Do When Your Guru Sues You* (Los Angeles: Prelude Press, 1994), p. 253.

11. Spokesperson for International Churches of Christ, "20/20," ABC TV (October 15, 1993).

12. "The Burning Times: Witchcraft, the Inquisition, and Christianity," KCET TV, Los Angeles (August 16, 1994).

13. Nathaniel Branden, "Taking Back the Disowned Self," in Zweig and Abrams, *Meeting the Shadow,* p. 281.

14. Carl G. Jung, *The Undiscovered Self,* trans. R. F. C. Hull (Princeton, N.J.: Princeton University Press, 1976), p. 21.

15. Abbé Francis Trochu, *The Cure d'Ars* (Rockford, Ill.: Tan Books and Publishers, 1927), p. 120.

16. David G. Lotto, "On Witches and Witch Hunts: Ritual and Satanic Cult Abuse," *Journal of Psychohistory* 21, no. 4 (Spring 1994): 383.

17 Daryl Sharp, *C.G. Jung Lexicon: A Primer of Terms and Concepts* (Toronto: Inner City Books, 1991), p. 62.

18. Austin Miles, "The Tax-Free Ride," in Tim C. Leedom, ed., *The Book Your Church Doesn't Want You To Read* (Dubuque, Iowa: Kendall/Hunt Publishing Company, 1993), p. 341.

19. John Bradshaw, "Work and Creativity," KCET TV, Los Angeles (December 4, 1993).

20. Carl G. Jung, *Memories, Dreams, Reflections,* ed. Ariela Jaffe, trans. R. and C. Winston (New York: Vintage, 1961), p. 346.

21. Leo Tolstoy, *War and Peace,* cited in McWilliams, *Life 102,* p. 47.

22. Carl G. Jung, *The Archetypes and the Collective Unconscious,* trans. R. F. C. Hull (Princeton, N.J.: Princeton University Press, 1969), par. 267.

23. CNN, Special Business News Report (June 27, 1992).

24. Carl G. Jung, *Psychology and the East,* trans. R. F. C. Hull (Princeton, N.J.: Princeton University Press, 1978), p. 55.

25. Carl G. Jung, *Mysterium Coniunctionis,* trans. R. F. C. Hull (Princeton, N.J.: Princeton University Press, 1970), par. 708.

26. Carl G. Jung, *Aion: Researches into the Phenomenology of the Self,* trans. R. F. C. Hull (Princeton, N.J.: Princeton University Press, 1969), par. 126.

27. Randall Terry, quoted by Americans United for Separation of Church and State (Washington, D.C., 1995).

28. Attributed to Carl Jung.

29. M. Woodman, *Holding the Tension of the Opposites* (Boulder, Colo.: Sounds True Recordings, 1993).

30. Cited in Zweig and Abrams, *Meeting the Shadow,* p. 164.

31. Lao-Tzu, *Tao Te Ching,* ed. Gia-fu Feng and Jane English (New York: Vintage Books, 1972), p. 2.

32. Robert Bly in *The Rag and Bone Shop of the Heart: Poems for Men,* ed. Robert Bly, James Hillman, and Michael Meade (New York: 1992), p. 196.

33. Arthur Koestler, *The Ghost in the Machine* (New York: Random House, 1976), p. 262.

34. M. Scott Peck, quoted in Zweig and Abrams, *Meeting the Shadow,* p. 179.

35. Robert J. Lifton, *The Protean Self: Human Resilience in an Age of Fragmentation* (New York: Basic Books, 1993), p. 202.

36. "Sixty Minutes," CBS (March 20, 1994).

37. Robert Godwin, "On the Function of Enemies," *Journal of Psychohistory* 22, no. 1 (Summer 1994): 89.

38. Sam Keen, *Hymns to an Unknown God: Awakening the Spirit in Everyday Life* (New York: Bantam, 1994), p. 116.

39. James Hillman, *A Blue Fire* (New York: HarperCollins, 1989), p. 125.

40. Ibid., p. 187.

41. Ibid.

42. Cited in Leedom, *The Book Your Church Doesn't Want You To Read,* p. 381.

43. Campbell, "The Hero's Journey."

Chapter 10. The Color of the Dream

1. Joseph Campbell, *The Hero's Journey,* ed. P. Cousineau (New York: HarperCollins, 1990), p. 224.

2. Gracian, *The Art of Worldly Wisdom* (1647).

3. Jolande Jacobi, cited in Connie Zweig and Jeremiah Abrams, eds., *Meeting the Shadow: The Hidden Power of the Dark Side of Human Nature* (Los Angeles: Jeremy P. Tarcher, 1991), p. 255.

4. Adapted from *The Graduate* (screenplay).

5. Lao-Tzu, *Tao Te Ching,* ed. Gin-fu Feng and Jane English (New York: Vintage Books, 1972), p. 2.

6. Juvenal, *Satires* (c. 100).

7. Sam Keen, *Faces of the Enemy: Reflections of the Hostile Imagination* (San Francisco: Harper and Row, 1986), p. 27.

8. "The War Against the Indians," Discovery Channel (January 16, 1994).

9. Keen, *Faces of the Enemy,* p. 29.

10. "The War Against the Indians," Discovery Channel (January 16, 1994).

11. Henry Hazlitt, *On Prejudice,* cited in John Gross, ed., *The Oxford Book of Aphorisms* (New York: Oxford University Press, 1983), p. 259.

12. Martin Luther King, Jr., Speech at Civil Rights March on Washington (August 28, 1963), cited in John Bartlett and Justin Kaplan, *Bartlett's Familiar Quotations* (Boston: Little, Brown and Company, 1992), p. 761.

13. Charisse Jones, "Bridges," *Glamour* (October 1995): 127.

14. "20/20," ABC TV (April 29, 1994).

15. Nathaniel Hawthorne, *The Scarlet Letter* (1850), p. 20.

16. Susan Wittig Albert, "Letter to the Editor," *Common Boundary* (October 1994): 9.

Chapter 11. Slaying the Collective Dragon

1. Adrienne Rich, "Necessities of Life" (1966), cited in John Bartlett and Justin Kaplan, *Bartlett's Familiar Quotations* (Boston: Little, Brown and Company, 1992), p. 762.

2. Rainer Maria Rilke, in *Selected Poems of Rainer Maria Rilke,* trans. Robert Bly (New York: Harper and Row, 1981), p. 199.

3. Kabir, *The Kabir Book,* trans. Robert Bly (Boston: Beacon Press, 1977), p. 17.

4. George Orwell, "Letter to Richard Rees" (1949), cited in *Essays, Journalism and Letters* (New York: Harcourt Brace Jovanovich, 1971), p. 250.

5. Joseph Campbell, *The Hero's Journey,* ed. P. Cousineau (New York: HarperCollins, 1990), p. 63.

6. Cited in Connie Zweig and Jeremiah Abrams, eds., *Meeting the Shadow: The Hidden Power of the Dark Side of Human Nature* (Los Angeles: Jeremy P. Tarcher, 1991), p. 6.

7. Carl G. Jung, *The Archetypes and the Collective Unconscious*, trans. R. F. C. Hull (Princeton, N.J.: Princeton University Press, 1969), par. 284.

8. Carl G. Jung, *Memories, Dreams, Reflections*, ed. Ariela Jaffe, trans. R. and C. Winston (New York: Vintage, 1961), p. 183.

9. Robert Johnson, *Owning Your Own Shadow: Understanding the Dark Side of the Psyche* (San Francisco: Harper and Row, 1991), pp. 15, 24–25.

10. Marie-Louise Von Franz, *Projection and Re-Collection in Jungian Psychology*, trans. W.H. Kennedy (LaSalle, Ill.: Open Court Publishing, 1980), pp. 83–84.

11. Carl G. Jung, *The Undiscovered Self*, trans. R. F. C. Hull (Princeton, N.J.: Princeton University Press, 1976), pp. 46–55.

12. Cited in Campbell, *The Hero's Journey*, p. vi.

13. Ibid.

14. Cited in Joseph Campbell, *The Hero with a Thousand Faces* (Princeton, N.J.: Princeton University Press, 1949), p. 345.

15. Ibid., p. xxii.

16. Mary Lutyens, *Krishnamurti: The Years of Fulfillment* (New York: Avon Books, 1983), p. 249.

17. "Introductory Essay to the Bride of Messina," in Friedrich Schiller, ed., *An Anthology for Our Time*, (New York: Frederich Ungar Publishing Co., 1960), p. 168.

18. Cited in Sam Keen and Anne Valley-Fox, *Your Mythic Journey* (Los Angeles: Jeremy P. Tarcher, 1989), p. xvi.

19. Ibid., p. 11.

20. Ibid., p. 303.

21. Blaise Pascal, *Penses* (1670).

22. James Hillman, *Revisioning Psychology* (New York: HarperCollins, 1976), pp. 12–13, 22, 48.

23. Thomas Moore, in James Hillman, *A Blue Fire* (New York: HarperCollins, 1989), p. 37.

24. Hillman, *Revisioning Psychology*, p. 22.

25. Ibid., p. 26.

26. Cited in Keen and Valley-Fox, *Your Mythic Journey*, p. 14.

27. Jung, *Memories, Dreams, Reflections*, p. 183.

28. Marie-Louise Von Franz, *Dreams: A Study of the Dreams of Jung, Descartes, Socrates, and Other Historical Figures* (Boston: Shambhala Publications, 1991), pp. 3–4.

29. Andrew Samuels, *The Political Psyche* (London: Routledge, 1993), p. 63.

30. Carl G. Jung, *The Structure and Dynamics of the Psyche*, trans. R. F. C. Hull (Princeton, N.J.: Princeton University Press, 1969), par. 509.

31. Carl G. Jung, *The Development of the Personality*, trans. R. F. C. Hull (Princeton, N.J.: Princeton University Press, 1969), par. 189.

32. Jung, *The Structure and Dynamics of the Psyche,* par. 546.

33. Von Franz, *Projection and Re-Collection in Jungian Psychology,* p. 189.

34. Marie-Louise Von Franz, "The Realization of the Shadow in Dreams," in Zweig and Abrams, *Meeting the Shadow,* p. 37.

35. Von Franz, *Projection and Re-Collection in Jungian Psychology,* p. 78.

36. James Hillman, *Going Bugs* (New York: Spring Audio, Inc., 1991).

37. Hillman, *Revisioning Psychology,* p. 39.

38. Thelma Jean Goodrich, "Women and Power," *Los Angeles Times,* October 3, 1993.

39. Cited in Samuels, *The Political Psyche,* p. 4.

40. Cited in "Acknowledging Our Inner Split," in Zweig and Abrams, *Meeting the Shadow,* p. 191.

41. Eric Fromm, *The Sane Society* (New York: Henry Holt and Company, 1955), p. 274.

Chapter 12. Putting Soul into Relationships

1. James Hillman, *A Blue Fire* (New York: HarperCollins, 1989), p. 20.

2. Goethe, *Maxims and Reflections* (early nineteenth century).

3. John Stuart Mill, *On Liberty* (1859).

4. John Bradshaw, "Mystified Love," KCET TV, Los Angeles (December 4, 1993).

5. Joseph Campbell, *The Hero's Journey,* ed. P. Cousineau (New York: HarperCollins, 1990), p. 65.

6. Inayat Khan, *Vadan Gayan Nirtan of Inayat Khan* (San Francisco: The Rainbow Bridge, 1974), p. 106.

7. Carl G. Jung, *Aspects of the Feminine,* trans. R. F. C. Hull (Princeton, N.J.: Princeton University Press, 1982), p. 10.

8. Lao-Tzu, *Tao Te Ching,* ed. Gia-fu Feng and Jane English (New York: Vintage Books, 1972), p. 76.

9. Carl G. Jung, *The Structure and Dynamics of the Psyche,* trans. R. F. C. Hull (Princeton, N.J.: Princeton University Press, 1969), par. 425.

10. Rosemary E. Guiley, *The Encyclopedia of Witches and Witchcraft* (New York: Facts on File, 1989), p. 369.

11. Ibid.

12. William Morris, ed., *The American Heritage Dictionary of the English Language* (Boston: Houghton Mifflin, 1981), p. 226.

13. Thomas Stearns Eliot, *Four Quartets* (1935).

14. Cited in Joseph Campbell, *The Hero with a Thousand Faces* (Princeton, N.J.: Princeton University Press, 1949), p. 89.

15. Ibid.

16. Carl G. Jung, *Memories, Dreams, Reflections,* ed. Ariela Jaffe, trans. R. and C. Winston (New York: Vintage, 1961), p. 196.

17. Hillman, *A Blue Fire,* pp. xvi, 68.

18. Edward F. Edinger, *The Creation of Consciousness: Jung's Myth for Modern Man* (Toronto: Inner City Books, 1984), p. 18.

19. Ibid., pp. 18–19.

20. Cited in Campbell, *The Hero's Journey*, p. 176.

21. Thomas Merton, *The Way of Chuang Tzu* (New York: New Directions Books, 1969), p. 30.

22. Edinger, *The Creation of Consciousness*, p. 19.

23. Jung, *Memories, Dreams, Reflections*, pp. 233–34.

24. Ibid., p. 329.

25. Cited in Maria Mahoney, *The Meaning in Dreams and Dreaming* (New Jersey: The Citadel Press, 1966), pp. 51–52.

26. Robert Johnson, *Owning Your Own Shadow: Understanding the Dark Side of the Psyche* (San Francisco: Harper, 1991), p. 111.

27. Diderot, *Rameau's Nephew* (1761).

28. Morris, *The American Heritage Dictionary of the English Language*, p. 1327.

29. R. Buckminster Fuller, *Synergetics: Explorations in the Geometry of Thinking* (New York: MacMillan, 1975), p. 372.

30. Jung, *Memories, Dreams, Reflections*, p. 345.

31. Rainer Maria Rilke, *Selected Poems of Rainer Maria Rilke*, trans. Robert Bly (New York: Harper and Row, 1981), p. 121.

32. Carl G. Jung, *Aion: Researches into the Phenomenology of the Self*, trans. R. F. C. Hull (Princeton, N.J.: Princeton University Press, 1969), p. 346.

33. Rilke, *Selected Poems of Rainer Maria Rilke*, p. 175.

34. Jean T. Clift and Wallace B. Clift, *Symbols of Transformation in Dreams* (New York: The Crossroad Publishing Company, 1984), p. 107.

35. Carl G. Jung, *The Archetypes and the Collective Unconscious*, trans. R. F. C. Hull (Princeton, N.J.: Princeton University Press, 1969), p. 41.

36. Connie Zweig and Jeremiah Abrams, eds., *Meeting the Shadow: The Hidden Power of the Dark Side of Human Nature* (Los Angeles: Jeremy P. Tarcher, 1991), p. 304.

37. Morris, *The American Heritage Dictionary of the English Language*, p. 11.

38. Jung, *Memories, Dreams, Reflections*, p. 143.

39. James Hillman, *Revisioning Psychology* (New York: HarperCollins, 1976), p. 20.

40. Jung, *Memories, Dreams, Reflections*, p. 311.

41. Rilke, *Selected Poems of Rainer Maria Rilke*, p. 189.

42. Carl G. Jung, "Two Essays on Analytical Psychology," in *The Portable Jung* (New York: Penguin, 1982), par. 78.

43. Ibid.

44. Friedrich Nietzsche, *Twilight of the Idols* (1889).

45. Steven Bocho, "Truth and Fiction," *Inc.* (Nov. 1993): 21.

46. Chuang Tzu, in Alan Watts, *Tao: The Watercourse Way* (New York: Pantheon Books, 1975), p. 43.

47. Cited in Bocho, "Truth and Fiction," p. 21.

48. Robert Bly, *The Rag and Bone Shop of the Heart: Poems for Men,* ed. Robert Bly, James Hillman, and Michael Meade (New York: HarperCollins, 1988), p. 112.

49. Emily Dickinson, cited in Rhoda T. Tripp, ed., *The International Thesaurus of Quotations* (New York: Thomas Y. Crowell, 1970), p. 25.

50. Bertrand Russell, "The Role of the Individual," *Authority and the Individual* (1949).

51. William Blake, "A Poison Tree," *Songs of Experience*(1794), st. 1.

52. Johnson, *Owning Your Own Shadow,* p. 11.

53. Sam Keen and Anne Valley-Fox, *Your Mythic Journey* (Los Angeles: Jeremy P. Tarcher, 1989), p. 16.

54. Carl Rogers, *A Way of Being* (Boston: Houghton Mifflin Company, 1980), p. 334.

Chapter 13. Life After Group

1. Rainer Maria Rilke, *Selected Poems of Rainer Maria Rilke,* trans. Robert Bly (New York: Harper and Row, 1981), p. 13.

2. Mary Oliver, *Dream Work* (New York: Atlantic Monthly Press, 1986), p. 51.

3. Cicero *De Officiis* 2.7.24 (44 B.C.).

4. Thomas Moore, in James Hillman, *A Blue Fire* (New York: HarperCollins, 1989), p. 11.

5. Carl G. Jung, cited in H. Westmann, "The Old Testament and Analytical Psychology," *Guild Lecture No. 10* (London: Guild of Pastoral Psychology).

6. Cited in Marilyn B. Snell, "Leopold Kohr: Visionary Economist," *Utne Reader* (September/October 1994): 44.

7. Carl G. Jung, "Two Essays on Analytical Psychology," in *The Portable Jung* (New York: Penguin, 1982), p. 27.

8. Andrew Samuels, *The Political Psyche* (London: Routledge, 1993), p. 85.

9. Ibid., p. 49.

10. Bill Moyers, "The Healing Mind," KCET TV, Los Angeles (March 22, 1994).

11. Joseph Campbell, *Beyond Dogma: The Vision Quest Experience* (San Francisco: New Dimensions Foundation, 1990), audiocassette.

12. Alan Watts, *Tao: The Watercourse Way* (New York: Pantheon Books, 1975), p. 43.

13. Joseph Campbell, *The Hero with a Thousand Faces* (Princeton, N.J.: Princeton University Press, 1949), p. 391.

14. Cited in Joseph Campbell, *The Hero's Journey,* ed. P. Cousineau (New York: HarperCollins, 1990), p. 205.

15. John Dryden, *The Hind and the Panther* (1687), 11.239.

Bibliography

Behar, R. "The Thriving Cult of Greed and Power." *Time* (May 6, 1991): 50–57.

Bennett, William J. *The Index of Leading Cultural Indicators: Facts and Figures on the State of American Society.* New York: Simon and Schuster, 1994.

Berghold, Joe. "The Social Trance: Psychological Obstacles to Progress in History." *Journal of Psychohistory* 19, no. 2 (Fall 1991): 221–43.

Bion, W. R. *Experiences in Groups and Other Papers.* New York: Routledge, Chapman and Hall, 1961.

Blakely, M. "Psyched Out." *Los Angeles Times Magazine* (October 3, 1993): 27–28, 46–49.

Bloom, A. *The Closing of the American Mind.* New York: Simon and Schuster, 1987.

Bly, Robert. *A Little Book on the Human Shadow.* New York: Harper-Collins, 1988.

Bly, Robert, James Hillman, and Michael Meade, eds. *The Rag and Bone Shop of the Heart: Poems for Men.* New York: HarperCollins, 1992.

Bocho, Steven. "Truth and Fiction." *Inc.* (November 1993): 21.

Booth, Leo. *When God Becomes a Drug: Breaking the Chains of Religious Addiction and Abuse.* Los Angeles: Jeremy P. Tarcher, 1991.

Bradshaw, John. *Homecoming: Reclaiming and Championing Your Inner Child.* New York: Bantam Books, 1990.

Breggin, Peter R., and Ginger R. Breggin. *Talking Back to Prozac: What*

Doctors Aren't Telling You About Today's Most Controversial Drug. New York: St. Martin's Press, 1994.

Campbell, Joseph. *The Hero's Journey,* edited by P. Cousineau. New York: HarperCollins, 1990.

———. *The Hero with a Thousand Faces.* Princeton, N.J.: Princeton University Press, 1949.

———. *The Mythic Image.* Princeton, N.J.: Princeton University Press, 1974.

———. *An Open Life,* edited by P. Cousineau and S. Brown. New York: HarperCollins, 1989.

Camus, Albert. *The Fall.* New York: Alfred A. Knopf, 1957.

Canetti, E. *Crowds and Power.* New York: The Noonday Press, 1962.

Carroll, M. *The Cult of the Virgin Mary.* Princeton, N.J.: Princeton University Press, 1986.

Carson, R. *Silent Spring.* Boston: Houghton Mifflin, 1962.

Clift, Jean T., and Wallace B. Clift. *Symbols of Transformation in Dreams.* New York: Crossroad Publishing Company, 1984.

Conger, John. *Jung and Reich: The Body as Shadow.* Berkeley, Calif.: North Atlantic Books, 1985.

Conway, Flo, and Jim Siegelman. "Information Disease: Have Cults Created a New Mental Illness?" *Science Digest* (January 1982): 86–92, 165–70.

Crossen, Cynthia. *Tainted Truth: The Manipulation of Fact in America.* New York: Simon and Schuster, 1994.

Cult Awareness Network. "Marks of a Destructive Cult." Chicago: C.A.N., 1988.

Cushman, P. "Why the Self Is Empty." *American Psychologist* 45, no. 5 (May 1990): 599

Dibbley, Dale. *From Achilles' Heel to Zeus' Shield.* New York: Ballantine Books, 1993.

Edinger, Edward F. *The Creation of Consciousness: Jung's Myth for Modern Man.* Toronto: Inner City Books, 1984.

———. *Ego and Archetype.* New York: Penguin Books, 1972.

Enroth, Ronald. *The Lure of the Cults and New Religions.* Downers Grove, Ill.: Inner Varsity Press, 1987.

Erikson, Erik H. *The Life Cycle Completed.* New York: W.W. Norton and Company, 1982.

Feinstein, Sherman C. "The Cult Phenomenon: Transition, Repression, and Regression." *Journal of Adolescent Psychiatry* 8 (1980): 113–22.

First, Michael B., ed. *Diagnostic and Statistical Manual of Mental Disorders,* 4th. ed.Washington, D.C.: American Psychiatric Association, 1994.

Frankl, Viktor E. *Man's Search for Meaning: An Introduction to Logotherapy.* New York: Simon and Schuster, 1984.

Fromm, Erich. *The Sane Society.* New York: Henry Holt and Company, 1955.

Fuller, R. Buckminster. *Critical Path.* New York: St. Martin's Press, 1981.

———. *Ideas and Integrities.* New York: Macmillan Publishing Co., 1963.

———. *Synergetics: Explorations in the Geometry of Thinking.* New York: Macmillan, 1975.

Godwin, Robert. "On the Function of Enemies." *Journal of Psychohistory* 22, no. 1 (Summer 1991): 91.

Gordon, James. *The Golden Guru: The Strange Journey of Bhagwan Shree Rajneesh.* New York: Penguin Books, 1987.

Gross, John., ed. *The Oxford Book of Aphorisms.* New York: Oxford University Press, 1983.

Gross, Martin. *A Call For Revolution: How Washington is Strangling America And How to Stop It.* New York: Ballantine Books, 1993.

Guggenbühl-Craig, A. *Power in the Helping Professions.* Dallas, Tex.: Spring Publications, 1971.

Guiley, Rosemary E. *The Encyclopedia of Witches and Witchcraft.* New York: Facts on File, 1989.

Guinier, Lani. *The Tyranny of the Majority: Fundamental Fairness in Representative Democracy.* New York: The Free Press, 1994.

Hassan, Steven. *Combatting Cult Mind Control.* Rochester, Vt.: Park Street Press, 1988.

Hillman, James. *A Blue Fire.* New York: HarperCollins, 1989.

———. *The Dream and the Underworld.* New York: Harper and Row Publishers, 1979.

———. *In Search: Psychology and Religion.* Dallas, Tex.: Spring Publications, 1967.

———, ed. *Puer Papers.* Dallas, Tex.: Spring Publications, 1979.

———. *Revisioning Psychology.* New York: HarperCollins, 1976.

Hoffer, Eric. *The True Believer: Thoughts on the Nature of Mass Movements.* New York: Harper and Row, 1951.

Horney, Karen. *Neurosis and Human Growth.* New York: W.W. Norton and Company, 1942.

Hubner, John, and Lindsay Gruson. *Monkey on a Stick: Murder, Madness, and the Hare Krishnas.* New York: Harcourt Brace Jovanovich, 1988.

The I Ching, translated by C. F. Baynes and Richard Wilhelm. Princeton, N.J.: Princeton University Press, 1977.

James, William. *The Varieties of Religious Experience.* New York: Penguin Books, 1982.

Johnson, David, and Jeff Van Vonderen. *The Subtle Power of Spiritual Abuse.* Minneapolis, Minn.: Bethany House Publishers, 1991.

Johnson, Robert. *Owning Your Own Shadow: Understanding the Dark Side of the Psyche.* San Francisco: Harper, 1991.

Jung, Carl. *Aion: Researches into the Phenomenonology of the Self,* translated by R. F. C. Hull. Princeton, N.J.: Princeton University Press, 1969.

——. *Alchemical Studies,* translated by R. F. C. Hull. Princeton, N.J.: Princeton University Press, 1969.

——. *The Archetypes and the Collected Unconscious,* translated by R. F. C. Hull. Princeton, N.J.: Princeton University Press, 1969.

——. *Aspects of the Feminine,* translated by R. F. C. Hull. Princeton, N.J.: Princeton University Press, 1982.

——. *The Development of the Personality,* translated by R. F. C. Hull. Princeton, N.J.: Princeton University Press, 1969.

——. *Memories, Dreams, Reflections,* edited by Aniela Jaffe, translated by Richard and Clara Winston. New York: Vintage, 1961.

——. *Mysterium Coniunctionis,* translated by R. F. C. Hull. Princeton, N.J.: Princeton University Press, 1963.

——. *On the Nature of the Psyche,* translated by R. F. C. Hull. Princeton, N.J.: Princeton University Press, 1968.

——. *The Practice of Psychotherapy,* translated by R. F. C. Hull. Princeton, N.J.: Princeton University Press, 1967.

——. *Psychological Reflections,* translated by R. F. C. Hull. Princeton, N.J.: Princeton University Press, 1970.

——. *Psychological Types,* translated by R. F. C. Hull. Princeton, N.J.: Princeton University Press, 1967.

——. *Psychology and Alchemy,* translated by R. F. C. Hull. Princeton, N.J.: Princeton University Press, 1968.

——. *The Structure and Dynamics of the Psyche,* translated by R. F. C. Hull. Princeton, N.J.: Princeton University Press, 1969.

——. *Symbols of Transformation,* translated by R. F. C. Hull. Princeton, N.J.: Princeton University Press, 1967.

Jung, Carl. "Two Essays on Analytical Psychology." In *The Collected Works*, vol. 7. Princeton, N.J: Princeton University Press, 1953.

——. "Two Essays on Analytical Psychology." In *The Portable Jung*. New York: Penguin, 1982.

——. *The Undiscovered Self*, translated by R. F. C. Hull. Princeton, N.J.: Princeton University Press, 1976.

Kabir. *The Kabir Book*, translated by Robert Bly. Boston: Beacon Press, 1977.

Keen, Sam. *Faces of the Enemy: Reflections of the Hostile Imagination*. San Francisco: Harper and Row, 1986.

——. *Hymns to an Unknown God: Awakening the Spirit in Everyday Life*, New York: Bantam, 1994.

Keen, Sam, and Anne Valley-Fox. *Your Mythic Journey*. Los Angeles: Jeremy P. Tarcher, 1989.

Kernberg, Otto. "Leadership and Organizational Functioning: Organizational Regression." *International Journal of Group Psychotherapy* 28, no. 1 (1978): 3–25.

Kline, Joe. "Looking for Enemies." *Journal of Psychohistory* 22, no. 1 (Summer 1994): 29.

Koestler, Arthur. *The Ghost in the Machine*. New York: Random House, 1976.

Kotkin, Joel. *Tribes: How Race, Religion and Identity Determine Success in the New Global Economy*. New York: Random House, 1993.

Kramer, Joel, and Diana Alstad. *The Guru Papers: Masks of Authoritarian Power*. Berkeley, Calif.: North Atlantic Books/Frog Ltd., 1993.

Kramer, Peter. *Listening to Prozac: A Psychiatrist Explores Antidepressant Drugs and the Remaking of the Self*. New York: Viking, 1993.

Lao-Tzu. *Tao Te Ching*, edited by Gia-fu Feng and Jane English. New York: Vintage Books, 1972.

Leedom, Tim C., ed. *The Book Your Church Doesn't Want You to Read*. Dubuque, Iowa: Kendall/Hunt Publishing Company, 1993.

Lifton, Robert J. *The Protean Self: Human Resilience in an Age of Fragmentation*. New York: Basic Books, 1993.

——. *Thought Reform and the Psychology of Totalism: A Study of "Brainwashing" in China*. Chapel Hill: University of North Carolina Press, 1989.

Lowen, Alexander. *Narcissism*. New York: MacMillan Publishing, 1985.

Lutyens, Mary. *Krishnamurti: The Years of Fulfillment*. New York: Avon Books, 1983.

Lutz, William. *Doublespeak: From "Revenue Enhancement" to "Terminal Living."* New York: HarperCollins, 1989.

McNeill, D., and P. Freiberger. *Fuzzy Logic: The Discovery of a Revolutionary Computer Technology—And How It is Changing Our World.* New York: Simon and Schuster, 1993.

McWilliams, P. *Ain't Nobody's Business If You Do: The Absurdity of Consensual Crimes in a Free Society.* Los Angeles: Prelude Press, 1993.

———. *Life 102: What to Do When Your Guru Sues You.* Los Angeles: Prelude Press, 1994.

Mahoney, Maria. *The Meaning in Dreams and Dreaming.* New Jersey: The Citadel Press, 1966.

Mayburry-Lewis, D. "Tribal Wisdom." *Utne Reader* (July/August 1992): 66–93.

Merton, Thomas. *The Way of Chuang Tzu.* New York: New Directions Books, 1969.

Milgram, Stanley. *Obedience to Authority.* New York: Harper and Row, 1974.

Milkman, Harvey, and Stanley Sunderwirth. *Craving for Ecstasy: The Consciousness and Chemistry of Escape.* New York: Lexington Books, 1987.

Miller, Alice. *Drama of the Gifted Child: The Search for the True Self,* translated by R. Ward. New York: Basic Books, 1981.

———. *For Your Own Good: Hidden Cruelty in Child-Rearing and the Roots of Violence.* New York: The Noonday Press, 1983.

———. *Thou Shalt Not Be Aware: Society's Betrayal of the Child.* New York: Meridian, 1984.

Mindell, Earl. *Earl Mindell's Herb Bible.* New York: Simon and Schuster, 1992.

Mithers, Carol L. *Therapy Gone Mad: The True Story of Hundreds of Patients and a Generation Betrayed.* New York: Addison-Wesley, 1994.

Moore, Thomas. *Care of the Soul: A Guide for Cultivating Depth and Sacredness in Everyday Life.* New York: HarperCollins, 1992.

Nelson, Mariah. *The Stronger Women Get, the More Men Love Football: Sexism and the American Culture of Sports.* New York: Harcourt Brace and Company, 1994.

Nelson, Shirley. *Fair Clear and Terrible: The Story of Shiloh, a Strange Fragment of American History.* Latham, N.Y: British American Publishing, 1989.

Orwell, George. *1984.* New York: New American Library, 1949.

Peat, F. David. *Synchronicity: The Bridge Between Matter and Mind.* New York: Bantam Books, 1987.

Peck, M. Scott. *The Different Drum: Community and Making Peace.* New York: Simon and Schuster, 1987.

———. *People of the Lie: The Hope for Healing Human Evil.* New York: Simon and Schuster, 1983.

Peele, Stanton. *Diseasing of America: Addiction and Treatment Out of Control.* Boston: Houghton Mifflin Company, 1989

Pratkanis, Anthony, and Elliot Aronson. *Age of Propaganda: The Everyday Use and Abuse of Persuasion.* New York: W.H. Freeman and Company, 1992.

Quinn, Dick. *Left for Dead.* Minneapolis, Minn.: Self Health Books, 1992.

Rilke, Rainer Maria. *Selected Poems of Rainer Maria Rilke,* translated by Robert Bly. New York: Harper and Row, 1981.

Roberts, Richard. *Tales for Jung Folk.* San Anselmo, Calif.: Vernal Equinox Press, 1983.

Rogers, Carl. *A Way of Being.* Boston: Houghton Mifflin Company, 1980.

Rukeyser, Louis., ed. *Business Almanac.* New York: Simon and Schuster, 1991.

Sagan, Carl. "The Fine Art of Baloney Detection." *Parade* (April 1987): 14.

Samuels, Andrew. *The Political Psyche.* London: Routledge, 1993.

Satir, Virginia. *The New Peoplemaking.* Mountain View, Calif.: Science and Behavior Books, 1988.

Schaef, Anne W., and Diane Fassel. *The Addictive Organization.* New York: Harper and Row, 1988.

———. *When Society Becomes an Addict.* New York: HarperCollins, 1987.

Schmookler, Andrew B. *Fool's Gold: The Fate of Values in a World of Goods.* New York: HarperCollins, 1993.

———. *The Illusion of Choice: How the Market Economy Shapes Our Destiny.* Albany: State University of New York Press, 1993.

Schwartz, Lita L. "The Historical Dimension of Cultic Techniques of Persuasion and Control." *Cultic Studies Journal* 1 (1991): 37–46.

———. "Psychological Manipulation and Society." *Cultic Studies Journal* 8 (1991): 91–254.

Sharp, Daryl., ed. *C.G. Jung Lexicon: A Primer of Terms and Concepts.* Toronto: Inner City Books, 1991.

Singer, Margaret T. "Thought Reform Programs and the Production of Psychiatric Casualties." *Psychiatric Annals* 20 (1982): 188–93.

Smith, Adam. *Wealth of Nations.* New York: The Modern Library, 1937.

Smith, Lendon H. "DTP Shots and Infants." *Total Health* (August 1994): 9.

Sullivan, Barbara S. *Psychotherapy Grounded in the Feminine Principle.* Wilmette, Ill.: Chiron Publications, 1989.

Volokh, Alexander. "The Agency That Never Loses." *Reason* (May 1995): 23–29.

Von Franz, Marie-Louise. *Dreams:A Study of the Dreams of Jung, Descartes, Socrates, and Other Historical Figures.* Boston: Shambhala Publications, 1991.

———. *Projection and Re-Collection in Jungian Psychology,* translated by W.H. Kennedy. La Salle, Ill.: Open Court Publishing, 1980.

———. *The Psychological Meaning of Redemption Motifs in Fairy Tales.* Toronto: Inner City Books, 1980.

———. *Psychotherapy.* Boston: Shambhala, 1993.

Watts, Alan. *Tao: The Watercourse.* New York: Pantheon Books, 1975.

Whitmyer, Claude, ed. *In the Company of Others: Making Community in the Modern World.* Los Angeles: Jeremy P. Tarcher, 1993.

Woodman, Marion. *Addiction to Perfection: The Still Unravished Bride.* Toronto: Inner City Books, 1982.

Wright, Lawrence. *Remembering Satan: A Case of Recovered Memory and the Shattering of an American Family.* New York: Alfred A. Knopf, 1994.

Yalom, Irvin. *The Theory and Practice of Group Psychotherapy.* New York: Basic Books, 1985.

Yeakley, Flavil R. *The Discipling Dilemma.* Nashville, Tenn.: Gospel Advocate Press, 1982.

Zweig, Connie, and Jeremiah Abrams, eds. *Meeting the Shadow: The Hidden Power of the Dark Side of Human Nature.* Los Angeles: Jeremy P. Tarcher, 1991.

Index

Abel, I. W., 158
Abilene Christian University, 113
Abrams, Jeremiah, 165, 290
Abuse
  child, 222
  satanic, 222
Active imagination, 255–57
Adams, Henry, 63
African Americans, 246–48
Aid to Dependent Children, 146
Albert, Susan Wittig, 249
Alchemy
  heretical nature, 29
  imagination and, 29
Alcoholics Anonymous, 177
Allaire, Paul, 158
Aman, Caryn, 60
American dream
  admission to, 239
  buying into, 300
  dream shaping, 238
  implanted images, 238
  media and, 238
American Indians, 31
American Medical Association, 159
American Petroleum Institute, 40

Anima
  inner imbalance and, 65
Animus
  inner imbalance and, 65
  possession by, 65
Ann Ree Colton Foundation, 50
Anti-Christ, 120
Archetypal psychology, 27, 306–307
Archetype(s)
  as metaphors, 213
  one-sidedness, 230
  possession, 212, 224
  savior, 213, 224–25
Aronson, Elliot, 63, 75–76
Arthur (king), 260
Aspartame (NutraSweet), 154–55
Atlas, Jerrold, 189
Auschwitz, 44

Babbs, John, 85
Beck, Melinda, 169
Becker, Ernest, 157, 161
Berghold, Joe, 110
Berlin Wall, 33, 89
Berry, Jason, 235
Bieber, Owen, 157

Binary thinking
  vocabulary and, 75
Bion, W.R., 169–70
Blake, William, 51, 166, 301
Blakely, Mary, 43
Bly, Robert, 193, 231, 296, 310
Bocho, Steven, 294
"Born Again"
  as a psychological process, 53, 175,
    225–26
Bosnia, 24, 115
Bottone, Joseph, 58
Bradshaw, John, 79, 117, 193, 225, 277
Brandon, Nathaniel, 219
Brant, Sebastion, 179
Breggin, Peter, 162
Brokaw, Tom, 92
Bronte, Emily, 21
Buddha, 24, 180, 213, 225
Butler, Samuel, 127

Callahan, Jean, 189
Campbell, Joseph, 15, 19, 21, 24, 35,
    46, 51, 59, 76, 99, 133, 189–90,
    216, 227, 236–37, 251, 254, 262,
    277, 282, 310
Camus, Albert, 185
Canetti, Elias, 80, 155, 207
Capitalism
  freedom and, 126
  monotheistic, 136–37
  polytheistic, 136
Catholic(s), 30, 98, 55, 103
Chakra, 67
Chi
  relationships and, 141
Child abuse, 222
Child labor, 107–108, 133
China, 24, 141, 168
Christian Coalition, 147
Christianity
  adaptation and, 270
  African Americans and, 246–48
  as an ideology, 26
  as self object, 229

being "chosen," 179
blaming victim, 219
born again, 53, 175, 225–26
complexes and, 112
conformity and, 28
dark side, 169, 216, 221
depression and, 94
dreams and, 269–70
dualism and, 198
environment and, 235
escapism in, 220
exclusiveness and, 99
fundamentalism, 231–33
homosexuality and, 233
intentional suffering, 110
martyrdom and, 233
missionary zeal, 182
one-sidedness, 222–23
opposites and, 223
original sin and, 94
persecution and, 178
psychotherapy in, 233
rationalizing evil, 181
repression and, 216
sadomasochism, 221
salvation in, 168, 170, 218
self-sacrifice and, 233
sexual shadow in, 218, 303
shadow in, 216–18
suicide and, 233
virgin births and, 98
witchcraft, 280
Chuang Tzu, 284, 295
Cicero, 305
Clay, Jason, 30
Clinton, Bill, 143
Cognitive dissonance, 180, 181
Collective
  adaptation, 16, 179
  authority, 25
  collision between individual and, 19,
    25
  complexes, 111–12
  compulsions, 219–21
  costumes, 249

dark side of, 16, 29
defined, 17
demons, 29
deprogramming, 19, 254–62
differentiating from, 29, 37
dragon, 29
dream game, 241
ego, 24
enchantment, 24
holding tension between, 16
hysteria, 224
implants, 265
individual and, 25
infection, 267
influence, 16
integrity, 24
media and, 309
merging with, 26
morality, 118
narcissism and, 81
normality and, 78
opposites, 269
panic, 114–15
pleasure principle, 258
psychology, 19
roles, 29
self, 211
shadow, 185
shame, 244
shaping, 26, 238
splitting, 31
statistics and, 78–79
stigmata, 224
suicide and, 117–18
tension producers, 119
threshold guardian, 255
totalism and, 27
truth, 178
unconscious, 32–36, 98
Collective unconscious
defined, 35
images from, 36
suffering and, 32
Colton, Ann Ree, 50–58
Columbus, 31, 242

Commager, Henry, 70
Communism
authoritarian, 28
Communist
thought reform, 27
Community
aspects of livability, 135
destructive features, 310
differentiation and, 26, 238
healthy qualities, 307–308, 310
inner, 263–66
need to belong, 29
opposites and, 309
rules, 310
size, 113
spirit, 309
tension and, 309
welfare and, 309
Complexes
collective, 111–12
cultural, 29
defined, 175–76
healthy factors, 113
identification with, 112
possession by, 216
splinter psyches, 111
Confession, 185
Conger, John, 215
Conscience
outside authority and, 175
Consciousness
collective, 235
drugs and, 163
enlightenment, 235
evolution of, 36
integrity of, 287–88
lowering of, 169
missionary, 227
opposites and, 228
raising, 228
spirituality and, 229
splitting of, 229
tension and, 289
Consumer Safety Act, 143
Conversion factor

in mass movements, 95, 98
Corpus Hermeticum, 29
Creative process, 293–95
Creativity
  in a box, 42
Crime
  consensual, 128–30
  war on drugs, 170–71
Crowd Soul, 40, 43, 98, 251
Cult Awareness Network, 18, 190, 191
Cult(s)
  defined, 17
  political, 142–48
  religious, 18, 111
Cultural
  censorship, 69
  cloaking, 206
  conditioning, 26
  dualism, 31
  editing, 69
  exclusiveness, 77
  implants, 27, 87, 117
  incest, 222
  one-sidedness, 212
  spaces-in-between, 30
  unconscious, 254–55
  values, 107
  witch hunt, 223
Curé d' Ars. See Vianney, Jean-Marie-
    Baptiste
Cushman, Philip, 207–208

Dalai Lama, 49
Davis, John W., 165
Davis, Monica, 103
Defense mechanisms
  denial, 89
  displacement, 118
  projection, 90
  rationalization, 90
  reaction formation, 90
  regression, 90–91
  repression, 216, 301–302
Delusion of reprieve
  leaving a group and, 58

Demons
  collective, 29
Department of Energy, 129, 156–57
Depression
  bipolar, 94
  in Jungian psychology, 42
Depth psychology
  collective and, 272–73
  defined, 28–29, 64
  enemy making and, 200
  many parts and, 27
  one-sidedness and, 91
  repression and, 42
  requires tension, 161
  shadow and, 184
  soul-based, 28
  soul honoring, 31
  soul making and, 115
Developmental stages, 194
Dickinson, Emily, 297
Diderot, 287
Discrimination
  defined, 77
Disraeli, Benjamin, 45
Donahue, Phil, 32
Dostoevsky, Fyodor, 63
Double speak, 71
Dream(s)
  formats of, 268
  imagery, 267
  journal, 267
  one-sidedness, 269
  political aspect, 267–68
  tension and, 268
  totalism in, 269
Drinkwater, John, 266
Dryden, John, 310
Dualism, 303
Dweller action
  as evil, 55, 67
  family, 55
  Hebrew, 55
  Hindu, 55
  psychological, 55

East Berlin, 33
Eddins, William, 169
Edinger, Edward, 283–84
Ego-inflation, 200
Eliot, T. S., 66, 281
Emerson, Ralph Waldo, 139
Enroth, Ronald, 99
Environmental Protection Agency, 80, 154–56
Erikson, Erik, 194–96, 210
Eros
    control, 91
    unconscious and, 91
    will to power and, 91
Evangelism, 226
Evil
    collective adaptation, 232
    extremes and, 231
    integrity and, 230
    obedience as, 231
    rationalizing, 180
    true, 29
Evolution
    defined, 36, 66
    tension and, 36
Exclusiveness
    assumption of omniscience, 101
    cultural, 77
    superiority, 102
Existential crisis
    being versus nothingness, 101
    collective role, 240–41
    groups and, 34, 44
    lack of meaning, 306
Existential sacrifice
    dispensing existence, 99
    exclusiveness and, 101
    in groups, 16
Existentialism
    conditional, 45
    freedom and, 45
    normal anxiety and, 45–46
Extroversion
    in Jungian psychology, 171–73

Falwell, Jerry, 100, 233
Family dweller, 55
Farrakhan, Louis, 248
Feelings
    anger, 297
    expressing, 296–301
Feinstein, Sherman, 195
Feres Doctrine, 145
Festinger, Leon, 180
Food and Drug Administration, 24, 152–55, 189
Francis of Assisi, Saint, 221
Frankl, Viktor, 44, 60, 108
Freud, Sigmund, 64, 89, 211, 271
Fromm, Erich, 26, 276
Frost, Robert, 284
Fuller, R. Buckminster, 33, 119, 121, 288
Fuller, Thomas, 181

Gambling
    jackpot consciousness, 130
    lotteries, 131
    religion of, 130–31
Gandhi, 24, 140, 205
Gangs
    as cults, 116–17
Gates, Bill, 128
Gingrich, Newt, 153
God hole, 44, 45, 50, 76, 102
God(s)
    as metaphors, 197
    called by, 30
    co-creator with, 29
    collective, 36
    dualistic nature, 217
    flat-earth, 96
    gender of, 235–36
    green-backed, 40
    idolatry, 37
    money as, 134
    "one God," 30
    polytheism, 265, 270
    will of, 105
    word of, 25

Godwin, Robert, 127–28, 170–71, 200, 234
Goethe, 277
Golden Horde, 52
Goodrich, Thelma Jean, 271
Gracian, 237
Greek city-states, 98
Griffin, Michael, 169
Gross, Martin, 148
Group mind
    differentiating from, 273
    hero's journey and, 15
Group(s)
    as self objects, 210
    baby boomers, 78
    basic assumption in, 170
    compulsion and, 219–21
    conscience and, 25
    containment in, 26
    dark side, 16
    defined, 17–18
    deindividualization in, 196
    depersonalization in, 196
    destructive, 16, 24, 27
    destructive features, 313–14
    dynamics, 28
    ego-inflation, 200
    exclusiveness, 100–101
    fantasied objects, 170
    harmful effects, 191
    healthy criteria, 303–304
    hypnotic effects, 227
    identification and, 191, 203–207
    infection by, 267
    integrity and, 285–86
    narcissism and, 81–82
    obedience in, 231–32
    organized, 24
    paranoia, 222–23
    projection in, 199–202
    racism in, 244
    recovery from, 260–62
    relationship to, 26
    rituals, 195, 234, 228
    splitting in, 203

support, 309
surrender to, 98, 103
voice, 69
Group speak, 71–72
Gunn, David, 169

Hassan, Steven, 57, 100, 108–10
Hawthorne, Nathaniel, 249
Hazlitt, Henry, 244
Hebrew dweller, 55
Hendrix, Harville, 208
Heraclitus, 64, 289
Hermes, 65
Hero's journey, 15, 37, 46, 59–60, 131, 213, 254, 282
Hillman, James, 27, 43, 92, 94, 96, 117–18, 124, 137, 159, 178, 198, 207, 234–35, 263–65, 270, 277, 283
Hindu dweller, 55
Hitler, Adolf, 24, 90, 108, 212
Hocking, Bruce, 150
Hoffer, Eric, 43, 85, 104, 106, 189, 217
Holy Grail, 218, 260
Holy War, 88, 184, 217
Horney, Karen, 211
Hubbard, L. Ron, 100
Huddle, Donald, 151
Hulme, T.E., 65
Human heartedness, 34, 133
Hypnosis
    mass, 109
    social trance, 110

Identification
    destructive groups and, 16
    ego-inflation and, 206
    individuation and, 18
    splitting and, 203
    with an archetype, 229–30
    with groups, 39, 64
India, 107
Individual
    dual nature of, 29
Individuation

collective images and, 36
consciousness and, 37
defined, 18–19, 37
persona and, 36
tension and, 38
Industrial Revolution, 139–40
Inner child
depth psychology and, 27
Insight gaps, 297
Introversion
in Jungian psychology, 173–74
Iran, 24
Iraq, 24, 114
Irish Republican Army, 40

Jackson, Andrew, 243
Jacobi, Jolande, 237
James, William, 49, 100, 230
Jarrell, Randall, 49
Jenk, Jeremiah, 151
Jesus, 24, 36, 67, 76, 94, 168,180–81,
186, 205–206, 213, 216, 218,
225 29, 231, 247
Johnson, Ben, 70
Johnson, Robert, 118, 256, 286, 302
Johnson, Sonia, 219
Jones, Charisse, 246
Jonestown, 50
Jung, Carl G., 18–19, 23, 26–29,
35–37, 39, 44, 50, 64–65, 70, 76,
77, 85, 87–88, 91, 95, 98, 102,
104, 108–109, 111–14, 169–70,
172–74, 176–78, 181, 185, 199–
201, 203–207, 212, 215–16, 220,
225, 227–28, 255, 258–59, 266,
268, 278–79, 282–85, 288–89,
290–93, 307–308
Juvenal, 238

Kabir, 56, 213, 253, 284
Kafka, Franz, 180
Karma
as cliché, 67
defined, 55
negative, 57

Keats, John, 95
Keen, Sam, 23, 76, 77, 100, 121, 180,
182–83, 189, 234, 242–43, 262,
302
Kernberg, Otto, 195
Kessler, David, 152
Khan, Inayat, 277
King, Martin Luther, Jr., 246
Kipling, Rudyard, 86
Klein, Joe, 32
Koestler, Arthur, 114, 119, 232
Kohr, Leopold, 308
Kohut, Heinz, 209
Korean War, 83
Krishna, 180
Krishnamurti, 260

LaBier, Douglas, 131
Lagom
as fairness, 158
Laing, R.D., 34
Lammi, Glenn, 152
Language
group, 16
group speak, 71
loaded, 67
polarizing, 74
politically correct, 70
Lao-Tzu, 180, 230–31, 238, 279
Law of large numbers, 78
Lee, Li-Young, 49
Leno, Jay, 32
Life
meaning of, 306
Life totem, 262–64
Lifton, Robert Jay, 27, 67, 83, 99–101,
105, 133, 138–39, 174–75, 178–
79, 182–83, 186–87, 202
Lobbying
effects of, 40–41, 144–45
political action committees, 40
Lotto, David J., 222
Love bombing, 91
Lovern, Beth, 121
Lowen, Alexander, 81–82

Luther, Martin, 24
Lutz, William, 71

McClelland, David, 83
Maccoby, Michael, 158
McNamee, Mike, 148
Madison, James, 143, 147
Maharaj Ji, Guru, 101
Mailer, Norman, 31
Mao Tse-tung, 24
Market system
  black markets, 129–30
  collective shaping and, 26
  conscience and, 122–24, 129, 140
  heaven and hell in, 132
  hero's journey and, 131, 139
  invisible hand, 122, 127, 151, 176,
    208, 279
  language of, 127
  rules in, 126, 139
  social chaos and, 125, 176
  totalism and, 124, 140
Marquess of Halifax, 15
Mass movements
  conversion factor in, 95
  dangers in, 29
  organizations, 28
  surrender to, 95
Mass paranoia, 222
Meaning
  groups and, 45
  identity and, 45–46
  in words, 70–71
  of life, 44–47, 306
  tension and, 44, 46
Meditation, 228–29, 234
Memory
  repressed, 222
Mercedes Benz, 135, 145
Meyers-Briggs Type Indicator
  group personalities, 113
Miles, Austin, 224
Milgram, Stanley, 168
Mill, John Stuart, 277
Miller, Alice, 81

Mills, Jeanne, 50
Milton, John, 170
Mind
  Cartesian thinking, 95
  crowd, 222
  shares of, 27
  totalitarian, 30
Mind control
  destructive groups and, 16, 62
  ritual and, 54
  technique of, 26
Minimum wage, 147–48
Mohammed, Elija, 248
Monotheism
  human psyche and, 27
Montaigne, 113
Montesquieu, 21
Moon, Rev. Sun Myung, 174, 198
Moore, Thomas, 95, 265, 306
Mormon Church, 100, 224
Mother Teresa, 30
Murdoch, Rupert, 128
Mystification
  society and, 79
Mythology
  defined, 262–63
  language of, 292

Nader, Ralph, 163
Narcissism
  collective, 81–82
  power and, 82
Nation of Islam, 248
National Reconnaissance Office, 145
Native Americans, 243
Neighborhood
  electronic, 309
Nepal, Kathmandu, 94
Neumann, Erich, 254, 272
Neumark, David, 147
Newspeak, 67
Nicole, Pierre, 75
Nietzsche, 77, 109, 197, 260, 293
Nigeria, 92
Niscience, 50, 51–54, 56–58

Noran, Eric, 116
Normalizing judgment, 79
Norton, David, 175
Novak, Robert, 70
Novalis, 165, 283
Numinous, 76, 180

Odyssey, 24
Oliver, Mary, 305
One-sidedness, 86–89, 92–94, 102, 111, 181, 197, 206, 212, 222–23
Operation Rescue, 229
Opposites
  active imagination and, 257
  awareness of, 302
  Christianity and, 223, 233
  community and, 309
  group-defined, 31
  in dreams, 286
  in life, 278–81
  insight gaps and, 296
  integrity and, 287–88
  midpoint and, 283
  one-sidedness, 86
  points of view, 34
  problem of, 41
  relationship between, 279
  societal, 119
  space in between, 41, 281–82, 286–87
  tension between, 41, 278
  tensional art and, 97–98
  transcendental function, 290
  union of, 283
Orwell, George, 67–69, 254

Pan, 115
Pascal, Blaise, 86, 263
Patriarchy
  environment and, 41
  rules, 117
Peck, M. Scott, 232
Peer pressure
  effects of, 108–109, 191
  reaction formation and, 90
Peoples' Temple, 50

Personality types
  cloning, 113
  group persona, 113
  in groups, 113
Phobia(s)
  collective, 115
Pirandello, Luigi, 169
Plato, 63
Political action committees, 40
Polytheism
  psychological, 26–27
Portman, Adolph, 46
Porzio, Laura, 189
Postrel, Virginia, 150–51
Pratkanis, Anthony, 63, 75–76, 181
Préault, Auguste, 24
Projection
  as a defense, 90
  halo effect, 200
  in groups, 16, 19, 199–202, 210, 226
  loss of soul and, 19
  taking back, 37
Propaganda
  defined, 77
  group, 16, 75–76
  psychological aspects, 26
Protestants, 103
Prozac
  social medication and, 162, 163
Psyche(s)
  defined, 17
  differentiated, 38–39
  integrity and, 106
  multiple nature of, 27
  plural, 26
  polytheistic, 26–27
  self-regulating, 285
  splinter, 111
Psychological dweller, 55
Psychological opportunity cost, 41–42
Psychology
  archetypal, 306–307
  phenomenology, 306–309
  soul, 307
Psychology of the pawn, 179

Psychotherapy
  as dogma, 28
  as mind-control, 271–75
  collective issues in, 271–72
  constructive, 275–76
  defined, 272
  destructive, 271–75
  modern, 29
  support groups, 309

Racism
  group-induced, 244
  guilt and, 244
Rand, Ayn, 219
Rebirth
  motifs, 226
Reed, Ralph, 138, 146
Regression
  developmental, 16, 189–96
Rejectivism
  as core pathology, 196
Religious Right, 18, 138, 198
Renaissance, 98
Repressed memory syndrome, 222
Repression, 216, 301–302
Republican party, 18
Reynolds, R.J., 40
Rich, Adrienne, 253
Rilke, Rainer Maria, 253, 288–89, 292,
  305
Roberts, Richard, 25
Robertson, Pat, 147, 233
Rogers, Carl, 159, 303
Roman Empire, 98
Romer, Roy, 68
Rostrand, Jean, 197
Rothman, David, 162–63
Roux, Joseph, 41
Rumi, 262
Russell, Bertrand, 297
Russia, 24, 27, 56, 92
Rwanda, 24, 33, 90

Sacred science, 186–87
Sacrifice

  existential, 16
Sagan, Carl, 61
Salk, Jonas, 155
Samuels, Andrew, 117, 267, 309
Sandifer, Robert, 116
Santayana, George, 197
Satanic
  abuse, 222
Schiller, Frederick, 262
Schmookler, Andrew Bard, 23, 42–43,
  82, 122, 128, 135
Schopenhauer, Arthur, 101
Schwartz, Lita, 196
Seldon, John, 66
Self
  archetypal paralysis and, 212
  archetype of, 212
  authentic, 16, 38
  collective aspects, 211
  concept of, 206
  cultural aspects, 207
  despised, 211
  disorders of, 209
  disowned, 208
  empty, 208
  esteem, 210
  estrangement from, 95
  false, 208, 210–11
  idealized, 211
  identification with, 212
  images of, 207
  introjection and, 212
  lost, 208
  narcissism and, 207
  one's relationship to, 206
  parts of, 19
  possession by, 207
  projection and, 210
  recovering the, 19
  reflection, 88
  respect, 211
  responsibility, 95
  sacrifice, 90, 106
Shadow
  addictive behavior and, 230

collective suppression, 29
  hero's journey and, 15
  humor and, 303
  religion and, 220
  repressed, 297
  shadow work, 290
  unintegrated, 29
Shakespearean, 19
Shaman
  inner, 266
Sharp, Daryl, 37, 224
Shaw, Bernard, 215
Sherrington, Sir Charles, 77
Simonds, Robert, 138
Singer, Margaret, 210
Smith, Adam, 123
Smith, Lendon, 161
Social chemistry, 92
Social trance, 16, 24
Society
  fragmented, 308
Soul
  crowd, 40, 43
  diversity and, 27
  in things, 306–307
  loss of, 16, 19, 95–96, 120, 124,
    306–307, 309
  meaning of, 17
  nonexclusive, 27
  psychology of, 307
  return of, 284
  soul making, 307
  soul-work, 29, 283
Space
  ritual, 309
Spiritual atoms, 56
Spiritual mantle, 58
Splitting, 115
Stafford, William, 211
Stalin, Joseph, 24
Statistical murder, 80
Statistical person, 78–79
Steindle-Rast, Brother David, 216
Storr, Anthony, 285
Sudden Infant Death Syndrome, 161

Suicide, 198
Surrender, 185
Systems
  economic, 43
  educational, 17, 133, 137–38
  free market, 17, 26
  immigration, 150–51
  medical, 159–62
  political, 17, 146–48
  totalitarian, 27
  welfare, 148–51
Szasz, Thomas, 206

Tagore, Rabindranath, 86, 165
Tao
  pivot of, 86, 284
  seeing both sides, 86
Teeley, Kevin, 139
Tension
  acknowledgment and, 291
  balance and, 289
  creative tension, 97–98, 293–96
  defined, 287
  healthy, 97, 286, 290–94, 300–301,
    309
  holding the, 277–81, 285, 288–89,
    292–93, 297, 302, 304
  insight gaps and, 295–96
  integrity and, 287–88
  meaning and, 38
  normal, 163
  opposites and, 277–81
  psyche and, 38
  repressed, 118
  surplus, 119
  tensional art, 96–97
  war and, 119
Terry, Randall, 229
Theosophy, 260
Therapy (therapists)
  meaning and, 42–43
  role of, 43
  suffering and, 43
Thought police, 70
Thought reform

in groups, 27, 83
Thought-terminating cliché, 67
Threshold guardian, 59
Tolstoy, Leo, 225
Totalism
    authenticity and, 83
    business, 141–42
    Chinese and, 83
    choices and, 68
    defined, 166
    demands of, 117
    either-or, 82
    government, 309
    ideological, 27, 83, 138, 178, 184,
        202
    in language, 67
    one-sidedness, 87
    organizations and, 17
    power drive, 83
    primary themes, 174–75
    psychology of, 27, 83, 184
    reward and punishment, 28
    theological, 182
Trochu, Abbé Francis, 221
Tzu, Chuang, 284, 295

Unconscious
    Freud and, 89
    programming, 57
    projection and, 90
Unions, 157–59
    United Auto Workers, 157
    United Steelworkers, 158
    Wagner Act, 157
U.S. Department of Agriculture, 144
U.S. State Department, 130

Vaughn, Jackie, 157
Vauvenargues, 67, 185
Vianney, Jean-Marie-Baptiste, 221
Vietnam War, 72
Viewpoints, 88–89
Volokh, Alexander, 152
Von Franz, Marie-Louise, 41, 95, 110,
        199, 207, 218, 251, 257, 267–70

Warm fuzzies trap, 53
Washington, D.C., 40
Watson, John, 126
Watts, Alan, 38, 156, 310
Welch, Finis R., 148
West Berlin, 33
White Paper, 52, 55
White, Rev. Mel, 233
Whitmont, Edward, 215
Wideman, John Edgar, 125
Wilde, Oscar, 186
Wilson, Thomas, 85
Witchcraft
    Christianity and, 216–17
    ritual abuse, 222
    women and, 159–60, 219, 280
Woodman, Marion, 86, 230
Wordsworth, William, 23, 38
Wright, Eric Lloyd, 165

Xenophanes, 197

Yeakley, Flavil, 113
Yeats, William Butler, 21

Zen Buddhism, 86
Zweig, Connie, 31